Geomodernisms

Geomodernisms

Race, Modernism, Modernity

EDITED BY

*Laura Doyle and
Laura Winkiel*

INDIANA UNIVERSITY PRESS
Bloomington and Indianapolis

This book is a publication of
Indiana University Press
601 North Morton Street
Bloomington, IN 47404-3797 USA

http://iupress.indiana.edu

Telephone orders   800-842-6796
Fax orders   812-855-7931
Orders by e-mail   iuporder@indiana.edu

The paper used in this publication meets the minimum requirements of
American National Standard for Information Sciences—Permanence of Paper for
Printed Library Materials, ANSI Z39.48-1984.

Manufactured in the United States of America

Library of Congress Cataloging-in-Publication Data

Geomodernisms : race, modernism, modernity / edited by Laura Doyle and
Laura Winkiel.
p.   cm.
Includes bibliographical references and index.
ISBN 0-253-34607-X (cloth : alk. paper) — ISBN 0-253-21778-4 (pbk. : alk. paper)
1. Race in literature. 2. Literature, Modern—20th century—History and criticism.
3. Modernism (Aesthetics) I. Doyle, Laura. II. Winkiel, Laura A.
PN56.R16G46 2005
809'.933552—dc22
2005011538

1 2 3 4 5   10 09 08 07 06 05

To our families and friends, ever close across distances.

CONTENTS

Part II   Modernisms' Contested States

Part III   Modernisms' Imagined Geographies

ACKNOWLEDGMENTS

Above all, we wish to thank our contributors for the care and thought they gave to their essays. Thank you for making this volume what it is and for your collegial cooperation at every stage of its making.

The idea for this collection grew out of two seminars organized for the Modernist Studies Association Conference in October 2000, "Race, Modernism, Modernity," and "Race and American Modernism." We continued this conversation at the 2001 Modernist Studies Association Conference in two panels on "Race, Modernism, Modernity" and at the 2003 Modern Language Association Conference in a panel on "Geomodernisms." We thank the participants in those seminars and panels as well as the organizers of these conferences for providing venues for our thinking about the global horizons of many modernisms.

To Robert Sloan, our editor, we owe thanks for his commitment to the project and his nimble shepherding of it. As modernists know, so much depends on the editor, that interested eye. Thank you, as well, to our anonymous reader for thoughtful comments and enthusiastic approval of the collection. We are grateful to all of those at Indiana University Press who helped to create the book, including Jane Lyle and Jane Quinet, who were always quick to respond to our concerns or questions, and the copy editor, Joyce Rappaport, who gave the manuscript scrupulous attention. We also thank Iowa State University for the financial support that enabled us to coordinate this collection between locations in North America and beyond.

Last, we thank our partners for their love and fortitude throughout the period when this book came to life. You know what we mean.

Laura Doyle
University of Massachusetts–Amherst

Laura Winkiel
Iowa State University–Ames

Geomodernisms

INTRODUCTION:

THE GLOBAL HORIZONS OF MODERNISM

Laura Doyle and Laura Winkiel

INTO THE DISTANCE

So much depends on distance, says Lily Briscoe—or an intimation of things distant, as Nella Larsen puts it. So much depends on a red wheelbarrow in the rain beside the white chickens. So much depends on *which* hill the jar sits atop—and whether, as Ortega y Gasset remarks, the eye seeing it is proximate or distant. So much depends, these modernist observers hint, on place, proximity, position.

Geomodernisms makes evident how fully this insight applies to modernisms themselves. In both the creation and the interpretation of modernisms, that is, so much depends on *which* modernism, written when and why and from what place—which city, which hillside, which seat on the train, which new nation or new colony, and before, after, or during which war. Encompassing aesthetic projects in Cuba, Taiwan, China, South Africa, Lebanon, Haiti, Brazil, India, Wyoming, the Congo, London, and New York, this collection reveals diverse modernisms formed against and through each other, proximate or distant, and constituted by their locations in the world.

Modernists of all kinds have apprehended or explicitly named this situation. Many implicitly began the dialogue about "placedness" that we want to continue here. Whether one considers Jean Toomer's Georgia and Harper's Ferry, Virginia Woolf's London, Gabriel García-Márquez's Macondo, James Joyce's Dublin, or William Carlos Williams's Paterson, local detail serves as the raw material for both their new formalism and their shifting angles of vision. And the local conducts the charge of the imperial and racial. In *Mrs. Dalloway*, the plane droning over London and the mysterious government limousine organize the gazes of the shoppers, veterans, street vendors, and Parliament men and so supply centrifugal pull that rallies the dispersed, postwar energies of empire. Lord Dudley's vice regal cavalcade in Joyce's *Ulysses* unites the Dublin promenaders in its insistent demand for obeisance to the British imperial presence. The sleeping sickness that afflicts the villagers in *One Hundred Years of Solitude* arrives from elsewhere, in synergy with the Buendía men's romance with technology and travel, killing memory and signaling modernity's contagious rupture of histories.

Some modernists, in their critical reflections on art, meditated explicitly on these experiences of encounter and dispersion, place and exile, global connection and local alienation. In "The Narrow Bridge of Art" (1927), Woolf considers it the burden of modern fiction to represent the strangely globalized privacy of the modern self:

> The long avenue of brick is cut up into boxes, each of which is inhabited by a different human being who has put locks on his doors and bolts on his windows to ensure some privacy, yet is linked to his fellows by wires which pass overhead, by waves of sound which pour through the roof and speak aloud to him of battles and murders and strikes and revolutions all over the world. (222)

Woolf foregrounded these contradictions, while others fashioned modernist art to resolve them. T. S. Eliot and the New Critics who followed him, for example, were often at pains to master the global surround, reconnect reassuringly across separations, and reassimilate modernist innovation into an ideal center. In "The Use of Poetry and the Use of Criticism" (1933), Eliot describes the modern critic as one who observes literary history from a "different and more distant perspective." Modernist literary works appear as those "new and strange objects in the foreground," whose newness displaces more familiar works that "now approach the horizon" (87). As the past is pushed to the periphery, the modern becomes the center. From this center, the critic, "armed with a powerful glass," can compare "minute objects close at hand" with the older works on the periphery and so "will be able to gauge nicely the position and proportion of the objects surrounding us in the whole of a vast panorama" (87).

But even as Anglo-American critics recentered both their position and that of metropolitan modernism by seeking to represent the whole, Ortega y Gasset questioned that centering perspective. In "The Dehumanization of Art" (1924), he argues that art "has moved toward the outer rings" and artists occupying the margins of modernity are best positioned to reconfigure art's functions (48). This off-center locale, says Ortega y Gasset, generates an alternative aesthetics of proximity, a "retraction from the object toward the subject, the painter" that exposes the processes of reification and normativity (105). In a sense Ortega y Gasset indicates that the Society of Outsiders Woolf yearns for already exists, and its members readily, almost necessarily, craft the kind of art she envisions. Such art includes both those Latin American movements that Anthony Geist and José Monleón call "modernism at the margins" and that Marshall Berman (thinking of Russia as well as Brazil) calls the "modernism of underdevelopment," which "nourishes itself on an intimacy and a struggle with mirages and ghosts" (232). If, from these locales, we look back toward Anglo-European modernisms, we can begin to glimpse, as Simon Gikandi suggests here, how canonical white Anglo modernism is itself determined by contact-zone clashes and reversals and how it, too, is haunted by ghosts—the repressed ghosts of an African modernity, an Atlantic modernity, a subaltern modernity. That is, we begin to see all kinds of modernisms as they make themselves and are made from the *outside in*.

To emplace modernism in this way—to think, rather, in terms of inter-connected modernisms—requires a rethinking of periodization, genealogies, affiliations, and forms. To some degree, this rethinking estranges the category of modernism itself. The term *modernism* breaks open, into something we call geomodernisms, which signals a locational approach to modernisms' engagement with cultural and political discourses of global modernity. The revelation of such an approach is double. It unveils both unsuspected "modernist" experiments in "marginal" texts and unsuspected correlations between those texts and others that appear either more conventional or more postmodern. Thus this collection includes essays on a sentimental Native American novel (Dymond), Lebanese postwar novels (Seigneurie), and Taiwanese cinema (Chang). We posit that across their differences, these works share something that allows them to be grouped together: a self-consciousness about positionality. Here, positionality is onto-social as well as geographical, entailing a sense of situated and disrupted social presence.

Thus in some sense, however local their settings, their horizon is global and their voicing is refracted through the local–global dialectic of inside and outside, belonging and exile, in ways that disrupt conventional poetics. Thus does Okanogan author Mourning Dove position her seemingly conventional "native" heroine Cogewea in a romance plot on a Wyoming ranch that, however, when viewed from Cogewea's favorite mountain haunt, appears instead as a site of lost Indian community. Thus does Brazilian poet Mário de Andrade defamiliarize the racialist discourse of modernist poetics by conjuring instead a distended spatial connection between the metropolitan poet and the northern rubber-plantation worker, the hidden source of Brazil's export economy and global influence. Thus does D. H. Lawrence create Gypsy characters who arrive and disappear into an elsewhere that makes his English characters appear strangely enclosed. Thus does the Indian photographer Raghubir Singh create a hybrid Anglo-Indian framing of color and noncolor, stillness and movement—as well as a miscegenous Anglo-Indian theory of his practice. Thus does the racism of vorticism arise defensively against the instability of a capitalist and "cabaret" modernity. Critics have sometimes considered self-consciousness about "literary artifacts" as a key point of continuity between modernism and postmodernism, as Astradur Eysteinsson notes in *The Concept of Modernism* (113). But the essays here clarify how, in a wider range of texts than these critics often have in mind, this aesthetic self-awareness expresses a *geocultural* consciousness—a sense of speaking from outside or inside or both at once, of orienting toward and away from the metropole, of existing somewhere between belonging and dispersion. These artists' engagement with aesthetic traditions are shaped, they know (some more consciously than others), by an uneven, often racialized global modernity. Their aesthetic forms take up this situation, managing the (in)coherence within it. Some of these artists are pointedly engaged with the notion of modernism, some not, but all are aware of it as a coordinate on the map they occupy.

To consider this global set of texts in relation to modernism, then, is not to dilute them or the term but rather to concretize both, insofar as they share, not strict national or temporal frameworks or even explicit aesthetic programs, but a global horizon that affects both content and form. The question of whether we should name these various works "modernist" is less pressing than the need to understand the circuits they share. We call this set of projects *geomodernisms* with the aim of indicating both their continuity with and divergence from commonly understood notions of modernism, especially as shaped by race and related categories within modernity. *Geomodernisms*, the collection and the word, thus responds to Homi Bhabha's call to understand modernism as an intersection of multiple and nonsynchronous temporalities. And, at the same time, it transforms Jürgen Habermas's suggestion that meditations on modernism may guide us toward a more complex understanding of modernity by straying from the Occidental path of modernity. Gathering the divergent yet linked texts of what we call geomodernisms, and foregrounding the persistent, structuring forces of race, place, and modernization within them, we hope to stimulate new conversations about aesthetics within the world of late modernity.

DEFINING TERMS: RACE, MODERNISM, MODERNITY

Because the terms *race, modernism,* and *modernity* themselves carry charged histories, the challenge in using them is to do three things at once: to acknowledge and excavate the histories they carry, to redefine and disrupt them by articulating counterhistories, and to resist their tendency to "absorb" and ultimately re-erase these other histories. Here we will define them with attention to these demands and as they function flexibly in this volume.

Race

Kinship ideologies that create economic and gender hierarchies are as old and wide as the hills. So the West has no special claim on *race* if one thinks of race as a variation of kinship ideology. But race *is* a particular Western formation of kinship ideologies. And of course *one* of the underlying connections of race and modernity is that the dominance of European states in the modern global economy has led to the prominence of race as a kinship vocabulary—that is, the modern European notion of kinship, in the form of biological race, has infiltrated other cultures as well. In some cases, therefore, such as in African, African American, Latin American, and Native American modernisms, race per se often structures the aesthetic imagination. More than half of the essays treat projects explicitly structured by such racial paradigms.

In other cases, however, race operates only at the margins, secondary to the influence of other identities and tensions, so that a strict use of the critical lens of race would distort more than it would reveal. This unevenness in race's relevance as a category itself reflects global history. In this volume, the title word *race* sometimes stands in for closely related categories, such as organically conceived expressions of nationalism or nativism, which often echo or overlap with racial categories but are not identical with them. For instance, in Sung-sheng Yvonne Chang's material, the Western notion of race is relevant mainly insofar as the incursion of Western "modernization" fomented an anti-Western "nativism" within China and Taiwan, but the terms and shapes of that nativism are not strictly "racial." In Cuba and Brazil, as Gerard Aching and Fernando Rosenberg note, due to the longstanding mixture of "races," the meanings of "miscegenation" diverge sharply from those in the United States, and race gets subsumed into nationalism in particular ways in each country. Yet more starkly, in Ken Seigneurie's Lebanese materials, race withers in importance, except insofar as the West's racial assumptions have helped to catalyze the state of "ongoing war" that Seigneurie considers the ruling influence on those writers. Susan Stanford Friedman makes clear that other categories, such as caste in Arundhati Roy's work, become more salient at times than colonialism and race and inflect the meanings of these latter terms. Thus, we often use the term *race* in quotations to indicate its contingent and uneven application.

Modernism

In the case of *modernism*, again, the term serves not as the center around which other projects get organized but as a contested and historical referent that suffers pressure from the affiliations, indifference, or antagonism of diverse twentieth-century writers and artists. In some cases, as in China and Taiwan, *modernism* per se is the catalyzing term, in other cases not. Our explicit aim is to collapse the margin and center assumptions embedded in the term *modernism* by conjuring instead a web of twentieth-century literary practices, shaped by the circuitry of race, ethnicity, nativism, nationalism, and imperialism in modernity, and by the idea or commodity of "modernism" itself. Building on recent works by Geist and Monleón, Scandura and Thurston, and Booth and Rigby that have stretched the borders of modernism, our goal is to foster more conversations among critics of diverse national literatures, unveiling the degree to which traditions are pitched against each other—or not.

The danger, of course, is that critics invested in the term's field-defining power may misconstrue or appropriate divergent cultural histories, wrenching them to fit under the canonical notion of "modernism," as some, such as Houston Baker, have felt is the case in studies of African American modernism. The globalization of criticism, like that of trade, inevitably sends forth the specter of appropriation, and this collection walks under its shadow. After all, this collection is in English. Only a few of us hail from universities outside the United States. The economy that supports us and these conversations (albeit less and less) is embedded in the "Western" capitalism many of these essays critique.

And yet at the same time, to proceed with this collection is to heed the evidence presented by its contributors. That is, first of all, the essays here remind us, as they foreground diverse agencies and locales, that many values and histories have formed modernity and modern aesthetics. The same follows for modern criticism. If we step back from cross-national conversations about "modernism" under the assumption that "the Western," English language economy defines and holds the conversation *utterly* in its grip, we collude in another way with an ideology of dominance. There is no pure path to be taken, in other words. The essays here show artists engaging with non-Western legacies and idiosyncratic worlds as well as with Western textual hegemony. This collection critically examines their practice.

Modernity

Poststructuralist critics have scrutinized the values of modernity, and postcolonial critics have deconstructed its ways of arising within and departing from non-Western sites. Our contributors substantiate and extend these understandings of modernity, and our three subsections of essays are organized in part around dimensions of modernity—its historical, its state-based, and its spatio-temporal facets. Many of the essays demonstrate, following Arjun Appadurai, how local forms arise in response to the global —including in the imperial metropole, no matter how autonomous and originating a "center" it may seem, as Simon Gikandi argues in the case of canonical modernism's aesthetic of epiphany. Other essays illustrate Nestor Canclini's observation that modernity cross-pollinates various locations differently and unexpectedly, as Eluned Summers-Bremner dramatizes in her juxtaposition of T. S. Eliot's *The Waste Land* and Langston Hughes's *Montage of a Dream Deferred.* A number of contributors, including Patricia Chu, Fernando Rosenberg, Sung-sheng Yvonne Chang, and Gerard Aching, probe the complex ways that twentieth-century aesthetics takes shape in and against the formation of nations within a global political economy, thus uncovering new links between modernism and international capitalism. Several essays expand our understanding of what Dilip Parameshwar Gaonkar has called "alternative modernities," pointing, in the case of Ariela Freedman, Ken Seigneurie, and Justine Dymond, to ancient, non-Western formations of subjectivity that inflect geomodernist texts. Virtually all of the essays trace multidirectional channels of influence.

As we noted above, the challenge with using words like *race, modernism,* and *modernity* is to acknowledge both their historical pasts and their historical present, that is to use them flexibly and nonappropriatively within a shifting historiography. We take courage from the fact that, within modernity, the rule of print has always spawned unruly or undisciplined texts. We hope that by placing a range of "modernist" projects beside those often assumed to be irrelevant to them (whether due to marginal location, historical belatedness, or apparently nonexperimental aesthetics) and for convenience calling these self-consciously situated projects *geomodernisms,* we will, in some small measure, "un-discipline" modernist studies.

GENEALOGIES, STATES, GEOGRAPHIES

Taken together, the essays certainly initiate this movement across boundaries —and they invite many more connections than one anthologizing order can map. We have chosen not to organize the essays by locale or by their relative attention to race, modernism, or modernity but rather to indicate their larger ways of interlocking these (or related) terms and to juxtapose closely the different locales they treat. The first essays, in "Modernisms' Alternative Genealogies," approach the long history of modernity in order to unsettle reigning assumptions about origins and effects and to reconfigure geomodernisms accordingly; those in "Modernisms' Contested States" highlight the way that state modernization interacts with geomodernist aesthetics; and the essays in the third section, "Modernisms' Imagined Geographies," chart various spatial orders of modernity while registering the desire for another geography of global relations—an *un*killing worldness—as expressed in a geomodernist handling of space. This organization works to foreground the woven strands of geopolitics, subjectivity, and aesthetics and so to indicate new and more interdisciplinary paths of study. It has the effect, we hope, of unhinging simple binaries (such as metropole and margin) and pointing beyond frameworks that, at this stage, may limit or repeat the field of modernist inquiry.

Modernity arises in diverse places and forms long before the twentieth century, of course, and the essays in "Modernisms' Alternative Genealogies" excavate some of these pasts with an eye to their influence on late modern aesthetics. These long-view accounts expand narrow periodizations and regionalisms of modernism by bringing submerged histories into our vision, with the effect, most explicitly in Ariela Freedman's essay, of reconfiguring the present and future of such aesthetics, especially in relation to postcolonial agendas.

Aldon Nielsen's opening essay focuses on the black Atlantic experience and, in light of it, renarrates the sources of deconstructive thought in the West. Tracking the collaborations of C. L. R. James and Jean-François Lyotard in cultivating a political existentialism in the United States and in initiating deconstructive practices, Nielsen then considers how black Atlantic writers such as Claude McKay extend these theoretical moves into the world of aesthetics. His account of black intellectuals' role in the development of critiques of modernity holds out an object lesson for critics of modernism who might unconsciously deepen what Nielsen calls the "mise en abyme" of history: this abyss holds captive the labor and thought of blacks that has propelled modernity and yet is absent from narratives of modernity.

Evoking this same colonial history yet keeping his attention on the figure of the continental African rather than the African Caribbean or African American, Simon Gikandi asks how the European modernist mode of epiphany might have required the imagined encounter with Africans. Gikandi looks closely at the work of the German ethnologist Leo Frobenius and tracks Frobenius's expressed desire for cultural transcendence through intimacy with African communities. Here Gikandi finds a model for the monumentalization of otherness within modernism and in critical treatments of modernism—an interesting counterpoint to Nielsen's emphasis on the invisibility of black Atlantic history.

Laura Doyle uncovers another overlooked genealogy for racial and aesthetic practices in modernity. Arguing that we must trace modernity's emergence to sources far earlier than the Enlightenment, she begins her account of Atlantic modernity with the racialized liberty discourse that spread with the English Revolution of the 1640s. There, Doyle traces a paradoxical discourse in which the will to free individual subjectivity is racialized as Anglo-Saxon, so that modernity forms itself around "liberty plots" that are racially coded, especially in the genre of the novel. She argues that Atlantic modernisms fail to disentangle themselves from race insofar as they adopt a liberty narrative for their own practices—a conundrum for which Nella Larsen offers metanarratives in *Quicksand* and "Sanctuary."

Fernando Rosenberg turns this set of transatlantic reflections south, to Brazil. In his genealogy of post-1890s Latin-American *modernismo* (cata-lyzed by Latin American states gaining independence from Spain), Rosen-berg seeks to shift the ground of debates that tend to align *modernismo*, reductively, with either Eurocentric or nationalist–liberationist agendas. Instead, in the Brazilian *modernisto* Mário de Andrade, Rosenberg finds a global *economic* consciousness; Andrade's alienated speaker conjures not the romanticized native but rather an utterly deracinated Brazilian miner. In light of Doyle's essay, we might say that, in eschewing race as a central trope, Andrade leaves himself no way to redeem the liberatory narrative of the modern nation—and he thus leaves exposed the capitalist genealogy of geomodernist poetics.

Ken Seigneurie's and Ariela Freedman's essays take us elsewhere alto-gether, away from the Atlantic triangle's race negotiations. Seigneurie faces us with post-1975 Lebanon and its state of "ongoing war"—a situation shaped by race only secondarily (that is, only insofar as the Western ad-herence to race has affected the geopolitics of the region and insofar as the legacy of Enlightenment principles is perceived as Western). And yet, Seigneurie suggests, modernity's crises of failed liberation and its states of war, expressed in a modern aesthetics of disorientation, disaffection, and identity aporia, are fully manifest in the Arabic novel of the post-1970s. He speculates, in addition, that these Arab novelists' ultimate rejection of a postmodern sensibility may derive from the influence of an Arab (rather than a European) humanist tradition of *"adab."* And so, Seigneurie offers another kind of "future anterior" genealogy of modernity, parallel to yet different from Aldon Nielsen's. In Ariela Freedman's essay, likewise, di-verse traditions inflect modern aesthetics and its political situatedness. Aligning himself with the photographer Cartier-Bresson and poet Ezra Pound as well as Indian filmmaker Satyajit Ray and ancient Indian minia-turist paintings, the later twentieth-century Indian photographer Raghubir Singh openly declared himself a modernist—both because he practiced a transnational aesthetic of borrowing—stock in trade of white modernists—and because at the same time he drew on a very old set of multicultural and "centrifugal" traditions within India. In a sense, as do the Arab nov-elists Seigneurie discusses, Singh shows his indifference to Western dis-tinctions between native and foreign—seeking instead, in the wake of co-lonialism and in the face of poverty, a "palpable humanism."

In this diverse set of genealogies, we can begin to glimpse a different modernity. That is, although Western thinkers have since the eighteenth century attributed to themselves *the* history and consciousness that gener-ated modernity and eventually modernism, these essays clarify how, in fact, many histories—kept in the shadows of mainstream Western accounts—have converged to create these geomodernist imaginings. As we know, the many "inventions" regularly attributed to Western modernity—from codification of laws and scientific discovery to industrialism and cosmopolitanism to an ethos of sentiment and humanist secularism—also arise earlier elsewhere. Putting this fact beside the diverse cultural legacies charted in these essays, the "modernity" that seemed to rise on the sixteenth-century Atlantic with the transport of goods and people across a vast ocean instead begins to appear as a part of an older, worldwide geography of tributaries and riptides. Although the Atlantic experience stands as an epitome of this modernity, it may not mark its origin or its telos. Thus the "hauntology" of modernism that Nielsen advocates might entail a broader gathering of spirits—witnesses, we might say, to ongoing war as well as trickster borrowing—from all four corners of the world.

Such a multifarious modernity might well be expected to entangle art in a range of political contests. The geomodernisms treated in "Modernisms' Contested States" form one such constellation: these projects more directly manifest the contradictory strains of state and market modernization on twentieth-century aesthetic practices. Accordingly, the essays are more materialist in their orientation. In the end, they create an image of the pressure cooker conditions under which some geomodernisms formed—strategically, nationalistically, and anxiously.

Sung-sheng Yvonne Chang and Gerard Aching shed light on how geomodernist discourses have formed in response to revolutionary state upheavals. Chang offers a narrative of modernisms per se in China and Taiwan that correlates them with distinct phases of state modernization and economic innovation. She argues that the timing and shape of modernist practice in these places—specifically understood by practitioners as modernist—reflect modernisms' power as cultural capital that could be used in ideological struggles within China and Taiwan, variously serving nationalist and communist modernizing platforms but always precariously positioned vis-à-vis anti-Western nativism. In his analysis of José Martí—Cuban poet, journalist, and advocate for Cuban independence—Aching shows that here, too, modernist discourse occupies a precarious middle position within an unfolding state drama. As in China, writers in newly independent Latin American states found that bold, innovative, high culture modernism could provide a cultural formation suited to modernizing change. At the same time, this modernism was also allied to elite, old world aesthetic standards and educated class leadership. Under the racialized pressures of nation building in Cuba, Martí critiques this *modernismo* and proffers a more politicized, *mestizo* version of *modernismo,* an abstract "fictive ethnicity," pitched against the rising hegemony of North American Anglo-Saxonism.

While Aching and Chang reveal geomodernisms working in tension with national modernization projects, Patricia Chu and Janet Lyon study works that resist modernizing trends, and Laura Winkiel, in the final essay of this section, exposes a racialized anxiety about modernization among avant-garde British modernists. Patricia Chu provocatively juxtaposes two texts with apparently opposite racial agendas—*The Birth of a Nation* and Zora Neale Hurston's *Tell My Horse*—and shows how they operate in unsettlingly similar ways, as reactions against a state-based, rational, and individualist modernity. In this discourse, the attraction of nativism for the implicitly protesting voice (white Klansmen in Griffith's film and the participant-observer of Haitians in Hurston's ethnography) is more than psycho-sexual: it derives as well from ambivalent envy of the "native's" canniness about the crimes and misdemeanors of state modernization, and his/her "license" to dis-affiliate with state rule. In Chu's reading, Hurston and Griffith both operate as strategic mediators of antimodern resistance.

Janet Lyon's essay reinforces Chu's political account of primitivist "other-envy" by considering how "Gypsies" became cathected objects of antistate autonomy for British modernists (expressed most clearly in the writings of the Gypsy Lore Society), especially in a period of new legislation against Gypsy "vagrancy." Arthur Symons's essay, "In Praise of Gypsies," for instance, resonates suggestively with Hurston's ethnography of the "lying" strategies of Haitians, insofar as he points sympathetically to the supposed "Gypsy faults" of secrecy and lying as strategies of antistate resistance and he predicts that Gypsies will outlive both nations and their citizen-inhabitants. In this light, Lyon suggests that white European modernists' adoption of supposedly "bohemian" social practices, as well as their fictional representations of "Gypsy" figures, took on a political cast as expressions of resistance to state modernity.

Laura Winkiel similarly uncovers how, from within the British center, modernist attraction to the perceived primitive expressed resistance to narrow nationalism and to the conforming pressures of modernity. But her account of the vorticists draws attention to an underlying vehemence, incoherence, and outrage within these expressions of resistance—as if the incongruity of being entitled citizens who nonetheless feel regimented and constrained created a near-apocalyptic panic. Winkiel traces how the cabaret aesthetics of the vorticists (in which textual, visual, musical, and outrageously racialized performances promised to break past all proper categories) finally provides, for Wyndham Lewis especially, a renewed Anglo-Saxon claim to dominance justified exactly by this performative, larger-than-nationalist, boundary-breaking aesthetic.

Cutting against the grain of these state-oriented and strategic geomodernisms, the five essays in "Modernisms' Imagined Geographies" consider texts in which a disrupted or multiple positionality works against a national or racial mapping of identity. They turn attention to ontologies, sexualities, and what Eluned Summers-Bremner calls "psychogeographies." They theorize geomodernist desire or weariness as these are ontologically rendered.

Ian Baucom turns to the trope of space in considering the collapse of distance enacted by modernity, finding in Frantz Fanon and Charles

Baudelaire two oddly complementary theorists of this collapse. He recalls Baudelaire's image of the apparently blasé gaze of the courtesan or dandy through which modernity is witnessed—blasé, Baudelaire says, because the epic scale of a diorama-like modernity has been punctured and collapsed, its magic exposed as mere performance. Baucom then juxtaposes this gaze against the estranged vision that sees the white colonial town from the perspective of a colonial or apartheid township. Baucom considers the ways that Fanon and Can Themba (a mid-1950s "township renaissance" author) hint at a suppressed energy within the township gaze and point toward a geomodernist aesthetic in formation.

Through the lens of Baucom's essay, we could say that Susan Stanford Friedman more directly enters *into* the subaltern text's gaze and attends to the disavowed longings and unspeakable desires in it. Stanford Friedman foregrounds how taboo sexuality, in particular, prompts a gaze that looks across caste divisions not only, for instance, compelling a collapse of colonial distance in the sexual spaces of E. M. Forster's *Passage to India*, but also much later in the cross-national, cross-caste, untouchable couplings of Arundhati Roy's *The God of Small Things*. By way of this pairing, Stanford Friedman argues that a paratactical approach to such works as Forster and Roy's—interpreted, in effect, as readings of each other—forces us to acknowledge the spatial network of sexual prohibitions and displacements shaping their (post)colonial modernisms.

Eluned Summers-Bremner carries out, in another locale, the cultural parataxis Stanford Friedman advocates. She reads T. S. Eliot's *The Waste Land* and Langston Hughes's *Montage of a Dream Deferred* as a pair of nostalgic, post-traumatic poems memorializing the exile entailed in modernity. Summers-Bremner clarifies how the post-emancipation, migrant conditions underlying Hughes's poem actually shape Eliot's past and poem as well—revealing the submerged ways that race propels those poetics that are apparently race-free or cosmopolitan. Implicitly echoing the suggestions of Nielsen, in Summers-Bremner's reading, Hughes and Eliot together establish how modernity is founded on the presence/absence of black influence—a matrix she finds expressed in the "psychogeography" of their poems.

The last two essays return to the questions of desire and distance in modernity that Baucom evokes. Offering a counterpart to Ian Baucom's account of collapsed distance, Jessica Berman shows canonical Anglo-European modernists aiming to map, and in a sense refill, that drained and failed space. Establishing, first of all, the presence of cultural geographers in the early twentieth century who worked to move beyond determinist models of race and geography, Berman tracks a parallel project in Joyce, Woolf, Rhys, and Stein, finding in their fiction a desire-suffused ethic of geo-social "possibilism" (geographer Vidal de la Blache's term). Justine Dymond's study of *Cogewea* (1927), an apparently simple, sentimental, Western novel by Okanogan-American author Mourning Dove, on the one hand, echoes Baucom's account of geographic collapse and, on the other, may offer its own kind of hybrid "possibilism." Dymond argues that by emplacing her "mixed-breed" yet apparently sentimental heroine on a Western ranch and tracking her bodily (dis)orientation, Mourning Dove shares the project of many white women modernists—to explore the non-normative phenomenology of disenfranchised experiences. Yet unlike those modernists, Mourning Dove must also create a hybrid form: first, so as to establish the sentimental interiority of her heroine and then by evoking both the racial violence and the geo-phenomenological possibilities that her heroine carries.

Taken together, these essays move readers well beyond familiar accounts of race politics and primitivism in modernism. They present geomodernisms as a global, complex, multidirectional, and divergent set of projects. Launched from different locations at different times under unequal conditions, these geomodernisms arrive at sometimes incommensurable reimaginings of the modern world they inhabit together. We hope this collection, in turn, heightens the reader's sense of cohabitation with these projects and these places, however distant, however disorienting, and however difficult their demands.

AN INVITATION TO READ ASTRAY

Taken together, these essays move readers well beyond familiar accounts of race politics and primitivism in modernism. They present geomodernisms as a global, complex, and multidirectional set of projects.

And yet these essays are just a beginning. They indicate the potential and the need for a new set of multidirectional, postcolonial conversations in our scholarly work, conversations that enable a still fuller excavating of our mutually implicated histories and of geomodernisms' frisson within them. All of the essays here move across established boundaries of some kind—of nation, race, caste, genre, or period—yet many also continue to work mainly within mono-cultural or single-language histories. This place- and language-specific work is crucial, but an understanding of modernism's geocultural force and its full positionality will require an even more historical, transnational dialogue in scholarship than has yet emerged.

The next step, then, would be to launch projects that bring into view the fullest circuits of relation within modernity and among modernist projects. How might the rise of modernist Taiwanese cinema, with its seemingly west-to-east trajectory, appear differently in view of the earlier, turn-of-the-century Western borrowings from Eastern visual arts traditions? What might cabaret performances in early-twentieth-century London have to do with such performances in Brazil or Cuba? And what light might a transnational account of the origins of cabaret culture shed on all of these modern nightclub venues? Or, how does the Spanish tradition of *picaro* play out within the English-language novel's transatlantic tale of seduction, ruin, and freedom—or vice versa?[1] And again, given the indirect yet real relation between the state of "ongoing war" that Ken Seigneurie identifies in Lebanon and that which has persisted in some Latin American countries (recall the Iran-Contra affair, and recall too the centuries-old competitive yet symbiotic relationship between trading companies in the Americas and in the Middle East), what happens when we consider the modernist or humanist or racialist aesthetic projects of these two world-regions together? The essays gathered here enable us to ask these questions more clearly, and yet answers will emerge only when we persist in configuring more global and longer histories for modernism than is typical.

Thus this volume leaves much work in the reader's hands. We offer it above all as an invitation to move across linguistic and national boundaries in scholarship, in order to re-see the circuits within which capitalist modernity has placed us and geomodernisms. If it is impossible to step wholly outside those circuits, we can at least travel them differently, open to ways of transforming them through thoughtful encounters with each other. Our closing plea, then, is that readers read widely in this volume, not limiting attention to essays in a specific tradition or region but actively straying into unknown histories and texts. For as we know, wherever we stand, in colony, metropole, or somewhere in between, it turns out that our histories are multiple and interconnected in surprising, unforeseen ways.

NOTE

1. We thank Doris Sommer for suggesting the possible relevance, in this context, of the *picaro*'s influence on the English-language novel, and for highlighting, more broadly, the limits of mono-cultural scholarship in modernist studies.

PART ONE

Modernisms' Alternative Genealogies

1   The Future of an Allusion: The Color of Modernity

Aldon Lynn Nielsen

> If the cynical consciousness of the "black" writers speaks the truth about bourgeois culture, ideology critique does not have anything in reserve to which it might appeal.
> —Jürgen Habermas, *Discourse*

> Toussaint's failure was the failure of enlightenment, not of darkness.
> —C. L. R. James, *Jacobins*

> This is the last great battle of the West.
> —W. E. B. DuBois, *Reconstruction*

1

> there are eight million unfinished projects of the enlightenment in
> the naked city. this is one of them.

In his oft-cited introductory chapter to *The Philosophical Discourse of Modernity*, Habermas takes up the question Max Weber raised as a problem for any "universal" history. "For Weber," Habermas reminds us, "the intrinsic (that is, not merely contingent) relationship between modernity and what he called 'Occidental rationalism' was still self-evident" (1). Weber had pondered why, "outside Europe, the scientific, the artistic, the political, or the economic development . . . did not enter upon that path of rationalization which is peculiar to the occident" (1). While Habermas recognizes that the intrinsic relationship of modernity to Occidental rationalization may have subsequently come into question itself, he does not pause here to inquire just where Weber might have stood to observe this "outside" of Europe. Neither does he appear to wonder at the seeming conflict between modern Occidental reason's pretensions to universalism and its simultaneous insistence upon its peculiarly Occidental character. In 1958, when Weber's *The Protestant Work Ethic* was published in New York, there was virtually no place on earth that had not been brought within the horizon of Occidental rationalization.

Clearly, though, Habermas does not have writers of African descent in mind when he addresses himself to the cynicism of "black writers" (still, there is no reason to suppose that an African writer might not indeed be a "black writer" in his formulation); Habermas's blackness is here entirely metaphorical. It is that same darkness invoked by C. L. R. James, but the failures that James attributes to Toussaint L'Ouverture are failures of the Enlightenment, failures of the always unfinished projects of modernity. They were failures of rationalization, not the metaphorical heart of darkness and ignorance. James's seemingly straightforward sentence is among the more overdetermined passages in his monumental history, *The Black Jacobins*. At one end of the sentence he is at pains to separate the "darkness" of which both he and Habermas speak from the black figures about whom Habermas is completely silent. James is intent upon the destruction of the epidermalization of moral darkness that modern reason had reified in the form of ideological racism, a racism that subsequent writers such as David Theo Goldberg view as a defining feature of state formation in modernity. In Goldberg's reading, "the racially conceived and reproducing state is characteristic of, not exceptional to, modernity" (114). But even as he separates a mode of Habermasian darkness from the bodies of dark peoples, James is bent upon demonstrating that the failures of Toussaint L'Ouverture's reasoning were the failures of a Western-inflected rationalization, not failures of reason per se. The Occidental claim to be the peculiar locus of a universal reason is just the sort of darkness that marks the unreason it would deride. In James's estimation, it is precisely because L'Ouverture had come of age within the slave-holding civilization of the modern West that he made the particular form of revolution that he did make, and that he failed to learn the most important lessons taught by the struggles of his fellow Africans in San Domingo to achieve freedom and independence, to constitute themselves as the very subjects of liberty and fraternity. In all senses, L'Ouverture's incomplete revolution was an unfinished project of the Enlightenment collapsed finally beneath the weight of opposition met within Western modernity.

When Toni Morrison speaks of "The overweening defining event of the modern world," in her essay "Home" (10), her title alludes to an earlier collection of essays by Amiri Baraka at the same time that her sentence alludes to a major thesis found in such works as C. L. R. James's *Black Jacobins* and *Mariners, Renegades and Castaways,* a thesis that had also been developed independently by W. E. B. DuBois, perhaps at greatest depth in *Black Reconstruction.* Paul Gilroy alludes to that same thesis in *The Black Atlantic* (originally titled *Promised Lands*) when he describes a conception of modernity periodized differently from that of Habermas, a conception "founded on the catastrophic rupture of the Middle Passage rather than the dream of revolutionary transformation" (197). When we follow Gilroy back to his sources we discover that this reconception of modernity projected by James and DuBois is, in fact, accompanied by its own dream of revolutionary transformation, a dream drawing its resources from earlier revolutionary movements carried forward by African peoples in the West, carried forward out of the profoundest rupture of Middle Passage.

James and DuBois both argue far more than the simple case that black people, whether in the New World or in Africa, have not in fact lived outside the horizon of Occidental modernity. DuBois asserts in *Black Reconstruction* that the "black worker [was a] founding stone of a new economic system in the nineteenth century and for the modern world" (15). He further argues that "Black labor became the foundation stone not only of the Southern social structure, but of Northern manufactures and commerce, of the English factory system, of European commerce, of buying and selling on a world-wide scale" (5). Both James and DuBois trace the emergence of new, modern world-encompassing economies to the rupture of Middle Passage and the monumental labors of black workers, but James's *Black Jacobins*, published just three years after DuBois's *Black Reconstruction*, audaciously broadens this historical thesis in two directions. In the first place, James holds that the New World's novel modes of social and economic organization brought New World Africans into a fundamentally transmuted life world. Fred Dallmayr, in his critical response to Habermas's works on modernity, argues that "Renaissance and Reformation (together with the discovery of the 'New World') heralded an implicit break with the classical and medieval past; but the notion of a distinctly 'modern' period emerged only slowly in the aftermath of these events" (61). As James develops the history of the revolutionary transformations wrought by New World Africans, he insists that the emergence of the distinctly modern as a fact on the ground was considerably less slow in the case of those who had experienced directly the more explicit break with the continuity of their own past. What he was charting here was the same phenomena that had brought DuBois to his revisions of the concept of double-consciousness, the same phenomenon about which Richard Wright was to remark so poetically: "We millions of black folk who live in this land were born into Western civilization of a weird and paradoxical birth" (12). In an appendix later added to the second edition of his history, James asserts

When three centuries ago the slaves came to the West Indies, they entered directly into the large-scale agriculture of the sugar plantation, which was a modern system. It further required that the slaves live together in a social relation far closer than any proletariat of the time. The cane when reaped had to be rapidly transported to what was factory production. The product was shipped abroad for sale. Even the cloth the slaves wore and the food they ate was imported. The Negroes, therefore, from the very start lived a life that was in its essence a modern life. That is their history—as far as I have been able to discover, a unique history. (392)

Where Weber wants to see the path to modern rationalization as peculiarly Occidental, James sees the unique history of Africans in the diaspora as not only determining a modern essence *avant la lettre* but as the very condition of possibility of Occidental development and the emergence of a world system. James had earlier established that the wealth generated from slavery in the Western hemisphere did much to fuel the remarkable capitalist expansion of European economies (in fact, it was this portion of James's thesis that inspired Eric Williams's still controversial volume *Capitalism and Slavery*). James saw that the altered material relationships created in Europe by these new sources of capital and power did much to instigate new modes of political thought. This leads him to conclude that "the slave trade and slavery were the economic basis of the French Revolution" (47). He cites Juarès's remark to the effect that it was the fortunes created by the slave trade that "gave to the bourgeoisie that pride which needed liberty and contributed to human emancipation" (47). Though later historians and economists have contested James's and Williams's estimations of the exact extent to which the changing economies of the slave systems in colonial production influenced the political agendas of abolition, James's central argument in this regard has never been displaced: that the labors of Africans in the New World created both the plantation wealth and much of the historical circumstances enabling the rise to power of the ideas of liberty, fraternity, and equality accompanied by the violent final era of the old regimes. (It is just this that is completely overlooked in Dinesh D'Souza's fatuous *The End of Racism* when he asserts, completely ahistorically, that only in the West has a society "ever on its own account mounted principled opposition to human servitude" [100], an assertion whose only source, it turns out when one reads his footnotes, is an editorial column by Stanley Crouch.) In *The Repeating Island*, Antonio Benítez-Rojo reaches much the same conclusions as did James regarding the plantation system and its role in Western history:

So much has already been written about all of this that it is not worth the effort even to sketch out the incredible and dolorous history of this machine. Still, something must be said, just a few things. For one: the singular feature of this machine is that it produced no fewer than ten million African slaves and thousands of coolies (from India, China and Malaysia). All this, however, is not all: the plantation machines turned out mercantile capitalism, industrial capitalism . . . [and] African underdevelopment. (9)

This is one of those truths about the narrative of emancipation that James, like DuBois, had good cause to believe "a venal race of scholars, profiteering panders to national vanity, have conspired to obscure" (51). Where other historians and philosophers had, following the logics of Occidental reason, held with Hegel that Africa was outside of history, James and DuBois simply adopted a tactic familiar to us now from the Watergate investigations of the 1970s: they followed the money. When we follow the money we find that Africans had made possible not just the growth of the Singer Sewing Machine Company, Montgomery Ward, Brown University, and so on, but the very course of modern history. Where venal scholars portrayed black people in the Americas as atavistically pre-modern, James held that they were among the first truly modern peoples.

Parallel to these theses of modernity as advanced by James and DuBois in their historical works has been an equally persistent thesis regarding aesthetic modernism. When Melvin B. Tolson wrote in his *Harlem Gallery* that "the listening ear can hear / among the moderns, blue / tomtoms of Benin" (59), he was not merely noting the immediate influence of American jazz on modern sensibilities, so easily heard in the compositions of Stravinsky, Milhaud, and others. That argument had been placed on the table by black writers of the Harlem Renaissance and their contemporary historiographers. In the special Harlem issue of the *Survey Graphic* and in the subsequent volume *The New Negro*, edited by Alain Locke, historian J. A. Rogers took note of remarks European musicians and composers had made quite openly regarding the importance of black music to the modernizing of Western composition. Serge Kousevitzky had acknowledged that jazz had not simply made a contribution to modern musical literature, but that it had an epochal significance and was now fundamental to composition. Leopold Stokowski had praised jazz musicians as "pathfinders into new realms." "Thus," concludes Rogers in *The New Negro*, "it has come about that serious modernists and musicians, most notably and avowedly in the work of the French modernists Auric, Satie and Darius Milhaud, have become the confessed debtors of American Negro jazz" (222). Tolson was to take these arguments much farther. Where Walt Whitman had held in the preceding century that the job of the American poet was "to give the modern meaning of things" (1328), Tolson was to argue that it was specifically in the African diaspora that those modern meanings were to be formed. Looking to the incredible influence on European aesthetics wrought by the sculptures brought from Africa by Van Luschan, Tolson had already claimed that it was Benin "whose ivory and / bronze statues gave lyricism and / space reality to modernistic art" (container 8). In his lyric practice, Tolson was rearticulating arguments about modernism in the arts that had been current among black intellectuals for more than three decades, arguments found in the writings of Sterling Brown, Carter G. Woodson, DuBois and, at considerable length, Alain Locke. Locke had prominently placed in his 1925 *New Negro* anthology an essay of his own in which he maps out just a few of the overtly acknowledged circulations of African art forms in Western modernism. In painting and sculpture he names Matisse, Picasso, Derain, Modigliani, Utrillo, Pechstein, Archipenko, Zadkine, Guillaume, and others. Locke further tracks this influence as it spreads through the arts. "Attracted by the appeal of African plastic art to the study of other modes of African expression," Locke observes, "poets like Guillaume Appolinaire [*sic*] and Blaisé Cendrars [*sic*] have attempted artistic re-expression of African idioms in poetic symbols and verse forms" (261). One need only look as far as the *Cantos* of Ezra Pound, with their invocation of the *Dausi* epic and the tale of Gassire's lute, gathered from his readings in Leo Frobenius, to see the decisive role African expressive forms have played in modernist poetics. And this association of black arts with the evolution of aesthetic modernism was not a thesis confined to black thinkers and writers. As John Hammond publicized the "Spirituals to Swing" concert he was organizing at Carnegie Hall, he boldly predicted in the pages of the *New Masses* that "what we now have promises to be an evening of great discovery, a presentation that may well be to modern music what the Armory Show of cubist painting in 1913 was to modern art" (2). Those very cubist paintings seen at the Armory Show, of course, had tangible roots in their creators' rediscovery of African art forms.

But as we retrace these critical genealogies of blackness and modernity from the vantage point of our newly arrived century, we find ourselves following an intriguing fold in historical narrative. In order for intellectuals of the African diaspora to posit New World Africans as progenitors of modernity, in order for us, now, to follow them in thinking of African peoples as not simply subjects encompassed by modernity but as active producers of the modern, we must have modernity already there before us, and this is why all such writings are haunted by a "post-" and why all such histories must immediately be seen as revisionist. This is why contemporary critics such as Mark Anthony Neal posit African American modernity "as a 'counter' or at least 'alternative' modernity" (4), for it is a modernity that is found already there within modernity. It is as if black writers have had to steal past the disciplinary boundaries erected by whiteness around modernity, to slip inside modernity to demonstrate that they had been there all along. This accounts for the real violence that surrounds these arguments even now, as well as accounting for the redoubling of consciousness required of any who would think a future of modernism. A particularly biting passage in Ishmael Reed's novel *Mumbo Jumbo* satirizes the violent resistance with which such "black" writers and thinkers of darkness have been met. Blustering with anger, one character offers a damning litany against the sheer audacity of black thought:

I've seen them, son, in Africa, China, they're not like us, son, the Herrenvolk. Europe. This place. They are lagging behind, son, and you know in your heart this is true. Son, these niggers writing. Profaning our sacred words. Taking them from us and beating them on the anvil of Boogie Woogie, putting their black hands on them . . . Why . . . why 1 of them dared to interpret, critically mind you, the great Herman Melville's *Moby Dick*!! (114)

It is characteristic of racist rationalizations that this speaker simultaneously derides the colored peoples of the world as atavistic, as unmodern, as unlike *us*, while at the same time he is horrified at the prospect of one such person not only reading but critiquing a classic of American literature. Reed's passage, though, is even more interesting as an example of just the sort of narrative fold, of the future anterior in writing, that we see in the historical commentaries of James, DuBois, Locke, and so many others. For the character is here denouncing a book that had not yet been written. The critic who dared to interpret, critically mind you, *Moby Dick*, is none other than C. L. R. James, in his book *Mariners, Renegades, and Castaways: The Story of Herman Melville and the World We Live In.* And *Mumbo Jumbo* is a comic novel set at the height of America's jazz age, a time when Americans bemoaned the "rising tide of color" even as they streamed to venues in which they could listen, dance to, play with black music. James's *Mariners* would not be written for another three decades, yet Reed has ingeniously transported that critique back to the age of the great American rediscovery of Melville. Further, at the time Reed wrote his novel, James's critique was long out of print, acknowledged by no more than a handful of Melville scholars, and James himself was only then being allowed to re-enter the United States after having been forced to leave at the peak of the McCarthy era. James has managed, in Reed's wild imaginings, to out-precedent himself, to borrow a term from William Carlos Williams, to be so far ahead of his time as to be ahead of himself. For Reed, such re-doublings are characteristic of black modernity, which must always unfold within the modern as a prescient post-.

We have no further to look than to the writers of black modernism themselves to see just how striking is this double fold, this postmodernity within modernity that *is* diasporic blackness. Just as modernism is identified as the "jazz age," so has modernism also been closely identified with the industry, apparatus, and art of cinema, whose invention preceded and prepared the way for the aesthetics commonly identified as modern today. Any viewer of *Birth of a Nation* is already acutely aware of the role race plays in the birth of modern cinema. Any viewer aware of the fact that the same white actors play the Klansmen and the blackface Negroes chased by the Klansmen in that film's climactic scenes has witnessed the sort of racialized *mise en abyme* that I am here identifying as the doublefold of blackness and postmodernity. Anna Everett, in *Returning the Gaze,* has given us the remarkable history of African Americans' love–hate relationship to the cinema, tracking through the writings of early black film critics the same ironies and tensions found in the writings of black literary figures. Rudolf Fisher, in "Miss Cynthie," alludes to these mixed feelings when he reports the thoughts of a character as she settles into the front row of a lower box in the theater: "A miraculous device of the devil, a motion-picture that talked, was just ending" (248). But if New Negroes were drawn to the modern sensorium of the cinema, as the case of *Birth of a Nation* would indicate, the theater was every bit as racialized a space as were the rest of the social spaces in America. And like those other spaces (the railroad car, the waiting room, the café), the very fact of their racial striation was premised upon the modern device of race. As DuBois writes in "The Souls of White Folk," "the discovery of personal whiteness among the world's peoples is a very modern thing,—a nineteenth and twentieth century matter, indeed" (*Darkwater* 30). This personal whiteness is determined by its relation to blackness, of course, which makes the modernity of whiteness again something that has blackness as its very condition of possibility. And this is why the very modernity of cinema has at the center of its project the projection of blackness. Film has never been a simple pleasure for black people. "After all, a cigarette with Charlie Chaplin," thinks DuBois wistfully as he stands outside a theater watching the white patrons enter after he has been told the only remaining tickets are in the smoking gallery:

> Suddenly that silly orchestra seat and the cavorting of a comedian with funny feet become matters of life, death and immortality; you grasp the pillars of the universe and strain as you sway back to that befrilled ticket girl. You choke and sputter, and she seeing that you are about to make a "fuss" obeys her orders and throws the tickets at you in contempt. Then you slink back to your seat in the darkness before the film, with every tissue burning! (*Darkwater* 224)

From here, things get, if anything, yet more tangled, for the spectacle on the screen is no mere reflection of the scene of racial insult enacted at the ticket booth. And, if we are to believe Claude McKay, "there is no better angle from which one can look down on a motion picture than that of the nigger heaven" (227). What McKay inscribes here is not a simple matter of racial solidarity in the upper balconies; he is remarking that vertiginous viewpoint which affords a particular understanding of the redoublings of modern film. There is little more certain than that the modern white audience knew that the white people in blackface on their theater screens were not really black people, but how certain could they be of anything in the face of such a spectacle? Wasn't one element of the specular pleasures available to the audience McKay describes in the higher reaches of a Broadway theater precisely the gravity-defying sensation of looking over the heads of white people at the productions and reproductions of blackness and whiteness on the screen? Where would white audiences be without the possibility of these representations? And in the "Negro Picture Theater" as McKay dramatizes it, the redoublings of representations were yet more dizzying:

> It was odd that all these cinematic pictures about the blacks were a broad burlesque of their home and love life. These colored screen actors were all dressed up in expensive evening clothes, with automobiles, and menials, to imitate white society people. They laughed at themselves in such roles and the laughter was good on the screen. They pranced and grinned like good-nigger servants, who know that "mas'r" and "missus," intent on being amused, are watching their antics from an upper window. (227)

Where the modernity of white people is premised upon their projections of themselves in blackface, black spectatorship is informed by the recognition that there is another blackness than their own already on the screen; that this other blackness is dependent upon them for its very origins, and yet has so little to do with them. In turn, they project a racial imaginary of their own, one in which they fictionalize themselves as occupying the spaces of whiteness, but without white people. Nevertheless, the spectatorial pleasure attendant upon that imagining is never quite free of the imagined gaze of the other, the policing and distorting view of "mas'r" and "missus" looking on from an upper window. This, for McKay, explains why the "nigger heaven" in the Broadway theater provides the better vantage point from which to look down on a motion picture than the "Negro Picture Theater." Better to *be* the amused gaze, looking down at the whites as the whites look to themselves as black, than to feel that uneasy itch of surveillance perpetually at the back of the neck.

This passage from McKay is cited in no discussions of the postmodern gaze that I have ever been able to locate, and yet what is surer than that this is a classic instance of *mise en abyme*? Traditional discussions of the modernity of the Harlem Renaissance, while attending to the theater and the cinema, tend to elide this very sense of the vertiginous, this moment in which black viewers see themselves in the shadows behind the figurations of race at the heart of modernity. If T. S. Eliot was able to absorb a lyric by James Weldon Johnson to shore up his "Fragments of an Agon" (North 88–89), few critics other than Michael North have proved able to absorb the significance of this black lyric at the heart of a racialized, white modernism. If, as Mark Anthony Neal argues, "even as African-American culture embraced modernity, it was already impacted by postmodern influences" (8), this was in large part explainable by the fact that modernity was born of that impossible effort of white Westerners to bring themselves into being by simultaneously embracing and distancing themselves from blackness.

When, at the close of *Black Reconstruction,* DuBois insists that black people be admitted to our understandings of modernity, part of what he demands is an admission that modernity has no future otherwise. "Such mental frustration cannot indefinitely continue," DuBois promises, prefiguring James Baldwin's *The Fire Next Time* in one of his "darkest" passages:

> Some day it may burst in fire and blood. Who will be to blame? And where the greater cost? Black folk, after all, have little to lose, but Civilization has all.
>
> This the American black man knows: his fight here is a fight to the finish. Either he dies or he wins. If he wins it will be by no subterfuge or evasion of amalgamation. He will enter modern civilization as a black man on terms of perfect and unlimited equality with any white man, or he will enter not at all. Either extermination root and branch, or absolute equality. There can be no compromise. This is the last great battle of the West. (703)

2

Can you say *"mise en abyme"*?

If our histories in progress of modernity and modernism have generally been written as if black people had little to do with the subject other than be subject to it, American discussions of postmodernism have tended to a curious oblivion regarding our own very recent past. Thus, for one telling example, no consideration of the postmodern, or of poststructuralism for that matter, has yet contended with African American poet Russell Atkins's essays on deconstruction, essays he published in the small press journal *Free Lance* in the decade prior to Jacques Derrida's first appearances in the United States. Nor has any discussion of the phenomenon of metatextuality that I have been able to locate attended to this passage from what has to rank as among Amiri Baraka's most continuously available volumes, *Blues People.* In this portion of his discussion, Baraka is describing the manifold ironies of racial exchange in American popular music:

> Northern Negro pre-jazz music was almost like the picture within a picture, and so on, on the cereal package. Ragtime was a Negro music, resulting from the Negro's appropriation of white piano techniques used in show music. Popularized ragtime, which flooded the country with song sheets in the first decade of this century, was a dilution of the Negro style. And finally, the show and "society" music the Negroes in the pre-blues North made was a kind of bouncy, essentially vapid appropriation of the popular-

ized imitations of Negro imitations of white minstrel music, which, as I
mentioned earlier, came from white parodies of Negro life and music. (111)

An entire encyclopedia of whiteness studies could be generated out of this
pixilating passage, though it remains largely overlooked in that discourse
(as, indeed, do nearly all texts that might be described as black nationalist
in outlook). E. L. Doctorow's novel *Ragtime,* with its white-face mimicry of
Ishmael Reed's *Mumbo Jumbo,* erupts within the hall of mirrors here described by Baraka, from a paradigmatic moment in the modernizing of our
quintessentially modern America, and still Reed and Baraka have been
read out of *Ragtime*'s repertoire of referents by most subsequent scholarship, much as Scott Joplin was morphed into Marvin Hamlish at one year's
Grammy Awards ceremony in the wake of *The Sting* soundtrack's runaway
success.

As intriguing as these phenomena may prove, there is often a still more
direct pathway from the modern and from modernism to postmodernity
to be found in the works of black thinkers and artists. One of these routes
brings us yet again to the passages of C. L. R. James.

In October 1966, in London, James met with a group of British and
American comrades for a discussion of existentialism and Marxism. Very
much a preliminary sketch for further thinking and research, James's exe-
gesis builds from his earlier work in *Notes on Dialectics* to establish several
initial lines of inquiry in the texts of Heidegger, Sartre, and others. Then,
near the close of his excursus, James introduces the works in progress of
an activist and philosopher he characterizes as "One of our comrades in
France, a man called Lyotard" ("Existentialism and Marxism" 19). James
especially recommends to his North American colleagues a recent work of
Lyotard's in phenomenology (though he does not name it in the talk),
promising to translate selected passages of the work and send them to the
United States for circulation and discussion. The passages he intends to
translate, he explains, will demonstrate "how closely related Phenomenology and Existentialism are towards a philosophy of everyday existence"
(19). James proceeds to advise his friends, Martin Glaberman and George
Rawick among them, that "Unless Marxism can incorporate these things
and still remain Marxism we remain saying the things that were said by
Engels in Anti-Duhring, etc. That is it and nobody bothers with us. But we
are going to deal with that" (19).

Part of the post- in Lyotard's postmodernism is, of course, the result of
his eventual conclusion that Marxism could not incorporate such things
and still remain Marxism. What I would like to pursue for the moment,
however, is the somewhat simpler itinerary that brought the Afro-Caribbean
philosopher and historian C. L. R. James to press Lyotard upon his associates in 1966, at a time when, for most American academics, the name of
Lyotard would quite possibly have been even less familiar than that of

James, whose works were known, albeit pseudonymously, to philosophers in the United States as prominent as Marcuse. In the late 1940s, C. L. R. James was living and working illegally in the United States. Two remarkable women with whom he was closely collaborating, Raya Dunayevskaya and Grace Lee Boggs, were delegated to represent James's political group at meetings in France where they were to develop close working contacts with a grouping of radical French intellectuals and political activists who would come to be best known collectively under the title of their publication, *Socialisme ou barbarie*. The central figure in the French group, then writing under the name of Chaulieu, was the very same Cornelius Castoriadis whose work is the subject of Habermas's penultimate excursus, on the "Imagining Institution," in *The Philosophical Discourse of Modernity*. Another crucial figure in the life of *Socialisme ou barbarie*, perhaps the most significant for James after Castoriadis himself, was Jean-François Lyotard, with whom the James group continued to correspond through the years following Lyotard's political break with Castoriadis.

Though North American intellectuals have long recognized the importance of the events of May 1968 in France to the international emergence of thought about the postmodern (American writers, we should note, had been discussing the explicit idea of a postmodern since at least the 1940s), the relationships between currents leading into the events of 1968 in Paris and similar currents in the United States remain insufficiently investigated and understood. The fact is that throughout the 1950s, the group known as *Socialisme ou barbarie* and the group of activists gathered around James in the United States were in frequent contact. James, Grace Lee Boggs, and Castoriadis worked together on a series of texts that eventually produced the volume *Facing Reality*, a major statement of the James group's evolving ideology. During this same period, the French group published contributions from members of James's organization in nearly every issue of their journal. Of special interest to the French activists was a text titled *The American Worker*, written by Phil Singer and Grace Lee Boggs, that was translated into French and serialized in successive issues. Appearing alongside some of these American contributions were critical dispatches sent from Algeria by Lyotard, whose contemporary analyses of the anticolonial struggles in North Africa (childhood home of none other than Jacques Derrida) have been reprinted in English in his *Political Writings*. When Lyotard later spoke of the moment more familiar to his readers in North America, that moment in 1968 when, as he puts it, "the student government foregrounded some of the motives that had been animated by Socialism or Barbarism" (167), it should be clear that these motives were formed in part in the North African crucible of his Algerian experiences, and in part in the correspondence with the C. L. R. James group. Both the James organization and *Socialisme ou barbarie* had devoted much of their energies to a thorough critical attack upon a particular set of problems of representation: an assault upon political vanguardism on the Left, and a more general anatomy of the problems of speaking for others. In both groups this eventually led to the demise of the small political organization itself over questions of what Lyotard was to term a "depoliticization" (169). In America, James, Dunayevskaya, and Boggs parted company in a series of devastating organizational splits at nearly the same time that Castoriadis and Lyotard began to move away from Marxism and from one another. James was to remain a Marxist to his death, but he remained a Marxist who rejected the modes of heroic representation typically claimed on the Left of his formative years. Lyotard was to take a different route out of the confrontation with the same set of problems. As he later wrote:

> The presumption of the moderns, of Christianity, Enlightenment, Marxism, has always been that another voice is stifled in the discourse of "reality" and that it is a question of putting a true hero (the creature of God, the responsible citizen, or the enfranchised proletarian) back in his position as subject, wrongfully usurped by the imposter. What we called "depoliticization" twenty-five years ago was in fact the announcement of the erasure of the great figure of the alternative, and at the same time, that of the great founding legitimacies. This is what I have tried to designate, clumsily, by the term "postmodern." (169)

This is exactly the point at which Habermas opposes himself to Lyotard, but in the act of calling for the ideal of communicative action on the part of the reasonable and reasoning citizen, Habermas re-enacts the stifling of discourse that his unfinished project of the Enlightenment was to have remedied. Despite his formalist turn in his efforts to avoid the Weberian presentation of a Eurocentric reason, his philosophical discourse of modernity again follows a peculiarly Occidental path, one that ignores its own reliance upon the enslavement of strangers, the insistence on maintaining them *as* strangers. That modernism, DuBois and James argued, has no future.

In Toni Morrison's reading, "The most valuable point of entry into the question of cultural (or racial) distinction, the one most fraught, is its language. . . . Such a penetration will entail the most careful study, one in which the impact of Afro-American presence on modernity becomes clear and is no longer a well-kept secret" ("Unspeakable" 377). Just such a penetration was called for by James and DuBois earlier in the twentieth century. It has been a well-kept secret that remained, like Poe's purloined letter, in plain view before us. James, for one example, enjoyed the support of Leonard and Virginia Woolf, who published his first British pamphlet, giving it, one would have thought, an impeccably modern imprimatur. If, as David Theo Goldberg observes, "it was thought that the native ought to be encouraged to shed his nativity, in part through language acquisition"

(153), it has also been the case that the native has always been held in the white mythology of modern Western imagination to be ultimately incapable of mastery of the master's tongue. That mythology has required a modernism that deafens itself to its own deepest intonations. If, as David Theo Goldberg believes, "Enlightened racism is camouflaged beneath its liberal historicist enlightenment" (88), it is thinly camouflaged indeed, vulnerable at every point to critical penetration by our "black" writers.

Studies in modernism and modernity have yet to offer adequate answer to the calls of James and DuBois. If such studies are to have a meaningful future they will have to undertake the penetration of the languages of modernism to learn how the theories of historical modernity advanced by black writers inform a view of the postmodern as a condition of possibility within modernism itself, a future anterior, or, to use the Hegelian terminology that would have been favored by James, the future in the present. This means as well that the future study of modernity must of necessity be a mode of Derridean "hauntology" that remembers Derrida's Algerian past, that confronts the revenant of the modern upon the battlements of our assigned post. Lyotard came to doubt that social and political struggles were the privileged realm of the voice of the intractable. Habermas insists upon the potential of "a comprehensive public sphere in which society as a whole fashions a knowledge of itself" (360), and yet his public sphere must appear to many Americans to have been evacuated as thoroughly as anything Lyotard has described. In DuBois's estimation, the Color Line had been laid across the spheres of the political and the social "as at least a partial substitute" ("Realities" 657) for the stratifications of class whose violent transformation accompanied the emergence of liberal thought. For C. L. R. James, the Color Line had produced the conditions of possibility for that revolutionary overthrow and for the fateful projection of the modern. Both authors' visions of modernity stand as a rebuke to the failures of memory that have marked the Enlightenment, and as a possible starting point of our cultural imaginary. In our twenty-first-century postlude to modernism we might pray, with Dubois:

> Let then the Dreams of the Dead rebuke the Blind who think that what is will be forever and teach them that what was worth living for must live again and that which merited death must stay dead. Teach us, Forever Dead, there is no Dream but Deed, there is no Deed but Memory. (*Autobiography* 422–23)

2   Africa and the Epiphany of Modernism

Simon Gikandi

1

It was perhaps Charles Taylor who first identified modernism as an epiphanic philosophical moment in the discourse of modernity. Instead of focusing on the accepted history of modernism as a reaction to the crisis of modernity and the rejection of its established doctrines on such important issues as the idea of the unitary self, identity, time consciousness, and instrumental reason, Taylor concluded *Sources of the Self* with the claim that modernism represented the epiphany of modernity—its moment of revelation and insight. Taylor's radical assertion was that epiphany was itself a sign of the newness of modernism, of its accounting for the gap between the objects of modern life and existing conventions of representation that were found wanting and inadequate. As the basis for "nonrepresentational art," Taylor argued, modernism was the European artist's search for a new way of accounting for experiences that could not be reflected through "the surface of ordinary things"; the epiphanic was the mode of recuperating "something only indirectly available, something the visible object can't say itself but only nudges us towards" (469). Accordingly, Taylor argued, modernism arose in response to a problem that had come to haunt the culture of (European) modernity in the nineteenth century: how to achieve "a kind of unmediated contact with the fullness of life" (469).

By its very nature, modernism sought to promote ideas about culture and forms of representation at odds with what Taylor called "the deadening, routinized, conventional forms of instrumental civilization" (469). But what exactly was involved in this deployment of an epiphanic moment was very much a matter of debate: "Did it mean simply throwing off the old forms and achieving a kind of unmediated contact with the fullness of life?" (469) or was the epiphanic a continuation of older forms of social mediation? Taylor's conclusion, derived from a careful reading of the artistic philosophies of a range of early-twentieth-century writers and artists, including James Joyce, T. S. Eliot, Paul Cézanne and Robert Musil, was that modernism sought the inner depths of life through something that comes "close to merging with the other" (471). What the other was for the modernists—and for us—continues to be one of the most vexing questions in the study of modern culture and its aesthetic ideology. Countless accounts in anthropology, literary studies, and art history have shown that the other—variously called the primitive or the barbarian—was constitutive of the aesthetic ideology of modernism.[1] But in spite of this thick archive, several significant questions remain: what was radical and different in modernism's deployment of the other? Was the other valued simply as a conduit to unmediated experiences, or was it to be recuperated as part of the edifice of a reconstituted modern culture, so that it could no longer be the sign of radical difference but part of a unified consciousness, what Taylor calls "an unmediated unity" (471)?

These questions lead to a set of oppositions that are the subject of my discussion: From one perspective, the epiphanic was motivated by the need to merge with the other as the most effective and instinctive rejection of previous forms of consciousness, the ones associated with tradition and modern industrial culture. From another perspective, however, the other could only be represented through the imposition of a frame of reference and set of categories that preceded its discovery. Thus, the notion of an unmediated experience would come to be defined both by its possibility and impossibility: once modernism had made an unmediated experience central to its aesthetic ideology, then it had no choice but to make the other "the alter ego of the modern poet" (Richards 206). And yet, what the modernists constructed as the mentality of the primitive was itself a set of ethnographic and psychological constructs developed within Western institutions and systems of knowledge, especially the ones enabled and authorized by colonialism.

Now, all prominent accounts of modernism's encounter with the other have called attention to the fact that modern writers and artists were themselves aware of the duality of their desire for the other and its elusiveness. What has not always been apparent is how this duality between artistic desire and its failure came to define the institutionalization of modernism and perhaps to account for its quick canonization in the twentieth century. Michael North has made the important claim that modernism could not escape the contradictions of European colonialism—"it was only because it pushed these to extremes that it could exist as a movement at all" (76). I explore the relationship between modernism and colonialism elsewhere.[2] My current discussion seeks to endorse but also to go beyond North's argument. I want to endorse his claim that it was in its engagement with what it construed as radical (colonial) difference that modernism derived its authority as a unique cultural moment. But I want to probe the usefulness of these contradictions for modernism by arguing that in the process of being institutionalized, the moment of modernism also valorized older, familiar, racial economies. As I show in the second part of my discussion, the narrative of how modernism was shifted from a transgressive, epiphanic event to a centerpiece of Western high culture—a museum event, as it were—involved an almost ritualized management of difference, a series of counter-epiphanic gestures (see Canclini, Doyle [*Bordering*], and Rainey [*Institutions of Modernism*]). In this context, there is the possibility, explored in the third and fourth parts of my discussion, that modernism was easy to institutionalize because it was also the product of a fundamental contradiction: it invoked the other and made it part of its schemata but also allowed for the differentiation of difference, so that some of its more radical forms could be exiled from its form through the ritual of canonization.[3]

Two narratives are involved in the discussion I present here. The first concerns the role of difference, in generalized rather than specific terms, as a specific insignia of the failure of the epiphanic desire of modernism in its moment of institutionalization. If what I sketch here is the monumentalization of modernism through the suppression of difference in general terms—or rather its cleansing to allow it to perform a high cultural role—it is because I am convinced that to limit alterity to purely racial matters is to fall into the trap of what we may now call the normativity of modernism, that of the canon and the art museum. My premise is that in order to raise the question of the influence of Africa and African bodies in the shaping of the culture of modernism we need to go beyond now familiar stories about primitivism. There are several good reasons to go beyond primitivism. The first and most obvious one is that primitivism is itself a product of the moment of monumentalization of modernism as the insignia of high culture. A second and perhaps more important reason is that almost without exception, notions of primitivism either explore the influence of African art objects on the works of modern painters and sculptures (which is often the case in art history) or focus on the African American body as the supplement for the African (which is the case in literary studies). Both approaches are problematic.

The first approach presents us with particular difficulties because it ignores how a focus on African art objects as essentially sources of influence allowed for an early incorporation of Africa into the institutions of modern art through a surreptitious suppression of the sense of radical difference that made the continent, in real or imagined terms, attractive to modernism. The second approach is inadequate because in focusing on the diasporic black as the stand-in for the African, the critical tradition negates the curiously privileged role of the African American—in modernism—as an American. I call this privilege curious because the African American body is endowed with the value of a primitivism that is more consumable because of its Western familiarity. Here, it is significant to note that in the same years that Josephine Baker was taking Paris by storm performing primitivism, Africans were still being displayed in cages at colonial fairs (see Petrine Archer-Straw 67–70). One form of primitivism was part of the art décor; the other was still locked in early modern economies of curiosity. My goal here is to shift emphasis from the figure of the primitive to the process by which the monumentalization of modernism came to negate the very radical alterity that was its condition of possibility. This is the argument I develop in the following part of this chapter.

But there is a second narrative here, and this concerns a more radical form of epiphanic desire that came to be relegated to the margins of official modernism. As I argue in the third and fourth sections of my chapter, the most radical form of epiphany, represented here by the work of the German ethnologist and explorer Leo Frobenius, was the one that sought to merge with the inner recesses of what was assumed to be a purer form of primitivism. It is my contention that the failure of this epiphanic moment provides us with important insights into what Taylor aptly calls an "uncollapsable distance between agent and world, between thinker and instinctual depths" (472). The last section of my discussion will explore the role of this distance in shaping our received and institutional accounts of modernism.

2

If we are sure about anything in the rise of an aesthetic ideology of modernism, it is that it was a moment that was initially defined by the desire to merge with the other (hence its revolutionary rupture) but ultimately one that produced forms of art and literature that now buttress the institution of culture in Europe and the United States. This issue might now appear tautological but it provides the thick description in which the movement of epiphany and counter-epiphany that concerns me here must be understood. Everything else is secondary. Why? Because one of the great ironies of the twentieth century is that modernism, a movement that began with an attempt to appropriate the practices and art forms of subjects and places considered to be the most removed from the culture of modernity, ended up institutionalized in museums and galleries as the visible symbol of the triumphant culture of capitalism. How did the history of modernism, which begins sometime in the 1900s with the European artist's enchantment with the primitive as a way out of what Freud called the discontent of civilization, end up encased in institutions funded by the most powerful agents of capital? This question is an important one because in spite of all the debates about primitivism in modernism, the institution of modern art would not allow for an origin of European art that existed outside the domain of the West.

Indeed, if primitivism seems to perpetually provoke debate and raise questions that appear unsolvable, it is because it was a palpable presence in modern art that, nevertheless, needed to be confined to the margins of the ideology of modernism, to be evacuated from its museums and institutions of interpretation. What is at issue here, then, is the gap that separates the artist as the agent of difference and the institution of interpretation as the force for stabilizing the aberrant. Consider this fact: what attracted Matisse to the African woman represented in his 1907 masterpiece, *The Blue Nude,* was her ugliness; if "I were to meet such a woman in the street," said the artist, "I should run away in terror" (quoted in Butler 107). Now enshrined in the Baltimore Museum of Art, Matisse's painting is not valued for its ugliness but for its high canonical capital. And so the question arises: How did ugliness become transformed into beauty?

In order to establish its authority, as Richard Brettell notes at the end of *Modern Art 1851–1929,* the wealthy patrons of modern art were keen to exclude forces and movements that might threaten their own vision of modernism. They wanted difference but not too much of it:

> There was almost universal agreement among these rich patrons about the nature of modern art. Many of them followed the intellectual lead of either Julius Meier-Graefe or Roger Fry in thinking that modern art had begun with Manet, that the Impressionists had invigorated and collectivized it (even if Renoir was the only artist with enough ambition to have triumphed over what seemed to them the limitations of the movement), but that it lacked masters until the next generation of artists, Seurat, Gauguin, van Gogh, and Cezanne. From these four artists, virtually all Euro-global modernism seemed to them to have sprung, and their work dominated exhibitions of modern art, before its ultimate triumph in the painting of Picasso and Matisse. (212)

The idea of modern art that has shaped our most cherished notions about culture and being cultured reflected the interests and tastes of a wealthy, primarily East Coast, American elite and the museums they constructed far away from the primitives who were supposed to have inspired this art:

> It is not accidental that modernism, being a product of the museum age, seems to have become the first period in the history of Western art that annexed the museum idea to its own project of definition and promotion. One can scarcely imagine the friends and patrons of, say, Rembrandt or Boucher or Goya getting together to start a museum that would present their work, and its conscious antecedents, in a seemingly independent way to what we call the general public. But that is exactly what Tretyakov, Shchukin, Lane, Barnes, Phillips, Courtauld, Bartlett, Kroeller-Mueller, Osthaus, Dreier, and

the small group of people who started MOMA succeeded in doing. These men and women perceived themselves as the selfless and generous proponents of neglected geniuses whose work deserved to be given the highest possible respect. In order to give it that respect, the art museum, with its ideas of political power or personal memorial, stretched itself to include the promotion of the taste and ideas of men and women with the means and the leisure to make the best judgements about contemporary works of art. All this is not to say that the public has not benefited enormously from this enterprise. Rather, it is to point out the fundamentally private, and hence limited, nature of the vision put forward by these worthy figures. (Brettell 212)

The vision of modern art determined by the culture of the museum and patrons is limited not simply because it negates the aberrant and the other, but also because the tastes and interests of the patrons of modern art have been at odds with all the familiar preoccupations of modern artists themselves—their concern with radical difference, their search for alternative forms of representation, and their desire to debunk the classicism that motivated and shaped European art. In this sense, modernism, especially the early phase that concerns me here, was clearly at odds with the institutions of modern art: the art of modernism derived its energy from the sites and objects that seemed to represent the unknown and to be against everything (see Malraux).[4] In contrast, the institution of modern art was set up to tame the new and transgressive and to rewrite it as part of a continuous aesthetic tradition. So-called primitive art thus came to occupy a significant place in the modern museum, but its institutionalization also emphasized its separation from modern art rather than its fundamental relation to it.

Thus, the modern art museum came to acquire what Néstor Garcia Canclini in *Hybrid Cultures* has called its ritualizing architecture, a spatial configuration whose goal, intended or unintended, was to separate the art object from the world around it and the one that produced it (24). Gone was Picasso's dream of an open space in which all art would be in one place, where African art would sit next to the statues of Minorca, and Goya could gaze on "Guernica"; gone, too, was André Malraux's dream of a Louvre in which the rooms of "Negro art will call into question those devoted to ancient arts, which are organized in accordance with the evolution of our history" (34–35). Our understanding of modern art has thus come to be circumscribed by the space in which it is enclosed, the space of the museum in art, replicated in the institutions of modes of criticism that sublimate difference (see Paul).[5]

Our inherited history of modern art is misleading for another reason: it assumes a unified and universal narrative of modernism. In fact, the global nature of modernism is easy to confuse for universalism. A careful separation of the two terms is perhaps urgent. The global dimension of modernism inheres in its willingness to draw energies from geographies located outside its European centers; its universalism, on the other hand, was predicated on the emergence of a dominant idea—sustained by the institutions of interpretation—that the economies of difference that had drawn artists to the other could ultimately be subsumed under the logic of a modern, cosmopolitan culture.[6] A more serious problem is implicit in the invocation of the universal in modernism: in our continuous and relentless focus on difference in the modern, we seem to have moved away from the normativity of high modernism. The question that remains to be addressed is whether we have actually transcended what Raymond Williams once called "the metropolitan interpretation of [modernism's] own processes as universals"—whether we have to yet explore the theory and practice of modernism "with something of its own strangeness and distance" (*The Politics of Modernism* 47).

My contention, then, is that so long as our accounts of the other in modernism always adopt the metropolitan location as its starting point—and this seems to be the case in almost all existing studies of primitivism—all attempts to explore modernism in its strangeness and distance are bound to return us to the very site we seek to deconstruct. The challenge of a new reading of difference in modernism lies not in reading notions of alterity that are already embedded in the high modernist norm, but in thinking through the limits of the difference modernism celebrated. As Robert Farris Thompson, the distinguished historian of African art, once put it: "[W]hat are the indigenous *African* definitions of the impact of African art forms on the artists of the cities of Europe (like Fang masks in Paris) at the beginning of this [twentieth] century? What do the traditional opinion leaders of *Africa* (as opposed to Western scholars) think about the redistillation of certain of their forms . . . ?" (190).

Scholars of African art history have come a long way to meeting Thompson's challenge (see Lawal and Strother), but students of modernism—especially in literary studies—have tended to focus more on the redistilled form of the African difference, the one that excludes the strange and distant. In order to comprehend modernism and other dominant Euro-American movements in their strangeness and distance, we have to travel to those places where the theorists and practitioners of these movements sought strangeness in its most radical form and thus also strove to distance themselves from the cultures of the metropolis. But we must also focus on the failure of modernism, in its foundational moment, to account for difference without redistillation. The following case study represents this effort and the forces, ideas, or notions that blocked it.

3

In retrospect, Leo Frobenius, the German explorer and ethnologist, never seemed in doubt that his expedition to Africa in 1905 had been motivated by the desire to counter the Hegelian image of the dark continent that seemed to have remained intact for most of the nineteenth century. Even with the wealth of information about the continent that the European institutions of knowledge seemed to have accumulated through four centuries of colonization, Africa remained, even in the crucial 1890s, either as an unfathomable mystery imprisoned in the figure of "the insensible fetish" or as the blank darkness Hegel had condemned it to in his lengthy introduction to *The Philosophy of History*.[7] In his introduction to *The Voice of Africa*, Frobenius recalls reading the following in a "very learned article" in a Berlin newspaper in 1891:

> With regard to its negro population, Africa, in contemporary opinion, offers no historical enigma which calls for solution, because, from all the information supplied by our explorers and ethnologists, the history of civilization proper in this Continent begins, as far as concerns its inhabitants, only with the Mahommedan invasion (Islamite would be more correct!). (1)

One of the most important reasons why Frobenius wanted to embark on a scientific expedition to Africa was to find evidence that the continent did indeed have a civilized culture and polity to counter the image of the continent as the depository of barbarism. But like many disenchanted modernists of his generation, Frobenius was not going to Africa for altruistic reasons: his goal was to find what one may call resources of difference to counter the whole narrative of Western civilization. For if the Enlightenment had predicated the superiority of the West on its ability to liberate itself from the irrational mind of the other, modernism was attempting to show that in spite of its claims to modernity, the European self was still in the hold of pre-modern forces. The encounter with Africa would hence serve two purposes, perhaps at odds with one another: First, it would show that Africans were not uncivilized and that what was called their barbarism was itself a mark of a different model of civilization, one that reconciled, rather than separated, nature and culture. Second, the African body and polity was to be recuperated as the radical opposite of civilization as the term was understood and circulated in the nineteenth century.

Frobenius's project was hence an attempt both to overcome the cognitive gap that separated the European and the African while at the same time holding on to the insignias of radical cultural difference. What he discovered in Africa, Frobenius asserted in his preface to *The Voice of Africa* published in 1913, was a cultural formation that was governed neither by "the insensible fetish" nor "power expressed in degenerate bestiality alone": "I discovered the souls of these peoples, and found that they were more than humanity's burnt-up husks" (xiv). Here, as elsewhere, Frobenius's goal was to recover what had been considered to be the savage and to translate it into an object of knowledge and contemplation. In effect,

Frobenius's goal was to make barbarism itself a condition of possibility of the idea and geography of culture that was beginning to emerge in the dawn of modernism (see Eagleton; Manganaro). In other words, instead of representing African peoples and cultures as Fetishes—objects of fear and repulsion—he would reinterpret savagery itself as a mode of cultural achievement. For example, Frobenius was not in doubt that the Bassonge were cannibals and that cannibalism was, in theory, practiced by "peoples on the most degraded level of human morality and without any general experience of spiritual refinement or progress" (14), but he did not want to stop there. He wanted to go further and probe what he considered to be one of the riddles of Africa: that established theories on the relationship between racial origins and cultural practices, on one hand, and morality and progress, on the other, did not seem to make sense when applied to the continent. Frobenius didn't question the presumed cannibalism of the Bassonge, but he wanted to show that this did not necessarily exclude them from the domain of human culture and achievement. Indeed, the cannibalistic Bassonge were, in Frobenius's account, the most aesthetic and skilled artists in the world:

These cannibal Bassonge were, according to the types we met with, one of those rare nations of the African interior which can be classed with the most aesthetic and skilled, most discreet and intelligent of all those generally known to us as the so-called natural races. Before the Arabic and European invasion they did not dwell in "hamlets," but in towns with twenty or thirty thousand inhabitants, in towns whose highways were shaded by avenues of splendid palms planted at regular intervals and laid out with the symmetry of colonnades. Their pottery would be fertile in suggestion to every art-craftsman in Europe. Their weapons of iron were so perfectly fashioned that no industrial art from abroad could improve upon their workmanship. The iron blades were cunningly ornamented with damascened copper, and the hilts artistically inlaid with the same metal. Moreover, they were most industrious and capable husbandmen, whose careful tillage of the suburbs made them able competitors of any gardener in Europe. Their sexual and parental relations evidenced an amount of tact and delicacy of feeling unsurpassed among ourselves, either in the simplicity of the country or the refinements of the town. Originally, their political and municipal system was organized on the lines of a representative republic. True, it is on record that these well-governed towns often waged an internecine warfare; but, in spite of this, it had been their invariable custom from time immemorial, even in times of strife, to keep the trade routes open and to allow their own and foreign merchants to go their ways unharmed. And the commerce of these nations ebbed and flowed along a road of unknown age, running from Itimbiri to Batubenge, about six hundred miles in length. This highway was only destroyed by the "missionaries of civilization" from Arabia towards the close of the eighteenth century. But, even in my own time, there were still smiths who knew the names of places along that wonderful trade-

route driven through the heart of the "impenetrable forests of the Congo."
For every scrap of important iron was carried over it. (14–15)

The significance of this passage to the project of rethinking difference
that we have come to associate with modernism can only be recognized if
we locate Frobenius's discourse in its time and place. The entry above was
made in 1905 during the German expedition to Africa. Frobenius tells us
that his desire to discover the real Africa was motivated by the reading of
an entry in a Berlin journal in 1891. *The Voice of Africa* was published in
1913. We can appreciate the significance of Frobenius's intervention by
simply recalling some crucial dates in the canon of modernism: Conrad's
Heart of Darkness, Nietzsche's *Genealogy of Morals*, and Freud's *The Interpretation of Dreams* were all published in 1899. Picasso discovered African
masks at the old Trocadéro in 1907 when he was in the midst of painting
"Les Demoiselles d'Avignon." Furthermore, 1910 was the year when, according to Virginia Woolf, human character changed.

The invocation of these dates and works is, however, not intended to
establish an affinity between Africa and the moment of modernism. No
one doubts that the discovery of African art objects was one of the key
points, indeed a significant fulcrum, in the radical transformation of European art. I start with Frobenius, however, because I want to insist that
while African art objects came to play a crucial role in the making of modernism, the appropriation and translation of these objects was surrounded
by an ambivalence that still dominates and haunts debates about the nature
of modern art, especially in its institutions of exhibition and interpretation. The source of this ambivalence is that the modernists' desire for African art objects, or even for an African, pre-modern mentality, was always
blocked and often haunted by the apparitional and haunting presence of
the African's body. Frobenius is an ideal case study because, unlike the
other members of the early moment of modernism, he assumed that you
could not get to African art objects without encountering African bodies
and cultural practices.[8]

In this regard, Frobenius's observations about the Bassonge contain
several useful insights into a rethinking of the epiphany of modernism as
an attempt to separate art objects from the bodies of their producers, or, in
more familiar language, to separate the aesthetic ideology from social formation. The first insight into this contradiction or dialectic can be found
in Frobenius's insistence on the civilizational authority of the Bassonge.
Contrary to what one might expect, Frobenius insisted, the civilization of
the cannibals preceded colonization. Indeed, Frobenius was adamant that
it was the Arabic and European invasions, usually considered to be the
agents of modernization in Africa, that had been responsible for the degeneration of the Bassonge, their fall from civilization as it were. Before the

foreign invasion, he contended, Bassonge culture contained all the trappings of modernity: it was an urban culture, its instruments of war were made from iron (the metallurgy of a modernized polity), they had a rational system of governance, and they upheld the values of the modern self, including hard work. In short, the Bassonge bore the ingredients of modernity in its classical European sense.

But why did Frobenius, who ostensibly had gone to Africa to escape the disease of modern civilization, seem eager to adduce this same civilization to an African culture? The truth is that we are so used to seeing the modernists' desire for primitivism as a counterpoint to modern industrial civilization that we often forget that the relationship between the European self and the other it came to celebrate on the wake of modernism was troubled. Like most modernists, Frobenius cast his journey into Africa as the quest for deep knowledge about the other. The figure of the savage was asked to make modernism possible because it could be the source of meanings and values that had been foreclosed from the civilized mind (Richards 189–217). This is how the "noble savages" came to be read, in Richard's memorable words, as "the very essence of modernism" and the force and field that made "the modern world possible for art" (211). But as Frobenius's encounter with the Bassonge illustrates vividly, the other could only be accepted as the essence of modernism, or the source of its energies, if it were also represented in a grammar familiar to us, ironically, the grammar of modern civilization—of organized culture, cities, metal, and rationality.

There is a second insight to be gained from Frobenius's encounter with the Bassonge: Frobenius wanted to go a step further and revise the terms of the epistemology that defined the relation between the self and the other. He saw his immersion into the African world, and some of its most profound rituals, as the first step in the rethinking of the terms of cultural contact itself—"the establishment of an understanding based, not on European critical analysis, but on an intimate knowledge of the African's nature" (48). Significantly, however, like other proponents of modernism, Frobenius did not seek to overcome the division between Europe and Africa. For if he were to adduce the civilizational authority of the European to the savage, then the primitive mind could not function as a conduit to what modernity had repressed; it would just be another extension of established notions of culture.

Consequently, a third insight to be gained from Frobenius's discourse is to be found in the careful separation he made between the cultural practices of the Bassonge, including their cannibalism, and their aesthetic objects. Frobenius's argument here was simply that aesthetic objects did not necessarily reflect the moral state of a people or the level of their culture. In this regard, what was unique in modernism, and what was unprecedented in the European encounter with the other, was the separation of the savages' bodies—and their beliefs and practices—from their aesthetic objects. This separation of the aesthetic ideology and morality was crucial.

4

As I have shown in other places, one of the central claims of modernity, especially in the Enlightenment, was that there was a deep affinity between the racial character of a people, their morality, and their aesthetic (see Gikandi). It is my contention that the ideology of modernism set out to transform this unquestioned relationship, but it did not go all the way. In order for modernism to appropriate the other and to see it as the condition of possibility of modern art, it needed to separate the body of the savage from its aesthetic objects so that the latter could be valued even in the face of hostility toward the former. The complaint that proponents of modernism could celebrate the art objects of an African people without raising a finger to protest the destruction of their cultures or bodies is a familiar one. But what does it tell us about the mind of the modernist at the end of the nineteenth century or the beginning of the twentieth century? It calls attention to the deep ambivalence at the heart of what appears to be modernism's revision of alterity: modernists wanted to seek new energies for art in the domain of the other; they wanted to rethink the whole project of representing modern culture from outside the axioms established by modernity itself; they wanted to use the weapons of the primitive to escape the impasse of civilization and its discontents. At the same time, however, modernism—which we have come to see as the radical critique of modernity—carried within it powerful residues of the civilization it sought to negate via the primitive. But in order to come to terms with this residuality, we have to stop thinking of modernism's celebration of radical difference as one of the marks of its antimodernity or, more specifically, its anti-Kantianism.

What do I mean by this? Let us recall that one of the bedrocks of modernity, the very condition of modern knowledge, was the call for the self to be liberated from the tutelage of tradition and to function as the source of its own understanding. As Immanuel Kant claimed in "An Answer to the Question: 'What is Enlightenment?'" (one of the key documents of European modernity), Enlightenment was "man's emergence from his self-incurred immaturity"; immaturity was "the inability to use one's understanding without the guidance of another"; it was self-incurred because one did not have the resolution or courage to have self-understanding "without the guidance of another" (54). In the terms represented by both the practitioners and theorists of modernism, this turn to the other for understanding would appear to be a supreme anti-Kantian moment, a reversion to a time when self-understanding was only possible through another, including others who appeared to be the most removed from us. In this sense, modernism's privileging of the other as its condition of self-understanding would seem to mock Kantianism by seeking knowledge in the most uncritical and unmediated fashion, against the tenets of modernity itself.

Here, again, Frobenius offers us a final lesson in the rethinking of modernism: he worked with the premise that the road to modern knowledge, which the Enlightenment had declared was only possible through liberation from superstition and tutelage, could be achieved solely through a return to ritual in its most radical form. Ritual was, of course, the embodiment of superstition and the tutelage of tradition. As he tells us at the opening of *The Voice of Africa,* one of his most important goals at the beginning of the African expedition was to be initiated into the Ogboni society, one of the most powerful and secretive Yoruba men's societies.[9] It is quite clear from the description he has left us that Frobenius's goal was not to enter the Ogboni society so that he could acquire insight into the African mind; on the contrary, what appealed to him were the society's rituals, especially those that seemed to go against the tenets of civilized behavior, because they would enable a glimpse into the pre-modern mentality:

In the course of a fortnight I had established amicable relations with most of the people of influence and taught them the depth of my pocket by all sorts of visits of the kind just described and other business transactions. Now was the time to deliver my "swashing blow." I declared that I wanted to join the membership of the Ogboni League. I said so to the head of the League, and in his eagerness for the cash which baited the hook, he was actually prepared to negotiate. A final agreement was arrived at by which not we, the Europeans, were to partake of the bloody "consecrated wafer" at the altar, but that a black man should be our substitute, and that the ceremony should be performed in my own house in secret with closed doors. That very same evening the not particularly aesthetic rite was celebrated in our hall by the light of our lanterns. It was an uncanny and, in its own way, sinister business. Naturally it was not carried out in all its details, because in recent times ducklings have taken the place of the hitherto customary human victims. But with this exception it corresponded in all other respects to the descriptions I had collected years ago which I now append for clearness' sake. The metal most in favor with the Ogboni, a prosperous association of wealthy men, had from all times been a yellow amalgam, or bronze, the materials for which were found in the country itself until the introduction of imported brass in recent years supplanted it. Every Ogboni possesses a little Eda figure as a charm, made of this substance. In the High Priest's, or Oluvo's, house hung the Abbebede mask of the same metal, and from time immemorial the holy draught of blood had been handed round in a great vessel made of this particular bronze. A pair of Eda idols, whose heads were connected by a chain and whose lower extremities are fitted with iron prongs, upon which individual Ogbonis and the High Priest place their sacrificial offerings, are also made of the same metal. The two figures were a man and woman, and "Eda-Malé" was their name. When the sacred apparatus was displayed at the initiation of a new member, those present stripped themselves to the waist, then stepped up to the bronze effigy in the lurid light of a huge fire and greeted it in chorus with a shout of "Hecqua!" Then the first sacrifice was offered up. A human being was beheaded in such a position above the pair of "Eda-Malé," that the blood poured over them. Occasionally, when a more important ceremonial was deemed necessary, several human beings were sacrificed. (60–61)

Frobenius provides this elaborate scene merging art and the sacrifice of human beings in a chapter of his book aptly entitled "The Road to Knowledge." He assumes that the return to primal rites, in which art objects play a significant role, is the real path to knowledge, and his only regret is perhaps that at his initiation into the Ogboni cult, ducklings had been substituted for human victims. The significant point, though, is that he assumes, as the surrealists were to assume thirty years after him, that human sacrifice represented the ultimate act of radical difference. He assumed that it was in such acts of difference that we could gain insights into both ourselves and the other and come to understand the "monumental majesty" that characterized human civilization before what he contemptuously called "modern times" (66). The lesson here, already elaborated by Nietzsche and Freud, was that ritual was the key to the essential experiences that negated critical and conscious reason. But still, Frobenius did not exhibit any desire to give himself up wholly to the forces represented in the Ogboni rituals of initiation. He was content to have black substitutes stand in for him on the Yoruba altar that, significantly, he could only conceive in terms of Catholicism. He wanted to be inside the domain of the other but also outside it; inside enough to acquire ethnographical knowledge, but not so completely inside the horror that he would be consumed by it.

I consider Frobenius's ambivalent relationship with the Bassonge and Yoruba crucial to our understanding of the economy of difference in modernism, and thus a challenge to the aura of monumentality that has come to surround the institution of modern art, because I want to displace the history of a dominant European idea—in this case modernism—by giving it an alternative genealogy. Given the extreme view of African difference promulgated in early modern cultural movements, the moment of modernism might appear to be different from either humanism or the ideology of the aesthetic because it was perhaps one of the first cultural movements in recent European history to appropriate the other as one of its conditions of being, or as an instrument for rethinking Western systems of thought and cultural representation. Unlike previous movements of art and culture, modernism is seen as having embraced the other as part of the same. Indeed, when it comes to questions of identity and difference, the canonical view of modernism is that it represents a positive form of ethnocentrism, what has come to be known as primitivism.

My goal here is not, of course, to adjudicate between different forms or levels of ethnocentrism, but to suggest that modernism did not entirely overcome the terror of the other associated with earlier movements of European art and culture. As a matter of fact, modernism brings into sharp focus the ambiguity that has been attendant to the emergence of Europe as the quintessential modern polity. And although there is a case to be made for the "modernity" of primitivism as it emerges in the works of modern artists such as Gauguin and Picasso, Matisse and Mondrian, there is a sense in which primitivism functions as the most visible sign of the ambiguity of the modern encounter between the self and the other as it has emerged since the eighteenth century or earlier. In effect, rather than seeing primitivism as the sign of a positive ethnocentrism, as some proponents of modernism have suggested, we need to identify it as the apotheosis of the dialectic of identity and difference that is so crucial in the making of modern culture. In other words, one cannot have a discourse of primitivism that is not at the same time an inscription of the radical difference of the other; but our relationship with this other is framed by the structure of what Mary Douglas has called purity and danger: it attracts and horrifies us at the same time; what makes the most outrageous order of difference attractive and energizing is precisely its distance from the moral convictions that define our own rules of civilized behavior (1–6).

In this sense, when we think about Frobenius, the amateur ethnographer and adventurer, so close and yet so far from the rituals of human sacrifice in Ibadan, we should remember that he had just set out to fulfill the desires and prohibitions of his age. As is well known, the great desire of the age of modernism was to detour the culture of modernity, to escape what was seen, Taylor argues in *Sources of the Self*, as "the restrictions of the unitary self" and to launch an attack "on the time consciousness and modes of narrativity associated with disengaged instrumental reason and Romanticism" (463). But it is my contention that once confronted with what they considered to be the opposite of disengaged reason, advocates of modernism fell back on a set of prohibitions, including the fear of the irrational and the fragmented self, that ended up reinforcing the authority of modernity and the claims of its culture. Proponents of modernism entered the domain of the other seeking what T. S. Eliot would consider to be the "mystical mentality" of the pre-modern, the pre-logical, and pre-critical, but they would return repelled by what they saw; and it is this repulsion, I want to argue, that provided the energy for modern art and modernism (see Richards 204–205).

The problem with this claim, however, is that except in a few instances—Conrad in Africa and South Asia and Lawrence in the Americas, for example—very few modern artists actually traveled in the domain of the other. Modernists seemed to be attracted to the other as a schemata or idea but to avoid its materiality. The irony of modernism, then, is that it seemed to have made the difference of the other constitutive of its project and yet, somehow, it felt uneasy with a serious engagement with this coveted other. How do we explain this paradox? We could speculate that the modernists feared a concrete engagement with the other precisely because they felt, intuitively perhaps, that a real encounter with the radically different would deprive it of its aura and thus lead to a reaffirmation of disengaged reason and modern civilization. It is interesting that modern artists rarely presented the problem of repulsion directly; none seemed to say explicitly that the horror they had encountered in the heart of darkness validated the culture of modernity. In fact, it is hard to find a modern work of art that posits the world of the primitive as a preferred alternative to modern civilization. The world of the savage is always written about retrospectively as a place of death and danger. Conrad's Marlow may compare the Thames and the Congo at the beginning of *Heart of Darkness,* but it would be a mistake to ignore his assertion that the barbarism of the former belongs to the past while that of the latter is very much part of the danger he has survived and must hence be retold, retrospectively, in what amounts to a powerful act of exorcism. The narrative of modernism, or its art objects, must hence be read not as the medium through which the Western self and the African other initiate meaningful encounters, but as a symbolization of their separation at their moment of recognition.

Ultimately, I want to suggest that although they rarely make it to the canon of modernism, adventurers and amateur ethnographers like Frobenius are central to the rethinking of the idea of modernism and its invocation of African difference for two closely related reasons. First, what we know about the other came to us through them.[10] This has been the case throughout Western history. It is the marginal figures of our institutions of knowledge who bring the others home to us. Second, these minor figures were the first to institute the crucial separation between the African aesthetic and African bodies and cultures. Throughout his travels in Africa, Frobenius would never cease to marvel at the great gap that separated African art from its social formation, and *The Voice of Africa* begs a question it never raises: How could a culture of barbarism produce such great objects of art? This differentiation of art and culture was to have a lasting impact on the ideology of modernism at different stages, and we need to keep it in mind so that we can better understand the central, and yet ambiguous, role that primitivism has come to occupy in the ideology of modernism.

5

Writing about African sculpture in 1920, for example, Roger Fry, one of the first theoreticians of modern art, had no doubt that "Negro Sculpture" belonged to the highest level of artistic expression, yet he considered it "curious that a people who produced such great artists did not produce also a culture in our sense of the word" (103).[11] Fry went on to observe that for a culture to be truly great, it needed more than creativity and genius; it also demanded a critical tradition, "the power of consciousness, critical appreciation and comparison" (103). In Fry's view, African culture was an anomaly in the history of the world because, in comparison to China, for example, the continent had not produced either a great culture or a critical apparatus to explain it: "It is for want of a conscious critical sense and the intellectual powers of comparison and classification that the negro has failed to create one of the great cultures of the world, and not from lack of the most exquisite sensibility and the finest taste" (103). It is my contention that one of the techniques used to manage African difference in the aesthetic ideology of modernism was to insist on the difference between African cultures (and bodies) and art objects.

But there is another dimension to this split between African culture and sensibility in the discourse of modernism. The issue, we always have to remember, is *not* that Africa had not produced great cultures comparable to those of China or India. European explorers and adventurers had encountered such cultures since the early modern period. The more intriguing fact is that the existence of such cultures did not, however, lead to the revision of European notions about their ostensible absence. The existence of African cultures that seemed to come close to those of the East (India and China) was explained away in one of two ways. They could be represented as anomalous institutions introduced into "black" Africa by invading "Hermitic" cultures. Case in point: Frobenius had gone to the country of the Yoruba to challenge the European image of uncivilized Africa and his expedition would discover terra cotta heads that seemed to confirm the existence of a powerful civilization, but when it came to explaining the origins of these remarkable artifacts in *The Voice of Africa*, he arrived at a familiar exegetical fix: how to explain the presence of great art in the absence of a powerful culture to match it:

> In discussing this, I, in the first place, maintain that Yoruban civilization must, in its present form, be unhesitatingly declared to be essentially African. By this I mean to say that it not only rests upon the surface of African soil like a bubble blown from abroad which a breath can also dispel, but,

rather, that it is actually incorporated with it. It is as much an integral part of, as deeply rooted in, the body and soul of the Yorubans themselves as the terracottas are part and parcel of the homogeneous soil of Yorubaland. Here there is a state of culture which has been realized in flesh and blood, drawing the breath of life from its aboriginal form. We are, then, faced with the question whether it was here developed or transplanted hither, *i.e.*, whether we are to regard it as autogenetic, or in symphonic relation to foreign civilizations. The question is, did it originate in this country itself, or, if it was brought from beyond, which was the road that it took? (322)

On the surface, the problem appears fortuitous: if the terra cottas of Ille Ife were made of Yoruba soil, why would their origin be up for debate?

On closer examination, the issue was how to explain the existence of insignias of civilization where none was supposed to exist. Thus Frobenius, after a meticulous comparison of Yoruba cultural objects and those of the ancient world, concluded that the culture of the Yoruba was "the crystallization of that mighty stream of Western civilization which, in its Euro-African form, flowed from Europe into Africa, and, when it sank in volume, left behind it the Etruscans as its cognate and equally symphonic exponents" (348). As readers of *The Voice of Africa* will recall, Frobenius would end his investigation with the lyrical claim that high Yoruba culture was the remnant of Atlantis itself!

The final point to consider in this separation of culture and art is its implication for the emerging idea of modernism in the years between 1895 and 1920. Let us recall that Fry had endowed Africans with artistic genius but denied them the capacity to make critical judgments. This was, of course, an advancement on the Enlightenment where the African was denied both genius and critical judgment. In terms of what one may call the internal economy of modernism, the separation of the work of art from its critical judgments was to have a greater implication than the division between culture and the aesthetic. One implicit, but quite central, assumption in Fry's essay on African sculpture was that the realm of creativity was natural and spontaneous while that of judgment was conscious and self-reflective. For Fry, art expressed deeper or higher powers outside the domain of reflection; in contrast, the critical sense was consciously motivated by the need for comparison and classification. Although Fry was applying this differentiation to African art, it was the source of a paradigm that, like Africa itself, was to define and haunt modernism. Under the domain of the ideology of modernism, the view that modern art, like African sculpture, was produced without a critical consciousness would become fundamental to artistic production and, ultimately, to the institution of modern art in the museum and university.

Under the circumstances, I want to insist that Fry did not deny African sculptors critical consciousness because he was ignorant of actual artistic practices among African peoples, as Christopher Green has insisted, but because he wanted to project onto African peoples the very claims of art that he wanted to make for modernism—the unconsciousness of impressionism, for example—without according them the civilizational authority of the modern. Even if he had traveled among the Fang and listened to their artists comment on their works, Fry would most likely have reached the same conclusion regarding the absence of an African critical tradition, for modernism needed Africa as both a site of experimentation and projection, not as a cultural force. If Africa did not exist as the site in which the fears and energies of modernism could be projected, it would have to be invented; by the same token, modernism emerged as an important cultural movement because while it could not do without Africa, it did not know what to do with the blackness it saw in the mirror that was supposed to reflect its repressed side. Africa is the unconscious of modernism—its "absent cause"—a force whose presence can neither be negated nor endorsed and must hence be repressed (see Althusser and Balibar 186–89; Jameson, *The Political Unconscious* 34–36). The history of modernism that interests me here is the one that is embedded in this repression, the moment when the European encounter with its others is also one of separation at the most subliminal level. In the end, modernism sought energies in the strangeness and distance of the other but it could only bring this other back in the terms that seemed to fit into its essentially Eurocentric framework.

NOTES

1. The literature on primitivism is now too extensive to list here, but for some important works on the topic in general see the books by Goldwater, North, Price, and Torgovnick.

2. I discuss these issues in greater detail in *The Modern Unconscious: Race, Art, and African Difference* (in progress). This chapter is an excerpt from that work.

3. I use the notion of contradictions in the Althusserian sense, a process of displacement and rupture: "In periods of stability the essential contradictions of the social formation are neutralized by displacement; in a revolutionary situation, however they may condense or fuse into a revolutionary rupture" (see Althusser and Balibar 311). My implicit claim is that modernism starts as a set of contradictions that fuse into a revolutionary rupture; however, in its institutionalized phase it is neutralized.

4. What thoughts flowed in Picasso's mind when he first encountered African art at the old Trocadéro in 1907? According to Malraux, this was Picasso's reaction: "I myself think that everything is unknown, that everything is an enemy!" (110).

5. In this study I focus primarily on works of art because they represent the most dramatic encasement of difference in the museum, but the same "ritualizing" process is at work in the establishment of a high modernist normativity in literary criticism. A notable example of the latter is F. R. Leavis's majestic reading of Eliot in *The Living Principle*.

6. This problem is explored in some detail by Raymond Williams in "What was Modernism."

7. This is how Hegel evacuated Africa from the discourse of history: "Africa proper as far as History goes back, has remained—for all purposes of connection with the rest of the World—shut up; it is the Gold-land compressed within itself— the land of childhood, which lying beyond the day of self-conscious history, is enveloped in the dark mantle of Night" (91).

8. Elsewhere in this project I argue that the figures who deployed Africa as the condition of possibility of modern art (Picasso, for example) found the African body revolting.

9. For the use of the "Ogboni" cult as an instrument of a "modernist" understanding suspended between the conscious and unconscious, see Wole Soyinka's *The Road* and *Death and the King's Horseman*.

10. Frobenius's work enters high modernism through his well-known influence on the thought and poetics of Ezra Pound. In Chapter 5 of *Masks of Difference*, Richards provides a detailed account of how the works of colonial travelers and missionaries such as J. Roscoe came to influence the works of Sir James Fraser, sequestered in his study at Cambridge, and, by extension to shape the informing mythologies of modernism. Conversely, these adventurers and missionaries had been inspired to undertake their projects by the theories of intellectuals such as Fraser.

11. The significance of Fry to the construction of the idea of modernism that dominated the first half of the twentieth century needs to be underscored because he tends to be absent in literary accounts of modernism. Not only was he a key member of the Bloomsbury group, but his first biographer was also none other than Virginia Woolf.

3   Liberty, Race, and Larsen in Atlantic Modernity: A New World Genealogy

Laura Doyle

> freedom, that blessed sense of belonging to herself alone
> and not to a race.
>
> —Nella Larsen, *Quicksand*

We keep arriving late at the drama of Atlantic modernity. Most English-language histories of Western modernity begin in the eighteenth century with the Enlightenment, glancing back only briefly to earlier signs of its ferment in science, print culture, or political economy. Likewise, most English-language histories of race thinking begin in the eighteenth century, linking new taxonomies of race to New World slavery and colonizing projects. But we've missed a crucial first scene: the English Revolution of the 1640s. The key English-language *vocabularies* of Atlantic modernity are coined here, I'll argue, especially the merged rhetorics of race and freedom; and we miss their full resonance if we ignore this English Civil War moment.

During the English Civil War, race unfurls as a freedom myth. Witness John Hare in 1647, in his Civil War pamphlet, *St Edward's Ghost or Anti-Normanism*:

> There is no man that understands rightly what an Englishman is, but knows withal, that we are a member of the Teutonick nation, and descended out of Germany: a descent so honourable and happy, if duly considered, as that the like could not have been fetched from any other part of Europe[. . . .] in England the whole commonalty, are German, and of the German blood; and scarcely was there any worth or manhood left in these occidental nations, after their long servitude under the Roman yoke, until these new supplies of freeborn men from Germany reinfused the same [. . .] Did our ancestors, therefore, shake off the Roman yoke[. . . .] that the honour and freedom of their blood might be reserved for an untainted prey to a future conqueror?" (Kliger 136–37)

Hare joins many others who yoke freedom and race in an Anglo-Saxon discourse of resistance to conquerors and tyranny. Over the next century, this discourse yielded the notion that some races are born to seek freedom—and therefore deserve it—and others are not. By the later eighteenth century and until Iraq in 2004, peoples or races must, from a Western point of view, demonstrate "their capacity" for freedom, or be ruined. In the Western idea of freedom, race and modernity join hands, for the will to freedom is the very essence, according to G. W. F. Hegel and others, of "world-historical," modern races. In modernity, it is above all the capacity for freedom that measures a race.

Yet it is important to recognize the seventeenth-century claims not just as the seedbed for slavery, Nazism, and American imperialism but also as the postcolonial revolutionary resistance they were intended to be. The early fashioners of the discourse of race and freedom understood themselves to be reclaiming their trammeled native rights from foreign usurpers —Norman, French, and popish. Only when we recognize this old and dissenting genealogy of race and freedom do we understand fully the power and dynamics of race in the modern West. And only then can we grasp how late-nineteenth- and twentieth-century English-language writers seeking to break "free" of literary shackles did so under the aegis of race.

Helga Crane in Nella Larsen's novel *Quicksand* (1928) senses the paradoxes in this genealogy of race. When she boards the train with Mrs. Hayes-Rore to escape her joblessness in Chicago, she uneasily enters a liberty plot that is also a race "uplift" plot. She attempts repeatedly to unhook her car from the freedom train's race telos. And at moments, especially when she launches out across the Atlantic, she thinks she has done so. On her first trip to Copenhagen, departing from black Harlem, she sighs with relief at what she feels as "freedom, that blessed sense of belonging to herself alone and not to a race." Like Helga Crane, we often think of race as an obstacle to freedom, something we can set out to get free *of.* But Helga's story tells us otherwise. In the end she fails, and she becomes sickly, reproducing children for the race identity she meant to transcend.

And, indeed, Nella Larsen continues to reproduce this race identity—as a now canonized African American woman author enlisted to forward the project of African American freedom. Larsen plays this part because the liberty plot drives not only transatlantic novels but also literary criticism, and critics face the same dilemma Larsen did: to pursue freedom—of story, of speech, of literary tradition—it seems one must invoke the telos of race. But is the goal race-freedom or freedom from race? How does one gain freedom by subscribing to a race identity; and yet for whom is the cultural freedom fight fought if not for the race? Underneath this dilemma lies the question faced by English revolutionaries in the Putney debate of 1647: how can the centripetal energy of liberty provide a centrifugal principle of community, of identity? And, in the end, perhaps we discover what they did: that, however paradoxically, the Atlantic economy demands the yok-ing of liberty to race. Certainly, in English-language stories a person, a protagonist, typically rises or falls in navigating the strained relation be-tween them.

Tracking this genealogy of race as it shapes Atlantic modernism re-quires that we look back before British and American slavery to England in the early seventeenth century, as I will do in the first section of this es-say. In my discussion of this earlier period, I will use the terms *nativism* or *racialism* to describe revolutionary forms of English race thinking that pre-pare the way for the imperialist racism we know so well—and yet which should not be read anachronistically as racism. Such an account then al-lows us to glimpse the ways that, in English-language novels since the late seventeenth century, from *Oroonoko* through *Moll Flanders* to *The Scarlet Let-ter, Billy Budd,* and *Of One Blood,* a liberty plot unfolds as a race plot and furthermore repeatedly does so as a story of struggle, ruin, and recovery on the Atlantic. When we notice how the narrative trope of a sea-crossing and an Atlantic experience of ruin structure diverse English-language lit-eratures, we can begin to answer Paul Gilroy's call to "take the Atlantic as one, single complex unit of analysis" and "use it to produce an explicitly transnational and intercultural perspective" (*Black Atlantic* 15). Here I can only sketch this perspective that I am elaborating in a larger project, so as to provide an outline of the patterns from which Nella Larsen so shrewdly fashions her fiction and by which she participates in the geoliterary phe-nomenon I call Atlantic modernism. This Atlantic modernism includes a range of protagonists who share Helga's story of a racialized, traumatic, seaside launching toward freedom: Woolf's Rachel, Rhys's Marya, Stein's Lena, Chopin's Edna, Forster's Adele, James's Isabelle Archer, and Hur-ston's Janie. All of these characters embark from a racialized place; they all suffer sexual and communal "ruin" on their water-crossing quests for freedom; they all end up radically alone or dead, and in any case prodigal race citizens. As I argue in the second half of this essay, Larsen's novel *Quicksand* and her story "Sanctuary" together offer a genealogical meta-narrative of this Atlantic modernism.

1

It is useful to think of John Milton's Satan as a roving Atlantic libertine, for doing so helps us to see the founding force of Atlantic colonialism in the modern English-language literary tradition. In *Paradise Lost,* as William Spengemann has noted, Milton emphatically casts Satan as the restless seeker "of foreign worlds" (10.441) and in particular a "new world" (1.650, 2.403, 4.34, 4.113, 10.257) across the "illimitable ocean" (2.892) where the downcast may "hope to change / Torment with ease" (4.892–93).[1] Milton accordingly fashions Eve as an "advent'rous" woman ("of her roving there is no end") seduced by this vision of new world liberation from God's tyranny (9.121, 8.189). I suggest that Milton thus accretes one allusive layer of a developing geoliterary formation—the transatlantic seduction plot—which Atlantic modernists revisit.

Spengemann draws attention to *Paradise Lost* in order to establish that the encounter with America is *the* catalyzing pivot in the modern English-language tradition, not just one important force. Yet he, too, erases a crucial earlier history. When he claims that "the single most important event in the history of the [English] language, rivaled only by the Norman Conquest, has to be its discovery of the New World" (43), he not only overlooks the impact of later linguistic encounters in the East but he also fatally excludes the effects of the English Reformation. His own evidence unwittingly indicates the importance of this earlier event, however. Milton's epic is above all, of course, a Puritan- and therefore Reformation-descended reimagining of the Fall, which provides the framework for its coded criticism of American colonialism. Further, when Spengemann argues that the exploration by Europeans of America introduced new words into the English language, he chooses words that actually point toward the legacy of the Reformation and the English Civil War—and these, *in turn*, prepare the way for discourse in and about America. That is, he attributes strictly to American Puritans the "invention of words like *independence* to describe the proper allegiance of a congregation to Christ, rather than to the bishops, and *primitive* to denote the original purity from which the church had strayed and to which it must return" (44). But both independent and primitive (the latter especially) are Reformation terms used to describe the pre-papal, Saxon church—although they do indeed come to have many uses in America.

And it is no coincidence that their later American resonance is racial. For the Reformation ultimately gave rise to a new racialization of English identity, initiating the turn toward a *Saxon* English identity—that would become racialized—in the search for links to the "primitive" German church predating Christianity's dependence on bishops and popes.[2] Henry VIII authorized Matthew Parker to gather from England and abroad all documents revealing the Germanic and Anglo-Saxon origins of the "true and primitive" Church that predated popery (Adams 11). As Parker's secretary, John Jocelyn, explains, Parker "was verie carefull and not without some charges to know the religion off the ancient fatheres and those especially were of the English Church. Therefore in seeking upp the Chronicle of the Brittones and the English Saxones [. . .] his mens diligence wanted not"; and accordingly, "he indevored to sett out in printe certaine of those aunciente monuments [. . .] which he thought would be most profitable for the posterytye to instruct them in the faythe and religion of the elders" (qtd. in Adams 20–21). Parker determined to put in print as many as he could of these documents, furnishing the printer John Day with the first Anglo-Saxon type and sponsoring the first Anglo-Saxon book, a collection of sermons, epistles, and prayers called *A Testimonie of Antiquities* (1566–67). As in his tract *A Defense of Priests' Marriages* (written in exile under Queen Mary), in his preface to this volume Parker draws on Saxon materials to authorize specific changes in Church practice, including that of the communion ceremony: so that "thou mayest knowe (good Christian reader) how this [sacrament] is advocated more boldly than truely, [. . .] here is set forth unto thee a testimonye of verye auncient tyme, wherein is plainly showed what was the judgement of the learned men in thys matter, in the days of the Saxons before the Conquest" (qtd. in Adams 24–25). Such prefaces were typical, as in the case of Foxe's address to Queen Elizabeth in the preface to his Old English version of the Gospels (*The Gospels of the former Evangelistes translated in the olde Saxons tyme out of Latin*), where he explains that his book shows "how the religion presently taught & professed in the Church at thys present, is no new reformation of thinges lately begonne, which were not before, but rather a reduction of the Church to the Pristine State of olde conformitie" (Adams 32–33). This notion of a return to the ancestors' primitive simplicity would be invoked throughout the next two centuries, echoed in 1698 by those who advised Edward Thwaite as he prepared his *Heptateuchus* (1698), emphasizing that his book could provide "undeniable evidence to all posterity that the belief of our Papists at this day is a very different thing from that of our Saxon ancestors" (in Adams 119–20, Appendix 8). By that time such urgings, as we will see, struck a familiar note in what had become a complex nativist concerto.

The Society of Antiquaries comprised one key institutional link between this Reformation collection activity and the later revolution that linked liberty and Saxonism. Although originally founded by Tudor kings to support this research and authorize the Reformation, under the Stuart kings James I and Charles I the Society of Antiquaries turned its attention increasingly to old Saxon legal documents and became incendiary. As scholars unearthed information about Anglo-Saxon law-making councils and the Magna Carta, their work posed a threat to the Stuarts' divine-right claims to absolute power. The Society's collected papers give ample record of their preoccupation with the origins of Parliament in the laws of earlier "races." Although unpublished in their own day, they eventually joined with such published works as Lambarde's *Archainomia* and "The Priviledges and Practices of Parliaments in England. Collected out of the Common lawes of this Land. Seene and Allowed by the Learned in the Lawes. Commended to the High Court" (London 1628) to provide fuel for the arguments of Sir Edward Coke and other Parliamentary lawyers in their battles with the Stuart kings (Kliger 126). As a result, the Society was disbanded, and Coke, John Selden, and other Parliamentary lawyers were repeatedly imprisoned or dismissed, their publications censored.

Matters reached an early crisis point—and the rhetoric of ancient Saxon rights found its legs—when in 1620 the king issued a proclamation restricting Parliament's right to discuss high matters of state. Parliament responded directly, coining a language that would not only become the basis of the 1628 Petition of Right but would also create the heart of the Whig politics and Saxon myth that lasted well into the twentieth century: "The privileges and rights of Parliament are an ancient and indubitable birthright and inheritance of the English, and all important and urgent affairs in Church and State as well as the drawing up of laws and the remedying of abuses, are the proper subjects of the deliberation and resolutions of the Parliament. The members are free to speak upon them in such order as they please, and cannot be called to account for them" (Brinkley 38). In further exchanges with the king, the Parliament reasserted its "Ancient and Undoubted Right, and an Inheritance received from our Ancestors," until the king "publicly tore these protests from the Journal of the House of Commons and dissolved Parliament" (Brinkley 38). Throughout the 1620s and 30s Parliament and the Stuart kings reached several such impasse moments. Finally, in 1629, Charles I dissolved Parliament—and it did not reconvene until 1640.

Meanwhile, however, other forces were gathering. Across the Atlantic, a group of men were building a new commercial network that would eventually help to break the impasse. Ultimately, this development would make the racialized rhetoric of liberty a transatlantic phenomenon, embedding it deep in the structures of English-language narrative. Although the British empire would turn east by the end of the next century, the American colonies served as the crucible for its alchemy of liberty and race. In a sense, the English Civil War and its aftermath, from Cromwell's Commonwealth to Queen Victoria's empire, find their necessary cause in the years from 1610 through the 1620s, in the form of a group of "new men"—middling-class and eventually Puritan-affiliated—who initiated the activities and alliances that would reshape the economic balance of power. For, with the Parliamentary crisis of 1628–29, culminating with Charles I's eleven-year dissolution of Parliament and renewed persecution of Puritans, a handful of Atlantic merchants who had been accruing land, power, and wealth in the west Atlantic throughout the 1620s joined hands with those interested in building colonies as safe havens for religious refugees. Together, to put it oversimply, these men overthrew the king.

This colonial growth formed a crucial condition for the Civil War in England—its tobacco and sugar profits, in fact, eventually fueled Parliamentary warships (Bliss 48). As Robert Brenner has documented, there evolved "growing ties between the American merchant leadership and the great Puritan aristocrats who ran the Bermuda and Providence Island companies, as well as the lesser gentry who governed the New England colonies" (Brenner 149). Men such as Maurice Thomson and his brother-in-law

William Tucker, who had begun as ship captains, had entered the breach left by the retreat of the king's trading companies in Virginia. Furthermore, the absence of Royal Company rules allowed these men to run both exports and imports and to set up shop on both sides of the Atlantic (a practice prohibited in the royal companies). As a result they quickly monopolized the import of supplies for settlers as well as the export of tobacco, and they accrued huge profits. Working together with a handful of others, they eventually expanded their reach south to the West Indies (where they headed interloping invasions against the colonies of other European powers) and north to the Massachusetts Bay Colony, financially backing the Puritan settlement of Massachusetts and helping to organize provisions for colonies both north and south.

These ties eventually laid the foundation for the "transatlantic network of Puritan religio-political opposition to the Crown" that included Massachusetts, Connecticut, Rhode Island, and, in the West Indies, Bermuda Island and Providence Island, all of which drew investors for religious and political reasons as well as for profits and all of which served as both "ports of exile and staging posts for revolt" (Brenner 113, 110). Under these conditions, the pursuit of religious freedom, so touted in American history books, was utterly involved with the pursuit of mercantile freedom: for, even when religious motives were paramount, economic "freedoms" were requisite to make the colonial settlements viable, as Karen Kupperman has shown (142). Furthermore, it was from this base, and for this base, that Thomson and his circle began to interlope in the slave trade and the East Indies trade, and then in turn to build the enormously profitable West Indies sugar plantations during the 1640s (Brenner 161–65). When Parliament finally reconvened in 1640, a new coalition of members, including Puritans backed by these merchants, succeeded in abolishing the Star Chamber (which had handled licensing and press censorship since 1586), purging those members they considered popish or unlawful, exerting powerful resistance to the king's demands, and eventually declaring war. They spoke a liberty rhetoric that loosely blended religious and economic meanings. It is this Atlantic rhetoric of liberty that, three hundred years later, Nella Larsen probes.

In this early phase, the cry of liberty was voiced against not only the king but also against those merchants of the east whom the king had sponsored and depended on—such as in a petition organized by the Thomson group calling for "freehold" conditions in the West Indian colonies (Brenner 166), or the petition challenging the Royalist Calverts who controlled Maryland, also signed by Thomson and associates (Brenner 166–67). Likewise, "A Remonstrance of Many Thousand Citizens, and other Free-Born People of England to theire own House of Commons" complains of "the oppression of the Turkey Company, and the Adventures Company, and all other infringements of our Native Liberties" (Haller III, 358). Via the notion of native liberty, the Atlantic economy joined the nation, and, in turn, native liberty extended across the Atlantic.

At the same time, throughout the 1640s, because of the uncensored press and the unregulated preaching of ministers, liberty rhetoric spread "downward" and its nativist overtones became louder. The Long Parliament had not immediately replaced the Star Chamber with any equivalent censorship organ, and so there circulated increasing numbers of polemical newspapers, pamphlets, and petitions that eventually made it impossible for the entrepreneurs and the Puritans to maintain control of the liberty discourse. Indeed, this is the moment when the Habermasian public sphere becomes a reality in England—briefly yet influentially.[3]

It is worth specifying the eruptions of this Habermasian moment before recounting the activist liberty language that helped to organize it. Between November of 1641 and April of 1642, there appeared eleven domestic weekly papers. By 1645, fourteen more regular newspapers were available in London (Thompson, *Media and Modernity* 67). At the same time, pamphlets and petitions spread like fire, readily accessible to a broad segment of what now became a "publick" literate enough through their Bible reading to comprehend such texts. Especially as the Puritan-slanted Parliament gained the upper hand in the war, numerous petitions were presented to the House of Commons, expressing the desire of soldiers, soldiers' wives, tradespeople, religious sects, and laborers for relief from painful economic conditions and for fuller representation of their voices. But relief and representation were not forthcoming, and so "the public" printed, agitated, and formed new coalitions. By 1647, the failure to hold new Parliamentary elections with an expanded electorate, to pay soldiers their arrears, to finance support for widows and orphans or for citizens who quartered the soldiers, to break up monopolies of trade in an already debilitated postwar economy, to allow for full religious toleration instead of new preferential treatment of the Puritans, and to repeal the tithes and taxes that weighed heavily on the poorest—all of these fed widespread disenchantment among a people who had sustained years of war for the sake of better living conditions. Increasingly politicized middle-rank women as well as men wrote petitions, held meetings, and joined or led public protests to address these injustices. Early in 1641, four hundred women gathered at Parliament to demand a response to a petition on the loss of trade. When they received no satisfactory attention, they penned the "Humble Petition of many hundreds of distressed women, Tradesmens wives, and widdowes" in which they claimed that "we have an interest in the common Privileges with them [who have petitioned for the] Liberty of our Husbands, persons, and estates" (qtd. in McEntee 93–94). In August 1643, some five thousand to six thousand women (as numbered by their critics) marched on the Commons for peace. By 1647, as women appeared so frequently on the steps of Parliament to petition or demand responses to petitions, the House of Commons enacted an ordinance against loitering and a directive to guards to clear away "those clamourous women, which were wont to hang in clusters on the staires"; the women must have kept returning for, later in the year, the Commons issued an order to apprehend and jail all such loiterers (McEntee 96).

These various groups, including the so-called Levellers led by Lt. Col. John Lilburne, spoke continually of "native rights" (Prall 134), "the people's just rights and liberties" (Prall 129), the "Nation's freedoms" (Prall 134), "the free-born people of England" (Prall 127), and the "free-born People's freedoms or rights" (Prall 128). Like John Hare, Nathaniel Bacon more elaborately laid out the Saxonist historical narrative underlying this rhetoric that would become Whig orthodoxy by the early eighteenth century. In his *Historical and Political Discourse of the Laws and Government of England,* which addresses the "Debate concerning the Right of an English King to Arbitrary Rule over English Subjects, as Successor to the Norman Conqueror" (1647), Bacon remarks that it is

> both needless and fruitless to enter into the Lists, concerning the original of the Saxons[. . . .] They were a free people, governed by Laws, and those made not after the manner of the Gauls (as Caesar noteth) by the great men, but by the people; and therefore called a free people, because they are a law unto themselves; and this was a privilege belonging to all the germans, as tacitus observeth[. . . .] The Saxons fealty to their King, was subservient to the publick safety; and the publick safety is necessarily dependant upon the liberty of the Laws. (Kliger 139)

Such pronouncements opened the way to more radical thinkers such as the Diggers, who nonetheless invoked the same nativist rhetoric. The Digger Gerard Winstanley echoed it in pronouncing that "the last enslaving conquest which the enemy got over Israel was the Norman over England" (Prall 179). The many migrations, rebellions, ironies, and crimes of Atlantic history follow from this inextricable intertwining of the colonial, revolutionary, and Saxonist roots of the modern notion of freedom.

Equally important, at this point the liberty rhetoric also took what we might call an "interior turn." Leveller pamphleteer John Warr signaled the shift when he claimed that "Justice was in men, before it came to be in Laws" (Kliger 269). In his political theology, Winstanley casts "the great Creator, who is the Spirit Reason" not only as "man's teacher and ruler within himself" but also as "the Spirit of universal community and freedom" (Prall 176). It is beyond the scope of this paper to consider the long path by which such claims led to the interiorization of both racial identity and modern narrative, and to the forms of power Michel Foucault analyzed, but suffice it to say for now that this legacy also conditions the "subjectivism" of Atlantic modernists three hundred years later. The work of

G. W. F. Hegel (*Philosophy of History*) gives a glimpse of the way the revolutionary nativist vision became an interiorized, racist one. For Hegel, too, "Reason" drives the "Universal History" of the world toward "Freedom" (10), but he declares German culture to be the ultimate incarnation of this process. Making explicit that which was incipient in the discourses of the seventeenth century—that "the History of the World is nothing but the development of the Idea of Freedom" (456)—Hegel announces that Africans and Native Americans lack Protestant subjectivity and the historical will to freedom, while "The German spirit is the Spirit of the new World. Its aim is the realization of absolute Truth as the unlimited self-determination of Freedom. . . . The destiny of the German peoples is to be the bearers of the Christian principle . . . of Spiritual Freedom" (341). The movement from the Reformation to the English Civil War to Hegel neatly encapsulates how a discourse of race merged into an interiorized discourse of freedom and, via the prosperous Atlantic economy, gave rise to an imperial chauvinism. In effect, I am arguing that Atlantic modernism inherits and variously resists this legacy—perhaps by our lights unsuccessfully but nonetheless revealingly.

Yet, despite its radicalism, it is already clear that Saxonism in the Civil War period began to provide a cohering, conservative, centripetal idea in a community that was experiencing radical centrifugal rupture of its geography, economy, social order, and historical identity. With the monarch under arrest, women protesting in the streets, families fleeing to colonies across the Atlantic that were themselves in struggle with the Indian peoples whose land they seized, all while at home the problems of poverty and hunger were finding unbridled expression in a new world of print—under these conditions, as contemporaries reported, "There is a great expectation of sudden destruction" for "The greatest powers in the kingdom have been shaken" (Woodhouse 42, 20). Alarmed, conservative Puritans like Prynne worked to remonopolize the liberty rhetoric, to discredit the radicals' use of it, and so to delimit it, charging that they aimed "to establish a *meere popular* Tyrannie" (Kliger 155, emphasis added). Others likewise predicted defensively that the dissenters would "destroy all distinction of degrees" until "there be nothing at all of civil constitution left in the kingdom" (Woodhouse 50).

It is this crisis—in which English society seems teetering on a cliff—that racialism works to contain. The 1647 Putney Debates between the Army and Cromwell (together with his son-in-law, Colonel Henry Ireton) mark this moment and reveal this ameliorating function. As I will argue in the next few pages, to quell the Army's protests Cromwell and Ireton conjured this threat of social leveling as well as the specter of control by "non-native" foreigners; and in the process they drew out racialism's possibilities—which could all at once supply a new principle of community, authorize radical, new claims to membership, rights, and property, and yet still draw a substitute boundary to counter the complete "leveling" of social hierarchies. Held after the close of the Civil War in response to the Army's demand for more representation and Cromwell's plans to re-move Army forces to Ireland (in part to defuse their political maneuverings at home while reinstating colonial rule over the Irish), the Putney Debates were specifically meant to take up the Army's objections as laid out in "The Case of the Army Truly Stated" and "An Agreement of the People." These documents enumerated what the writers considered their "native rights" such as a more representative electorate and a biennial Parliamentary elec-tion, which emerged in tension with the new and more radical notion that liberty is a universal principle.

In resisting the idea of a universalized "natural right," Cromwell and Ireton momentarily lift the veil covering the elitist basis of the state. When in the Putney Debates the Army spokespersons proclaimed that "every man is naturally free," Ireton (apparently)[4] responded by scorning those who "fly for refuge [for their arguments] to an absolute natural right" (Woodhouse 61, 53). He insisted that such a natural right would be "no right at all" because no one could lay claim to anything in the form of property, and thus it would imperil both civil rights and property. If each man "hath the same [equal] right in any goods he sees—eat, drink, clothes," he can supposedly "take and use them for his sustenance"—in other words, steal them from others (Woodhouse 58). Ireton argued that only "law" can install "rights," especially property rights, and law exists to protect those rights: "For matter of goods, that which does fence me from that [right] which another man may claim by the Law of Nature, of taking my goods, that which makes it mine really and civilly, is the law[. . . .] This is the foundation of all the right any man has to anything but to his own person. This is the general thing: that we must keep covenant one with another when we have contracted with another" (Kliger 278–79).

Ireton circles an absent origin: how can it be that men both constitute themselves in law to protect property and that such constituting itself "founds" property? He would make "property" the anchoring term so as to elide the question of its legitimacy in the first place. The note almost of defensiveness one hears in his comments is not surprising, given that Ireton and Cromwell are facing not only the possible extension into democ-racy of the Army's liberty claims but also the exposure of the circular logic, and absent center, of any contract theory of the state. In short, the debate opens up the question of how the state with which one contracts comes into being—circling around the question of what founds property. Here is that same missing center that readers of Jean-Jacques Rousseau have noted in his attempts to imagine the moment of original contract with the state that simultaneously founds the state.

To cover the gap and push back the claims of the opposition, Ireton in-vokes the threat of foreign control as the final disastrous effect of liberty understood as a universal interior right. When he does, the Army's and Ireton's shared interest in property surfaces clearly and so, simultaneously, does nativism's power to delimit and counterbalance the principle of liberty. As the debate heats up, Ireton poses the question of what is to stop "a foreigner coming in amongst us—or as many as will coming in amongst us, or by force or otherwise settling themselves here" and claiming rights of representation, if a man need not have any land and so no "real or permanent interest in the kingdom" underlying his bid for representation (54). He goes so far as to align the propertyless of England with foreigners when he points out that even if renters who have lived their whole lives in England pay rent "for two years, or twenty years" they may always take their property out of the kingdom and therefore have not "a local, a permanent interest" in it (Woodhouse 62). Offended, his opponents shift away from the claim that "every man is naturally free," and instead insist that they speak only of "birthright"—that is, the rights of those born in England (Woodhouse 69). They stand on "the examples of our ancestors" who often fought for "the recovery of their freedoms" (Woodhouse 445). And so we glimpse the pressure toward nativism that the competition over property and power exerts.

In short, the Putney Debates foreshadow how the notion of native liberty would both challenge and reconstitute the state. It served as a political and rhetorical pivot for the turn from a domestic, land-based economic order to a colonial and trade-based one and so allowed the new accumulation of mercantile wealth to exert its force. The model of "free contract" served to rationalize this shift in the nature of power—drawing strategically, as David Zaret notes, on the spiritual language of covenant and so further merging Protestantism and Atlantic mercantilism (Zaret 6–10). But in a state that maintained unequal distribution of private property as its economic norm while cultivating liberty as its political principle, the property interest of the emergent social contract would have to be effaced. And some other principle of "commonwealth" that would at once rationalize hierarchy and reconstitute community would have to be generated. Anglo-Saxonism served that function. At the same time, in a deep ontogeographical sense, more Englishmen were inhabiting a space "outside" the traditional political center—in colonies far from the island of England—and this geography also embodied their other outsider conditions in terms of class and religion. Under these conditions, they worked hard to establish their claims, assertively dethroning royalist fictions and disseminating a nativized, interiorized, and contractual fiction.

It is within these currents of thought that there began the "westward transatlantic movements of peoples" that Bernard Bailyn has called "one of the greatest events in recorded history" (5). "From 1500 to the present," he points out, "it has involved the displacement and resettlement of over fifty million people, and it has affected indirectly the lives of uncountable millions more" (Bailyn 5). This resettlement took off after the English Civil War, so that in the course of the seventeenth century the population on the Atlantic seaboard grew to 400,000, and by the end of the eighteenth century it numbered four million (Bliss 1; Wood 125). When the Scotsman Charles Tisbet visited the United States shortly after the American revolution, he saw a "new world . . . unfortunately composed . . . of discordant atoms, jumbled together by chance, and tossed by inconstancy in an immense vacuum"; and he concluded that the society "greatly wants a principle of attraction" (Wood 305). What Tisbet did not see was the way that the colonists, entrepreneurs, and founders had been fashioning race to provide just this "principle of attraction." Under the pressures of these migrations and dispersions, novels plot the interiorized and deracinating—yet race-bearing—story of trans-Atlantic liberty.

2

By the eighteenth century, in the genre of the English-language novel, a liberty plot that encodes this racialization increasingly took the form of a transatlantic tale of rupture, and ruin, and, in some cases, redemption. Initiated by Aphra Behn's *Oroonoko* and soon shaping English identity in *Robinson Crusoe* and *Moll Flanders,* this plot surfaces again and again. We see it in Gothic novels such as *The Monk,* in which all the trouble begins when two lovers elope to Cuba to marry against their family's wishes, or Charles Brockdon Brown's *Wieland,* which tells of the trauma of a family that emigrates from Saxon Germany to the United States, faces rupture and rape, and ends with the American Saxon son murdering his family— all of which is narrated by the nearly unhinged sister. Early sentimental U.S. novels such as Susanna Rowson's *Charlotte Temple* align the seduction plot directly with an Atlantic crossing, and more broadly, as Cathy Davidson has tracked, most early American novels used the seduction plot as an interrogation of the new nation's liberty principles. Such novels make explicitly Atlantic the story organized as an English epic by Richardson's character Clarissa—that paragon of "native dignity" (1073) who asks her seducer-conqueror "whether it be, or be not, your intention to permit me . . . the freedom which is my birthright as an English subject?" (934).

In telling of how the seductions of liberty can end in isolation and loss of community, these novels offer a deeper allegory of modernity—whose free-floating citizens each contract with a laissez-faire capitalism in exchange for an eroticized if troubled interiority and the promise of material comfort—even while sentimental endings make heroic and native these cautionary tales of freedom. At the same time, white English and American authors repeatedly enfold African characters into their fiction, positioning their white protagonists as the liberty-wise friends of those Africans who seek escape from captivity, as in Aphra Behn's *Oroonoko*. These stories cast English characters as mediators between Africans and freedom and in the process appropriate the African's freedom struggles as adjuncts to their own freedom story. Thus Friday is both saved and enslaved by Robinson Crusoe, that man located, in isolation, at the center of an Atlantic and colonial economy. In turn, writers such as Olaudah Equiano wrest back these tropes to tell their own transatlantic freedom stories, yet meanwhile in the process enter into the story's racial telos—that of securing freedom for an oppressed race.

Herman Melville's *Billy Budd* perhaps best embodies the palimpsestic way in which white authors' narratives simultaneously acknowledge and subsume the Olaudah Equianos of the Atlantic. His tale begins with the portrait of "a common sailor so intensely black that he must needs have been a native African with the unadulterated blood of Ham," yet whose substitute role for an "ancient" European is foreshadowed by his "Highland bonnet with a tartan band" (291). Then there enters the young Billy Budd, a man of "free heart" (298) who was "cast in a mould peculiar to the finest physical example of those Englishmen in whom the Saxon strain would seem not at all to partake of any Norman or other admixture" (299). And of course, the African "cynosure" disappears altogether as Billy's tale takes center stage. The Atlantic allegory embedded in this novella finds further expression in the fact that Billy with his Saxon soul launches on the Rights of Man, a mercantile ship, but soon finds himself impressed into service on the Bellipotent, an imperial warship pursuing that enterprise in which even a chaplain "subserves the purpose attested by the cannon" (374), and operating under the strict code of martial law by which, as Captain Vere says, men "cease to be natural free agents" (362). On the morning of his execution, chained in irons, Billy resembles all at once "a Tahitian" indifferent to the rituals of Christianity, an angelic blond with the look of the ancient "Angles," and "a condemned vestal priestess in the moment of being buried alive" (372–73). Clearly, his deadly passage on the Bellipotent substitutes for the Atlantic falls of Others.

3

In *Quicksand,* Larsen retells this palimpsestic Atlantic story. The very name of her protagonist, Helga Crane, alludes to the Germanic and Atlantic layers of the palimpsest (echoing, also perhaps, Stein's use of "Melanctha" for her mixed-blood heroine, apparently named after the sixteenth-century German Reformation scholar, Melancthon).[5] Larsen further indicates this troubled Euro-African genealogy in the name of the school where Helga teaches—Naxos. The name not only refers to a Greek island of Dionysian affiliations and thereby an erotic struggle, but it also suggests "Saxon" spelled backwards—a neat encapsulation of Larsen's revisionary project.[6] Larsen's heroine suffers the abandonment and betrayals of this noxious Saxon history, and Larsen writes her way "backwards" through it.

Helga's struggle with the double bind of race and freedom finds its first and most compact expression in her reflections on colorful dress. Alienated by the regimented routines of Naxos, Helga indicts the school's "suppression of individuality and beauty," taking its disapproval of color and boldness in clothing as one instance of this suppression.[7] Yet she also understands her own love of color as the "inherent *racial* need for gorgeousness, . . . [for] bright colors" (20, 18, emphasis added). These desires are contradictory. Is dress an expression of the individual or the race? Is it unfettered individuality or racial actualization that Helga seeks? Freedom from race, or freedom *for* the race? She seems to desire both, and the novel tracks her swerving movement between the two, as well as her insights into their incommensurability.

In her travels back and forth across the Atlantic, the objective *and historical* correlative for her mixed desires, Helga becomes acutely conscious of the Catch-22 in the culture of freedom. In Copenhagen, first noting the "odd architectural mixture of medievalism and modernity," she observes that "Here there were no tatters and rags, no beggars"—for "begging, she learned, was an offense punishable by law" (75). She reasons that the appearance of settled order and naturally well-bred modernity rests on punitive laws that are justified by the notion of everyone's "duty somehow to support himself and his family" (75). The State apparently feels "bound to give assistance" to the impoverished—yet only, she wryly adds, as help "on the road to the regaining of independence" from the others (75). Helga precisely pinpoints the tension between group and individual in the orthodoxy of Anglo-European modernity: everyone *must* be an independent individual in order to be a member of the group; and conversely, one can only be a group member by assenting to the laws of laissez-faire economy and individual self-support.[8] This orthodoxy is the essence of a racial Saxonism parading as social contract, and it creates the incoherence of Helga's desires for race and for escape from race.

Helga sees that her Harlem circle of friends is similarly caught in these contradictions, especially through their simultaneous identification and dis-identification with race. She observes that Anne Grey "hated white people with a deep and burning hatred" but "she aped their clothes, their manners, and their gracious ways of living" (48). Conversely, "while proclaiming loudly the undiluted good of all things Negro, she yet disliked the songs, the dances, the softly blurred speech of the race" (48). Helga's friends seek the freedom to appropriate whichever customs serve them best, yet like the whites, these middle-class Harlem blacks do not scrutinize too closely exactly what this supposedly deracialized freedom is. As *Negroes* they deserve freedom—freedom to be Negroes no longer, to live

un-raced. Although at moments Larsen manifests her own racial dissocia-
tion,[9] she nonetheless exposes the way that Anne and friends take up the
whites' most shrewd strategy—using race as a way to authorize their escape from race into an ostensibly neutral selfhood and freedom.

Larsen most clearly builds her meta-fiction of the Atlantic freedom plot
when she mobilizes the correlation between sexual ruin, race, and the transatlantic seduction into liberty.[10] For Helga's "alien" position originates in
her Scandinavian mother's affair with an African American man. Helga
remembers her mother as an innocent immigrant—"A fair Scandinavian
girl in love with life, with love, with passion, dreaming, and risking all in
one blind surrender. A cruel sacrifice. In forgetting all but love she had forgotten, or perhaps never known, that some things the world never forgives.
But as Helga knew, she had remembered, or learned in suffering and longing all the rest of her life" (23). After her lover leaves her, Helga's mother
becomes the social pariah who, out of "grievous necessity" eventually marries a white man, "for even foolish, despised women must have food and
clothing" (23). In the aftermath, scorned by her white stepfamily, Helga the
biracial daughter leaves them to attend a school for Negroes, which eventually lands her at Naxos as a teacher. Yet at Naxos, she can no more speak
of her white kin than she could, in her white family, embrace her African
American heritage. "No family. That was the crux of the whole matter," she
realizes in brooding on her sense of distance from everyone at Naxos (8).
She stands outside both racial communities, giving the lie to their ostensible devotion to freedom as the principle of *community*.

Hereafter, the plot of the novel might accurately be characterized as
Helga's vacillating movement toward and away from race as a ground of
identity, a series of racial reaction-formations in a quest for freedom.[11] In
New York, as at first in Chicago, Helga feels again "that magic sense of
having come home," for "Harlem, teeming black Harlem, had welcomed
her and lulled her into something that was, she was certain, peace and contentment" (43). She loses "that tantalizing oppression of loneliness and isolation" in her identification with African American community, looking on
the "white world" as a collection of "sinister folk ... who had stolen her
birthright" (45). The old language of birthright resurfaces here, just as later
Larsen's narrator describes Helga as feeling "yoked" to race (55). At first in
Harlem, she feels a contentment that "she knew sprang from a sense of
freedom, a release from the feeling of smallness which had hedged her in,
first during her unchildlike childhood among hostile white folk ... and
later ... among snobbish black folk in Naxos" (46).

Yet, as the rest of the novel makes clear, "it didn't last, this happiness"
for "somewhere, within her, in a deep recess, crouched discontent" (47).
Soon she again feels "boxed up, with hundreds of her race, closed up with
that something in the racial character which had always been, to her, in-
explicable, alien" so that now she wants no longer to be "yoked to these

despised black folk" (55). Although she experiences "self-loathing" for this last emotion ("'They're my own people, my own people' she kept repeating"), she finds that "The feeling would not be routed" (55). Feeling a sharp "necessity for being alone," she takes her uncle's offer of a trip to her mother's relatives in Copenhagen and, at the very center of Larsen's novel, on board a ship sailing across the Atlantic to northern Europe, Helga feels a "returned sense of happiness and freedom, that blessed sense of belonging to herself alone and not to a race" (64). But instead of freedom from race, in Copenhagen Helga finds that she is paraded by her aunt and uncle "like a veritable savage" and soon she is "homesick not for America, but for Negroes" (92). Recrossing the Atlantic, she forgives her father his abandonment of her mother and his "surrender to the irresistible ties of race, now that they dragged at her own heart" (92). Yet, once in America—though she feels "the appeasement of that loneliness" and how "absurd" it was to think that "other people could liberate her from the ties which bound her forever to these mysterious, these terrible, these fascinating, these lovable, dark hordes" (95)—finally she realizes that, because of the cruelty and cramping Negroes faced in America, "she couldn't stay. Nor, she saw now, could she remain away." No. Her condition will be forever ambiguous, forever transient: "Leaving, she would have to come back" (96). She is the "race woman" in modernity, in a sense that Mrs. Hayes-Rore might not want to recognize.

4

Just when Helga begins to face that her freedom is always in some way a return to race, and so her only freedom is flight—Robert Anderson kisses her. His kiss reopens the "wound" of her childhood, that sensation, as she describes it, of being "an obscene sore" in other people's lives, which she repeatedly says Anderson recalls for her (29). In Atlantic modernism, such kisses mark the turning point in the heroine's voyage out—the moment of racial crisis, when the promise of social entry into a community is revealed as self-alienation. As Richard Dalloway kisses Rachel Vinrace, as Rochester kisses Bertha, as Adele *says* Dr. Aziz kisses her, Anderson's kiss reignites an old tainted history, the Gothic racial and sexual core of the liberty plot. In a back hall at Helen Tavenor's polyracial party, "he stooped and kissed her, a long kiss, holding her close" as "she fought against him with all her might" until "strangely, all power seemed to ebb away, and a long-hidden, half-understood desire welled up in her with the suddenness of a dream" yet after which "sudden anger seized her" (104). At this crisis, one can fairly hear the ghosts rattling their chains, or see what Rachel Vinrace imagines as the mocking goblins munching in their wet, dark corners, and what Helga calls the "skeletons that stalked lively and

in full health through the consciousness of every person of Negro ancestry in America" (96). As Edna Pontellier in Kate Chopin's *The Awakening*
learns about Robert Lebrun, Helga comes to realize that "[Robert Ander-
son] was not the sort of man who would for any reason give up one particle
of his own good opinion of himself. Not even for her" (108). Women who
kiss transgressively (or lay claim to a kiss, in Adele's case) ostensibly step
outside the group with its history, its sexual codes, and its borders, but
in the end they enact the will of the group—for the threat they embody
calls characters (like Robert Anderson) and readers back into the racial
fold. The married Robert Anderson brushes off the kiss and leaves Helga
to suffer once more the "wound" of racial "freedom"—experienced as a
casting out.

Overcome by mortification, feeling herself "alone, isolated from all other
human beings, separated even from her own anterior existence," Helga the
modern woman gets drunk and then later wanders into an urban storefront
revival meeting. This experience returns her to race as an ancient force,
and yet her final embrace of it comes, ironically, in an act of utterly arbitrary, unabashedly sexual freedom. Entering the storefront meeting—a
peculiarly urban setting and modern phenomenon (Esteve 279–80)—she
enters an ancient history: "people were singing a song which she was conscious of having heard years ago—hundreds of years it seemed" (111). She
is called out with "Bacchic vehemence" by the crowd of worshipers, who
recognize her as a "pore los' Jezebel!" a "scarlet 'oman," "our errin' sistah"
(111–13). Suddenly she holds herself very still because she feels she may be
sick, and "in that moment she was lost—or saved" (113). Her Kohutian loss
of self, as Barbara Johnson reads this scene (258), is also her entry into a
racialized or Bacchic modernity. She too begins to "yell like one insane"
until "the thing became real" and "A miraculous calm came upon her"
(114). The chapter ends with Larsen's narrator stepping back from her heroine's interior to acknowledge that "to the kneeling girl time seemed to sink
back into the mysterious grandeur and holiness of far-off simpler centuries" (114). Helga has returned to the ancient fold, that ideal on which modernity contradictorily depends for cohesion and progress. She is freed
into modern acceptance in confessing herself a lost Jezebel.

Larsen pulls even tighter the knot of paradoxes binding her protagonist
when Helga's final entry into this ancient community requires an "abandoned" sexual agency. While most critics read this scene as part of Helga's
struggle with sexual repression, I see no such struggle against "repression"
in Helga but rather a struggle with her *position* as a sexual subject.[12] Helped
home after her conversion experience by "the fattish yellow man," the Reverend Mr. Pleasant Green, she realizes that he is attracted to her (for, when
she leans on his arm "to keep herself from falling," he shudders involun-
tarily with desire). She has a flash of insight; she could sleep with him:
"across her still half-hypnotized consciousness little burning darts of fancy

had shot themselves": "That man! Was it possible? As easy as that?" She rejects the idea at first: "No. She couldn't. It would be too awful" (115). But then she realizes just how completely free her "lack of family" and her root-lessness have made her: "Just the same, what or who was there to hold her back? Nothing. Simply nothing. Nobody. Nobody at all" (115). So she takes the Reverend home and sleeps with him, and the next day marries him. She thinks perhaps she has freed herself finally into a true community. She goes "home" to the South, but there she will learn that she is from the North.

For Helga is free, after all, only to choose race. Freedom keeps entrap-ping her in the form of race, and race fails her again. At the end of the book, after giving birth to several children and coming to despise her hus-band, she is once again overcome with "this feeling of dissatisfaction, of asphyxiation" (134). Although she spends sickly hours in her bed dream-ing of "freedom and cities," and listening to a nurse read Anatole France's fiction about republican polity,[13] the book closes outside her consciousness "as she began to have her fifth child" (135).

As in *Passing*, in this novel Larsen restricts her narrator's access, focal-izing only through one character and at crucial moments blocking access even to that character's interiority, as in this closing moment. This narra-tional choice reinforces her protagonists' isolation, establishing their inte-riority as a source of separation and alienation from community; and it forces our participation in it as such.[14] In *Passing*, Larsen brings us to share Irene's paranoia about Brian's and Clare's desires, while in Helga's case she leaves us lost in her ruin. Larsen masterfully places her readers in a relation to her characters that mirrors her characters' relations to their communities—and so indicates how the community established in the print sphere forms around a fallen, exiled, yet racialized individual.

Larsen might have been surprised at the positive reviews of *Passing* and *Quicksand*, given her dark vision and her acerbic critique of African American community. On the contrary, however, these outsiders' stories solidified her role as a Harlem insider. For her acts of defiance proved her brave embrace of freedom—her transcendence of race, for the race. Like earlier authors of all kinds, Larsen used the interior struggle with lib-erty to create a racial place of narration for herself. She depended, neces-sarily, on race to tell her story of Helga's individuality—exactly as narra-tors of history and fiction had been doing for centuries. With her stark lucidity, Larsen may have known this—I think she did. She went forward undaunted, for she was a kind of kamikaze queen of race. She seems to have been ready to watch herself go up in flames if that's what it took to explode these paradoxes. The fact that her writing career did go up in flames, perhaps through an act of her own, offers a final lens through which to view Larsen's work as emblematic of Atlantic modernisms' nar-rative crises.

5

Instead of *Quicksand* or *Passing,* it was Larsen's ironically titled story "Sanctuary" that "ruined" her. Whether or not this story about theft is meant to resonate with an authorial act of theft, it certainly conjures a transatlantic history of theft. As we know, Larsen was accused of plagiarizing this story from the English writer Sheila Kaye-Smith's story "Mrs. Adis," but no one will ever know if Larsen did indeed read Kaye-Smith's story and consciously, unconsciously, or half-consciously take its material for "Sanctuary." The stories are strikingly similar. In both, a man on the run seeks asylum with the mother of a friend after having shot one of the pursuers who caught him in the act of stealing. In both cases the flinty mother reluctantly harbors the man, in both cases for the sake of their son who has been a friend and protector of the renegade man, as well as out of solidarity with the dispossessed—in "Mrs. Adis" with poachers against keepers and in "Sanctuary" with Jim who is a "po niggah" pursued by "white folk" (23). Though Kaye-Smith's story is set in Sussex County, England and Larsen's in the southern United States, they both open remarkably similarly, with a man approaching the lonely cottage of a woman, looking in surreptitiously through the side window before circling back to enter through the door, without knocking—the latter detail emphasized in both. In each case, it turns out that the man whom the renegade has unintentionally shot is his old friend, the son of the woman who gives him sanctuary (before she learns of her son's death). Similarly in both, when the authorities arrive to tell the mother the news of the son's death and the hiding man trembles in the next room, the mother chooses not to betray her son's murderer.

Given the large and small similarities, it is hard to imagine that Larsen had never read the story. It seems likely she did and lodged it somewhere in her mind. I am going to proceed as if she did and then later reconfigured it within the American frame of race—with whatever degree of (un)consciousness—rather than try to explain or dismiss this possibility.[15] For this allows me to give Larsen the credit she deserves for this act of expropriation and to appreciate the piercingly astute anatomy of Atlantic history inscribed in it. In focusing on both the plot they share and those crucial details that are different, we can see how Larsen overlays the story of race in the United States on Kaye-Smith's story of class in England, as is historically appropriate.

If we heed the history narrated by Peter Linebaugh and Marcus Rediker in *The Many-Headed Hydra* as well as the colonial history outlined above, the characters in these two stories have much in common in terms of material conditions and historical causes, which Larsen implicitly acknowledges in her merging of the two stories. That is, the enclosure of land and the practice of poaching that create the drama of the first story intersect powerfully, in history, with the slave legacy that creates the drama of the second. Just as she links the middle classes of Harlem and Copenhagen in *Quicksand*, in creating this palimpsestic "Sanctuary," Larsen juxtaposes the ruthless policing and impossible predicaments of laborers on both sides of the Atlantic economy. As Linebaugh and Rediker document, the privatization of common lands in England in the sixteenth and seventeenth centuries, prompted in large part by the turn to an international mercantile and manufacturing economy, led to a massive impoverishment and displacement of peasants. These displacements and the wage-labor economy found their "outlet," quite literally, in colonization schemes in the Americas whereby displaced people and petty thieves would be exported as bond servants to the colonies, laying the foundation for England's manufacturing and trade wealth. As reviewed above, colonization led in turn to the creation of the Atlantic triangle, the slave trade, and the virulent black–white racism of the United States.

Thus the enclosure of commons that began the centuries-long war between "poachers" and "keepers" depicted in Kaye-Smith's story prepares the ground for the racial drama of theft in Larsen's story. From this angle, Annie Poole the mother and Jim Hammond the thief in Larsen's story do indeed descend from Mrs. Adis and Peter Crouch in Kaye-Smith's. When Larsen "steals" from an English woman to tell her story, in fact she is stealing back what was long ago stolen—a story of herself initiated in effect by the propertied forces in England that generated the terms of both the original story and her own. Larsen indicates that her story is a later and grimmer symptom of the same modern economy underlying Kaye-Smith's when she replaces Kaye-Smith's "great tongue of land [that] runs into Kent by Scotney Castle" with "a strip of desolation . . . between the sea and old fields of ruined plantations" and places Annie's house along a road "little used, now that the state has built its new highway a bit to the west and wagons are less numerous than automobiles" (21). Kaye-Smith may be the unfortunate loser in this borrowing, through no fault of "her own," but judging by her story, Kaye-Smith herself had an inkling of the impossible positions, the irrecoverable losses, the paradoxes of complicity and compassion created when the principle of ownership reigns supreme. For, plagiarism itself—its designation as theft—is likewise an effect of the forces of modernity that make all things property, all art individual, and all assertions of common land—or writing—criminal.

And it is no coincidence that the tale Larsen "steals" narrates an isolated woman's decision about communal loyalty—her entrapment within a group loyalty founded on male-homosocial racial bonds that in the end turns against her through her son and leaves her utterly alone. Interestingly, in both stories the murdered sons have been upright citizens—good boys working within the system, who have struck some kind of compromise with the ruthless order that will kill a man for stealing a rabbit or a tire, as the lawmen assure the mothers they will do when the catch the thieves. In Kaye-Smith's story, Mrs. Adis's son is indeed in company with the keepers of Scotney Castle when his outlaw friend Crouch shoots and runs; and in "Sanctuary," Annie's son Obabiah is among those who chase his friend Jim for stealing tires. In their flight, the outlaws unwittingly kill their upright friends, the sons of the women who later harbor them. Larsen reinforces this irony when the white sheriff calls Annie's son "a mighty fine boy" and wishes "they was all like him—" (27).

Initially, before they know of their sons' deaths, both women accept the acts of theft by the sons' renegade friends. Mrs. Adis remarks that "shooting a keeper ain't the same as shooting an ordinary sort of man, as we all know, and maybe he ain't so much the worse"—though she will "have it on my conscience for having helped you to escape the law" (122). In Larsen's "Sanctuary," as "a look of irony, of cunning, of complicity passed over her face," Annie Poole finds herself "'siderin' all an' all, how Obadiah's right fon' o' you, an' how white folks is white folks, Ah'm gwine hide you dis one time" (23). Their remarks inadvertently align their sons with the very forces that the women are willing to subvert. The women's "complicity" is with illegality, while their sons have been affiliated with "the law" that protects property. These stories thus return to that question of property that haunts and impels the Putney Debates and the whole matter of the social contract. Larsen reinserts the racializations that historically have eased the elision of this question.

Informed of their sons' deaths by officers of the law, both mothers feel the impossibility of the positions they occupy between law and lawlessness, Annie Poole more sharply. In Annie, race-loyalty and rage are fused. After the officers leave, Tom's mother Mrs. Adis simply opens the door of Peter's hiding place in her lean- to and walks away from him without speaking. Notably, Larsen revises this detail, conjuring the intimate violations entailed in the Atlantic pursuit of liberty.[16] In "Sanctuary," Jim has hidden in Annie's bed, laying "his soiled body and grimy garments between [Annie's] snowy white sheets," over which she then places "piles of freshly laundered linen" (24). Once the sheriff leaves, she goes to her bedroom and speaks with "a raging fury in her voice as she lashed out, 'Git outer mah feather baid, Jim Hammer, an' outen mah house, an' don' nevah stop thankin' yo' Jesus he done gib you dat black face'" (27). The "dirt-caked feet" he pushes out from the covers and uses for his final flight from her house leave their physical marks on her bed, as her paradoxical authorizing of her own son's death leaves its marks on Annie's creased face.

In short, perhaps Larsen recognized her story in Kaye-Smith's and performed her own act of expropriation. She daringly, perhaps inescapably, walked the line between truth and theft, fiction and history—as her fictionalizations of her own family history indicate.[17] Fiction was, in effect, her only point of entry into history, her only access to its "liberties," which in the Atlantic setting are always already raced. And perhaps her borrowing from "Mrs. Adis" betrays a subconscious wish to see this fictive discourse with its false distinctions between fiction and history or one race and another collapse, so that the social death she lived privately would become visible in the public sphere. This seems credible given the hints in her fiction that she well understood the terms offered by a contractual yet racialized society especially to a woman without "people" (and also married to an "unfaithful" husband, as she herself apparently was). Indeed, in this light, a pattern of suicide in Larsen's fiction takes on new significance. In *Quicksand*, Helga considers but rejects suicide. *Passing* ends with a woman falling to her death out of a window, an act that might or might not be suicide.[18] An early short story similarly closes with a man jumping out of a window, despairing when he learns of the death of a mistress he earlier cruelly abandoned. This story is called "Freedom." In the aftermath of her divorce (provoked by her husband's infidelity), newspapers carried rumors that Larsen herself fell from a window and broke her leg. Once more we encounter the window to freedom that is no exit.[19] All of these ironical "falls" replay the story of Atlantic modernity that Larsen so adroitly made into fiction.

6

Larsen narrates how citizens sink within modernity's quicksands, its unnavigable Bermuda Triangles of racial and sexual treachery on the Atlantic—what Aldon Nielsen calls in his essay in this collection the *mise en abyme* of modernity's racial spirals. This abyss may be one place that diverse Atlantic modernisms wander into together without finding an exit.

Yet, paradoxically, for readers and writers, the telling of this story has seemed liberating. The narration of liberty's failures seems to offer an antidote for them. DuBois found Larsen's novels inspiring for the future of black America; while more recent critics understand her heroines as "powerful, independent" and "resisting subjects" (Bettye J. Williams 165–66). One critic unwittingly pinpoints the paradox when she remarks that Larsen's *Quicksand* "marks the beginning of greater freedom for self-examination and narrative experimentation in the writing of black American women" (Hostetler 36).[20] Thus is the reading and writing of novels bound up with the promise of entry into another, freer yet still race-centered future, which finds its fullest realization in print culture.

Deconstructing the tale of race frees the race. But from what, and into what? Into racial freedom? Yet if a race is fully free, is it a race anymore, by modernity's lights? Is it not simply then a collection of individuals, who can wear any colors they choose?

So perhaps instead such fictions free readers and characters into a deracialized, universal, and natural freedom. But the history I have reviewed here, as well as the contemporary conflicts now being fought out across the Atlantic between the United States and the Middle East, which reveal the vocabularies of freedom and race to be joined at the root, these histories should make us skeptical about all talk of freedom. Freedom's seeming innocence and individualism, even its revolutionary or postcolonial vanguardism, so often herald yet another racial imperialism. Many of the geomodernisms discussed in this collection reveal as much.

These conundrums suggest that the notion of freedom is as much in need of scrutiny as the notion of race. What is this freedom we speak of so readily, with our every breath? And if we bring this question to bear on what have been considered the signature forms of Atlantic modernism, we might ask, for instance, what—and whose—liberty story is expressed in such projects as "free verse" and "experimental fiction." Or if we aim to construct more progressive literary histories, we might wonder which communities we are hoping to rally around this better liberty. Can the principle of liberty—at once so empty and so full of history's weight—move us forward out of a traumatic Atlantic history?

NOTES

1. See Spengemann's discussion of Satan, pp. 107–108, and, of Eve, 111–12.

2. See Kliger, Brinkley, and Adams for discussion of the ways that the Reformation in England led to the antiquarian interest in Anglo-Saxons. All further reference to these works will be cited parenthetically in the text.

3. See John B. Thompson on how such publications shaped the pivotal role that the media would play in modernity. See Norbrook and Backscheider on literature's development of this public sphere in the later seventeenth century.

4. The manuscript and later print editions of the debates present several problems of correction and interpretation, based as they are on handwritten notes. See Mendle, Part I.

5. Although Silverman does not explore the Germanic parallel, she interprets *Quicksand* as a rewriting, in effect, of "Melanctha" in *Three Lives*—a collection of stories that Larsen read and found fascinating.

6. A number of critics have commented on the name Naxos, including as an anagram for Saxon and as a hint of sexual struggle, but George Hutchinson has provided the fullest reading of the latter through close consideration of the original Ariadne story, which involves both "miscegenation" and the abandonment of a woman. See Hutchinson, 179–80; Hostetler, 38; and Gray, 265.

7. For discussion of color and dress in the novel, see Barnett, 575; du Cille, 94; Gray, 263; Rhodes, 191. None of these notes the contradiction in Helga's desire for color as it is both individualist and racial.

8. Carby and Rhodes offer readings that complement mine here, Carby sug-

gesting that the novel captures "the full complexity of the modern alienated individual . . . embedded within capitalist social relations" (170) and Rhodes reading it as "a critique of the capitalist division of labor that necessitated the invention of racial difference" (184). Esteve develops a different and valuable reading of Larsen's interest in modernity, reflected in Larsen's representations of crowds and anonymity.

9. I suggest that the night club scene may express Larsen's anger toward race itself, an anger at raciality that gets misdirected toward *a* race, toward blackness, evident in the racist-associated language of the scene. Although much of the language is cast as Helga's (including references to "a black giant," a waiter "indefinitely carved out of ebony," and the "savage strains of music" [59]), it is also the case that exactly in the moment when Helga is finally uncritical and most lost to the joy of it all, the narrator steps away from her—as if she, too, must resist being caught up in it. "For a while, Helga was oblivious of the reek of flesh, smoke, and alcohol, oblivious of the oblivion of other gyrating pairs, oblivious of the color, the noise, and the grand distorted childishness of it all" (59). In this moment, the narrator perceives the reeking smells and the "childishness" that Helga is temporarily overlooking, and in turn beckons her readers to join her in this condescension. Most discussions of the scene attribute ambivalence to Helga but not to Larsen: see Esteve, 278; Monda, 27–28; Rhodes, 192; Silverman, 610; Wall, 100. Linda Dittmar, however, notes that Larsen expressed ambivalence about blackness in this scene, wishing both "to affirm and castigate" it (147).

10. For the most relevant discussions of Larsen's novel as a racialized revision of the classic sexual plot, see Barbeito, Kaplan, Sisney. Kaplan, in particular, understands this revision as an engagement with citizenship questions. She implicitly signals the relationship to liberty and gives a parallel interpretation of Helga's conflicts when she mentions that Helga seeks "freedom from identity" as well as recognition of her "complex identities" (165). Nunez likewise reads the novel as concerned with citizenship, as coded in its references to Brazil. I aim to highlight the longer, transatlantic history of these concerns.

11. Clemmen and Gray also study the vacillating movement of the novel. Gray especially emphasizes the European dimension of this movement and suggestively argues that "racial indeterminacy and indeterminacy of geographical 'place' become one question" (259).

12. Critics seem to conflate Helga Crane with Irene Redfield, assuming that she makes the same sublimating trade-off between sex and security that Irene does. She does not, though—from the moment she flees Naxos, she refuses this trade. For readings that assume Helga is grappling with psychological "acceptance of her sexual self" (Carby 169), see Carby, McDowell (141), Monda (23), Rhodes (190), and Silverman (612).

13. For a full reading of this allusion, see Hutchinson (190).

14. For a related reading of style in Larsen's novels (as practicing a "holding back"), see Dittmar (145).

15. Johnson and Haviland also analyze "Sanctuary" as plagiarism, combining psychoanalytic approaches with an analysis of Larsen's relationship to the social and racially inflected category of "authorship." Their account of the historical context of Larsen's story does not extend beyond the general categories of race and gender.

16. Haviland reads this revision psychoanalytically, as expressing Larsen's anger at the effects of her mixed-race parentage, although since she frames this rage as directed primarily at Larsen's white mother for abandonment, her account requires some unpersuasive contortions (304).

17. For the most complete account of Larsen's life, see Davis.

18. For a compelling reading of suicide in Larsen and in others, see Katy Ryan.

19. See my essay on Faulkner's *Light in August* for this reading of windows, 354.

20. George Hutchinson upsets this racialization when, in deconstructing the way criticism reinstalls race, he notes that we could also call Larsen a "Scandinavian modernist" (185).

4   The Geopolitics of Affect in the Poetry of Brazilian Modernism

Fernando J. Rosenberg

It is fairly common to find scholars of Latin American literature whose theoretical approach to their field is based on the idea that literature is *solely* an instrument of oppression. In one of the prevalent paradigms of my field of study, the general attitude of the critic toward the writer is one of resentment. From the idea of a perennial lettered man (the *letrado* introduced in *The Lettered City* [1996] by the Uruguayan critic Angel Rama, as a self-reproducing, self-justifying class), to the discussion around *testimonio* and against literature, to the more recent articulations of subaltern studies, literature, its practitioners and supporters, are many times examined just to be vilified.[1] I am aware of the major, contentious theoretical and political differences that I am trying to map out perhaps too roughly, but the fact remains that, in the search for new modes of social solidarity and emancipation, literature is accounted for as a single, homogeneous field, perpetuating itself as a discourse of authority that paved the way for an exclusionary hegemonic project of nation building and modernization. Latin American turn-of-the-century modernism, the avant-gardes, and the new narrative of the 1960s are placed along the same line; internationalized many times under the general banner of "modernist aesthetics," as the primary, monumental examples of the constitution of the modern literary field—while, at the same time its status is one of a survivor of past eras, is postulated as relevant, its social value *still* asserted, only to be more significantly debunked.[2] Without disavowing the overall reconsideration of the place of literature that the critical current outlined above has promoted (thus not taking refuge in the defense of a perennial aesthetic worth or on its unalienable autonomy), a shift of focus can be attempted that, while preserving the desire for a politically situated reading, is also able to recognize the potential of literary texts to articulate problems beyond the mere preservation of their own institutionalized value.

The poetry of Brazilian modernism (as is the case with many modernisms from the peripheries)[3] opens up issues that actively question its role in the nation's makeup, while simultaneously enacting larger geopolitical inquiries about its situatedness (of the nation, and of the literary) in the modern/colonial world system.[4] The interest of the first poem we are about to read, by Mário de Andrade, lies in part in its exemplarity: it actually stages a drama within which there is a lettered intellectual who is, sure enough, very eager to represent through literature the struggles of an oppressed subject who doesn't speak for himself. The stage is set for the kind of ideological criticism of the lettered elite—the poet, through the co-option of the subaltern's authority, as an accomplice of the oppression and exploitation effected by colonial power, by the state, or by international capital. But I would like to demonstrate how, through an aesthetic of the sublime—one that is geographically specific, and in which the universality of aesthetic judgment is also put to the test—two major poets of Brazilian modernism, Mário de Andrade and Carlos Drummond de Andrade unsettle any aesthetization of political representation, and point to the geopolitical articulation of the nation in capitalist modernity.[5]

Mário de Andrade was a key figure of the *modernista* movement that organized the multiartistic Week of Modern Art of 1922 in the city of São Paulo, the first full-swing outburst of an avant-garde aesthetic in Brazil. Famously, the *modernista* group (through the most outspoken of its participants, Oswald de Andrade) introduced the idea of cultural anthropophagy. Proposed as a tool for an understanding of cultural and economic exchange on a global level, *antropofagia* represented a tongue-in-cheek vindication of alleged (by European accounts) cannibal practices of the native inhabitants of Brazilian territory. Through this imagery, Brazilians proudly incorporated the foreign, civilized and modern, and digested it at their convenience to reinforce their own stock.[6] This idea can be located within a continental movement that, in parallel to and interwoven with the avant-garde, questioned organic notions of culture and identity and forwarded a mixed, constructed, hybrid sense of the cultural makeup of Latin American societies, under the name of *mestizaje, transculturación,* and in the Brazilian case, *antropofagia.*

Mário de Andrade's "Dois Poemas Acreanos" [Two Poems from the Acre], included in his 1927 collection *Clan do Jabotí,* provide a good starting point for my discussion. Bear in mind that the distant Acre is one of the states of the Amazonian basin and one of the centers of Brazilian rubber exploitation, and that the sudden, ghostly apparition of the first poem, who is also the addressee of the second poem, is a rubber tapper, a *seringueiro*—a worker of the *seringa,* a rubber plantation.

Two Poems from the Acre. I. Discovery

Sitting at my desk in São Paulo
in my house of Lopes Chaves street
suddenly I felt a coldness deep inside.

I got shivers, very touched
with the dumb book gazing at me.

Don't you see, I remembered that there, in the North, oh my God! very
far away from me,
in the active darkness of the fallen night,
a pale, thin man whose hair is pouring over his eyes
after making a skin with the rubber of the day;
he went to bed not long ago, now he is sleeping.

That man is as Brazilian as I am . . .

II. Lullaby of the Seringueiro (fragment)

. . .
In order to sing a song
That would make you sleep.
What an enormous difficulty!
I want to sing and I can't,
I want to feel and I don't
The Brazilian word
That would make you sleep . . .
. . .
Seringueiro, seringueiro,
I would like to watch you . . .
To touch you while you sleep,
Tenderly, don't be afraid,
. . .
Some things I do know . . .
Bulky you are not
But short and fragile
So pale, our Lady!
It seems you don't even have blood.
Even though, resilient guy,
You are there
. . .
I don't feel the seringueiros
That I love with unhappy love! . . .
Nor are you able to think
That some other Brazilian
Who is a poet in the South
Is worrying
With the sleeping seringueiro,
Wishing for the one sleeping
The good of happiness . . .
Those things for you
Must be indifferent,
Of an enormous difference . . .
Although I am your friend

And I want to try if I can
Not to pass through your life
In an enormous indifference.
My desire and my thought
    (... in an enormous indifference ...)
Go around the rubber plantations
    (... in an enormous indifference ...)
In an enormous friendly love ... [7]
  ...

The Americas have a tradition of the sublime of their own, we know—that of the grandeur of untamable spaces whose power annihilates the capacity of the mind to chart the territory, to conquer a space for convivial domesticity. This is in fact where the continent, in this tradition that comes from the conquest and is taken up in the process of nation building, purportedly finds its unalienable originality, constituting by the same token the source of its promise and novelty. In other words, the American sublime springs from a tradition that, from Hegel to Euclides da Cunha, envisions a promised land without history that, at the same time, the mind abhors because it threatens its intellectual power.[8] The task of the Latin American poet, famously proposed by Andrés Bello's "Alocución a la poesía" (1823) at the inauguration of the republican period, would be to assess the sublime, inherent in American nature, only to call it back to the house of the symbolic father, the national signifier, or other mark of identity. But the sublime is a foundational moment of the constitution of the Western consciousness, inasmuch as it entails an exploration of the limits of reason and representation. Is not the foundational character and its American inscription at stake in the title of the first poem? Does this "discovery" not point to the continuing redeployment of a foundational myth of the encounter between Western consciousness and what falls beyond representation? Yes and no. It is a fact of Brazilian cultural history that the Amazon region exerted the promise of a continuing, unending discovery, a tradition to which European travelers contributed a great deal.[9] This can be regarded as a spatial case of what Carlos Alonso has shown to be master discourses in the constitution of Latin American modernity; that is, the discourse of futurity and the discourse of novelty, both entangled with the history of coloniality and postcoloniality.[10] However, I want to advance the notion that, while acknowledging this tradition and weaving on its premises, the intellectual operation deployed here radically departs from just imaginarily endowing an uncharted land with the promise of a future. Instead of sublating colonization within the national frame, the poetic series moves away from the preoccupations surrounding the construction of the unified nation and toward a thinking of a broader geopolitical space.

    The sublime is not lodged in the Amazons, ready to be treasured up; it is actually nowhere to be found except in what the poem enacts as a failure of representation, a failure that has to do more with the historical position of this poet in the periphery of the West than with a transcendental, universal subject bewitched by the particularities of the American landscape. Let me make a disciplinary excursus. The alleged final demise of the place of art and literature is attributed to the unfolding of separate and related causes: the dismissal of the notion of the beautiful and the deconstruction of its universal subject and the radical relocation of the role of the nation as a frame for an understanding of cultural production. Fair enough. But as much as I attempt to introduce the question of the sublime, prime in Western aesthetics, let me make clear what I find problematic in taking refuge from the situation outlined above in an updated refashioning of art's alleged universality—one that, as is well known, instantly leaves certain artistic products, those coming from the periphery, in a state of subordination and abjection. A universality that is not one, as Bruce Robbins (62) has ingeniously paraphrased Luce Irigaray. Instead, I propose to use the category of the sublime in order to look at the modern subject of nationhood from outside its claims of universality—a theoretical position that, I claim, is enacted already in the poem.

The sublime always brings about the problem of borders from the perspective of what cannot be contained. Consequently, its use for the cultural production from the peripheries of the West is potentially rich, and the domesticating tradition of the sublime gaze sketched above is by this strategy challenged. Through an aesthetic of the sublime, let me now advance, Mário de Andrade (and others) problematizes the idea of literary and political representation and unsettles the inherited tradition of the national intellectual in Latin America on which he only *appears* to rest so comfortably. Because what is apparent is that, at a certain point of the first poem, his own position turns out to be spectral, when the book he is reading gazes back at him.

Let us return to the text in order to point out three very striking features of the poetic sequence: the disruptive appearance of this distant other in the intimacy of the São Paulo night; the spectral character of the apparition; and the ultimate lack of bonds and feeling that the figure of the poet intends, unsuccessfully, to overcome in the lullaby section. The "discovery" entails a poetic persona that invites us to perform the act of reading by ourselves only to reproduce its interruption. Now, how and when is it that the flow of signifiers traversed in the lyric subject's act of reading comes to a halt? Why, one might ask, does that intrusion appear just to disjoint the act of reading? Is perhaps the *seringueiro* represented or misrepresented in the discourse of that book that is read? What we know is not what is in the book, a blank book that ends up gazing at its reader, but what lies outside—that something is not signified in the archive of the private library of this national intellectual, not represented in the archive of the nation, and thus its appearance can only be abrupt. At one level, the book is a narcissistic justification for the reader poet, for only this self-confirming monad exists at the height of the night; at another level, the book is a representation of what lies *outside* the book, a representation of its representational capabilities. Both of these levels (imaginary and symbolic, we can call them) fail, due to the unannounced apparition of something that it is neither outside the representational chamber nor inside the all-inclusive self-consciousness of the reader poet and his book.

The sublime is, of course, not only present in what the poet claims he feels (the shivering, the commotion—that is, the symptomatic level), but in the fact that something has fallen beyond representation, and the consciousness of the poem strives to find an idea for it. But how can the sublime be without an object, neither mighty nor grand? The *seringueiro* is not something received through the senses to defy the imagination's capability, because the senses of the poet are obliterated, seemingly fully satisfied: the poet is at home, enjoying the solitude of his study, far from the demands of the day. This state is in fact indicative of the poet's availability to pursue intellectual abstraction, free from the body and its constraints. He is awake in the height of the night because he is awake from the state of necessity, as opposed to the *seringueiro*. To put it in romantic lingo, his social position guarantees the autonomy of this subject and opens the free play of his imagination. As the only one whose disinterest disposes him to universal judgment, this subject would be "naturally" selected to occupy the position of representative. All this (which constitutes the kernel of the critique of the Latin American intellectual sketched at the beginning, as elaborated only some decades later) is just a preamble to what is eventful in the poem; it represents its imaginary foundation (the foundation and the self-reflective criticism of it), what is presupposed. Because here comes the unexpectable, because this freedom, which constitutes the basis for the freedom of aesthetic judgment in modernity, is haunted. This is one of the great statements of this poem, which installs the subject of aesthetic judgment in a very comfortable and cozy environment so as to show its limits (and pull out the chair from underneath him). His body is suddenly implicated and his free consciousness arrested in an ecstatic moment—that is, carried outside the self, as has been pointed out in the conceptualization of the sublime from Longinus to Burke to Bataille (although Kant understood this moment as a the crisis of the imagination, calling for reason as an interventionist savior). Why does the poetic subject present itself as being approached by this other, and not the other way round? This question is a fundamental one for a reconceptualization of the relationship of politics and art that is not just contemptuous toward the latter. Why doesn't Mário depict himself as a poet in the heroic quest for the *seringueiro*, addressing him as Pablo Neruda did to all that was subaltern, dead or alive, almost losing his breath in the "Heights of Macchu Picchu"?[11] The answer is perhaps because, unlike Neruda, Mário de Andrade recognizes that he is, in his own chair, too full of himself. This poet is out of his mind, and it is from there that I want to shake loose the usual understanding of the place of poetry in relation to representation and the political realm.

Let us recall the European romantic enterprise of expanding the realm of the sensitive through the empathic incorporation of the wretched of the earth, as a token of cultural roots, an elegy for a situatedness of life experience that is perceived as fading away. This operation—which Neruda can be said to have continued—is archetypically exemplified by what Geoffrey Hartman called the "halted traveler" whose wandering is suddenly interrupted by the unexpected—the sublime encounter—, an archetype that is reversed in Mário de Andrade's poem.[12] For if, according to Hartman, empathy is haunted by the "specter of the failure—of lack of emotional response or inspiration" (15), what is apparent is that the specter, and not the illusion of a recovered presence, is there from the beginning. There are two specters, to be precise, that without empathy are left exploring the contours of that lack. It is a spectrality that distances itself from the Kantian final recuperation and points, I contend, to the irrecoverable quality of this recognition without affection for a notion of national culture and its universal subject.

Now, this other subject haunting São Paulo domestic life, this subject that does not belong there, is neither a cultural nor a racialized one—he is neither indigenous, nor black. In contradistinction to the European case in which, following the romantic tradition, sublime recognition of "the folk" was met with self-aggrandizing incorporation into a homogeneous national body, in Latin America the racial stock was assumed to be mixed (although this mix was mostly understood in the nineteenth century as an unnatural inconvenience to be superseded).[13] But through *antropofagia* and *transculturación*, the racial or cultural internal other was incorporated into mainstream Latin American national cultures in the twentieth century, and some intellectuals were in fact very operational in this construct. They were what Ángel Rama called at the end of the 1970s *los transculturadores*: translators of cultural differences, who weaved the representation of a multifarious whole, and complementarily allowed the foreign and the regional to melt into the national in good measure, selectively composing a renewed patchwork of cultural remnants.[14]

But what to do, then, with the *seringueiro*, that is, not with a racial or cultural other but with a position in the economic structure? It is a very particular position indeed, since rubber was, at the beginning of the twentieth century, one of the main Brazilian exports. The international market of commodities was outside representation in the scheme of the triumphant teleology of the three races (black, indian, white) that *antropofagia* happily reinscribes onto the national body.[15] The international economic order falls outside of the national self-understanding; it is what is not represented in the archive of its anthropophagic, ethnological ideations. There is something in this economic order that cannot be incorporated into an understanding of the national, and that nevertheless constitutes the national space from the outside. And the sublime, let us remember again, is about borders.

Allow me to make a historical excursus. Starting with the name Brazil, which derives from the tint extracted from Brazil Wood, the rainforest and its value in a symbolic economy is at the core of Brazilian definition as a nation. The extraction of latex to fabricate rubber, a primary product required for the auto and other industries, reinstated the promise that the forest always had for the Brazilian imagination, linking the rainforest with the development of industrial production in the centers of capitalism. But concomitantly, the ups and downs of the value of rubber, its spectacular booms and crashes, was a factor of the competition with other peripheral economies (Central American, African, and South East Asian) within a design that was very much subjected to investment capital from England and the United States. Just to give a prominent example: in the 1920s, when Mário was haunted by the *seringueiro,* Ford developed plans to settle a permanent operation, popularly dubbed Fordlândia in the Tapajós River of the Amazonian region. Ford began the construction in 1928, amidst heated debates about, never surprisingly, state corruption, bribes, and too-generous concessions in favor of the foreign investor.[16] At the level of labor, there is a remarkable transregional and transnational history as well, since rubber plantation workers were recruited from other regions of Brazil (particularly the northeast) and there were also plans to import a foreign workforce from Asia. The region of Acre in particular was, in the nineteenth and early twentieth centuries, more transnational than national; historically disputed between Brazil and Bolivia, the area was subject to few attempts by the central government to integrate it with the rest of the country (different, for example, from the parallel coffee economy that was instrumental to the industrial growth of the São Paulo state). But "even at the height of the [global rubber] boom," says Weinstein, "the Amazon occupied a peripheral position in the national economy" (230).

So, going back to the poem: this pale, effaced, spooky subject, the *seringueiro,* is, unsurprisingly, even bloodless. Doesn't he have ancestry? Doesn't he belong? Is it that this national extracting exploit, rubber (*borracha*), sucked his blood, as it sucks the blood of the tree? The very puzzling homonymy (one that my Brazilian dictionary leaves unexplained) between that tree called *seringa* and the other *seringa,* the syringe, is exploited in our poem in bewildering, although not at all explicit, ways. The *seringueiro* extracts from the *seringa* (a process that is called *sangria:* that is, bleeding) and this extraction leaves the worker himself bloodless (the theme of vampirization being further emphasized by the nocturnal staging of the scene). Is the worker black, indian, or white? Probably a very Brazilian mix of the three stems, but one that for the armchair poet of the beginning is not inscribed as Brazilian at all, and hence his surprise and the secondary moment of recognition—a recognition that nevertheless renders both parties indifferent (iteratively "in an enormous indifference"), thus failing to fulfill its promises. If for Burke the sublime is tied to an experience of physical terror that threatens us with extinction, that puts us on the verge of disappearance, terror is here the sudden presence, in the body, of something that threatens the national order of things.

The effaced *seringueiro* might be an unrepresentable race, an enigma in the body of the nation, outside of the colorful array that was the task of the *modernista* movement to inscribe into the Brazilian imagination (from Tarsila do Amaral's surreal painting of black women to Heitor Villa Lobos's mix of Indian and European classical tunes, the examples of racial mixes promoted by the *modernistas* abound), but that cannot possibly include this colorless subject's position, which is more a factor of transnational (economic) variables than of national (cultural) synthesis. *Modernismo* has been accused of perpetuating the myth of racial democracy in Brazil, in face of striking social inequalities among races.[17] Race is not a factor in this poem, I contend, not because of any carnivalesque multiracial construction, but because what it is trying to make relevant are the social and economic conditions of the production of racial inequalities. David Lloyd has brilliantly argued that the universal subject of aesthetic judgment is the precondition for the construction of the racial discourse, inasmuch as it is through the alleged neutrality and abstraction from particularity (of the senses, of taste, of his own culture, etc.) that the rest of the world can be first mapped out in different degrees of subalternity and heteronomy, and secondly, represented.[18] The national signifier—in this case, Brazilian—provides a momentary point of suture at different stages of the poem, allowing the national intellectual, through his identification with universality, to assimilate the other. But then the poetic discourse opens again, and what it makes clear is that there is no pedagogic recognition. In fact, the *seringueiro* in his nonracial being, in his effacement, seems to echo the broken universality of this intellectual, his failure to stand as the representative, that is, in the place of the universal.

That the recognition fails again and again, that it falls short of sublating the elements into a greater whole, that the operation of the poet as an awakened consciousness actually leaves a residue, to all of these the poem bears witness ("I want to sing and I can't, / I want to feel and I don't"). How can the failure to represent be made present? One of the ways is the iteration of the parenthetical remark that is outside of the discursive flow, that keeps coming back in the lullaby section: "(. . . in an enormous indifference . . .)." First, the vastness of the separation between the poet and his addressee, which surely alludes to the enormity of the Brazilian territory (usually a source of excitement and pride among the *modernistas*), is not recovered in a unifying sense of identity. In fact, it is to this irrecuperability that the poet is pointing when the enormity is a propos of indifference. In the representation of territory, in mapping this continuity, something is discontinuous, out-of-joint and without affect. The reader of the Brazilian landscape, the hermeneutic mind of the armchair poet, is beyond all capacity to interpret, represent, and feel a self-contained continuity.

Indifference is an interesting word indeed; it points to the desire of filling what seems to be an insurmountable gap by abolishing differentiation altogether and producing a fusion between subject and object. But, needless to say, we are talking about the affective (dis)charge of indifference, thus about what inextricably separates subject and object beyond any possible empathetic recognition that would do away with distance. A desire that recognizes its impossibility, and that Mário de Andrade sustains only by renouncing his privileged position in the representational economy—from which he departs, being the only one awake, being the one who produces the discovery. Leaving vacant the position of master of representation, what we find at the end of the poem is friendship as a floating affective charge that cannot be claimed for any symbolic wholeness: "Although I am your friend / And I want to try if I can / Not to pass through your life / In an enormous indifference. / My desire and my thought / (. . . in an enormous indifference . . .) / Go around the rubber plantations / (. . . in an enormous indifference . . .) / In an enormous friendly love . . ."

Indifference keeps coming back, indigestible by the main flow of the discourse. How does it feel, indifference? How can that be an affect, if it is the negation of affect? It does not really feel like anything, but it does exist, bracketed, outside of the array of possible feelings and as a negation of them. Is it related to a Stoic *apathy*, to an aristocratic ethics of withdrawal and noninvolvement? Is it something like modernist nihilism? Of course, the figure of the poet as presented in the first poem is very much aligned with the preservation of aesthetic distance upon which modern irony is based. *Antropofagia*, the intellectual operation set to explain Brazilian nationality as a unity in diversity that Mário's peers were articulating at this time, takes ironic distance for granted: it is through an adequate distance from any primary attachment that the incorporation of the foreign into the national body, which *antropofagia* proposed, can be achieved. But the indifference here is essentially not ironic, since it is not predicated upon the preservation of good distance. It is more a way to do without the self-involvement of subjective feelings and to mobilize the affective beyond the entrapment of subjectivity and empathic consciousness—that would only position the poet in a patronizing role toward the worker. Notice that indifference is attributed to both the poet and the *seringueiro*; it doesn't belong to anyone, it is not a proper feeling and doesn't dwell in the interior. "My desire and my thought / (. . . in an enormous indifference . . .) / Go around the rubber plantations / (. . . in an enormous indifference . . .) / In an enormous friendly love." This feeling of indifference is not felt by any-one, it is the background of every feeling, as a primary separation that friendship tries to overcome—an equalitarian friendship that moves away from the politics of empathy and incorporation. Beyond the capacity of the subject to represent it, indifference signals the structure of this recognition (recognition of the singularity of the other, recognition of the primary separation and of the desire of attachment unattended to by the nation, its intellectual and his mandate). Let me recall that Kant conceptualizes the sublime as an affect of the mind and notices that the absence of affection pertains to the sublime inasmuch as the mind follows principles that are unrepresentable—since the sublime is about a failure of the imagination to represent. But unlike the movement of reason overcoming the failure of the imagination in order to achieve mastery, what indifference articulates are two contradictory ideas. If indifference can be an affective consequence of the nation-state itself, inasmuch as it operates as an imaginary guaran-tor of every particularity as *already* inscribed within its realm, on the other hand indifference is what comes before the distribution of roles operated by the nation-state, before the assignment of identity markers, a primal state of nonseparation that points to the untamable desire for community ("I don't feel the seringueiros / That I love with unhappy love!").

The presence of an international, globalized market is everywhere in a poem that is seemingly framed by national borders. The nation's very in-scription as such in the seriality of nations depends on something, the rub-ber worker, that for its own map of cultural understanding is indifferent, beyond representation—so the poem seems to suggest. The Kantian ver-sion of the sublime always implies the possibility of abstraction, since it entails standing apart from primary attachments in order for the object of sublimity to be treasured up, gained for a cause. But the *seringueiro* is the opposite of the subject of belonging (to soil, to blood) and therefore offers no material for incorporation. In this way (and going back to the polemic with which we started), the poem goes from a dialectic of universality and particularity (where the intellectual stands as the one who is able to ab-stract and speak for the whole, where the poet represents, translates, and synthesizes for the achievement of a national signifier), to a problematic of positionality (that is, to a question of the particular conditions of possi-bility from which a peripheral intellectual can speak, the object, and the limits of his speech).

But the *modernista* and other Latin American vanguard movements from the 1920s and 1930s are not immediately linked to apathy and lack of af-fection, but to intellectual engagement, often carrying a charge of exultant optimism and enthusiasm. A conference given by Mário de Andrade in 1942 (a puzzling exercise in retrospection called "The Modernist Move-ment") will provide a chance for further interrogating this (global) posi-tionality and its associated affects. As a mature writer and cultural critic,

Mário is able to locate the causes for a *modernismo* that came to be recognized as the ur-Brazilian movement in a broader scenario of global historical shifts: "the transformation of the world with the gradual weakening of the major empires, as well as the European practice of new political ideals, the speed of new means of transportation and thousands of other international causes, and the development of American and Brazilian consciousness" (231).[19] Despite the adequate timing of the movement that he among others led, his retrospective gaze is full of feelings of estrangement toward his young intellectual persona; a sense of pride mixed with guilt and regret taints his discussion with very ambivalent tones. Pride for having participated in an intellectual movement that was necessary to shake a stagnant cultural atmosphere; regret and guilt, because this "intellectual orgy" (as he puts it) impelled his generation to "dance at the top of the volcano. . . . Full of doctrines, drunken with theories, saving Brazil and inventing the world, in truth we consumed everything including ourselves, in the bitter cultivation of delirious pleasure" (241). Let us hear Mário again when he affirms that the modernists consumed themselves—a claim no doubt related to that theory of cultural consumption called *antropofagia*, which points to *antropofagia*'s limits. The international moment outlined by Mário gives to some Latin Americans a sense of a historical mission. As it is well known, new Americanist philosophies of history surged with emphatic optimism in the interwar years, in what seemed once more the promising dusk of Western European culture and the announcement of the new.[20] But why does Mário struggle to recognize his young self? Because also from this different perspective he is again outside of himself, exceeded by the sublime enjoyment of his own epochal enthusiasm. Following Kant, although "comparable to madness," enthusiasm can be thought of as the subjective sign of history progressing toward the Idea, whose inscrutable character "cuts it off from any positive presentation" (144). Enthusiasm is only recognizable inside the self but beyond its limits, because there is no positive representation to account for this affective charge. This is the excess, the intoxication where Mário loses himself beyond self-recognition, which strikes him twenty years later as lack of authenticity. In 1942, it is perhaps more obvious that, once again, the Ideal will not deliver its promise: that the volcano erupted in Brazil and elsewhere, and that the Idea imposed upon history is bound to bring about social terror.[21] From a Kantian, teleological optimistic moment of the 1920s, to the very Adorno–Horkheimerean moment of the 1940s, Mário's career is marked by suspicion of his own modernist alliances.

The atmosphere of optimism seems at odds with the image of the poet depicted by the 1927 text. Enthusiasm (through the cultural construct of *antropofagia*) hints at participation in a new syntax of cultural exchange between ex-colonies and the West in which history is advanced through an intelligent consumption made by the former, thus effecting an inversion of previous geopolitical hierarchies. The poem is a symptom of this promising mapping; that is, it reveals what does not work. It shows a remnant of the symbolic exchange economy, an indigestible element that, although very much a factor of the global market, persists inside the body of the nation. Haunting São Paulo nights, the ghost of this *seringueiro* of invisible face appears to come from outside the border, from a remote backland that is too close but fails to be incorporated, that doesn't take part, and thus constitutes the daunting "discovery" of the nationally minded lyric subject.

National indifference seems to be in Mário de Andrade the displaced presence of a broader, cosmopolitan affect; that is, an affective charge built in relation to national longing but echoing an enigma that can't be solved from inside the national form. We can now redirect the question about cosmopolitan affects to Carlos Drummond de Andrade's (without question one of the greatest poets of the twentieth century) collection of poetry written between 1935 and 1940, appropriately called *Feeling of the World* [Sentimento do mundo].[22] Without leaving aside the interrogation of what constitutes Brazil, what can be seen in many poems by Carlos Drummond is an initial concern with a larger geographical picture combined with a guilty awareness of the limitation of their grasp, due to the lack of a grand narrative that renders them incapable from the start to represent their own burden:

> I just have two hands
> and the feeling of the world,
> but I am full of slaves,
> my memories are flowing
> and the body yields
> in the confluence of love

So go the opening lines of the book.[23] As is well known, the Spanish Civil War (1934–36) and the fight against fascism were sources of new articulations between the literary establishment and international politics, a net of solidarity that was the ideological breeding ground for many writers of "international" modernism.[24] The feeling of the world (and the opening poem that bears that title was first published in 1935) has been attributed to that particular transnational movement, but as the quotation illustrates, it sways deeper into (colonial) history and geography. The poem continues with "I feel dispersed / prior to frontiers / humbly I ask you / to forgive me,"[25] as if the moment prior to nation building could provide a standpoint from which the project of modernity should be redirected toward a cosmopolitan feeling of reparation and justice.[26]

The poem "Big World" bypasses once again the national concern. The market, an actual existing universality that effectively unifies the world, is confronted with the very absence of the fictive universality that is the legacy of modernity—universal rights, universal justice.[27]

> You know how big is the world.
> You are acquainted with the ships that carry oil and books, meat and cotton.
> You have seen the different colors of men,
> the different pains of men,
> you know how difficult it is to suffer all of that, to accumulate all that
> in a single man's chest . . . without exploding it.[28]

We will have to come back to this final sudden disruption. For now, let us concentrate on what remains as the position of this intellectual in a world where books are clearly part of the realm of deterritorialized commodities. We are a world apart from the closed chamber of the personal library from which Mário departed. In the logic of total, worldwide commodification, things can be clearly represented ("You know how . . . / You are acquainted with"); even difference and race, although not yet redeemed by social justice, are part of this world of complete representation ("You have seen the different colors of men,") and in a way they might be imaginarily redeemed by their simple recognition. Race can be represented and commodified as are meat, oil, and cotton (and coffee and rubber) as mere signs of, perhaps, the variety of the world. But emotions and representations seem to go different ways here, and only the former, accumulating chaotically inside the body, stand for the allegory of what in the world escapes representation, and thus threatens to produce this sublime, deadly excess. What makes this blast that annihilates individuality different from the typical self-immolation of the romantic-modernist writer entrapped in a monadic sovereign subjectivity is the cosmopolitan affect for the world, the affective mapping announced in the title, related in a way to Mário's proposed friendship, and with which Carlos Drummond tries to dissolve total commodification.

Now, the *sentimento do mundo*, the feeling of the world: does it refer to a feeling coming from the world, or a feeling toward the world? Perhaps to both, but it is not the same, mirrored feeling. If there is an affect present in that world, an affect that strikes the poetic voice all throughout the book, that affect is indifference—again, the lack of affect. Let me also add that indifference is an enigmatic affective remnant of every genocide of the twentieth century: just hear the survivors try to cope with the fact that, in a world of increasing information availability where everything can be readily represented, nobody responded on time. That is why Mário de Andrade, very different from just representing the subaltern, wanted to transcend the enormous, numbing indifference he found first in himself, then everywhere else, by creating an affective bond beyond the mirage of (national) representation. Drummond, for his part, plays out indifference as the sheer stuff that molds the relationship between the modern world and subjectivity: "You work without joy for a dying world / where the shapes and the actions don't present any example" ("Elegy 1938").[29] This achieved universality is the inverted mirror image of any cosmopolitan ideal: instead of an effort to transcend local attachment through a desire for multiple, interconnected alliances, world and subject are only related through indifference and detachment, the triumph of total rationality and instrumentality, the colonization of every space inside and outside. But pay attention to how Drummond finishes his "Elegy": "And you accept rain, war, unemployment, unfair distribution / because you can't, by yourself, dynamite the island of Manhattan." How would you digest, hypocrite and detached reader, *mon semblable, mon frère,* these uncannily shocking final lines? Can we find a reason for this outburst of rage coming from a subject so (un)moved by dispassion? The fact is, what this subject without joy and affection is giving witness to (beyond his leftist politics of suspicion toward the world market, which can be located, historicized, and consequently dismissed as somewhat passé) is that in a world of free-floating representation, nothing is perceived any longer unless it is the most shocking, extreme, unrepresentable event. What is important for us to notice, if we care to read the poem today, is that the impossible of past eras ("you can't, by yourself, dynamite the island of Manhattan," as the lyric subject gauges his personal limit) became possible, perfectly imaginable. That is, in fact, what a modernity of possessive individualism has dreamed about all along, the kernel of its promise in total individual agency: that everything for the individual might be possible; and that we can tame, only through individual autonomy, the unspeakable horror that is thus rendered indifferent. It is not, in Drummond's "Elegy," an aesthetic of the sublime but an announcement of the ghosts, the archaic anxiety raised by the anesthetic dream in a world of achieved, total representation. In the floating affective charge of friendship and world-feeling, in Mário and Drummond respectively, poetry bypasses representation and reconnects with the exclusions and the horrors that different representational regimes (that of the nation, that of global capital) pledged to have overcome, but have only made invisible.

NOTES

1. Ángel Rama's book *La ciudad letrada* (1984) has been translated as *The Lettered City* (Durham, N.C., and London: Duke University Press, 1996). The originally South Asian project of subaltern studies has been a gravitational field of discussion for mostly U.S.-based Latin Americanist scholars since the nineties. The foundational statement of the Latin American subaltern studies group can be found in *The Postmodernism Debate in Latin America,* ed. John Beverley, José Oviedo,

and Michael Aronna (Durham, N.C., and London: Duke University Press, 1995). Alberto Moreiras's *The Exhaustion of Difference: The Politics of Latin American Cultural Studies* (Durham, N.C., and London: Duke University Press, 2001) provides a solid theoretical ground for a reconsideration of subalternism from the perspective of a new order of Latin American studies. I am using the expression *against literature* in reference to the controversial book by John Beverley (*Against Literature*. Minneapolis and London: University of Minnesota Press, 1993), that cogently argued for a rearticulation of the intellectual field in relation to new conceptions of political emancipation. *Literature* stands for an elite practice that weaves together the hegemonic ideology of the national creole.

2. It is always necessary, in the context of comparative modernisms, to make the following clarification. *Modernismo* in Hispanic American contexts names an artistic tendency introduced by Rubén Darío as early as 1888, and entails an art-for-art's-sake poetic school informed by Romanticism, Parnassianism, and Symbolism. A Latin Americanist spirit of search for cultural identity (clearly related to the post-1898 "Pan-Americanist" U.S. rise as a world power) was also a by-product of this cultural current that the apparition of the avant-gardes in the early 1920s finally canceled. The movement spread across the Atlantic to become cross-continental Hispanic. The same word, *modernismo*, but now in Portuguese, refers to the Brazilian movement that sprang out of the *Semana da Arte Moderna* of February 1922, in the major city of São Paulo, and it is more akin to an avant-garde aesthetics. Parallel to the Brazilian movement, a number of avant-garde schools (mostly in literature and in plastic arts) came out in many of the Latin American countries, in connection but also differentiated from the Europeans, and with sometimes striking similarities. Vicky Unruh (*Latin American Vanguards: The Art of Contentious Encounters* [Berkeley: University of California Press, 1994]) provides an excellent introduction to many problems and debates concerning the avant-gardes in Latin America, including the Brazilian case. A transatlantic history of the avant-gardes remains to be written. The new narrative that emerged in Latin America in the 1960s and 1970s and that came to be dubbed the boom (*narrativa del boom*), and to which many of the most translated Latin American authors are ascribed (Mário Vargas Llosa, Gabriel García Marquez, Julio Cortazar, Carlos Fuentes, etc), represented the first major inception of literature from the subcontinent into the First World reading market. They are, no doubt, heirs of a high modernist aesthetic, as is much of the Latin American tradition of intellectual agency.

3. According to George Yúdice, the avant-garde in Latin America "is the first global expression, in the field of culture, of the struggles to 'integrate,' that is, to dominate the world on the part of several competing imperial and industrialized powers and, also, to resist these attempts locally" (54).

4. I take the compound expression modern/colonial world from Walter Mignolo, who among others contends that coloniality is a condition (necessarily negated) in the construction of modernity.

5. The three Andrades that I will mention in my essay—Mário de Andrade, Carlos Drummond de Andrade, and Oswald de Andrade—were not related by blood.

6. There are many analytical accounts of the Brazilian avant-garde movements. For a useful survey, see Wilson Martins (*The Modernist Idea: A Critical Survey of Brazilian Writing in the Twentieth Century* [New York: NYU Press, 1970]). Roberto Schwarz (*Misplaced Ideas: Essays on Brazilian Culture* [London: Verso, 1992]) highlights the paradoxes entailed by one of the characteristic *modernista* strategies for cultural definition: the festive juxtaposition of modern and archaic, foreign and native. Neil Larsen (*Modernism and Hegemony: A Materialist Critique of Aesthetic Agencies* [Minneapolis: University of Minnesota Press, 1990]) performs a thought-

ful Marxist critique of the Brazilian movement, particularly of the idea of *antropofagia*, in the context of the construction of hegemony in Latin American countries.

7. All translations from the Portuguese are mine. I extract these texts from the author's *Poesias completas*. Below is the original Portuguese version: "Dois Poemas Acreanos." I. "Descobrimento." "Abancado à escrivaninha em São Paulo / Na minha casa da rua Lopes Chaves / De sopetão senti um friúme por dentro. / Fiquei trêmulo, muito comovido / Com o livro palerma olhando pra mim. // Não vê que me lembrei lá no norte, meu Deus! muito longe de mim, / Na escuridão ativa da noite que caiu, / Um homem pálido, magro de cabelo escorrendo nos olhos / Depois de fazer uma pele com a borracha do dia, / Faz pouco se deitou, está dormindo. // Esse homem é brasileiro que nem eu . . ." (203)

II. "Acalanto do Seringueiro" (fragment) ". . . / Pra cantar uma cantiga / Que faça você dormir. / Que dificuldade enorme! / Quero cantar e não posso, / Quero sentir e não sinto / A palavra brasileira / Que faça você dormir . . . // . . . / Seringueiro, seringueiro, / Queria enxergar você . . . / Apalpar você dormindo, / Mansamente, não se assuste, // . . . / Algumas coisas eu sei . . . / Troncudo você não é. / Baixinho, desmerecido, / Pálido, Nossa Senhora! / Parece que nem tem sangue. / Porém cabra resistente / Está ali . . . // . . . Eu não sinto os seringueiros . . ." (203–206)

8. I am referring to Hegel's pronouncement about the New World in *The Philosophy of History* (1830–31). In mapping the evolution of the Spirit, America stands outside its trajectory, in a permanent state of immaturity—it is, in fact, in the geographic considerations that are logically prior to history itself that Hegel locates America ("Geographical Bases of History" 79). Da Cunha, a military man and journalist, wrote *Os sertoes* (published in 1900 and translated into English as *Rebellion in the Backlands* in 1944 for a University of Chicago edition, later re-edited) —a puzzled, tragic account of the failure of national modernity to come to terms with and integrate the northeastern Brazilian landscape (the desert *sertão*) and social practices into its projected wholeness. I mention this text here because of its prominent role among Brazilian foundational texts and its participation in what I refer to as the tradition of American sublime.

9. See *A pátria geográfica. Sertão e litoral no pensamento social brasileiro*, by Candice Vidal e Souza (Goiânia: Universidade Federal de Goiás, 1997).

10. See particularly Chapter 1.

11. In the most famous section of the massive *Canto general* (a poetic account of the history and geography of Latin America), the poet depicts himself as a perennial wanderer who has finally achieved personal realization through an act of poetic recognition and redemption of what is Latin American, performed as a meditation in the ruins of the Inca city of Machu Picchu. The poet stages the set for an exercise of the sacerdotal role of mediator between the dead (by Inca, colonial, national, and transnational rule) and a continental political redemption. For a solid analysis of Neruda, including of course his *Canto*, see Enrico Mário Santí's *Pablo Neruda: The Poetics of Prophecy* (Ithaca, N.Y.: Cornell University Press, 1982).

12. Geoffrey Hartman coined that expression in reference to Wordsworth, particularly as his poem "The Solitary Reaper." See Hartman's *Wordsworth's Poetry 1787–1814* (New Haven, Conn.: Yale University Press, 1964).

13. For an enlightening rendition of the problem of race in Europe in relation to the nation and the colonial enterprises, see Laura Doyle ("The Racial Sublime," in Alan Richardson and Sonia Hofkosh, *Romanticism, Race, and Imperial Culture, 1780–1834* [Bloomington and Indianapolis: Indiana University Press, 1996]). The volume *The Idea of Race in Latin America*, ed. Richard Graham (Austin: University of Texas Press, 1990), provides a good introduction to the subject title.

14. In *Transculturación narrativa en América Latina* (Mexico: Siglo XXI, 1982).

See "Transculturación y Género Narrativo," p. 32. The idea of *transculturación* was originally coined by Cuban anthropologist Fernando Ortiz, who in 1940 elaborated the category in opposition to the only negative view on cultural encounter as acculturation. See his *Cuban Counterpoint of Tobacco and Sugar* (Durham, N.C.: Duke University Press, 1995) backed up by the authority of the original Malinowski prologue.

15. I purposely do not capitalize the word *indian*, although this goes against the common usage. I do this for a matter of consistency with the other two "races," and because the capitalization would single out the natives as a unified people under a common ethnic identity. The scheme of the three races was in fact Brazil's foundational racial myth at least since the German philosopher Carl F. P. von Martius won, in 1843, the Brazilian Historic and Geographic Institute prize for his seminal essay "Como se deve escrever a historia do Brasil" [How to Write Brazilian History]. *Antropofagia* both surpasses and preserves the blatantly hierarchical racial division set up by the German historiographer, allowing the three-race model to survive within a more modern, flexible model of transformation and exchange. For a general account of the history of race in Brazil, from abolition until World War II, see Thomas E. Skidmore's *Black Into White: Race and Nationality in Brazilian Thought* (New York: Oxford University Press, 1974).

16. The information about the exploitation of *borracha* is extracted from Warren Dean's *A luta pela borracha no Brasil* (São Paulo: Nobel, 1989), 112–13.

17. See, for example, Zita Nunes, "Race and Ruins," in *Culture/Contexture: Exploration on Anthropology and Literary Studies*, ed. Jeffrey M. Peck and E. Valentine Daniel (Berkeley: University of California Press, 1996), 235–48.

18. See also Laura Doyle for a more historically explicit elaboration of Kantian universals vis-à-vis the colonial expansion.

19. In *Obra escogida* (Caracas: Ayacucho, 1979).

20. Oswald Spengler's *The Decline of the West* and its prophecy of the ascendance of an American spirit was read, reverenced, followed, and mocked among Latin American intellectuals of the interwar period. Waldo Frank was among the socialist-minded First World intellectuals of the time who saw, through the twilight of the West, the rise of Latin America as a novel force in the world. Virtually all the Latin American avant-garde movements pronounced themselves in manifestos and literary journals on the issue of Latin Americanism. For an overall assessment of this last body of texts, see Vicky Unruh, Chapter 3. Roberto González Echevarría's *Alejo Carpentier: The Pilgrim at Home* (Ithaca, N.Y.: Cornell University Press, 1979) provides an excellent analytical account of this interwar cultural climate.

21. Brazil, as other Latin American economies, was of course deeply affected by the ebbs and flows of the global markets. A major turning point is the collapse of the stock market in 1929 that prompted a debacle in the coffee trade on which base Brazilian "development" depended, and that would mark the 1930s as a decade of socially engaged, revolutionary, and internationally concerned Latin American artistic production. "The worldwide crisis that erupted in 1929 had a rapid and devastating impact on Latin America. The clearest indication of it was the collapse, in most countries, of existing political arrangements" (Halperín Donghi 208). For Brazil, this era marked the beginning of the authoritarian military rule of Getulio Vargas in 1930 that in many ways forwarded an economic modernization of Brazilian still under aristocratic domination, while forcefully suppressing any hint of profound social change. See Chapter 6 of Túlio Halperín Donghi's *The Contemporary History of Latin America* for a comprehensive account of the period.

22. Carlos Drummond de Andrade was close to the *modernista* group, but did

not participate in their group activities. He published poems in the *Revista de antropofagia,* the magazine that the *modernistas* edited. He and Mário de Andrade corresponded for many years.

23. Although all of these translations are mine, Drummond's poetry has been widely translated into English, most remarkably by the poets Elizabeth Bishop and Mark Strand. I quote from *Poesia completa e prosa* (1973): "Tenho apenas duas mãos / e o sentimento do mundo, / mas estou cheio de escravos, / minhas lembranças escorrem / e o corpo transige / na confluência do amor" (101).

24. Among the Latin American poets that pronounced themselves and wrote engaged poetry in favor of the Spanish Republic and against fascism were perhaps the most recognized poets of the avant-garde: Pablo Neruda, Vicente Huidobro, and Cesar Vallejo (the latter, although reluctant toward vanguard artistic movements, both belongs to this epochal climate and goes well beyond it).

25. "Sinto me disperso, / anterior a fronteiras, / humildemente vos peço / que me perdoeis" (101).

26. I use the expression "cosmopolitan feeling" with an awareness of the theoretical problematic surrounding it. Feelings have been traditionally attributed to (national) belonging, and a charge of detachment and coldness was the character of cosmopolitan ideals, more akin to Kantian rational universality than to the realm of affect. In his discussion of Benedict Anderson and Richard Rorty, Bruce Robbins has debunked this construct. For an excellent compilation of current debates surrounding cosmopolitanism, see Amanda Anderson's article "Cosmopolitanism, Universalism, and the Divided Legacies of Modernity," in Pheng Cheah and Bruce Robbins, eds., *Cosmopolitics: Thinking and Feeling beyond the Nation* (Minneapolis and London: University of Minnesota Press, 1998).

27. I am drawing here on Étienne Balibar's article "Ambiguous Universality." Balibar differentiates between real universality, fictive universality (defined above), and ideal universality—this latter being more related to insurrection again homogeneous normalcy as the effect of the Enlightenment's heritage of fictive universality.

28. "Mundo Grande" (fragment): "Tu sabes como é grande o mundo. / Conheces os navios que levam petróleo, livros, carne e algodão. / Viste as diferentes cores dos homens, / as diferentes dores dos homens, / sabes como é dificil tudo isso, amontoar tudo isso / num só peito . . . sem que ele estale" (116)

29. "Elegia 1938" (fragment): "Trabalhas sem alegría para um mundo caduco, / onde as formas e as açoes não encerram nenhum exemplo. / . . . / Coração orgulhoso, tens pressa de confessar tua derrota / e adiar para outro século a felicidade coletiva. / Aceitas a chuva, a guerra, o desemprego e a injusta distribuçao / porque não podes, sozinho, dinamitar a ilha de Manhattan" (115)

5   Ongoing War and Arab Humanism

Ken Seigneurie

> The war is over even if the peace hasn't started yet!
> —Rashid al-Daif, *Techniques of Misery*

The notion that wars begin and end on specific dates is thoroughly quaint by now, but the corollary, that war is an enduring, nomadic feature of late modernity, has entered public discourse only recently. This is strange because the developed world has been engaged in ongoing military operations since at least World War II (Arnold xi–xviii). The longer these ostensibly separate operations become and the more they are recognized as interconnected within a global network, the more they look like a structural feature of the modern world.[1] Yet the dawning consciousness of ongoing war is not uniform or homogeneous the world over. Entire peoples have lived through it as a palpable reality for decades while others have been insulated by distance and a pharmacopoeia of cultural mediators. It exists in low-level states such as military occupations, cold wars, and embargoes, and it develops, splits, and grafts onto other institutions, discourses, and conflicts. When, for example, open war swept over Lebanon in 1975, secular-ideological issues featured strongly, but the conflict very soon morphed into a retrograde ethnic-sectarian struggle of the kind that has since washed over much of the planet.[2] This rapid transformation dissolved numerous ideological illusions about the Promethean human and triggered a pointed cultural response as a handful of young writers began to reconceive the Arabic novel.

The history of the Levantine novel in Arabic cannot be separated from the political history of the region. In a companion to this essay, I explore how since its beginnings in the early part of the twentieth century, this novel vectored the ideals of the Enlightenment to the Arab world ("A Survival Aesthetic"). Whether championing the imagination in its romantic mode, or standing up to entrenched feudal authority in its realist mode, or positioning itself against Zionism in its committed avatar, the Arabic novel consistently stood for progress, the rule of reason, political liberation, and individual conscience.[3] By the late 1970s, however, these ideals faded as the absurdity of the Lebanese war mocked any pretension to understanding reality. Progressive forces in the war had been defeated (Petran 13–18) and, as Rashid al-Daif shows in his novel *Dear Mr Kawabata,* realist commitment had proven no more immune to false consciousness than any other aesthetic doctrine. At the same time, poststructuralist thought also undermined commitment by decentering the subject and exposing reality as to some extent a language construct. As if to drive the point home, by the early 1980s the war itself resembled a poststructuralist nightmare. Car bombings, sniper attacks, kidnappings, and shellings of civilians fluttered over the country like Derridean postcards, but what they signified, who sent them, and for whom was seldom obvious. In the midst of this infernal textuality, writers looked a pitiful lot with their pens, papers, and discredited aesthetic doctrines, whence perhaps the common notion in Lebanon that writers are separate from "real life." In response, some stuck heroically by ideological commitment (*iltizām*), and others produced a literature of alienation (*ightirāb*) (Harlow 164), but both assumed that it was possible to assume a position of truth and authenticity outside moral corruption. Yet others, however, sought a way to speak of human dignity while recognizing that the corruption of war, like the text, dwelled within as well as without.

Today, Hoda Barakat, Rashid al-Daif, and Hassan Daoud are among the most well known Lebanese novelists. During the war and in the postwar period their novels brought critical esteem, but a trip through Beirut bookshops today reveals that some of their best war novels are no longer available in Arabic. Booksellers express the common feeling that the war is passé and that its literature has nothing to say to the present generation. This essay will try to demonstrate that the survival aesthetic for ongoing war that these writers formulated remains timely today, and perhaps not only in the Arab world.

For Western readers, however, this aesthetic may initially appear to have fallen to Earth from an alien yet still carbon-based planet. The words are the same: *modernity, modernism,* and *race,* but their configurations are different. As an early-twentieth-century cultural import, the novel has always been associated with a "foreign" modernity, whether in its realist, romantic, existentialist, modernist, or postmodern modes. As a result, this novel has tended to explore the social effects of modernity more than its epistemic foundations, which means in turn that modernist techniques function differently as well as they become indigenized in the Arabic novel. Moreover, the presumed foreignness of modernity inflects "race" as well, a concept that compared to its role in the West, is both more and less central to Arab modernity: more in that the effects of modernity cannot be separated from their origins in the Western "races"; less in that race is not otherwise commonly enshrined as an important constituent of identity in the Arab world.

So let us reconsider Barakat's *Hajar al-Dahik* (translated as *The Stone of Laughter*), Daoud's *Binayat Mathilde* (translated as *The House of Mathilde*), and three short novels by al-Daif: *Fusha Mustahdafa Bayna al-Nuʿas wa-al-Nawm* (translated as *Passage to Dusk*), *Taqniyyat al-Buʾs* (untranslated, "Techniques of Misery"), and *Nahiyat al-Baraʾa* (translated as *This Side of Innocence*).[4] All but one of these novels were published during the last seven years of open war, between 1983 and 1990. The fifth, al-Daif's *This Side of Innocence,* was published in 1997 and testifies to the continuities between the war and postwar periods.

* * *

The particularity of these novels rests on how four categories of narrative techniques often associated with postmodern literary practice are re-inscribed into a modernist aesthetic in order to respond to the exigencies of ongoing war.[5] The first is indeterminacy of narrative voice and focalization. The plot of Daoud's *House of Mathilde* follows a Beirut apartment building's decades-long slide into ruin. Nothing could be clearer than the relentless decay of this microcosm of the nation, yet the identity of the novel's narrator is never clear. He is both a boy participant in the diegesis and an adult observer at a temporal remove, which increases perceptual range over spaces and time (Aghacy, "To See" 205). The first-person subjectivity of the boy and the third-person objectivity of the adult provide a synoptic but actually impossible view of the building. The reader intuits the mutually contradictory points of view without sensing that they mar the novel any more than violating the dramatic unities mars a play. Yet despite this narrative sleight of hand and the complete absence of dialogue in the novel, which further concentrates the reader's line of vision through that of the narrator, character motivation and causality remain opaque. The misanthropic Mathilde surprisingly, but not implausibly, invites a strange man to board in her home and the polite and gentle man, even more surprisingly, murders her and dismembers the body. It is as if Daoud uses indeterminacy to achieve greater narrative control and a coherent vision of the war, but in the end has to confess befuddlement before its madness.

Hoda Barakat's *Stone of Laughter* recounts another catabasis into the disorder of war as a gentle, androgynous young man slowly transmogrifies into a militia thug. Narrative voice and focalization are even more indeterminate than in Daoud. One page begins in the third-person heterodiegetic mode and passes seamlessly into the first person as the narrator suddenly mentions how "we" spend evenings during the war. The narrator then melds her point of view with that of the protagonist, Khalil, in free indirect discourse before addressing him directly in the second person. And finally—still on the same page—Khalil narrates several lines in the first-person, homodiegetic mode (96). The source of narration is everywhere and nowhere at once. Likewise, the proliferation of tropes, which at rare moments is almost overwhelming, also introduces indeterminacy as tenor and vehicle are blurred. It is, for example, clear enough that stray dogs morphing into wolves parallels the transformation of rootless youths into militiamen and opportunists (33, 37, 221–22), but personified "death" is more cryptic:

> Death is the master of clarity and precision but, so precise and clear is he that he rises up from the city like a spirit and is tormented whenever he has to define his features or forms. In his buildings he suffers the torment of one concerned with God's incarnation in man and man's incarnation in God, buildings which perpetually fall a little short, which are always tight across his infinite shoulders. (153)

This lyrical excursus and the slurring of narrative voices are not so much demonstrative of epistemological confusion as performative. The indeterminacy of voice betokens a near-frantic effort to circumscribe a mounting and protean menace. Likewise, indeterminacy at the plot level is a survival mechanism. Khalil clings to his indeterminate gender identity as if to parry the corruption of a war that is coded as hypermasculine. At last, however, he realizes the war's potentiality within himself and assumes the determinate but pathological role of militia thug. In *The Stone of Laughter* as in *The House of Mathilde*, indeterminacy does not function primarily to reveal the undecidability or potential plurality of worlds as they presumably often do in Western literature; rather, they function performatively in the desperate—and vain—effort to grasp one chaotic world.

Al-Daif's *Techniques of Misery* is apparently quite different as it maintains a rigorous external focalization. The narrator is centered as if in the eye of a camera, but unlike similar experiments in Isherwood or Hemingway in which external focalization actually casts character into relief, in this novel the technique draws attention to the ontological emptiness of the narrator. The characters, too, are strangely contentless, doing things but apparently thinking and feeling little. Such a narrator and characters are well suited to the plot of the novel, which traces the various ways in which the war demands behaviorist adaptations—the "techniques of misery"—humans must acquire in order to survive. As the protagonist arranges his life around war's contingencies: car bombings, kidnappings, sniping, searches, garbage pileups, and outages of plumbing, electricity, and telephone—it becomes excruciatingly clear that psychological interiority is an obstacle to survival. The irrelevance of thought, opinion, emotion, and desire is thematized in the narrator's mantra that he has "seven million ideas" stillborn in his head at any given moment. The result is a panorama of a feral city, ill-mannered and malevolent, as pedestrians calmly dodge rubbish underfoot and falling objects overhead. To these and other indignities the hapless protagonist is forced to adapt, hovering frantically at one point between lovemaking in the bedroom and doing battle with an overflowing toilet in the bathroom. External focalization in *Techniques of Misery* thus demonstrates the unknowability, but mostly the irrelevance, of the human "spirit" in a state of ongoing war.

Indeterminacy reaches a paroxysm in al-Daif's *Passage to Dusk*. Within the first few lines of the novel, the narrator is shot dead at the door of his apartment, or so it seems, as his mind continues to mull over the event and numerous other deaths and maimings he undergoes throughout the novel. In the process, indeterminacy extends to the narrator's identity as he loses his name and gender identity and eventually his very existence as insects devour his body:

> After my blood had been drained, after all my water had dried, it was the turn of crawling and creeping insects, especially ants. The ants disintegrated me and carried bits and pieces to every quarter of the city. There wasn't an anthill in all of Beirut without a shred of me in it. (32)

The literal diffusion of the narrator's body throughout the city suggests the war's inevitable phagocytosis of civilian life. This narrator seems consequently a ghostlike voice from a subject position outside the space and time of the diegesis.

In sum, indeterminacy in these novels certainly rehearses what is by now a familiar refrain that the subject is constitutively plural and decentered, the product of myriad discourses and therefore indeterminate. But the context of war means that this fact is not primary. In these novels indeterminacy is not postmodern in the sense of demonstrating epistemic limitations or ratifying difficult freedoms. Rather, indeterminacy is part of the context surrounding the more proximate task of dealing with war. It underscores a victim's anxiety about one violence-saturated world, not a victor's Promethean *jouissance* in the multiplicity of possibilities.

The second technique common to these novels is an unemphatic narrative tone. In *The House of Mathilde,* the narrator's deadpan dovetails with the subject matter of everyday life in one apartment building. This documentary tone and the absence of dialogue imbue the building's slow dilapidation with formal dignity. Its decay and tragic end may therefore be implacable but they are never miserable.[6]

Although apparently quite different, the tone of al-Daif's most disturbing novel to date, *This Side of Innocence,* achieves much the same effect. The novel recounts the torture and rape of a man accused of tearing the poster image of a political figure. Like Daoud, al-Daif eschews the agon, building a character of consummate good faith and cooperation. The narrator-protagonist is at pains to rationalize the actions of his tormentors and give them the benefit of the doubt at every turn. It soon becomes clear that he embodies an idealized Enlightenment rationality; if, at times, he verges on the frenzied, it is seldom when one would expect it. Left alone by his interrogators in an empty room, he suffers a self-reproachful dark night of the soul over what to do with his cigarette ash in the absence of an ashtray, concluding at last, "Oh vile self!" (38). On the other hand, after spending hours in illegal custody, he reasons:

> If I were to put myself in the interrogator's place, how would I myself be-have? Undoubtedly exactly the same way, maybe even worse. In view of what they could do and had the right to do, they were treating me humanely. Yes! (68)

The ironic humor that emerges from such incongruities precludes any hint of a moralizing tone and, indeed, directs attention to the narrator's matter-of-fact attitude toward torture and violence. Consequently, the novel thematizes not the perpetration of violence, which is all but assumed as normative, but rather the blindnesses and self-deceptions of reason faced with violence.

Al-Daif's *Techniques of Misery* also features an indomitable fool who contrives—always in vain—to avoid unpleasantness. His failure to find a modus vivendi with war does not lead, as one might imagine, to cynicism or stoicism, but rather to ever-greater sensitivity to conditions. At one point, the protagonist, Hashem, is cramped three abreast in the front seat of a collective taxi on a rainy day:

> His [Hashem's] jacket pocket was situated at about the level of his stomach. He slipped his hand inside, pulled out a paper handkerchief, blew his nose and folded it. As he was folding it, a small shred of the paper fell on his knee. He blew on it and the shred of paper flew up and landed on his neighbor's left thigh near the knee.
>
> The man wore dark gray trousers and the shred of paper was white. It didn't seem to bother him!
>
> But Hashem's eyes were transfixed on the shred of paper. He tried several times to turn away, but he couldn't keep from looking at it. He couldn't look elsewhere.
>
> As for the man, he gazed through the windshield in front of the driver where only one wiper worked properly.
>
> It seemed to Hashem that at one point the man glanced out the corner of his eye at the shred of paper. (92)

The narrator's obsessiveness about the marginalia of life contrasts with the flatness of his tone around great events. In this way the novel ironically de-emphasizes the political-military foreground while casting into relief the psychological depredations of the war on civilian life.

The Stone of Laughter displays perhaps the most engaged tone of these novels, although even here this sense emerges obliquely, often through the use of ellipses in otherwise unemphatic passages. The protagonist spends hours listening to callers on late-night FM talk shows:

> They are people, but they are not real. Only their voices are real and this was what gave Khalil pleasure . . . voices that existed in corridors. For the pleasure of benign corridors, voices which had no wish to come in at all . . . real voices, empty and false, they were the real voices of a city like this. . . . the real city, people like me exist, then, they are real and they talk on FM. (75)

Without the ellipses, the tone of this passage would flat-line. With them, some authorial pathos seeps in, but it is more often the case that Barakat's tone remains unemphatic, especially during moments of extremity or violence such as when Khalil performs oral sex on the gang leader (224) or when he rapes his neighbor in the novel's culmination (230). Thus Barakat, like Daoud and al-Daif, resolutely avoids an impassioned tone, especially at moments of extremity.

The use of unemphatic tone in these novels is akin to the postmodern "banalization of the fantastic" (McHale 76–77), but it betokens nothing of a postmodern "waning of affect" (Jameson, *Postmodernism* 10). Within the context of enthusiastic but ever-less plausible ideological commitment in the 1970s, unemphatic tone sharply distinguished these novels.[7] At the same time, however, the rejection of unchaste language and utopic programs did not signal an abdication of responsibility, but rather a properly modern yearning for coherence as a prerequisite to action. Indeed, the willfully subdued tone is anything but unprecedented in modernist literature that focuses on civilian tragedy. Consider in this regard Walter Kalaidjian's analysis of "the numbed monotones and understated ironies" in Dos Passos's account of the Armenian genocide (110).[8]

The third category of techniques common to these novels includes iteration and recursivity. Iteration, the repetition of "little stories" on the same narrative level within a novel, is distinguished from recursivity, in which "little stories are a structural component of a larger constituent, to which they contribute input" (Marie-Laure Ryan 122). Iteration stutters forward in time; recursivity constantly sets back the clock (122). By this light, story motifs in the diegesis are iterative, and repeated narrative focalization on the same event is recursive. The novels under study here employ both these structures as a way of gesturing backward to trauma.

Numerous motifs in *The House of Mathilde* convey a sense of slow change; as they are repeated, the context shifts slightly, drawing attention to the changes that have taken place in the meantime. A sizzling frying pan, dusty balconies, elegant bathroom faucets, and oft-repainted doors are among the motifs that draw attention to the constantly reiterated message that "the building was no longer habitable." These iterative structures function not only to gauge the distance between what was and what is, but also to suggest at each stage that things could have turned out differently. Each time the narrator notices the "elegant" lines of the building, for example, he is also implying that the potential for redemption remained at that point, that the narrative could have followed a different path but instead proceeded one step closer to the destruction of the building and by extension the nation.

In *The Stone of Laughter*, iteration takes the form of a spiraling narrative. The protagonist, Khalil, lives through three fundamentally similar situations, each of which builds on the preceding one. The pattern proceeds as an investment in love, followed by corruption, violent loss, and hopelessness. Khalil loves Naji, his neighbor, who gets mixed up in the war and is killed. After a bout of depression, Khalil develops a similar attachment to Youssef, whose corruption by war and subsequent death trigger another depression. Out of hopelessness, Khalil finally enters the spiral himself, joining a gang of drug and arms dealers, delivering himself to violence, and becoming at last a militia thug. As in Daoud's novel, the repetition of the cycle of corruption, violence, and death suggests a relentless drive toward debacle. Each time, alternatives that could yield a different outcome are rigorously eliminated. In this sense, these are resolutely antipostmodern novels inasmuch as they foreclose the kind of open-endedness that characterizes much postmodern fiction.

In *Passage to Dusk*, a recursive structure apparently adheres more faithfully to the postmodern tenet of open-endedness. The murder of the first-person protagonist is recounted some half-dozen times, each time with a difference. Likewise, the narrator's paranoia in a collective taxi—a preferred site of terror throughout al-Daif's work—and his bleeding into a gutter are recounted several times. The effect of these multiple tellings most certainly suggests unknowability and ontological contingency—but only to a certain extent. Unlike Barbara Herrnstein Smith, who once masterfully demonstrated the dizzying range of narrative contingency by showing how *Cinderella* could plausibly span hundreds of often contradictory versions, al-Daif never strays far from his central preoccupation. Whether the protagonist is the object of torment or the subject, such as when he participates in poisoning the well of an enemy village, recursivity always ends in coercion, humiliation, and violence. The novel ends as it begins, with the knock at the door that announces the narrator's death, implying that recursivity has entered an infinite loop with no hope for forgetfulness.

Thus, again techniques that often imply one state of affairs in the West are used in these novels to utterly different effect. Iteration and recursivity here point not to the givens of open-endedness and infinite potentiality but beyond these to a compulsion to bear witness. Thus it is not so much the techniques that differ as the attitudes toward them. These novels have little to do with a postmodern fascination with surfaces and much to do with a modernist anxiety about the depths of trauma.

A fourth feature is the focus on everyday spaces, which implies a corresponding de-emphasis on high relief elements of narrative such as heroic characters, epiphanic events, and teleological time. Space conceived of as "a mutually conditioning network of character, event and place," is an attempt to account for the relational and decentered nature of subjectivity that we find in these novels.[9] Few characters possess the wherewithal to initiate or carry through significant change, and no single action or event functions as a turning point. Character, place, and event are interwoven into a loose sourceless subjectivity not unlike that once described by Louis Althusser:

> [T]he relations of production now appear to us as a regional *structure,* itself *inscribed* in the social totality. [. . .] [T]he structure of the relations of production determines the *places* and *functions* occupied and adopted by the agents of production, who are never anything more than the occupants of these places, insofar as they are the supports [*Träger*] of these functions. The true "subjects" (in the sense of the constitutive subjects of the process) are therefore not these occupants or functionaries, are not, despite all appearances . . . the "real men"—but the *definition and its distribution of these places and functions.* [. . .] But since these are "relations," they cannot be thought within the category *subject.* (179–80; emphasis in original)

Althusser is here unwittingly describing the situation of those who survive ongoing war. In these novels, even when significant individual acts or events do occur, they yield no compensatory changes of circumstance or knowledge. Things, mostly bad, just keep happening. Yet characters are not resigned to their plight and there is no Beckettian "reveling in wretchedness" (Sheehan 157). Instead, these novels reveal a painstaking and sometimes almost quirky attention to conditioning contexts, not unlike an autopsy performed on a cadaver's furniture.

As Samira Aghacy has shown, Lebanese war novels dramatize the diffuse links between war and society by polarizing and gendering spaces of war and refuge ("Domestic Spaces"). In *The House of Mathilde,* each home in the apartment building is a separate socioeconomic and ethnic-sectarian space. Vast social forces are telescoped down into the concrete spaces of the building: the arrival of refugees, the sudden flight of long-term inhabitants, the flux of businesses, the retreat into the interior of homes, growing penury, the rise of suspicion and fear. Likewise, these symbolic spaces enter into conflict as when Mathilde, a Beiruti Christian, and her male tenant, presumably a Shiite Muslim from the south, set up borders between each other in the apartment. The border is initially breached through sexuality but ultimately in violence as Mathilde is murdered and dismembered in the "Arab-style" bathroom, the domestic crime standing for the breakdown and disintegration of Western-oriented Christian authority in Lebanon.

The patient and inductive tracing of war's inroads into everyday life is also a feature of *The Stone of Laughter*. Early in the novel, Khalil's fastidious cleaning of his apartment after a battle corresponds to an effort to preserve his home and mind from the corruption of war. His actions may border on obsessive-compulsive behavior but they preserve a kernel of his sanity. The rhythms of everyday life in the neighborhood remain separate by accommodating themselves to the naturalized rhythms of ongoing war.

> [T]he way we reckon our days has come apart from the way that time is generally reckoned by the sun. [...] When the sun is high in the sky the markets are packed with latecomers. [...] The darkness of what we know as night settles, while people begin to listen out for the moment [...] so that their heads will be able to respond quickly to the dangers and surprises that the night of afternoon brings. (28–29)

But war gradually encroaches on even this civilian redoubt in space and time as Khalil's friends and neighbors, Naji and Youssef, die one after the other and their families flee. A warlord bringing arms and drugs with him invests the neighborhood and occupies an apartment in Khalil's building. Khalil no longer deludes himself that housework can keep the war at bay and explores with little satisfaction spaces of frenetic, vacuous escape in nightclubs and parties. He eventually understands that he cannot live alone and realizes that survival itself depends on his adaptation to what is troped as a fellowship of vermin (98–99). He enters the space of the warlord by attending his parties and eventually interiorizing their norms. His identity soon goes into flux and he begins speaking of himself as split and feminized: his "self tried to control herself" (220). Shortly thereafter, Khalil begins his life as a warlord's catamite, a rapist, a militiaman, and ultimately a "laughing stone."

The gendered demarcation of spaces is central to all of these novels with violence and sexuality flashing at the borders. Khalil bursts into his neighbor's flat and rapes her near the threshold. The protagonist of *Passage to Dusk* is forced at gunpoint to share his apartment with a pregnant woman and her boundary-mad brother who nevertheless fails to prevent contact between the narrator and the woman during the brief times when the door between their sections of the apartment is open. In all of these novels, war pervades physical spaces of refuge and character psychologies simultaneously. Barakat's Khalil loses control of his space and of his protective androgyny. Al-Daif's narrator in *Passage to Dusk* loses his masculinity and his sectarian identity as he temporarily adopts the alternative identities of woman and Muslim, as if hoping thereby to escape from the threat of war (88–92). Unsurprisingly, he experiences no liberation or respite from his torments and the novel ends shortly afterward with the narrator taking sleeping pills to avoid the knock at the door that signals the eternal return of war into his home and into his psyche. In other literatures, borders are often zones of productive intercultural encounter as Susan Stanford Friedman has shown in *Mappings;* in these novels, however, one can almost go as far as to say that nothing good comes from border zones, so thoroughly has war corrupted the potential for intercultural encounter.

The nexus of space, sex, and violence tightens even further in al-Daif's novel *This Side of Innocence,* published in 1997, seven years after open war ended. When the narrator allegedly tears a poster of a leader, he is treated like a captured enemy. That his offense is far less serious than those committed during open war only suggests that leaders and warlords are not all that different from each other and that the burdens of "peacetime" sometimes exceed those of war. The spaces of this novel, however, are apparently very different from the dilapidation depicted in the war novels. The first half of *This Side of Innocence* takes place in a clean, very well lighted office furnished with leather couches, a coffee table, and a desk. After an initial interrogation, the narrator is left alone where he, an eminently rational man, ponders the equally rational system that produced the office and the efficient young men who apprehended him. The focal point of his thought is the lighting, the source of this rationality:

> I couldn't make out anything outside, as though that curtain preceded a block of light instead of a window. As if this block of light, which was the same dimensions as the window, had been secured into the wall. [. . .]
> [I]t was impossible to see through it. It was white as a block of ice. So where was the light coming from, then? (25)

Early in the novel the sourceless light tropes instrumental reason. Later, the narrative concentrates on how this cold rationality becomes indistinguishable from barbarism when directed on the body. The men, whom the narrator describes at one point as "real men," beat and sodomize him, giving him a derogatory and feminized identity. In the second half of the novel, the interrogation moves to the narrator's home and continues in front of his family. As in the other war novels, spaces here too are rigorously policed and sexualized, such as when the narrator is forbidden to go to the bedroom where his wife is kept with an interrogator. Through these spaces, the novel thematizes the overwhelming power of instrumental reason over the self-reflexive but feckless rationality of the narrator.

In this novel, spaces map the unleashing of modern order just as they map the penetration of chaotic violence in the others. These novels indict both as twin aspects of the engine of ongoing war. In this way, the characteristically postmodern technical emphasis on space over time serves the characteristically modernist function of exposing the violence of instrumental reason but without fetishizing its presumed opposite, the irrational.

* * *

Identifying the hybrid modernism of these novels is all well and good, but none of the four categories of techniques—indeterminacy, unemphatic tone, iteration-recursivity, or spatiality—are particularly new or noteworthy in themselves. Nor are the topics of corruption, coercion. or the thematization of war through gendered spaces and sexualized violence. On the other hand, the particular blend of these techniques and thematic preoccupations reveals a great resilience and strength in Arab culture to withstand the onslaught of ongoing war. It is worth exploring the character and sources of this cultural strength.

At first blush, these novels might appear to be halfhearted postmodern experiments: they employ postmodern techniques and accept the decentered self as a given. Yet for all this, the authors do not seem to have the nerve to take the final step, to make their peace with the contingency of meaning and value. Throughout their work flows a tense, unpostmodern yearning for . . . what exactly? Well, it is never clearly stated but it seems, surprisingly enough, akin to a noncontingent sense of human dignity. Which is strange because in these novels the autonomy of every subject is compromised. Every struggle ends in corruption and failure. Every moral polarity deconstructs. Every vestige of essential human dignity is proven illusory. Yet they still refuse to jettison the normative idea and apparently lay themselves open to the charges of naïve or nostalgic hopes for coherence—after having painstakingly shown that such coherence is impossible! This is all so curious that it is a relief to see another critic grope toward a similar claim. Magda al-Nowaihi remarks about a novel by Moroccan writer Muhammad Barrada:

> [I]n distinction from western texts where postmodernity and commitment often seem to be mutually exclusive, we have here a narrative that is postmodern in sensibility and structure, but is also fiercely concerned with the here and now and committed to struggling for its improvement. (387–88)

It is easy enough to see how this tension between contraries emerges. Indeterminacy and iteration-recursivity imply a proliferation of perspectives and possible worlds whereas unemphatic tone and spatiality are deployed in a countervailing effort to render a single phenomenological reality. The result is the tension between radical contingency and a tortured refusal to dissipate the afterimage of essential human dignity. These writers are therefore cognizant of the impossibility of fathoming reality but no less committed to the belief that their work can intervene productively. They harbor no pretension whatsoever to noncontingent truth and yet there exists in their work an underlying seriousness of moral purpose that functions as if there were. Hence their narratives are like Philomela's tapestry, pointing to a ghostly reality that cannot be spoken because it cannot be fathomed, but which they believe exists despite their awareness of contingency in all its forms.

This faith in human understanding in the face of all evidence to the contrary is especially curious because, in philosophical terms, if the Western metaphysics of presence has been undergoing steady demolition since Nietzsche, why should Arab writers, who arguably have a good-size bone to pick with the Enlightenment, cling to the ghost of humanism? Perhaps because for historical reasons theirs is a different kind of humanism. Recent Western antihumanism emerged in the wake of two world wars that shattered the faith in the notion of innate human dignity. Heidegger, Fanon, Horkheimer, and Adorno were all ambivalent about humanism and Sartre was too, but in his preface to Fanon's *Wretched of the Earth,* he positively excoriates the hypocrisy of this humanism that "was nothing but an ideology of lies, a perfect justification for pillage; its honeyed words, its affectation of sensibility were only alibis for our aggressions" (25). So humanism, ostensibly concerned with the dignity of all humans, is part and parcel of the project to dehumanize most of humanity, Arabs included.

The intellectual focal point of Western antihumanism was Paris in May 1968. Its principal thinkers—Lacan, Barthes, Foucault, Derrida, Kristeva, and Althusser—exposed the hidden coercions in a highly rationalized society as well as the illusion of autonomous subjectivity. Kate Soper's distillation of the issue is still valid:

> Where the humanist sees a confrontation between agents possessed of will and reason and the "unwilled" and "irrational" products of their concerted actions, the anti-humanist views the wills themselves as "unwilled" and the "reason" in whose name every "progress" is supposedly made as no more obviously to be privileged than the "madness" it opposes. (122)

Without making any claim for determinism, one can note that the antihumanist argument springs from a particular social context of long-overdue opposition to colonial war and political stagnation in the West. It was the West speaking to the West of the Western subject's self-deception. But May 1968 and its sister movements elsewhere in the West failed to overturn the system, leaving a good deal of resentment and untested utopianism that arguably found its way into criticism and theory.

Lebanon in the early 1970s was both like and unlike Paris. Like the Parisians, these Beirut-based writers experienced the moral bankruptcy of instrumental reason in the cynicism of the nation-state, so they could not very well ignore the various critiques of Enlightenment and humanism. At the same time, however, these writers also witnessed a deeply reactionary sectarianism in the form of Zionism and its mirror images in local Islamic and Christian fundamentalisms. The historical focal point was wartime Beirut in 1975–76 when secular ideologies, including programmatic Leftism, were discredited and the balance of conflict shifted to age-old ethnic-sectarian animosities, foreshadowing a worldwide shift along the same lines as in the Iranian Revolution and the breakup of Yugoslavia, down to this day.[10] In this paroxysm of violence, unlike Paris, the nation-state did break down, but there was no subsequent liberation, only chaos and the atrocity of ongoing war. In this catastrophic state of affairs, Barakat, Daoud, and al-Daif did not see antihumanism as a viable response. After all: "The political message [of antihumanism] . . . tends to pessimism, emphasizing the obstacles presented by language or by the psyche itself to the remaking of social institutions" (Soper 122). Nor did they go for the optimism of utopian commitment, nor for the hand-wringing of alienated consciousness, nor either for the opportunistic complicity with ongoing war. Instead, they explored the thorough perfusion of war into society and the self but without denying human dignity as a base standard in their work. It was both a clear-sighted admission of human limitations and a voluntaristic adherence to humanism nevertheless.

There may be yet another, frankly more speculative, reason for these writers' attachment to the ghost of humanism. A companion to this essay stresses the role of the West in the development of what is termed here an "Arab humanist" aesthetic. It argues that these novels keep faith with Enlightenment values at the very moment that they are under attack not only in an Arab world where ethnic-sectarianism is in the ascendant but also in the postmodernizing West. The present essay explores the obvious fact that the Arabic novel is not only a product of the West but of more than fifteen centuries of literary culture in Arabic.

Of the numerous currents within the Arabic cultural heritage that might explain these writers' refusal to reject humanism, one is most suggestive: that humanism was already firmly planted on Arab soil long before the first Arabic novel was written, long before even Napoleon's Egyptian expedition disembarked in 1798. Within the past two decades a number of scholars have disputed the received wisdom that medieval Arab arts and scholarship were mere placeholders between classical antiquity and the early modern "Renaissance." In the sciences, George Saliba has unearthed key Arab contributions to human (as opposed to Western) science. In the humanities, several scholars have traced links between the medieval Arab-Islamic tradition of *adab* ("literature" and "refined literary culture") and what much later became known as Renaissance humanism in Italy. In *The Rise of Humanism in Classical Islam and the Christian West*, George Makdisi argues persuasively that what is most often taught as the indigenously European movements of scholasticism and humanism were actually borrowed from the Islamic Arab tradition.[11] Scholasticism and humanism, he writes,

> carry the signatures of classical Islam clearly legible on their essential constituent elements. [. . .] The parallelism may be seen in all areas: in the institutions of learning, in the organization of knowledge, in the humanistic studies, in the cult of the book, in the cult of eloquence, in the methodology of instruction, in self-teaching, in all phases of the humanist community. (348)

Makdisi concentrates his efforts on showing how the major fields of humanism —grammar and lexicography, poetry, oratory, letter writing, speechmaking, history, and moral philosophy—were drawn from classical Islam in the second half of the eleventh century ("Inquiry" 18).[12] The conceptual overlap between the terms *adab* and humanism is surely imperfect, but Makdisi stresses that two concepts of fundamental importance to the *adab* tradition are "eloquence" and "the dignity of man" (19). The notion of human dignity is, of course, a mainstay of Renaissance humanism and a distinct departure from classical antiquity (Kinney 4). This is not to argue that *adab* humanism was necessarily more important than, say, Christianity in the emphasis on human dignity, but to suggest it as an important source among others. Nor is this to claim that there has existed a continuous and unchanging thread of *adab* humanism in the Arab world to the present. It is to suggest, however, that *adab* humanism may be one of the ways that Islamic Arab culture made a significant contribution to what might be referred to as a common "structure of feeling" in the medieval Mediterranean basin. Just as a notion such as Homeric *techné* can find modern-day descendants in cultural predispositions, so too could the institutionalized and rich *adab* humanist tradition. *Adab,* therefore, may also help to explain these Lebanese war authors' reluctance to fully embrace postmodern consciousness.

The humanism of these writers, however, differs from that commonly espoused in the West by such thinkers as Tsvetan Todorov. Humanism for Todorov is an "anthropology" that "tells how men are" (30). According to Todorov's Kantian definition, humanism is a Promethean exercise of the will; one acts "in conformity only with those principles and maxims accepted by the subject" (30). The humanism that emerges from the work of these Lebanese war writers is less ambitious. It makes no claims to what human beings essentially are or are not. Nor does it define itself by the subject's will to accept or reject principles and maxims. Instead, it is a conviction that there exists beyond all our ignorances, and especially beyond our reason, an essential human dignity which must not be flouted. This conviction is learned, not assumed as an ontological truth. As Fedwa Malti-Douglas remarks about the *adab* tradition: it is "a spirit, but more concretely . . . a discourse" (51–52). In other words, this humanism is a willfully acquired and maintained ideology, a product of culture and education. Part of what "human dignity" means in this discourse may be gleaned from one of the meanings of *adab,* "refined manners": "Everything that the term *manners* implies can be assumed to underlie the combination of correct demeanor, comportment, and diction encompassed by the word *adab*" (Carter 31). From within a Kantian discourse of dignity as "acting in conformity with only those principles accepted by the subject," this is all so much inauthentic verbiage. Yet, from a poststructuralist perspective, the sovereign subject is no less a product of inauthentic verbiage. The Promethean subject and the well-mannered subject are therefore both products of discourse, the latter having the advantage of at least knowing it is not autonomous.

It is therefore perhaps a good time to consider lifting the banishment of manners and decorum from the notion of human dignity. Such a replacement of education at the center of human identity may temper the excesses of the Promethean human—"the overcoming animal, the transcending being, the superseding species" (Sheehan 89). Today, as ongoing war spreads on a world scale in a way reminiscent of the Lebanese militia wars, it is worth considering whether Beirut in 1975–76 more than Paris 1968 better embodies the predicament of culture today. If so, Barakat, al-Daif, and Daoud have much to offer, showing how the novel can animate humanism to meet the ill-mannered arrogance of ongoing war.

NOTES

1. This essay's interest in ongoing war stops at its facticity and does not speculate on its causes. Marx's claim that capitalism "ruthlessly forces the human race to produce for production's sake" (739) seems central to much subsequent thought on the causes of ongoing war, from Fanon's account of the anticolonial struggle (40–41) to even the liberal analysis of capitalism's powers of "creative destruction" (Schumpeter 81–86; Thurow 67). Other thinkers have identified a range of alternative causes for ongoing war, from Horkheimer and Adorno's claim that Enlightenment as such is totalitarian (4) to Baudrillard's notion that the contemporary world is prey to "metastatic disorder" (15). The purpose of this essay is to explore ways in which some Lebanese novelists have responded to ongoing war.

2. This is not in any way to privilege the Lebanese Civil War, commonly dated from 1975 to 1990, over other contemporaneous conflicts such as the Vietnamese or Cambodian debacles or the Iran-Iraq War, the Soviet-Afghan War, or civil wars in Angola, Mozambique, El Salvador and Nicaragua, or the Israeli-Palestinian conflict. Lebanon, however, by virtue of its small size, its multicultural profile, and its socioeconomic conditions, was arguably a crucible case for a wider phenomenon. Prior to the war, the tiny nation was renowned for being a tolerant, hedonistic, bold, and resourceful country, displaying an economic liberalism "exuberant almost to the point of wildness" (Picard 3). It had a form of democracy, freedom of speech, and independent political parties. Its service- and financial-

based economy made Lebanon a "merchant republic" open, not unlike many nations today, to market and political whims (45–47). Again like many other nations today, Lebanon accepted with considerable aplomb a yawning disparity between rich and poor—among the world's largest at the time (90). Finally, entrenched sectarianism and a social predilection for solving political disputes through violence also made Lebanon a trailblazer in contemporary identity politics and clientelism (see Michael Johnson). At the time, the breakdown of the nation-state into ethnic-sectarian chaos was commonly referred to in the West as "Lebanization."

3. This claim is also argued in, for example, Badawi, 14; Jabra, 18; and al-Daif ("Al-Nitaj" 167).

4. Quotations are taken from available translations whenever possible; if none exists, translated passages are mine. Transliterations of Arabic follow the guidelines established by the *International Journal of Middle East Studies*.

5. I am aware that any formal distinction between postmodern and modern literary practices is impossible to uphold with any rigor. Nevertheless, I do find the distinction useful in describing general formal differences. More important, I choose to see an implicit attitude—the serene acceptance of ontological contingency—as a defining feature of postmodern literature. Without denying that this attitude can be found in pre–World War II literature, it seems to me important to identify its spread and influence in a variety of post–World War II Western novels such as Beckett's *Molloy*, Robbe-Grillet's *Les Gommes*, and Pynchon's *V.*

6. I argue this claim more thoroughly in "The Everyday World of War in Hassan Daoud's *House of Mathilde*."

7. Naturally, Arabic literature in the mid-1970s was more varied than the close focus on commitment literature would indicate. Nevertheless, the polemical tone of much post-1967 literature is evident in Mahmoud Darwish's declaration: "There is no life for our literature except as an arm and supplement for man" (23). So urgent was the cause that some writers called for imitation of the most successful commitment literature to date, Israeli social realism. Thus Ahmad Mohammad Attiyeh called in 1974 for writers to "fight then write" in order to equal the spirit of Zionist literature, which he observed was, "committed, institutionalized and focused on creating a national identity" (9).

8. Kalaidjian notes that deadpan voice "deflects the full emotive impact of mass murder" (110). He argues, however, that this traumatic impact can return in the figure of the "phantom" at a "second- or even third-generational remove" (116). For the purposes of this essay and without excluding the pertinence of Kalaidjian's claim, we can note that deadpan can also ironically defamiliarize trauma.

More broadly, Kalaidjian's work intersects with this essay at several points, not least in the claim that "genocide persists as the unthought underside to the so-called progress we have witnessed in the twentieth century" (108). I am grateful to the editors of this volume for drawing my attention to his article.

9. The definition of social space as a dynamic that exists among structures, practices, and discourses is drawn principally from Henri Lefebvre (16) and Michel de Certeau (117). Other pertinent work on space and narrative would include Michel Foucault's stress on the organizational aspect of space in "Of Other Spaces"; David Harvey's discussion of space and aestheticization (201–308); Fredric Jameson's identification of a homologous relationship between spatial and social mappings ("Cognitive Mapping" 353); and Bill Brown's work on the relationship between objects and subjectivity.

10. Al-Daif's ʿ*Azizi al-Sayyid Kawabata* (*Dear Mr Kawabata*) vividly recounts the disaffection (but not the capitulation) of the Left during this period.

11. See also Arkoun, Carter, Kraemer, and Malti-Douglas.

12. Another scholar of Islamic Arab humanism, Joel Kraemer, shows how this

mutually beneficent relation among Mediterranean cultures stretches back to classical antiquity. His claim is that

> The humanism that flourished in the Renaissance of Islam was an offspring of the humanism ideal that germinated in the period of Hellenism and Greco-Roman antiquity. Its primary features are: (1) adoption of the ancient philosophic classics as an educational and cultural ideal in the formation of mind and character; (2) a conception of the common kinship and unity of mankind; and (3) humaneness, or love of mankind. (10)

6   On the Ganges Side of Modernism: Raghubir Singh, Amitav Ghosh, and the Postcolonial Modern

Ariela Freedman

> Today we have descended into a kind of schizophrenia where people feel they have perforce to choose whether they should dress (or decorate their houses) in a way which they call "ethnic," or in a style which they term "modern." This is ridiculous, because India is one of the few places in the world where you could do both at the same time.
>
> —Charles Correa, "India Seminar"[1]

When Raghubir Singh died in 1999, Max Kozloff wrote of his work, "If you can imagine what a Rajput miniaturist could have learned from Henri Cartier-Bresson, you'll have a glimmer of Raghubir Singh's aesthetic."[2] Singh's last book, *River of Colour,* intended as a retrospective for an artist in the middle of his career but left as a final word in consequence of Singh's untimely death, lays out the central principles of this aesthetic in an introductory essay. Kozloff's coupling of the Rajput miniaturist and the French Modernist photographer is lifted right out of the pages of Singh's essay, which begins with an evocation of the courts of Rajasthan and continues with anecdotes about Cartier-Bresson and Atget, as well as the Indian modernist filmmaker Satyajit Ray. Singh seamlessly blends the European modernist manifestos of artists as diverse as Cartier-Bresson and Pound with his own sense of Indian vernacular art. He argues for "the Ganges side of modernism, rather than the Seine or East River side of it" and claims, "Indian photography needs to develop its own kind of adaptation of the modernist canon."[3] Here we can find what this collection of essays has titled "alternative genealogies," different "geomodernist imaginings"[4] that allow us to both place and displace a conventional understanding of modernism. This persistent attempt to reconcile European modernism with Indian art is not, of course, Singh's alone. India remains one of the few countries where the discourse of modernism continues to be actively transformed as a source of inspiration for architects like Charles Correa and Balkrishna Doshi,[5] sculptors like Anish Kapoor, writers like Amitav Ghosh and Anita Desai, and photographers like Raghubir Singh. In fact, these days one is more likely to locate modernism along the Ganges than along the Seine.

In this chapter, I want to inquire into Singh's retention of the terms of modernism, and his continued understanding of modernism as an aesthetic that allows him to occupy both the past and the future, to reinvent Indian culture in a new vernacular and retain its vitality for another generation. I will show the light this sheds on Amitav Ghosh's fascinating portrait of a young modernist photographer in his new novel, *The Glass Palace*. With these instances in mind, I want to ask why postcolonial criticism seems so blind to the continued reinterpretation of modernism in Indian literature and art, and to trouble the presumed affinity between postcolonialism and postmodernity.[6] Under this definition, Indian artists who do not fit under the rubric of the second will rarely be engaged by critics of the first unless they can be adequately read according to the demands of what Kwame Anthony Appiah calls "the alterity machine." Or, as Aijaz Ahmad succinctly puts it:

> [W]e live in the postcolonial *period*, hence in a postcolonial *world*, but neither all intellectuals nor all discourses of this *period* and this *world* are *postcolonial* because, in order to be a properly *postcolonial discourse* the discourse must be *postmodern*, mainly of the deconstructive kind, so that only those intellectuals can be truly *postcolonial* who are also *postmodern*. (284)

One might object that it is perverse to claim the continuing value and relevance of the discourse of modernism to Indian art when so much of postcolonial criticism has been occupied with the repudiation of the project of modernity. Appiah calls the postmodern into question, but as a continuation of the logic of the modern; "what the postmodern reader seems to demand of Africa is all too close to what modernism—in the form of the postimpressionists—demanded of it."[7] Modernism has become a byword in postcolonial criticism, even as postmodernism has become an invocation. Yet modernism is a term no more easy to define than postmodernism, and a term no less easy to scapegoat. Recent criticism continues to chip away at our own myth of the modern, so that it seems clear that modernism is no monolith but a loosely organizing term that encompasses a wide variety of aesthetic and political positions, private and public preoccupations, and uneven developments. After all, which hegemonic modernism are we scapegoating? Joyce, who has become the pillar of postcolonial Irish studies? Woolf, whose writing reads the end of empire in the anxious play of Peter and his knife? Even Lawrence, whose "misogyny" must be counterbalanced by the slipperiness of signification in his novels and his extreme skepticism about nationalism, British nationalism in particular? While elements of European modernism were either inhospitable to Indian art or appropriative of it, other elements were quickly and productively reappropriated. As Henry Louis Gates points out, "there are no one-way flows."[8] Raghubir Singh and Amitav Ghosh argue that elements of postmodernism are not conducive to their art, but they readily appropriate aspects of modernism for their own purposes. We might name the act of appropriation itself modernist: the artist borrows, or borrows back, the habit of borrowing. The difference between this and postmodernist pastiche is that the borrowing is not done to flatten or parody the object but to enhance it. Modernism is attractive to the postcolonial artist because it allows for an art that in Ghosh's terms is both "placed and dis-placed" and provides a strategic vernacular that claims both aesthetic autonomy and cultural groundedness. While a postmodernist postcolonial criticism may be the appropriate lens through which to explore hybridized and self-consciously postmodernist writers like Salman Rushdie, or migrant intellectuals like Homi Bhaba and Gayatri Spivak, it is a lens that, applied indiscriminately, inevitably produces distortions.[9]

Kwame Anthony Appiah's article "Is the Post-in Postmodernism the Post-in Postcolonial?" was one of the first to call the elision of the two terms into question. I want to suggest, following Appiah, that there is something inappropriately omnivorous in the category of the postcolonial postmodern and in the theoretical structures it entails. Appiah is writing of African art. In Indian art one of the alternatives to the postmodern is modernism, and modernism as it has been interpreted by Indian artists has provided the cultural vitality, continuity, and optimism that Appiah heralds at the end of his essay through weaving the modernist and the traditional together. Reading Indian or African authors in the United States or Canada may contribute to our own sense of existing in a postmodern plurality of cultures. However, multiculturalism, which is a central preoccupation of postmodernism, has been an element of Indian life for thousands of years. To take one example, the architect Charles Correa's syncretism is closer to T. S. Eliot's *The Waste Land*—which uses a mixture of western and eastern texts to point to a connection between them—than it is to postmodern pastiche. The hijrah is not a postmodern phenomenon; the technicolor kitschy posters of Ganesha and Saraswati bought in a market in Mysore may be postmodern on my wall, or on the wall of my friend's high-rise in Juhu, but we are not who they were primarily made for and that is not how they are primarily deployed. I am not arguing for the replacement of postmodernism with modernism as *the* key to postcolonial Indian art, but I am saying that it is worth exploring the points that western modernists and a number of influential Indian postcolonial artists have in common. These Indian artists diverge from European modernism in service of an embedded Indian aesthetic, but this divergence is significantly different from the rebellion of postmodernism. The dialectic between traditional and modernist art creates a series of possibilities for postcolonial artists in India, and this dialectic is itself a modernist paradigm.

Raghubir Singh was one of the most elegant practitioners of modernism in Indian art. He dedicated his last book to "Devika, a teenager of two worlds," and "Satyajit Ray, who showed us how to bridge them, without the loss of one's identity." The mention of Satyajit Ray, India's pre-eminent modernist filmmaker, points to Singh's central preoccupation in his photographs, as articulated in the preface to the book: the attempt to create a modernist Indian vernacular in photography. The title of the preface, "River of Colour: An Indian View," proclaims the situated attempt to explore a national aesthetic, while the epigraph, by Sri Aurobindo, one of the finest twentieth-century theorists of Indian aesthetics, engages both a universal notion of beauty and a particularized understanding of different aesthetic standards. These are the two poles of Singh's aesthetic, which trickily desires to claim autonomy and authenticity, universality and a sense of place. Singh's essay has two main arguments: it is a defense of modernism in Indian art, and it is a defense of Indian art against the claims of European modernism. Singh writes, "the new kind of Indian artist—the world-wise artist and photographer—will very selectively borrow more aspects of the modern and less of the postmodern" (15). This borrowing must be careful, and must be rooted in the particularities of Indian culture. In borrowing itself there is no shame. He affirms, "Grand Indians, like Satyajit Ray, were not afraid of borrowing from the west," and quotes Rabindrath Tagore:

> The sign of greatness in great geniuses is their capacity for borrowing . . . only mediocrities are ashamed and afraid of borrowing for they do not know how to pay back the debt in their own coin . . . our artists were never tiresomely reminded of the fact that they were Indians . . . they had the freedom to be naturally Indian in spite of all the borrowings that they indulged in. (12)

Singh himself claims to borrow from the west and from Bengal, "the first place in the subcontinent to attempt a fusion of the modern arts with the centrifugal force of India" (12).

What might it mean to be naturally Indian? To assert identity here is to claim to transcend it. The artist according to Singh is only naturally Indian in his or her willingness to go outside native culture. In implicit defense against nationalist ideas of art that would claim the influence of other cultures as a taint, Singh here takes the very action of going outside the culture as a proof of the insider status of the Indian artist he envisions. Singh transforms the paradoxical double bind of the artist who desires to be both outside and inside the native vernacular into the strength of the

Indian artist, able to have his cake and his kulfi too. In so doing, Singh redefines the original and natural as the already borrowed and impure. This is not a strategic essentialism as much as it is a revisioned figure of original essence, crafted to anticipate the cosmopolitan identity Singh claims. The power of the "centrifugal force" of India is to appropriate outside influences without itself being decentered or displaced.

Later Singh cites Eliot and Pound in another moment of both affiliating with and distancing himself from European modernist masters. He cites an especially pressing debt to Cartier-Bresson, a photographer who he claims laid "a photographic bridge between the pictorialism of Europe and the pictorial life of Asia" (13). Yet he sees Cartier-Bresson as having adopted a sympathetically Indian vision in his photographs of the country, having "intuitively distanced himself from the core of the western canon in which his early work was squarely planted" (14). Singh contrasts this instinctive empathy and willingness to surrender to another aesthetic with Lee Friedlander who, when seeing a dust storm heading toward Jaisalmer, wondered out loud, "What would Atget have done?" (15).

Singh's introduction is an eloquent defense of color in Indian art, and of his own exclusive use of color photography. He points out that in the west the word *color* is a mild put-down. When we say a person is colorful we mean *not like us* or *not from here*. He then contrasts his own position with the western photographer's modernist insistence on black and white. Singh writes, "Before colonialism and before photography, Indian artists did not see in black and white" (9). Color had a central place in Indian aesthetics, not simply as ornament but as mystical essence.[10] Certain colors were considered sacred or auspicious, but black, the color of Kali, was and is considered taboo for India's majority Hindu population. White, in turn, was associated with mourning. Moreover, black-and-white photography was the medium for what was often a stark aesthetics of alienation, which Singh claims is also alien to the Indian sensibility. "For these reasons," Singh concludes, "I believe that however much we Indians genuinely admire the black and white arts of the west, the Indian photographer cannot reproduce the angst and alienation rooted in the work of western photographers such as Brassai, Bill Brandt, Robert Frank and Diane Arbus" (10). While Singh imagines a monolithic Indian aesthetic, he does so as a counterweight to the overwhelming influence of western photography. His countercanon cannot acknowledge the differences and hybridity among Indian artists if he desires to give his own aesthetic the weight of tradition. Instead of acknowledging the multiplicity of Indian artists, Singh imagines a single artist who is already hybrid and multiple.

In Singh's account, the "camera became an instrument of colonialism" (12). He furthermore claims that colonial photography helped destroy Indian miniature painting. Yet the process of western infiltration was dialectical, as Indian photographers began to exploit the western instrument for their own purposes. Singh writes that the Indian photographers who hand-colored their photographs did so with "a rich palette . . . very different from that done in other cultures" (12). The nineteenth-century Indian photographers, coloring in photographs in vivid colors rather than in taupe and pink, were the descendants of miniature painters; they also set the stage for the Indian color photographer of today. The miniature, handheld camera in its turn ended the static and posed shots of British colonial photography. Singh states his affiliation to the "masters of the miniature camera" (13) like Cartier-Bresson rather than to the nineteenth-century British photographer. There is, then, a crucial difference between the English colonial photographer, tied both to a static tripod and to a set notion of ideas about "the native," taking India as object, and Singh's rather romantic vision of the French photographer Henri Cartier-Bresson roaming through India after independence, camera in hand, being able to dislocate himself from the European canon he primarily works in while bending his art to the demands of his subject.[11]

In his introduction to a collection of Cartier-Bresson's photographs of India, Satyajit Ray congratulates his "palpable humanism" and notes that Henri Cartier-Bresson's eye is drawn to people, not landscapes. Cartier-Bresson is fascinated with the faces of India. His photographs are filled with people, with landscape or architecture as background. Contrast this with the majestic—yet oddly empty—famous colonial photographs of the Taj Mahal at Agra or the Red Fort in Delhi, photographs that not only, as Singh points out, see without problem a country soaked with color in black and white, but also see a densely populated and vibrant country as a series of beautiful but elegiac monuments to the past. It takes a great deal of effort to photograph an empty Taj Mahal. Singh's own photographs of the landmark in *The Grand Trunk Road* (1995) are portraits: a man and his grandson slumped on a bench, oblivious to the storied palace behind them; a random grouping of three visitors, each moving in different directions and shot close up and from below, with the famous wall behind them barely recognizable. Through displacing this iconic monument to desire, which has also stood in for the western desire for India, Singh emphasizes the Indian subject rather than India as object.

Most striking in Singh's essay is his virulent rejection of postmodernism, which he claims "stands at odds to the very values of India" (15). He particularly disavows the "anti-religious stance" of postmodernism, which he argues, "cocks a snook at the spiritual foundations of Indian culture" (15). Singh seems to reject the attitudinal stance of postmodernism as well as its inability to engage with or accept spiritual value. His list of postmodernists, "George Bataille, Gilbert and George, Ingmar Bergman, Don DeLillo," is rather eccentric but concentrates on what he calls in relation to Lee Friedlander's photography "the abject as subject" (15). Singh insists on "beauty, nature, humanism, spirituality" (14) as the cornerstones of Indian culture. The Indian photographer, who "stands on the Ganges side of modernism, rather than the Seine or East River side of it," needs to emphasize these artistic qualities and "develop his own kind of adaptation to the European canon . . . in spite of the great danger of sentimentality that modernism attaches to these values" (14). Singh's redefinition of the "Ganges side" of modernism stands in opposition to postmodernism, which Singh believes will only triumph in India if India becomes "completely Westernized" (15).

The "Ganges" side of modernism also recognizes the claims of religion on modernism. As a modernist artist, Singh retains proximity to traditional ways of life; by this, I mean both the religious and the social. In the first half of the twentieth century, religion was still a strong element of the west, and secularization existed in inconsistent pockets. This situation presented both a problem for modernist artists and a productive source of reaction (in Joyce's case) and inspiration (in Eliot's). The same is true in India today. When Singh points to the particularity of India, he writes "what makes India different is its great and ancient bond with religion" (14) and assumes that the Indian artist cannot ignore this aspect of Indian culture. In an Indian context, postmodernism, which has little language to deal with religion, risks not only irreverence but also irrelevance.

In Singh's view, multiculturalism and globalization work as checks against westernized postmodernism. He lauds an international community of artists, including Abbas Kiarstomi, Alfredo Jarr, Gu Wenda, Shazia Sikander, Ravindra Reddy, Seydou Keita, and Nhem Ein, who retain their own artistic traditions and integrity yet also help create an international language of humanist art. In an essay in *Art in America*, P. C. Smith asks, "Could it be, though, that Singh was still fighting yesterday's battles? In his essay for *River of Colour*, his earnest call for a 'humanist photography' comes at a time when nihilist feeling dominates serious art."[12] Smith leaves his own question unanswered, but Singh, as we shall see in our discussion of Amitav Ghosh, is far from alone in his turn to a modernist humanism.

An important element of Singh's modernist humanism is his insistence on responsibility to beauty. Beauty is omnipresent in his lush and detailed photographs, and is understood in a moral context, along with nature, humanism, and spirituality. He sees the celebration of beauty as an intrinsic part of the Indian aesthetic. Perhaps in this he can be accused of sentimentality, for though his photographs do not ignore the more unattractive aspects of India—the poverty, the urban blight—they also do not transvalue or romanticize them. Yet none of his photographs can be said to take "the abject as subject"; they all provide delight to the eye, primarily through the use of color. Smith quotes Singh at a slide talk in March 1999: "I realized fairly early there was no contradiction between sadness or poverty, and color" (99). Photographs that would seem pessimistic in black and white provide their own compensations in color; a slum dweller in Mumbai, photographed in 1990 in the photograph most reminiscent of Walker Evans's collection on impoverished farmers in the South, peers over a corrugated iron makeshift wall, beside the figure of a woman cut off at the waist and seated on a stepladder. One gets the feeling that what attracted the photographer was not the poverty of the surroundings but the man's bright and inquisitive gaze, and the way the green border of the woman's pink sari is picked up in the fading green of the iron wall. Singh writes that the *Rasas* of Indian aesthetics dictate "an enchantment of sight and sense" (10). He demonstrates this by contrasting a painting of the murder of Khan Jahan Lodi from the seventeenth-century *Padshahnama* with David's *The Death of Marat* (1793), and writes, "In the Moghul work the Indian artist had the power to see simultaneously the most gruesome murder as well as a kingfisher catching fire" (10). V. S. Naipaul compared viewing Singh's photographs to looking at Moghul miniatures.[13] In the context of Singh's statement, we can understand this as a reference to the inclusiveness of his vision and his ever-open eye for beauty, as well as to the promiscuous detail of his pictures.

Yet the beauty of Singh's photographs differs from that found in European modernists like Stieglitz and Weston in the use of color and in the emphasis on the group. His photos nonetheless participate in modernist paradigms through an emphasis on form and the abstraction of shadow, or, as Satyajit Ray expresses it in discussing Cartier-Bresson's photographs, "the eye seeking the subject matter and, at the same time, its most expressive disposition in geometrical terms."[14] In the introduction to the book, Singh notes that British colonialism brought not only aesthetic traditions but also ideas, including "the concept of the individual—the assertiveness of the *I* replacing the passivity of the *we*—as well as the traditional anonymity of the Indian artist" (12). Modernism elevated the individual still further; Singh's photographs form a compromise with modernism through a portraiture that emphasizes an always-contextualized individual. The photograph that opens the book, "Morning on Panchganga Ghat, Benares, Uttar Pradesh, 1985," carefully sets the tone. The ghats, or ceremonial stairs, are a favorite spot for Singh to photograph, since they are a locus for the juxtaposition of religious devotion and everyday life. As is typical of most of Singh's photographs, the picture is drenched in color, most strikingly seen in the bright red, blue-topped structure that appears to be a roadside shrine. Behind the shrine is a shuttered window, colored with red graffiti. The only word legible is *Rama*, scratched again and again on the side of the shrine and along the stair's wall. Inside the frame, Singh has caught an assortment of men, women, and children, most in the midst of action: two boys walk, one boy's hand on the other's shoulder; two women gossip in the road; another, in a bright green silk sari, drags her child up a set of stairs. The world he captures is diverse and vibrant, with religious devotion as background and the human community as foreground. One solitary figure stands out, a boy, caught in the dead center of the photograph. He is wearing a dirty white shirt and a red lunghi patterned with gold circles, and his arms are tightly crossed against his chest as he stands in classic contrapposto. The contrapposto seems a wink to the art of the west, just as Singh notes Cartier-Bresson's photographs of devotees at Tiruvannamalai parallel Massacio's murals in the Brancacci chapel in Florence. In a photograph filled with action, the boy is a still point. The photograph ascends in a strong diagonal to the left, emphasized by the staircase, but the boy marks a central horizontal line reinforced by the stairway's post directly behind him, and by his own sharp shadow. His passivity and isolation are difficult to read in the context of the photograph. He seems a contemplative figure, but his face is half-hidden and his eyes are lost in shadow. Though he creates a point of stillness in the midst of motion, the eye is always drawn out to the more active and engaged figures in the photo. This is less a portrait of an isolated individual than a figure momentarily outside the flux of motion that swirls around him. In this he mimics the photographer who must be facing him directly, still for a moment to capture the action of the photograph and to create a "timelessness [which] emerges out of time" (15), yet about to return to the moving crowd.[15]

The photographer rarely appears in his photographs. Only in "Pavement mirror shop, Howrah, west Bengal, 1991" do we catch a glimpse of him, his face hidden behind the lens of the camera and his hands blurred in the rectangular mirror at the top center of the frame. If we are looking closely, we will notice, at the bottom and slightly to the left in a red-framed oval mirror, his camera case and bent elbow. In the assortment of mirrors on the pavement stall, people are reflected back to us in varying perspectives. It is difficult to tell where the images end and the road begins. Mirrors are layered on top of mirrors. One figure, in the corner, is divided and fragmented into two mirrors placed side by side. The scene reflects both the people and objects of street life: a bicycle, peeling posters, a potted plant, colorful print skirts hanging at a neighboring stall, the golden tiled roof of a building. The point of the mirrors is not a reflexive one. They do not reflect back to us an unreal world, a world as image or surface, a society of the simulacrum. Instead, they help cram maximal life into the photograph, adding depth and detail. None of the figures is focused on the mirrors, except Singh himself.

Among the people Singh thanks for comments on his essay is Amitav Ghosh, the Indian novelist and journalist. Ghosh returns the favor in the author's notes at the end of *The Glass Palace* (2000). There, Ghosh writes that Singh "was my mentor and my teacher in all things relating to photography. It is my great regret that I was unable to acknowledge my gratitude to him during his lifetime. If I do so now, it is not in the hope of making amends, but rather, to record an unpayable debt."[16] Ghosh critiques the logic of imperialism far more explicitly than Singh, but in his writing it is evident that he is equally committed to an internationalist and humanist vision of art and an appropriation of modernity rather than its rejection.[17] This appropriation of modernity recognizes modernity as already appropriated, already hybrid and borrowed.

It is difficult to do justice to the complex plot of Ghosh's multigenerational saga, which is set in Burma, Malaya, and India. The book tells the story of an Indian orphan, Rajkumar, working in a stall in Mandalay, and Dolly, the Burmese attendant to the queen with whom he falls in love the day the Burmese king and queen are exiled, along with their children and Dolly, to India. Rajkumar finds Dolly as an adult. Their story, as well as the stories of their friends, children, and grandchildren, spans the collapse of the British empire.

Rajkumar's grandson, Dinu, is the only artist in the book. His experiments with photography provide Ghosh with a way to address the methods, beliefs, and role of the artist. Dinu is a self-consciously modernist photographer; he brings his Rolleiflex to a Calcutta railway station because he has seen "railway shots by Alfred Stieglitz," but as he looks through the lens he says, "I think this is even better than the pictures I had in mind . . . because of all the people . . . and the movement" (274). After seeing Singh's photographs, it is difficult not to imagine Dinu's picture as one of Singh's own. His realization that the movement and bustle of the porters and tea boys adds to Stieglitz's static photograph is the melding of what Singh calls "the pictorialism of Europe and the pictorial life of Asia" (13). I am not claiming that Dinu's views belong to Ghosh; if Dinu's method as an artist is modeled on anyone, it is probably modeled on Singh, as Ghosh seems to indicate in his afterword. However, Dinu is a locus for the discussion of art in the novel. He is an observer, a witness, and one of the only characters Ghosh follows into old age. Finally, Dinu is a hero in the cultural guerilla war that he carries out in his old age from a crumbling photography studio that bears the name of Ghosh's novel.

These last chapters, especially in Dinu's speeches, seem to reflect ideas closest to Ghosh's own positions on art and freedom, and show the novel at the point where it is most gently polemic. The photographic studio contrasts sharply with the glass palace at the opening of the narrative. The glass palace is a monument to wealth and royal power, an elite and forbidden place. Dinu's glass palace, by contrast, is a crumbling apartment crowded with books and people. It is also the locus of a weekly salon, Dinu's "glass palace day." When Jaya finds the apartment and hears the voices inside, she wonders whether she has stumbled on a clandestine political meeting; then she recognizes the names of the modernist photographers Edward Weston, Eugene Atget, Brassai, and slips inside. The room is crowded with people listening to Dinu, who is sitting on an old rattan chair and lecturing on Weston's photograph of a nautilus shell. The room is ringed with books and photographic reproductions including Weston's shell, a Cartier-Bresson photograph from his trip to Asia, and "a Raghubir Singh picture of an old house in Calcutta" (507). Modernist art, and the discussion of this topic, provide Dinu with the tools for a subversive language; more accurately, it *is* a subversive language. As if anticipating a possible reader's objection, Dinu translates a piece of one of the arguments in the room for Jaya:

> "They're arguing about the picture I was talking about—Weston's nautilus . . . some of them see themselves as revolutionaries . . . they insist that aesthetic matters have no relevance to our situation . . ."
> "And what was your answer?"
> "I quoted Weston . . . Weston reflecting on Trotsky . . . that new and revolutionary art forms may awaken a people or disturb their complacency or challenge old ideas with constructive prophecies of change . . . it doesn't matter . . . every week this comes up . . . every week I say the same thing." (510)

The defense of the revolutionary role of the aesthetic against the exclusive desire for action of the revolutionary is never complete, but must be continually reiterated. Having long ago abandoned his own photography, Dinu takes the propagation of aesthetic value as his vocation.

Through Dinu, Ghosh aligns himself with the modernist insistence on the autonomy of the aesthetic realm, often as a response to or a compromise with the continued dominance of faith discourses and repressive social structures. In cases like that of Joyce, the insistence on artistic autonomy involved both a rejection of the British colonial insistence on the ownership of the English language and the nationalist Irish demands for a purified Gaelic art. Again, we see this situation echoed in Singh, who sees India's independence as the shift of patronage from the British colonialist to the Indian politician and nationalist, and who rejects both patronage systems. He cites Satyajit Ray's refusal to film a documentary on Indira Gandhi and his refusal of a seat in the Indian parliament: "'I am an artist!'—he shouted in anger, when the offer was made to him by a Bengali politician" (12). The autonomous aesthetic realm is rarely preserved without risk; Dinu's Glass Palace Studio is a subversive space, and Dinu defends not only its aesthetic but also its political value.

In his award-winning essay, "The March of the Novel through History: The Testimony of My Grandfather's Bookcase," Ghosh describes the contents of his uncle's bookcases, which lined his grandfather's walls in Calcutta. They were filled with a disparate group of international authors; Ghosh later realizes that they represented the winners of the Nobel Prize in literature. Ghosh writes:

> [T]he Nobel prize was itself symptom and catalyst for a wider condition: the emergence of the notion of a universal "literature," a form of expression that embodies differences in place and culture, emotion and aspiration, but in

such a way as to render them communicable. This idea may well have had its birth in Europe but I suspect it met with a much more enthusiastic reception outside.[18]

Ghosh describes re-encountering such a bookcase in the home of the writer Mya Than Tint. He is taken aback by the variety of Mya Than Tint's books, a collection gathered by ragpickers from the garbage of diplomats and kept despite the aggressive censorship of the Burmese regime. Incidentally, as well as achieving fame as a Burmese writer, Mya Than Tint was also a translator, a mediator between literatures through language, who translated not only Tolstoy's *War and Peace* but also *Gone with the Wind*. Readers of *The Glass Palace* will recognize this library and its unlikely genesis; Ghosh has given it to Dinu. Ghosh locates the novels on his grandfather's bookcases, and the novel itself is caught between internationalism and a particular sense of place. Ghosh concludes the essay: "It is the very vastness and cosmopolitanism of the fictional bookcase that requires novelists to locate themselves in relation to it."[19] The novel must at once be placed, and dis-placed. It must respond to the expectation and desire of an international readership and the utopian bookshelf where New York and New Delhi meet, but will only gain a place there through being what Ghosh calls "parochial," by which he means rooted in a specific location.

Ghosh's fictional bookcase includes Solzhenitsyn and Bulgakov, Bellow and Doctorow, Naipaul and García-Márquez. When writing *The Glass Palace* he claims to have self-consciously gone to the bookshelf to "look for help." Like Singh, Ghosh heralds the strategy of borrowing. When the interviewer asks Ghosh the inevitable question about Rushdie's influence, he replies that "one of the greatest things that Rushdie did was that he opened up a kind of political space where it was possible for Indian writers to exist" (*Interview* [online], Pt. I, 3). Yet Ghosh emphasizes not Rushdie's originality, but the fact that Rushdie participated in the "fabulist moment" of García-Márquez, Grass, and Pynchon and "opened up a political space where we could also work with the ways that people around us were working" (Pt. I, 3). Ghosh claims that Naipaul and James Baldwin were the writers "I read most carefully in college." He states, "For us, Naipaul was more important than Rushdie" (Pt. II, 3). Who is the "us" Ghosh is claiming? Ghosh seems implicitly to be resisting the positioning of Rushdie at the vanguard of Indian writing, and to claim that Naipaul, though less heralded, has in fact been more influential. V. S. Naipaul's clearheaded analysis of the wave of Muslim fundamentalism that has swept Asia and Africa as another, *non-European* form of colonialism has received little attention from postmodern critics.[20] In drawing attention to Naipaul, Ghosh seems to be constructing an alternative postcolonial canon far less dependent on Rushdie's influence. While Rushdie's postcolonial writing is also postmodern, a genealogy originating in Naipaul would work against the alignment of postmodern and postcolonial literature. Ghosh writes that "the postmodern kind of English language writing is so ironic. The whole effect of it is based on irony. With Indian writers there is a, sort of, very real reaching out towards emotions" (Pt. II, 6). Rushdie's writing, located more in the ironic than in the affective sphere, seems implicitly excluded. Like Singh, Ghosh rejects the postmodernism that "cocks a snook" and argues for the legitimate expression of "open, frank emotionalism" despite fear of the accusation of sentimentality. The defense of the emotional lines up with the defense of color. Singh and Ghosh both reject the postmodernist stance, postmodern irony, alienation, and distance and instead emphasize aesthetic modernism as a form of humanism. Smith notes that Singh recognized "that acceptance of his work has perhaps been helped by notions of postmodernism, but that he himself tried to play down irony, lest its facility play down other feelings."[21]

In contrast to their rejection of postmodernism, Singh's and Ghosh's appreciation of modernism is less an effect of techniques borrowed from the modernist avant-garde—though they do borrow, with both of their styles being predominantly realist—than a translation and transformation of certain modernist attitudes, and a retention of universalism and humanism.[22] Their work lines up with the mood Ann Douglas identifies in the late-modernist first generation of World War II artists, when "art and thought still seem grounded in specific geographical places and historical times; new forms, political and artistic, are believed to be possible."[23] Singh's emphasis on color and group find their correlative in Ghosh's insistence through Dinu that modernism is a way of seeing.

Singh and Ghosh at once demand the creation of a new vernacular and retain an integral link to the past that in Faulkner's words "is not dead. It is not even past." For modernist writers, the past may be a threat but it must always be reckoned with; in Eliot's *Wasteland*, in Joyce's *Ulysses*, modern art is the collision of past and present. Contrast this with the postmodernist deconstruction of history, with Eric Hobsbawm's insistence that we are losing our sense of the past, with Jameson's analysis of postmodernism as a condition of ahistoricity. In her essay "Notes on the 'Post-Colonial'" Ella Shohat critiques the inability of postmodernism to connect back to the past. She writes: "At times the anti-essentialist emphasis on hybrid identities comes dangerously close to dismissing all searched-for communitarian origins as an archeological excavation of an idealized, irretrievable past. Yet, on another level, while avoiding any nostalgia for a prelapsarian community, or for any unitary and transparent identity predating the fall, we must also ask whether it is possible to forge a collective resistance without inscribing a communal past."[24]

While Shohat insists on the necessity of the "retrieval and reinscription of a fragmented past" for communities that "have undergone brutal ruptures," she, puzzlingly, suggests the form of fragment for its reinscription:

"a notion of the past might thus be negotiated differently; not as a static, fetishized phase to be literally reproduced but as *fragmented sets of narrated memories and experiences* on the basis of which to mobilize contemporary communities."[25] In other words, Shohat trades hybridity but inserts another postmodern commonplace—the idea that fragmented narration and experience are the best way of relating (postmodern) history. Perhaps one of the reasons that the multigenerational, historical, realist novel-epic has become such a popular form for Indian writers (Seth, Ghosh, Mehta, Singh, Baldwin) is that it reconstructs the past, not in a fragmented form, which is how it has been left, but in the form of a continuous history that allows the writer to make connections between different locations and communities, and of course, between past and present. Singh and Ghosh both retain realism even as they flirt with innovation for narrative and sentimental power.

Ann Douglas writes, "Postmodernism seems to be in part a denial of postcoloniality . . . postcolonialism has the power to explain and contextualize postmodern thought, as postmodernism does not seem fully able to situate or deal with colonialism."[26] There is too much that a postmodern postcolonialism cannot comprehend; the most significant elisions seem to me to be the place of religion in postcolonial societies, especially of religious fundamentalism, and the existence of local forms of oppression, on which Naipaul and Correa have been eloquent. Finally, the postmodern denial of subjectivity holds little appeal for people who, in Fanon's words, exist in a time that "transforms spectators crushed with their inessentiality into privileged actors with the grandiose glare of history's floodlights upon them."[27] In Marshall Berman's grandly inclusive description of modernism as the attempt "to become subjects as well as object of modernization"[28] these Indian artists are still committed to the process of becoming modern, and of existing, as the introduction to this volume would have it, "somewhere between belonging and dispersion."[29] Singh and Ghosh insist on their freedom to arrange their fictional bookcases freestyle; to absorb whatever influences they will, to resist when they feel they must, to mix traditions, eras, and styles as they choose, to turn to modernism as a source of pleasure and delight, and to be, as Tagore personified art, the "solitary pedestrian, who walks alone among the multitude, continually assimilating various experiences, unclassifiable and uncatalogued."[30]

NOTES

1. Charles Correa's own architectural work is, of course, an exemplary instance of a happy marriage of modern and traditional style.
2. Max Kozloff, 96.
3. Raghubir Singh, 14.

4. *Geomodernisms*, 9.

5. In *Rethinking Modernism for the Developing World: The Complete Work of Balkrishna Doshi,* James Steele writes that the "modern models contributed by such important architects as Le Corbusier and Kahn have been of such high calibre that they have established an enduring framework or 'filter' for everything that has followed it." (Steele 8).

6. Critics of the conflation of postmodernism and postcolonialism include Kumkum Sangari (1987), Kwame Anthony Appiah (1991), Aijaz Ahmad (1997), Chidi Okonkwo (1999), and Patrick Colm Hogan (2000). The editors of *The Post-Colonial Studies Reader* insist that "the 'post' in post-colonial is not the same as the 'post' in postmodernism" (118) in their introduction to a selection of essays on the relationship between the two terms. In the anthology *Past the Last Post: Theorizing Post-Colonialism and Post-Modernism,* Linda Hutcheon argues for a significant overlap and "conjunction of concerns" between the postmodern and the postcolonial (169). Other inclusions in the anthology take a more skeptical approach to the conjunction of these two terms. The critics of the conflation of postcolonialism and postmodernism can be divided into two groups: those who, like Sangari and Appiah, believe that postmodernism continues the logic of modernism and is "just as imperious as bourgeois humanism" (Sangari 146), and those who, like Hogan, wish to argue for the continued presence and relevance of humanism in postcolonial discourse. All the critics above, including Hutcheon, agree that there is considerable divergence between the politics of postmodernism and of postcolonialism.

7. Kwame Anthony Appiah, 356.

8. Henry Louis Gates Jr., 65.

9. Arif Dirlik makes the most explicit link between postcolonial criticism and the migrant intellectual, writing that postcolonialism as currently practiced is "a discourse that seeks to constitute the world in the self-image of intellectuals who view themselves as postcolonial intellectuals" (333).

10. Singh seriously underestimates the significance of color in western tradition, conveniently eliding the medieval period in art when the colorful flat pictorialism of manuscript illumination hews very close to the art of the Indian miniature. When Singh writes that Judaism "had no sense of color and representation until as late as Chagall," he must be unaware of the illumination of *ketubot* (marriage certificates) and *megillot* (holy scrolls).

11. Singh's distinction between the British colonial photographer and the French postcolonial one is significant. There is not *one* colonizer, always certain to behave in the same malignant way, any more than there is a single colonized subject. Anne McClintock notes that "post-colonialism" is rarely "used to denote *multiplicity*"—she is concerned that the term recenters global history and risks being monolithic, a "bogus universal" (85). By contrast, David Chioni Moore concludes an essay that interrogates postcolonialist's blindness to post-Soviet studies by saying that "the colonial relation at the turn of the millennium . . . becomes as fundamental to world identities as other 'universal' categories, such as race, and class, and caste, and age, and gender" (David Chioni Moore 125).

12. P. C. Smith, 103.

13. V. S. Naipaul, "Obituary."

14. Satyajit Ray, "Foreword," *Henri Cartier-Bresson in India,* 5. One might also evoke the words of Cartier-Bresson himself, who speaks of photography as "the recognition of a rhythm in the world of real things" (Cartier-Bresson 7).

15. Henri Cartier-Bresson, whose book *The Decisive Moment* profoundly influenced Singh, writes that the photographer's aim is to "'trap' life—to preserve life in the act of living. Above all, I craved to seize the whole essence, in the confines

of one single photograph, of some situation that was in the process of unrolling itself before my eyes" (2).

16. Ghosh, *The Glass Palace*, 551.

17. Ghosh here seems to conflate modernity and modernism, perhaps agreeing with Marshall Berman that the second is a consequence of the first.

18. Ghosh, "The March of the Novel," 16.

19. Ghosh, "The March of the Novel," 23.

20. Chidi Okonkwo points out that "the spread of Islam into Africa (and Europe) by Arabs of the Arabian peninsula constitutes a colonization enterprise whose beginnings predate those of Europe and whose effects have proved equally enduring" (26).

21. Smith, 102.

22. *The Glass Palace* is in fact far less experimental than some of Ghosh's earlier work; particularly *The Calcutta Syndrome* (Toronto: Vintage, 1995), which fluctuates between a dystopic near-future and a colonial past, and *In An Antique Land* (New York: Knopf, 1993), which combines elements of travelogue, autobiography, scholarship, and fiction.

23. Ann Douglas, 84.

24. Ella Shohat, 109. Shohat's reasoning is very like that of Gyan Prakash, who writes in "Postcolonial Criticism and Indian Historiography" that the historian's goal should be "not to restore lost forms of telling and knowing but to pick apart the disjunctive moments" (17).

25. Shohat, 111.

26. Ann Douglas, 73.

27. Frantz Fanon, *Wretched of the Earth*, 14.

28. Marshall Berman, *All That Is Solid Melts into Air: The Experience of Modernity*, 5.

29. *Geomodernisms*, 4.

30. Rabindrath Tagore, *Angel of Surplus: Some Essays and Addresses in Aesthetics*, 38.

PART TWO

Modernisms' Contested States

7   Twentieth-Century Chinese Modernism and Globalizing Modernity: Three Auteur Directors of Taiwan New Cinema

Sung-sheng Yvonne Chang

Modernism in twentieth-century Chinese literature has belatedly been entered as a topic for scholarly discourse in the West, witnessed in part by the publication in the last decade or so of three books in English devoted to the subject: my own book *Modernism and the Nativist Resistance: Contemporary Chinese Fiction from Taiwan* (1993); Xudong Zhang's *Chinese Modernism in the Era of Reforms: Cultural Fever, Avant-garde Fiction, and the New Chinese Cinema* (1997); and Shu-mei Shih's *The Lure of the Modern: Writing Modernism in Semicolonial China, 1917–1937* (2001). An important observation to be made here, however, is that these are not studies of different phases of a single, overarching movement, but rather of three separate instances of modernist literary trends that have occurred in modern Chinese history, in three distinct historical epochs. Shih tackles the notion of modernism in terms of Chinese literature in the middle period of China's Republican Era (1911–49), during which the Nationalist government nominally united the whole country, torn by warlords and "semi-colonial" imperialist rule, through consolidating its power in central China, with such coastal cities as Nanking and Shanghai as its political and economic base. My book focuses on the U.S.-influenced flourish of modernist literature in Taiwan during the 1960s and 1970s, where the Nationalist-ruled Republic of China resettled after losing sovereignty of the mainland China to the communists in 1949. Finally, Zhang's study treats the more recent modernist phenomenon in the post-Mao era of the People's Republic of China (PRC)—founded on mainland China by the Chinese Communist Party in 1949—when the regime rescinded the socialist system after the debacle of the Cultural Revolution (1966–76).

    Separated by war and revolution, and each entangled with specific epochal politics, these three modernist waves were essentially independent developments, with very little direct or indirect lineage to speak of. Nonetheless, the fact that modernism has always "come back" to influence the same cultural and linguistic site within the larger historical frame of "modern China" invites us to probe more deeply into the question of continuity beyond actual contacts. The first part of this chapter considers some broad implications of the patent structural affinities found in these modernist trends, both within the Chinese contexts and in relation to Western modernism's global spread. The focus is on how artistic modernism, taken out of its original context, was re-embedded in the Chinese cultural field under its own peculiar cultural logic. This logic includes the ongoing transformation of "literature" into a modern institution, and the tug-of-war between political and cultural legitimacies within the cultural field. Both of these legitimacies are dictated by a "high culture" imperative, which in turn is closely associated with the notion of Chinese modernity.

Toward the end of the twentieth century, some dramatic transformations occurred in the general cultural system in both Taiwan and the PRC, causing the influences of the last two modernist trends to be largely dispersed and fragmented in these societies' market-dominated cultural milieus. While after this Great Divide individual artists continue to employ modernist thematic tropes and aesthetic conventions, their appropriation of modernism now is no longer driven by some prominent collective agenda. The second part of this chapter illustrates this phenomenon by examining works of three auteur directors of the Taiwan New Cinema. Modernism, no longer an integral part of the local cultural landscape in Taiwan today, functions as a useful tool for these individual artists to insert themselves into the restructured global cultural system.

MODERNISM AND CHINA'S CONVOLUTED COURSE OF MODERNIZATION

Of the three texts about Chinese modernist literature mentioned above, only my own pays primary attention to the "literary modernism." The other two authors define *modernism* more comprehensively to encompass a wider range of cultural responses to the conditions of modernity. This difference may of course be explained by the fact that Taiwan's modernist trend sustained a longer tenure and hence acquired a more distinct status in the literary universe. However, even Taiwan's modernist literature is so deeply entrenched in the overall sociopolitical milieu as to require a more holistic treatment, a subject explored in my later book, *Literary Culture in Taiwan: Martial Law to Market Law* (2004). Similarly, Leo Ou-fan Lee's *Shanghai Modern: the Flowering of a New Urban Culture in China, 1930–1945* (1999) and Jing Wang's *High Culture Fever: Politics, Aesthetics, and Ideology in Deng's China* (1996), which cover roughly the same periods as those in Shih's and

Zhang's studies, also treat the Chinese modernist trends within the larger historical contexts.

By and large, newer approaches to "Chinese modernism" are moving away from the conventional influence–reception model, with its potentially demeaning implication that Chinese modernism is in some sense "derivative" or "inauthentic." At the same time, aided by postcolonial and postmodern discourses, recent scholarship has favored more local-centered definitions of Chinese modernity, as witnessed by the popularity of such terms as *alternative modernity, repressed modernity, colonial modernity,* and *translated modernity.*[1]

These critical paradigms have definitive advantages over the New Critical style text-centered approach that had dominated Chinese literary studies in previous decades. But the enlargement of the scope of inquiry to include sociopolitical dimensions has also resulted in methodological infelicities, many of them deriving from the lack of distinction between the more specific, artistic dimension of modernism and that which is denoted by the more inclusive definition of the term.[2]

The Contextual Approach

I would therefore like to stress the importance of a more refined, theoretically sound conceptual framework in discussing the relationship of literature to the conditions of Chinese modernity. First and foremost, it is useful to perceive the modernist literary trend as one particular artistic formation, competing and interacting with other formations within the field of cultural production. The cultural field, following Pierre Bourdieu, is governed by its own internal laws, while at the same time it is embedded in the society's general field of power, in particular the political and economic power.

There is a patently intimate relationship between the modernist artistic formation's positional struggles within the cultural universe and the "real" politics generated by Chinese societies' torturous and convoluted course of modernization. It is worth noting that all three Chinese modernist trends occurred in historical periods during which the Chinese government (either the nationalist or the communist) launched a modernization program after the capitalist model with Western assistance. The reasons are obvious. In these periods—i.e., the mid-Republican, post-1949 Taiwan, and post-Mao China—communication channels with the outside world were more widely open; Western-educated and bilingual intellectuals occupied influential positions in the society; and cultural agents in general gained easier access, through translation or other forms of mediation, to creative works and aesthetic doctrines (in this case, modernist works and aesthetic conceptions) that had been consecrated in the metropolitan West.

Despite a climate conducive to the importation of modernism, resistance existed. Each modernist trend was heralded by a ground-clearing debate in the public sphere over the relative merits of "traditional Chinese civilization" and "Western civilization" (*zhongxi wenhua lunzhan*). But this battle was relatively easy to win, given the fact that the legitimacy of Western culture had already been firmly established in the earlier part of the twentieth century, through the May Fourth new culture movement (roughly between 1919 and 1927). Under the movement's two banners, *qimeng* (enlightenment) and *jiuwang* (national salvation), Western civilization was deemed as possessing the power to enlighten the Chinese people and thus could enable them to rescue the nation from dismemberment by the imperial powers. In these opening rituals of the "China versus the West" debate, radical voices advocating "wholesale Westernization" (*quanpan xihua*) were heard through such famous spokesmen as Hu Shi, Li Ao, and Liu Xiaobo. Emboldened by their self-denying gestures, writers and artists launched earnest re-examinations and harsh critiques of the traditional social relations, ethics, and such longstanding institutions as Confucianism, helping to set a basic "modernist" tenor for what subsequently unfolded in the literary arena.

The more formidable resistance to the modernist trend came from nationalist-minded left-wing intellectuals. Shortly after the May Fourth movement came an ideological split in the intellectual community, resulting in political struggles between the nationalists and the communists, and transformed into a prolonged tug between the capitalist and the socialist models of modernization. Modernism became linked with liberal ideology, capitalist economy, individualism, cosmopolitanism, and pro-West diplomacy; while "sino-realism," or a modified version of nineteenth-century European realism, was sanctified by the leftist intellectuals who espoused socialist ideology, egalitarian economic principles, collectivism, local nationalism, and an anti-imperialist agenda. Numerous particularly militant and embittered "literary debates" and factional feuds within the literary sphere surrounding these two -*isms* were not at all concerned with the aesthetic issues. They were rather thinly disguised political struggles between two ideological camps that embraced different models for modernizing China.

It is an understatement to say that the modern Chinese literary sphere is enormously politically charged; in Bourdieu's terms, there has been a high degree of interpenetration between the political field and the field of cultural production. At times, such as during the Cultural Revolution, the two were completely collapsed. It was no surprise, therefore, that just as the three modernist literary trends were facilitated by the government's launch of capitalist modernization, they were also brought to sharp decline by brute forces in the political realm. The first wave of Chinese modernism was cut short by the outbreak of the Sino-Japanese war in 1937. The second, in post-1949 Taiwan, was disrupted in 1977–78 by a nativist literary debate, which culminated a trend of cultural resistance triggered by Taiwan's forced resignation from the United Nations in 1972. Finally, the 1989 Tiananmen Incident abruptly ended a decade of reformist intellectual fermentation in post-Mao China, in which the modernist literary trend played a pivotal role.

The Institutional Dimension

The foregoing discussion demonstrates how deeply the Chinese modernist trends were embedded in the society's general field of power, which was driven by contending forces that pushed for modernization through either the development of capitalist economy or a socialist vision of modernity. There is, however, another dimension of Chinese modernism, the institutional dimension, that more directly connects it to the global expansion of modernity in general, and the spread of artistic modernism to the non-West in particular. I will approach this topic with conceptual frameworks provided by Anthony Giddens, in *The Consequences of Modernity*, and Pierre Bourdieu, in *The Field of Cultural Production*.

Giddens gives a ballpark definition of modernity as follows: " 'modernity' refers to modes of social life or organization which emerged in Europe from about the seventeenth century onwards and which subsequently became more or less worldwide in their influence."[3] Underlining the inherently globalizing tendency of modernity, he carefully tracks the relationship between major dimensions of globalization (including the nation-state system, world capitalist system, international division of labor, and world military order) through four "uniquely modern" institutions: surveillance, capitalism, industrialism, and military power.[4] Yet I would add that literature—I will use this form to stand for other cultural genres in this discussion—as we know it today can be appropriately regarded as a modern social institution, a sub-institution of capitalism for that matter, in the sense that the production, dissemination, and consumption of literature today are increasingly dependent on the publishing industry, which is ultimately conditioned by the logic underlying "capital accumulation in the context of competitive labor and product markets."[5]

Bourdieu's analysis underlines this point. In outlining the development of the modern field of cultural production in nineteenth-century France, Bourdieu says that intellectual and artistic life in that country had progressively freed itself from the domination of external sources of legitimacy, namely the aesthetic and ethical demands of the court or the church in the preceding centuries, and had steadily marched toward greater autonomy.[6] Embedded in the larger field of political and economic power, the cultural field thereafter unfolded as a site of constant struggle between two opposing principles of legitimacy, the *autonomous* and the *heteronomous*—exemplified respectively by the art-for-art's-sake principle of "pure art" and the commercial logic followed by best-sellers. The rise of "pure art," and the advocacy of absolute non-utilitarianism, was a reaction against the commoditization tendency of the market.

In China the development of literature as a modern institution was extremely convoluted in the twentieth century, as the entrenchment of modern forms of culture industry were repeatedly disrupted by civil war, foreign invasion, and the communist revolution. Usually, the literary field was governed by legitimacy principles quite different from those focused on by Bourdieu in the French case.

Facing imminent threats from imperial aggression, the founders of modern Chinese literature and their successors in the May Fourth movement projected a "high culture" role for literature as a vehicle to enlighten the people and build China into a modern nation-state. Their legacy persisted: literary discourses in modern China were overburdened by this agenda, making writing practices highly susceptible to appropriations by both the government's cultural control and the intellectual's political resistance. The principle of political legitimacy therefore dominated the modern Chinese cultural field.

At the same time, the institutional dimension of literature inevitably subjected its modes of production, circulation, and consumption to the workings of the modern culture industry. Rather than pursuing an *autonomous* principle of legitimacy in literature and the arts, however, the Chinese cultural agents were in quest of a properly cultural legitimacy principle with enough potency both to contain and to rival the dominant discourses within their own cultural universe. Artistic modernism, I argue, well answered this need. Consecrated in the metropolitan West, modernism was perceived as the most "advanced" form of art in a linear evolutionary model. Modernist literature and art compared favorably to traditional art with contents and forms supposedly determined by the rhythms of modern life, and enjoyed a competitive edge over the technically crude leftist works. As scholars have repeatedly pointed out, behind the Chinese cultural agents' fascination with modernism was a nationalistically motivated desire to modernize Chinese aesthetic sensibilities.

There was, therefore, a significant political dimension to the Chinese modernist trend, despite its palpable goal to replace political legitimacy with cultural legitimacy. Different from the institution of "pure art" that developed in the West with the rise of bourgeois capitalism, the "artistic autonomy" espoused by the Chinese modernists (e.g., the *xiandai pai*, or the modernist school in Taiwan; the *menglong shi*, or "misty poetry," the *xungen pai*, or the "root-seekers" and the fifth-generation filmmakers in post-Mao China) functioned primarily to critique the politically instituted dominant culture and to be a ground for resisting political interference and mobilization. In the heydays of the last two Chinese modernist trends, namely the 1960s and 1970s in Taiwan and the 1980s in the PRC, modernist artists were close allies of, and deeply influenced by, the country's vigorous liberal intellectuals. Pitted against authoritarian governments that rushed economic modernization while withholding political reform, Chinese liberal intellectuals welcomed the imported modernist aesthetics and their underlying ideological assumptions, and strategically used them as tools for challenging the state monopoly of legitimate cultural discourse. This alliance and symbiotic relationship between modernist artists and liberal intellectuals produced perhaps the best examples of literary and cinematic works in modern Chinese history; these are fully documented in the scholarly works, mentioned above, on these periods.

A New Genealogy

Incorporating the institutional perspective enables us to consider the "continuity" between the three separated instances of Chinese modernism in a meaningful way. As mentioned earlier, the first modernist wave was disrupted by the outbreak of Sino-Japanese war (1937–45). Recent scholarship has demonstrated how this eight-year, all-out "resistance war" caused mass relocation of cultural agents and the breakdown of cultural and publishing establishments in the urban centers. More important, the writers' patriotic war participation activities shifted the power of cultural control into the hands of paramilitary personnel, and a wartime model of literary mobilization and censorship was developed.[7] This legacy was carried over through the civil war (1945–49) and continued to exert strong influence in the Chinese cultural fields after 1949, in both the PRC and Taiwan.

Viewed from this perspective, the second modernist wave experienced by Taiwan in the 1960s, and the third wave felt in mainland China in the 1980s, occurred at times of marked relaxation of the collective, paramilitary control of literary production. These waves corresponded with the resumption of the cultural field's progression toward greater autonomy and the cultural agents' quest for new principles of cultural legitimacy to govern the field. Fulfilling better the field's own intrinsic logic, artistic modernism significantly aided in its process of moving away from political subjugation. These two spots in history nurtured an impressive number of accomplished artists.

This "golden age" of Chinese modernism, however, was again short-lived, a phenomenon that, in hindsight, may be explained by the accelerated speed with which the Chinese cultural fields raced toward a market-authorized autonomy. Although on the surface the fever for modernism in Taiwan of the 1960s and mainland China of the 1980s was quenched by such high-visibility events as the nativist debate and the Tiananmen Incident, what really had stunted the growth of the modernist trends was the internal transformation of the structure of the field, generated by the rapid advancement of capitalist modernization. Receiving a boost by the lifting of martial law in Taiwan in 1987 and Deng Xiaoping's south China tour in 1992, the Chinese cultural fields on both sides of the Taiwan Strait became more differentiated, specialized, and professionalized in the last decade of the twentieth century. The shift of academic interest to the new category of "popular culture" dealt a considerable blow to modernism—its elitist, high-culture image was now tarnished and had almost become a stigma.

In sum, the introduction of modernism into Chinese societies was inextricably intertwined with the spread of market-dependent literary institutions as part of a globalizing modernity. Prior to the 1990s, the contextual dimension of Chinese modernism (namely, how it functioned as an artistic formation interacting with multiple layers of forces at the local level and partaking in the general process of societal modernization) was of paramount importance. And the Chinese artists' employment of modernistic thematic tropes and aesthetic conceptions was to a high degree determined by specific dynamics and governing laws within the Chinese cultural field. Previous scholarship had often evoked the notion of "transplantation" (*yizhi*) to highlight this "glocalization" phenomenon. Further dwelling on this metaphor, the fact that the Chinese modernist trend either was aborted prematurely or had developed within a compressed timetable, typically consumed within a span of ten to fifteen years, had made it difficult for modernism to firmly take roots in the Chinese soil.

But this is not the whole story. Even after the Great Divide that occurred in about the late 1980s and early 1990s in both Taiwan and mainland China, the question of Chinese modernism still remains relevant, but must now be examined within a different frame of reference. In short, the practice of artistic modernism has become dispersed and fragmented, more of an individual affair, the result of yet another momentous change in the institutional environment of cultural production.

MODERNISM AND THE TAIWAN NEW CINEMA IN AN ERA OF INTENSIFIED GLOBALIZATION

Whereas the last two modernist trends in Taiwan and post-Mao China had already faded by the 1990s, the residual influences have lingered on, finding outlets in certain individuals or cohorts of artists. This phenomenon is explained by some fundamental changes in the institutional environment of creative practices after the Great Divide at about the turn of the 1990s. In mainland China, the privatization of the culture industry has unleashed formidable forces of mass consumption, creating a sense of crisis among cultural agents engaging in more elitist forms of artistic pursuit. In Taiwan, the more differentiated, specialized, and professionalized cultural field, bearing greater resemblance to that of advanced capitalist societies, is now populated by aggressive cultural brokers and calculating artists busily adapting to the new rules of the game. In short, the market is propelling the progression of the cultural field toward greater autonomy in both places, successfully reducing direct political interferences while marginalizing "elitist" artistic endeavors. Halos surrounding modernism, previously valued for its potency in combating political dominance, are disappearing. No longer a viable artistic formation in the cultural field, the modernist trend has begun to fragment and disperse, retaining its grip on fewer members of the community.

Unexpectedly, however, classic modernist themes and aesthetics are given a new role to play in the current era, thanks to the intensifying globalization process. That postsocialist (mainland) China and post-martial-law Taiwan are particularly susceptible to influences of global capitalism has to do with the political regimes' reform policies featuring centrally the economic liberalization. Whereas a diversity of cultural products on the global marketplace have become available for domestic consumption, some Chinese cultural products are also entering the international market.[8] Cinematic products, including works of the fifth-generation directors from mainland China and the Taiwan New Cinema, not to mention the more popular genres of Hong Kong films, have played a vanguard role in this process. For our purpose, the case of Taiwan New Cinema is of particular interest, as artistic modernism has played a vital role in shaping the individual styles of its best-known representatives: auteur directors Hou Hsiao-hsien, Tsai Ming-liang, and Edward Yang. Before more detailed discussions of their works, a brief introduction of the Taiwan New Cinema movement is in order.

Taiwan New Cinema

Taiwan New Cinema arose around 1982–83, as part of the cross-regional Chinese New Wave cinematic trend that took place in a staggered manner in Hong Kong, Taiwan, and mainland China since the late 1970s. Within the context of Taiwan, this trend received impetus from the coming of age of the baby boom generation of artists and the disintegration of the ruling Nationalist regime's ideological domination. One significant source of influence was the nativist literary movement of the previous decade, which called upon artists to get out of the ivory tower and pay greater attention to contemporary Taiwanese sociopolitical reality. There was also an important chance element: the Party-owned Central Motion Pictures Corporation, formerly a government propaganda machine, adopted a new policy and supported serious-minded young filmmakers as part of its desperate attempt to salvage Taiwan's bankrupting film industry. The movement was initially a middle-class affair, catering to Taiwan's rather homogeneous mainstream audience through a mixture of nativist realism and sentimental melodrama. However, some of its members, notably Hou Hsiao-hsien and Edward Yang (Yang Dechang), harbored a high-culture agenda bearing definitive imprints of the earlier modernist literary trend.

Then a turning point came in the late 1980s, around the lifting of martial law in 1987, as accomplishments of individual Taiwan New Cinema directors began to be recognized outside Taiwan. Like many other third world film cinemas, Taiwan New Cinema entered the sphere of transnational cinema through the international film festival circuit, making its debut with Hou Hsiao-hsien's now classic *City of Sadness*.[9] Also characteristic of such transnational cultural phenomena in a postcolonial era, the Taiwan New Cinema's rise to international fame had a distinctive political edge. A decade after its re-emergence, the mainland Chinese government began more aggressively to pressure members of the international community to reject Taiwan's national status (PRC considers Taiwan, or formally the Republic of China, a renegade province, and to this date Taiwan is still denied membership in most international organizations, including the World Health Organization [WHO], which became a focus of controversy during the SARS outbreak in 2003). Increasingly isolated, the Taiwan government enlisted services from its cultural agents. That the international film festival was seen as a venue for Taiwan's struggle to expand its "international living space" benefited the Taiwan New Cinema filmmakers in more than one way. Most of their products—even such daringly transgressive works as Tsai Ming-liang's *The River* that touches on the incest taboo—received government subsidies. The government-funded annual trips to film festivals across the globe further allowed the New Cinema filmmakers to gain exposure, build connections, and eventually find their niche in the global art-film circle.

The Taiwan New Cinema filmmakers' penchant for modernist tropes and aesthetics, a legacy of Taiwan's own modernist trend, helped initially to position them in the global art-film circle.[10] In the meantime, in Taiwan's more thoroughly commercialized domestic market, this same tendency gave their films a "box-office poison"—even critics who used to champion the New Cinema now fault them for their arrogance and "self-indulgent" elitist pursuit. Before long, the more established auteur directors—chiefly Hou, Yang, and Tsai—turned to foreign funding sources for their production, and no longer targeted their films primarily at Taiwan's mainstream moviegoers. In a typical scenario of cultural globalization, these auteur directors have been "lifted out" of their local context and have been "re-embedded" in a transnational cultural system.[11] The taste of global art-house film audience has necessitated even deeper assimilation of "classic modernism" by these directors, forcing them to employ modernist thematic tropes and formal devices in original ways. In the process, they are given excellent opportunities to offer personally meaningful aesthetic reflections on the arrival of a capitalist modernity in a former third world region toward the end of the twentieth century.

Hou Hsiao-hsien (b. 1947)

Whereas stylistic lyricism has been a distinctive feature of Hou's cine-matic work as a whole, for the domestic audience of the early products of Taiwan New Cinema what stood out even more prominently was a "na-tivist humanism": *Boys from Feng-kuei* (1983) and *Dust in the Wind* (1985) dealt with straitened plights of youngsters who have moved to the city from the rural areas during Taiwan's economic takeoff; *Dust* and *A Time to Live and A Time to Die* (1985) used the Min-nan and Hakka dialects and reflected Taiwan's polyethnic and multilingual reality that previous films had tried to ignore for reasons of political propaganda. Hou's works of this period are also subtly political. Tacitly endorsing the nativist champi-ons' critical views on the ills of capitalist modernization, a preoccupation of the ruling regime, Hou often made critical insinuations about the au-thoritarian nationalist government's self-delusional political myths, and its "successful" use of culture as a tool of ideological indoctrination. Im-mediately following the lifting of martial law, then, Hou used the hitherto taboo February 28 Incident of 1947—a historical trauma in which the na-tionalist army massacred tens of thousands of native Taiwanese in sup-pression of a riot—as background to state his powerful condemnation of the encroachment of politics onto individual lives.

In one sense, Hou's work in the first half of the 1990s, in particular the historical trilogy—*City, The Puppetmaster* (1993), and *Good Men Good Women* (1995)—continued to participate in Taiwanese intellectuals' collective en-deavor to retell a history distorted in official narratives. While this the-matic dimension has been widely discussed, for our purpose Hou's evolu-tion toward purer aestheticism at the expense of popular audience appeal still deserves close scrutiny. The excessive use of Hou's hallmark "long take" technique in *The Puppetmaster*, the intricate play with narrative con-ventions in *Good Men Good Women*, and the fragmentary plot lines in *South Goodbye South* (1996) turned away local moviegoers, while allegedly elicit-ing only a lukewarm reception from the film festival's more aesthetics-savvy audience. Even Peggy Chiao, influential critic of Chinese-language cinema and Hou's longtime promoter, was displeased with this develop-ment.

Hou's movement toward the pole of "pure form" culminated in his 1998 *Flowers of Shanghai*, a piece of exquisitely executed showmanship that has drawn polarized reception even from the art-film audience. Adapted from a late Qing dynasty popular novel, the film comprises a series of ro-mantic entanglements between courtesans and their wealthy patrons, set in high-class brothels of Shanghai's British concession in the late nine-teenth century. Ostensibly devoid of direct local references to Taiwan, the film bears distinctive imprints of its cultural politics and the ideological makeup of Hou's artistic cohort—namely, mainstream artists of the baby boom generation who have internalized the nationalist-instituted, conservative, conformist, and neotraditionalist dominant culture in the martial law period. As the nationalist-endorsed sinocentric cultural ideology is severely debunked by supporters of the ascending Taiwanese nationalism in post-martial-law Taiwan, middle-aged artists like Hou and his long-time partner, screenwriter Zhu Tianwen, find themselves in a painfully ambivalent position. Artistic modernism functions to empower them with its potent cultural legitimacy, while at the same time allowing them to make an oblique political statement. *Flowers,* in particular, embodies an "aesthetics of the commonplace" that celebrates the mundane reality of everyday life and upholds the benign elements of human nature—a central element in the nationalists' official literary discourse (as part of its anticommunist strategy). The film's highly refined and stunningly beautiful rendition of what is trivial and inconsequential emphatically foregrounds the notion of modernist aestheticism, as ordinary experience is translated into *style,* a privileged source of meaning. At the same time, with fastidious attention to the quotidian reality and social mannerism, the film transforms the exotic nineteenth-century brothel house into something intimate and familiar, pregnant with quintessentially humane qualities.

Different aspects of this particular aesthetic ideology have been articulated on several occasions in Hou's films and in the fictional work of Zhu Tianwen, who plays a crucial role in Hou's artistic development. For instance, in *The Puppetmaster,* a film based on the biography of legendary folk artist Li Tianlu, the real-life puppeteer comes on the screen and tells an anecdote: in the chaotic lawlessness of the first days following the Japanese surrender to the Allies in 1945, he often joined other fellow Taiwanese to loot a fallen airplane. And the proletarian folk artist goes on righteously to defend himself: the money he got from selling its parts was the only means to enable him to carry on his puppet performance, and to deliver the gift of art to the Taiwanese people. Or, in the concluding passage of Zhu's highly acclaimed 1994 novel *Notes of a Desolate Man,* the gay protagonist Xiao Shao finds that the only way to overcome existential nihilism is to continue writing. One sees strong echoes of modernistic aestheticism in both the affirmation of art as possessing values beyond the mundane law and morality, and the attribution to the creative act of writing a quasi-religious redemptive power. Such aesthetic notions are easily traced to Taiwan's own modernist literary trend in the works of its representatives such as Wang Wenxing and Li Yongping, who have dedicated exceedingly long periods of time to linguistic and formal experimentation and whose fiction is underscored by distinctive modernist ideology.[12]

With the exception of *Flowers,* the majority of Hou's films in the 1990s—*Good Men Good Woman, South Goodbye South,* and *Millennium Mambo* (2001)—are specifically concerned with the confused and confounded state of being that was experienced by individuals thrown into the quicksand of fin de siècle Taiwan. Showing profound sympathy for vulnerable, emotion-

ally wounded individuals living on the margin of prosperous contemporary Taiwan society, these films echo the 1970s nativist criticism of an approaching capitalist modernity. And I can characterize Hou's particular
response to modernity with the aid of a taxonomy given by Anthony Giddens. In *The Consequences of Modernity,* Giddens lists four types of "adaptive
reactions to risk profile of modernity"—"pragmatic acceptance," "cynical
pessimism," "sustained optimism," and "radical engagement"[13]—which I
interpret somewhat more broadly as "responses to the negative impact
of modernity on our life world." Hou's reaction to the negative consequences of modernity may be appropriately described as one of "pragmatic
acceptance"—only he has channeled the bitter sentiments of sympathy
and powerlessness generated in this involuntary process into something
vicariously empowering: the modernist aesthetics that allows him to create
a substitution-text for life, in which the troubling realities of modern life
are captured, frozen, and transformed into sources of pleasure for the cultured audience. In the following sections I will also consider Tsai Ming-
liang's and Edward Yang's attitudes toward the question of modernity in
relation to Giddens's other categories.

Tsai Ming-liang (b. 1957)

If the majority of Hou's films are rich in exuberant details with vivid references to Taiwan's sociopolitical history, Tsai Ming-liang's work has a
minimalist outlook and easily lends itself to parabolic readings. The mon-
strosity of the modern city, emblematic of capitalist modernity, is a theme
that runs through all his films: *Rebels of the Neon God* (1992), *Vive L'Amour*
(1994, a Golden Horse winner), *The River* (1997), *The Hole* (1998), and *What
Time Is It There?* (2001). The affluent metropolitan setting of these films is
a far cry from the bleak scenes of poverty-stricken slums seen in works of
the Taiwan New Cinema in the 1980s. If characters in those earlier human-
istic films are often overburdened with social (especially family) responsibilities of the traditional type, Tsai's films are populated by agonized mo-
nads in anxious, but futile, search for meaningful human contact, a theme
effectively conveyed in his award-winning *Vive L'Amour* through a "motif
of displacement." The main characters are three well-dressed "homeless"—
a new species in a city with skyrocketing real estate prices—who take temporary lodging in an empty apartment that Mei, a real estate agent, is
trying to sell. The gay loner Hsiao-kang, whose job is to distribute adver-
tisement flyers for a columbarium, rings the doorbell to make sure that *no
one is in* before entering the luxurious apartment with a stolen key. Mei's
alarm clock fakes the crowing of a rooster, a once-familiar sound no longer
part of the background noise for city folks rising in the morning. And,
of course, the empty apartment, in which the characters dine, bathe, do
laundry, attempt suicide, daydream, make love, and masturbate, is only a
phony replacement of the real *home,* something the characters deeply yearn

for. Tsai uses the device to call attention to what are conspicuously absent in the characters' lives—home, and more permanent interpersonal relationships—to underscore the salient modernist theme of alienation.

What are the implications of a Chinese artist making such "classic" modernist films nearly half a century after the heydays of their Western models? In an interview, Tsai suggested that having grown up in a backwater region of Malaysia and having moved to Taiwan during the economic boom to personally witness its runaway urban expansion made him particularly sensitive to how drastically capitalist modernity transforms our life world. That Tsai studied Western drama in college and directed Sartre's plays perhaps help to explain why he has chosen to depict this recent arrival in Taiwan of an alienating, dehumanizing modern condition in familiar terms of classic modernism. Sure enough, there are numerous echoes of the early-to-mid-twentieth-century existentialist literature in Tsai's later films, *The River, The Hole,* and *What Time Is It There?* In particular, the apocalyptic, doomsday scenario and biblical symbolisms that imply sin and salvation through providence are so palpably alien to the native Chinese tradition that they are clearly "borrowed" tropes.

Younger than the first generation of Taiwan New Cinema filmmakers, Tsai began his film career in the early 1990s, when Taiwanese cinema was already drawing international attention. His emulation and mastery of a highly consecrated Western artistic tradition quickly earned him recognition and respect in the international art-film circle. And the increasingly self-referential quality of his later films further invokes a time-honored modernistic device that has been valorized in that circle. The insertion, in *The Hole,* of surrealistic dance scenes in the style of 1950s Hong Kong musicals and, in *What Time Is It There?* of clips from François Truffaut's *Four Hundred Blows* pays homage to and acknowledges both Chinese and Western sources of inspiration for his own art.

Tsai, therefore, has consciously structured his personal reflection of a "belated" modernity in artistic terms recognizable to a global audience, coding his cinematic representation in established modernist tropes. This practice of conscious imitation cannot but be imbued with a quality of parody, which reinforces the cynicism implied in Tsai's pessimistic vision of modern life: its psychological vacuity, the latent threat of large-scale catastrophe beyond human control, and the erosive power of physical decay that is part of our daily existence. I therefore characterize the informing spirit of Tsai's work as "cynical pessimism," à la Giddens.[14]

Edward Yang (b. 1947)

Even after the Taiwan New Cinema moved into the transnational space, the Taiwanese locality is still very much foregrounded, whether in Hou's national epics or Tsai's urban parables. Since the mid-1990s, however, there has been a subtle mutation of this thematic core; *Flowers*, for instance, is set in late-imperial China, and about half of Tsai's *What Time Is It There?* was shot in Paris. The latest Taiwan New Cinema products, therefore, increasingly display a universalism that tends to vitiate the very particularities associated with its nominal identifier, "Taiwan." This tendency may be accounted for by another crucial factor: that is, Taipei, the object of representation in most of these films, was already very much a postmodern "global city" by the end of the twentieth century. This is eminently obvious in Edward Yang's latest masterpiece, *Yi Yi* (*A One and a Two*): the upper-middle-class Taiwanese in the film go by English names, work for transnational corporations, invest in American mutual funds and Yahoo! stocks, and make frequent trips between Taipei and the United States, Japan, and mainland China.

In this film, Yang has revisited some distinctively modernistic themes and devices that have appeared and reappeared ever since such early films as *That Day, on the Beach* (1983) and *The Terrorizer* (1986). The emotional crisis experienced by N.J.'s wife Min-min and his old girlfriend Sherry, for instance, is conveyed by visually powerful scenes shot with Yang's hallmark "reflection" technique. In these scenes, both women are literally "drowned" by glittering fluorescent images of cityscapes, of Taipei and Tokyo respectively, that have penetrated into the interior space through the buildings' glass walls. The film also recapitulates such motifs as the sudden attack of existentialist angst, and confused or misguided self-quest that leads to accidental death in suicide or murder. However, comparing *Yi Yi* with those earlier works of Taiwan's modernist literary movement that treat similar themes, such as Chen Yingzhen's 1967 short story "My First Case,"[15] one gets a clear sense of evolution. Most notably, in *Yi Yi* Yang introduces a positive character type—represented by Ata, a Japanese software engineer, and Yang Yang (standing for Edward Yang?), N.J.'s eight-year-old son—to launch his critique of contemporary Taiwan society and offer an answer to the confused spiritual quest that torments many of his characters.

Yang's engineering background—he has earned a master's degree in electrical engineering from the University of Florida—may have contributed to his insight about the detrimental impact of the combination of two major modern institutions, capitalism and industrialism. As a link in the global production chain of information technology (Taiwan supplies a high percentage of the world's personal computers), Taiwan is caught in ferocious competition internationally and domestically, and one surviving strategy many have resorted to is piracy (N.J.'s company lost its business to a "copycat" of Japanese software). The film, however, shows that the people of Taiwan have paid a price for economic prosperity: spiritual impoverishment, hollow lifestyles, and loss of moral integrity. Ata, the idealized Japanese character, serves as a sharp contrast to their spiritual dilemma. While versed in high culture (he is a talented pianist), Ata also maintains a harmonious relationship with nature, due to his sincere guilelessness (as revealed when pigeons, feeling safe, rest on his shoulders). He assumes the aura of a "wise man from the Orient" with the dictum: "Life shouldn't be that complicated." Most important, he envisions the possibility of enhancing humanity through technological innovation, observing that virtual-reality technology has so far only produced fighting and killing video games because "we humans do not understand ourselves."

The characterization of N.J.'s son Yang Yang, the would-be philosopher, scientist, and artist, completes the director's positivistic vision of scientific creativity as part of modern life. The young boy "experiments" in the bathtub for ingenious ways to resolve problems he encounters in everyday life, such as getting revenge on the evil school master. He once makes a stack of photos of the back of people's heads, to show them half of the reality that "they themselves could never see." And, in the funeral service scene that concludes the film, Yang Yang reads a letter to the deceased grandmother, telling her that he has figured out a way to make his life meaningful after growing up: "I would like to show people what they cannot see." This scene can be readily interpreted as the auteur director's comment on his own career motive, as an affirmation of the value of his own pursuit in cinematic art. In light of the film's repeated equation of visual access to human knowledge, the boy's wish points to the quest for an ideal combination of technology and humanity. That the film ultimately evokes Enlightenment ideas of self-knowledge and providential reason as possible correctives for the spiritual malaise in contemporary Taiwan reveals a fundamentally rational and optimistic attitude toward modernity.[16] Yang's particular vision of modernity thus seems to be closer to the "sustained optimism" on Giddens's list.[17]

CONCLUSION

Viewed within a larger context, the three Chinese modernist trends in the twentieth century all took place in historical periods of government-endorsed capitalist modernization through Western assistance, and part of their valence came from the attendant, imported ideologies, such as liberalism and Enlightenment rationalism. As an artistic formation within the cultural field, the modernist trend was deeply immersed in the Chinese intellectuals' high culture quest, and enjoyed a competitive edge in the field's struggle between "cultural legitimacy principles" and "political legitimacy principles." The latter, for historical reasons, dominated the modern Chinese cultural field. The situation has drastically changed in both mainland China and Taiwan since the late 1980s and early 1990s. Dramatic political and economic liberalizations and a higher degree of openness have accelerated the cultural fields' progression toward a market-authorized autonomy. Globalization forces have also come into play; there has been a boost in the importation of foreign cultural goods for domestic consumption, and Chinese artists now assume greater international presence.

The second section is a case study of this last phenomenon, using as examples three internationally renowned auteur directors of the Taiwan New Cinema. Taiwan New Cinema filmmakers have inherited from Taiwan's earlier modernist trend a penchant for artistic modernism, which has served as a useful cultural currency in positioning them in the world's art-film circles through international film festivals. That their primary target audience has shifted from a domestic to an international one means that they rely even more heavily on established modernist thematic tropes and artistic devices to ensure their products' appeal. At the same time, a significant value of such "belated" modernist practices rests in the fact that they have meaningfully registered the individual artists' different reactions to the impact of a globalizing modernity, at a time when its consequences "are becoming more radicalized and universalized than before."[18]

Finally, I would like to make some preliminary observations on a new development that may eventually render the Taiwan New Cinema filmmakers' brilliant modernist achievement a swan song of sorts. As transnational film production is a dynamic force field reigned supremely by the law of competition, the newcomers must always find a different niche in order to establish themselves. Competing for the limited investment resources available to Asian filmmakers, Peggy Chiao, a veteran Taiwan New Cinema critic and promoter, has adopted a new strategy: in a project nicknamed "A Tale of Three Cities," she has packaged a group of six films and invited young talents from China, Taiwan, and Hong Kong as directors.[19] The project successfully attracted investments from seven different sources from France, Taiwan, and China and has already won two awards.

For our purpose, it is important to note that this new investment strategy could be pointing to a new direction for younger Taiwanese—as well as mainland Chinese—filmmakers. Significantly departing from the previously dominant art-film model, the project sets as its goal the design of well-produced, commercially viable works that would cater to both the Chinese and the global audience. The central image in the award-winning *Beijing Bicycle,* for instance, is chosen for its ready association with "China" in the electronic media. The film also uses popular culture icons—well-known movie stars and fashion models—in the cast for their market draw. This abandonment of the "modernistic" high culture premise injects an element of uncertainty into the future of the impressive minor renaissance of "Chinese modernism" that the Taiwan New Cinema created in the last decade of the twentieth century.

NOTES

1. See, for example, the following books published since the 1990s: David Der-wei Wang, *Fin-de-siècle Splendor: Repressed Modernities of Late Qing Fiction, 1849–1911* (Stanford, Calif.: Stanford University Press, 1997); Tani Barlow, ed., *Formations of Colonial Modernity in East Asia* (Durham, N.C.: Duke University Press, 1997); Lydia He Liu, *Translingual Practice: Literature, National Culture, and Translated Modernity—China, 1900–1937* (Stanford, Calif.: Stanford University Press, 1995); Ping-hui Liao, *Linglei xiandai qing* [On alternative modernities] (Taipei: Yunchen chubanshe, 2001); and Rey Chow, *Women and Chinese Modernity: The Politics of Reading between West and East* (Minneapolis: University of Minnesota Press, 1991).

2. In her review of Leo Lee's and Shu-mei Shih's books in *Chinese Literature: Essays, Articles, Reviews,* for instance, Letty Chen addresses the same methodological issue from a different perspective.

3. Anthony Giddens, *The Consequences of Modernity* (Stanford, Calif.: Stanford University Press, 1990), 1.

4. Giddens, 55–64.

5. Giddens, 59.

6. Pierre Bourdieu, *The Field of Cultural Production: Essays on Art and Literature* (New York: Columbia University Press, 1993), 112.

7. See Charles Laughlin's article, "The Battlefield of Cultural Production: Chinese Literary Mobilization during the War Years," *Journal of Modern Literature in Chinese* 2.1 (July 1998): 83–103.

8. Previously Chinese cultural products were mostly exported to Chinese diaspora in different parts of the world, in particular to Southeast Asia.

9. The film won the Golden Lion award at the Venice Film Festival in 1989.

10. In the same vein, national epics, with the Cultural Revolution as centerpiece, have helped to place the films by the PRC directors, like Zhang Yimou and Chen Kaige, in the mainstream global film market.

11. These are Anthony Giddens's terms for discussing the mechanisms of the globalization of modernity. See *The Consequences.*

12. See my discussion in Chapter 4 of *Modernism and the Nativist Resistance.*

13. Giddens, 134–37.

14. Ibid.

15. Chen Yingzhen is a key figure in Taiwan's modernist/nativist literary and cultural formation.

16. It is worth noting that among the three Taiwan New Cinema directors, no one comes close to exhibiting the kind of activist spirit that informs Giddens's fourth category, "radical engagement." This is especially conspicuous considering the thriving radical cultural trends in Taiwan between the late 1980s and the mid-1990s. One plausible explanation is that these directors are deeply indebted to influences of Taiwan's earlier modernist trend, which had a strong elitist, "disengaged" tendency. By the 1990s they had already passed their formative years.

17. Giddens, 134–37.

18. Giddens, 3.

19. Trained in film criticism at the University of Texas at Austin, Chiao has served as juror at various international film festivals in the last decade and is a crucial link between the burgeoning Chinese-language cinema and the international film circles.

8   Against "Library-Shelf Races": José Martí's Critique of Excessive Imitation

Gerard Aching

In José Martí's seminal essay, "Our America," the Cuban intellectual and anticolonial activist posits late-nineteenth-century, Spanish American identity as a terrain of competing epistemologies, and reasons that "America began enduring and still endures the weary task of reconciling the discordant and hostile elements it inherited from its perverse, despotic colonizer with the imported forms and ideas that have, in their lack of local reality, delayed the advent of a logical form of government" (292).[1] For Martí, this reconciliation of "discordant and hostile elements" and "imported forms and ideas" was not only politically urgent but would also enhance nation-building processes that had been transpiring over a presumably brief historical period. "Never before," he writes, "have such advanced and consolidated nations been created from such disparate factors in less historical time" (289–90). Structurally, the "Hispanoamerican enigma" (294) emerges imperiled because "the colony lives on in the republic" (293); that is, political autonomy from Spain did not eliminate important colonial institutions and practices, including the region's reliance on goods manufactured overseas and ideas generated abroad. Discursively, the region's "enigma" arises as a "weary task" of reconciliation that is further exacerbated, in Martí's view, because political, commercial, and intellectual leaders in the new republics locate the modern in European and North American metropolises and compulsively imitate the epistemologies, theories, policies, fashion, art, and literature that "originate" there. In repudiating these imitative practices, Martí simultaneously challenges a specific historical disavowal: he advocates a racially inclusive Spanish Americanism, a *mestizo* America about which he declares, "our bodies a motley of Indian and *criollo* we boldly entered the community of nations" (291).[2] I am interested in how Martí articulates this entrance into an international community as the "racialized" advocacy of a nonimitative Spanish Americanism.

The idea of "boldly enter[ing] the community of nations" means viewing Spanish Americanism or Hispanoamericanism in a particular way. "Our America" has often been read in biologistic racial terms as the promotion of a Hispanoamerican identity in response to Anglo-American economic and cultural hegemony. I would like to posit late-nineteenth-century Spanish Americanism as a contested discursive site of historical and cultural self-consciousness within a Hegelian "rational process" of "world history" (Hegel, *Lectures* 27).[3] Martí writes that "the problem of independence was not the change in form, but the change in spirit" (292). According to Hegel, "the aim of world history . . . is that spirit should attain knowledge of its own true nature, that it should objectivise this knowledge and transform it into a real world" (64). Knowledge, he argues, is the "form and function" of spirit, and the "spirit of the nation"—or, in my study, that of a transnational region—represents a stage of self-consciousness that "varies according to the kind of awareness of spirit that it [the nation] has attained" (53). Embodying "universal spirit in a particular form" (53), Spanish Americanism emerges through ongoing debates about the relationship between local self-awareness and "world history"; about the ways of belonging to a "community of nations" either, for example, through the imitative cosmopolitanism that the politically conservative but economically liberal ruling oligarchies practiced toward the close of the nineteenth century or the cultural autochthony that the weak but more politically liberal middle classes were beginning to espouse.[4]

An important premise in this chapter is that the relationship between these debates about the region's status and promotion of self-conscious knowledge and the penchant for imitation is constitutive of the ruling classes' discourse on *raza*. Loosely translated as "race" but both grounded in and hampered by idealistic, mid- and late-nineteenth-century theories about racial and cultural "purity," *raza* articulated a transnational consciousness of Spanish America during a period when racial-cultural theories in Europe posited "race" as "the be-all and end-all of history" (Augstein x).[5] Étienne Balibar argues that racial theories in the nineteenth and twentieth centuries define communities of language, descent, and tradition that transcend the borders of historical states and that "the dimension of universality of theoretical racism . . . plays an essential role here: it permits a 'specific universalization' and therefore an idealization of nationalism" ("Racism and Nationalism" 61).[6] In this study, I define *raza* as an idealistic discourse about Spanish America's place in "world history," a "specific universalization" in a nineteenth-century Hispanoamerican process of historical and cultural self-consciousness. My claim that the discussion of "race" in "Our America" in fact describes competitive epistemologies within national and regional geopolitical institutions and practices is corroborated by the observation that despite the visibility of diverse racial subjects in Latin America, the widespread interest in encouraging white immigration, and the burgeoning influence of the United States in the region, discourses on *raza* employed abstract or nonspecific "fictive ethnicities" as they advanced competing forms of self-knowledge.[7]

In order to comprehend the ideological value of such abstractions, close attention to ruling class formations is also crucial. According to Beatriz González Stephan, conservative *criollo* oligarchies came to power after independence and remained there into the early twentieth century through the adroit assimilation of economic liberalism (22–59). Against the promotion of the Eurocentric conceptualization of *raza* that they reified through the imitation, acquisition, and even fetishization of European cultural objects and ideas, Martí advocated a *mestizaje* (miscegenation) that affirmatively valorized local knowledge, cultures, and peoples. In this opposition to Spanish American Eurocentrism, Martí's views have often been juxtaposed to the ideas and aesthetic practices of the region's *modernistas*.[8] Their specific universalization of Spanish Americanism and also of Pan-Hispanism was not simply aligned with the ruling oligarchies' self-image and material interests but was frequently elaborated through the cultivation of aristocratic sensibilities.[9] It is in this light that one might account for why Rubén Darío, perhaps the most famous *modernista* poet, should proffer the following remark in the prologue to his second and arguably most accomplished book of poems, *Prosas profanas* (1896): "Is there in my blood some drop of African, or Chorotega or Nagrandano Indian blood? That could be, in spite of my marquis' hands: but behold you see in my verses princesses, kings, imperial things, visions of far-off or impossible countries: What do you wish? I detest the life and time in which I happened to be born" (9, my translation). Through this aristocratic imaginary, he chooses cosmopolitanism over Spanish American autochthony and evades the issue of racial ancestry altogether.

Yet because of the sheer breadth of *modernista* literary production in Spanish America—it was the first "movement" from Spanish America to influence Spanish literature—juxtaposing Martí's appreciation for the autochthonous and Darío's penchant for cosmopolitanism tells us less about *modernismo* than it does about the region's historical and cultural self-consciousness in two areas, which, due to spatial constraints, I can only mention briefly.[10] The first is the relationship between Hispanoamerican ruling classes and the art and literature that they sponsored. As opposed to Fredric Jameson's assertion that Darío's introduction of the term *modernismo* into Spanish letters was something of a "scandal" because it predated the usage of the term in other languages and could not account, because of its "historical precocity," for the second break that *vanguardismo* later represented (2002: 100–101), it would be more worthwhile to interrogate the difficulty of conceptualizing class-informed aesthetic ruptures and "radicalism" in the region when it was conservative, land-owning oligarchies that, instead of idealizing the land, encouraged the *modernistas'* imitative cosmopolitanisms and their taste for "far-off" and "impossible" countries.[11] The second area of inquiry that transcends the Martí–Darío juxtaposition and describes the region's modernity is the awareness that autochthony, as Carlos Alonso demonstrates for the regional novels that emerged in the 1920s, is also an instrumental set of discursive strategies; this discursivity suggests that Martí's idealization of a mestizo America partook of representational strategies and practices that were already available in racial-cultural formations such as the discourse on *raza*.[12] The choice between cosmopolitanism and autochthony is undoubtedly class-informed; but the fact that a Eurocentric, Spanish American *raza* and a *mestizo* America articulate ideological positions through racial abstractions is, as I suggest, a symptom of a Spanish American quest for a special place in "world history." With respect to Martí, his ideas about Spanish America's specific universalization are founded on a critique of what he calls "library-shelf races"—racial abstractions produced by questionable scholarship ("sickly, lamp-lit minds")—and the imitative strategies that gave rise to them (295).

My goal in this study is twofold. First, I examine how Martí's critique of the imitative practices that informed the idealization and promotion of a Eurocentric, Spanish American *raza* also provides a modern shift in thinking about "race" and its connections to nationhood and regionalism. I contend that even though he destabilizes the discourse on *raza* by pointing out the dangers and fallacies of its particular universalizing abstractions, Martí's *mestizo* America is also the product of an ideologically motivated abstraction even as it appeals for autochthonous leadership and knowledge. The challenges to Martí's conceptual *mestizaje* would come shortly afterward as he attempted to reconcile his critique of rampant imitative practices and the racial ideologies that they facilitated with racial antagonisms in Cuba's struggle for independence. My second aim, therefore, is to describe and interrogate how Martí negotiated these ideological and political challenges in "The Abolition of Slavery in Puerto Rico" and "My Race," essays that he wrote two years after "Our America." In these later chronicles, Martí adapts the idealism of a *mestizo* America to the ideological demands of the independence struggle with some difficulty; he shifts his discussion from race as the product of intellectual reflection to an idealization of the nonexistence of races in Cuban society. In my reading of these chronicles, I do not treat universalism and racialism as antithetical but as dialectically constitutive of the discourse of the nation.

A CRITIQUE OF EXCESSIVE IMITATION

Martí's "Our America" argues for an alternative path toward Spanish America's place in "world history." What has greatly contributed to the canonical status of his essay in Spanish American letters is the way in which the Cuban intellectual conceptualizes the region's cultural identity not in terms of essentialist, biologistic racial categories but as a critique of the presence, limitations, and/or absence of specific kinds of self-conscious knowledge in the Hispanoamerican racial-cultural formations of his day. Martí grounds his discussion of Spanish American identity in a discourse that privileges ideas as "weapons of the mind" and "trenches" (288). In this intellectual call to arms, he draws connections between knowledge and identity by opposing the "prideful villager['s]" complacent awareness of his locality (an initial stage of self-consciousness in Hegelian terms) to two related geopolitical concerns of which the villager remains unaware (288). The first geopolitical concern that Martí mentions focuses on the conflicts among Spanish American nations that prevent the region from realizing its political and cultural potential; the second entails the imminence of U.S. hegemony in the region. By insisting that the internal construction of a Spanish American cultural identity is inextricably related to knowledge about the other America, Martí discards the epistemological and ideological comfort of purportedly autonomous, unilaterally imagined cultural definitions in favor of a dialectics of identity construction that is more reminiscent of some contemporary approaches to the issue.

In his discussion of Spanish American cultural identity, Martí critiques the politics of knowledge that he observes in both Americas on two levels. The first level posits knowledge as the possession of facts about the world beyond limited local or national borders. From the vantage of exile in the United States, Martí warns the "prideful villager" (or the Spanish American reader who assumes this attitude) that the "sleepy hometown in [Spanish] America must awaken" (288). Cautioning against the other America's ignorance, Martí refrains from essentializing North Americans, declaring that "we must not, out of a villager's antipathy, impute some lethal congenital wickedness to the continent's light-skinned nation simply because it does not speak our language" (296). According to him, the gravest danger that the United States poses is not its citizens but the "disdain" that emerges from a nation that "does not know" the rest of the continent (295). Hence, in making this distinction between a people and what it does not know, Martí suggests that "weapons of the mind" and "trenches of ideas" are appropriate for combating the detrimental effects of U.S. ignorance on its neighbors. Indeed, one of Martí's most valuable contributions to the discourses on Spanish American identity construction has been this shift in the terms of the debate away from scientifically and pseudoscientifically derived genealogies that failed to account for Spanish American identity at the end of the century and toward ideas and arguments that elucidate specific kinds of knowledge, their dispositions within geopolitical structures of power, and the degrees of self-consciousness that inform the social antagonisms within such structures.

The second level in Martí's assessment of the relationship between Spanish American cultural identity and its politics of knowledge is epistemological-pedagogical. His essay can be read as a treatise on the critical selection, foundations, scope, and validity of epistemologies that ought to sustain the Spanish American racial-cultural formation that Martí calls "our America." Grounded in a profound understanding of the history of the region and the political challenges that the "new" nations face, the text decries a rampant and, for Martí, misguided politics of cultural knowledge that privileges imitative cosmopolitanisms over local knowledge and governance. Almost as if he were a contemporary theorist of the region's "postcolonial" educational requirements, Martí writes that "[o]ur own Greece is preferable to the Greece that is not ours; we need it more" (291). Referring to discrepancies between knowledge and place, he asserts that "no Yankee or European book could furnish the key to the Hispanoamerican enigma" (293–94). Conscious of the relationship between knowledge and political power, he laments the fact that no American university teaches the "art of governing," which he equates with "the analysis of all that is unique to the peoples of America" (291). Out of this reasoning emerges one of Martí's famous dictums: "To know is to solve. To know the country and govern it in accordance with that knowledge is the only way of freeing it from tyranny" (291). These statements take aim at post-Independence leaders and intellectuals for alienating themselves from their societies and, consequently, for failing to provide a proper understanding of and leadership for the region.

If Martí is disturbed because the "youth go out into the world wearing Yankee- or French-colored glasses and aspire to rule by guesswork a country they do not know" (291), then his essay can also be taken as a critique of those *modernista* practices that reinforce the ways in which "the colony lives on in the republic" (293). Besides rejecting the fetishization of "the imported book" and the "artificial intelligentsia" (290) that this obsession produces, he repudiates practices that have typically been identified with *modernista* decadence. Associating autochthony with virile nation building and cosmopolitanism with a weak, effeminate, and decadent dandyism, he writes:

> Only runts whose growth was stunted will lack the necessary valor, for those who have no faith in their land are like men born prematurely. Having no valor themselves, they deny that other men do. Their puny arms, with bracelets and painted nails, the arms of Madrid or of Paris, cannot manage the lofty tree and so they say that the tree cannot be climbed. We must load up the ships with these termites who gnaw away at the core of the patria that has nurtured them; if they are Parisians or Madrileños then let them stroll to the Prado by lamplight or go to Tortini's for an ice. These sons of carpenters who are ashamed that their father was a carpenter! These men

born in America who are ashamed of the mother that raised them because she wears an Indian apron. (289)

In stark contrast to the way in which Darío celebrated his "marquis' hands," Martí identifies the region's cosmopolitans with "puny arms" that belong to Madrid or Paris and admonishes them for failing to contribute to nation building from within. *Modernista* cosmopolitanism involved not only the acquisition of intellectual and artistic capital from European centers of "high culture" but offered *modernistas* the social advantage of positioning themselves as consumers and producers of this capital for a transatlantic pan-Hispanic readership. Martí did not oppose the development of a cosmopolitan readership; in fact, he insisted that knowing various literatures was the best means of liberating oneself from the tyranny of some of them ("Oscar Wilde" 60). What he did reject was the unreflexive incorporation of a fetishized cosmopolitanism that distorted the way in which the region would be viewed by its own political and intellectual leadership.

Martí's strong stance against an overdetermined cosmopolitanism does not exclude him from the literary phenomenon that came to be known as *modernismo*. While there is a uniqueness to Martí's thought—Ángel Rama describes him as one of those "lucid thinkers [who] strove to fashion more inclusive, syncretic cultural models that might reconcile the irresistible attractions of universalism with the maintenance of national traditions" (*The Lettered City* 81)—the Cuban intellectual also shared traits with his *modernista* interlocutors. Just as the latter drew from a multiplicity of sources in order to create their literature, so he, as one of the most traveled *modernista* thinkers of his day, assessed the validity of the ways in which cultural fragments (objects, gestures, referents, and allusions) were being combined to produce a modern literary and cultural expression. In other words, Martí's critique of the politics of knowledge at the epistemological-pedagogical level is also a valorization of the eclectic cultural fragments (the "disparate factors" giving rise to these "advanced and consolidated nations") that lay at the disposition of Spanish American leaders, intellectuals, and artists so that, not surprisingly, "Our America" is frequently punctuated by synecdoches and metonymies.[13] In examining the unique "body" of Spanish American culture, Martí observes: "What a vision we were: the chest of an athlete, the hands of a dandy, and the forehead of a child. We were a whole fancy dress ball, in English trousers, a Parisian waistcoat, a North American overcoat, and a Spanish bullfighter's hat" (293). Martí is not opposed to (re)arranging selected cultural fragments—for he is aware that this is a creative, critical task for such modern ("new") nations—but to the way in which this cultural work was being done. Drawing connections between discordant elements, imported forms, and governance, Martí underscores the urgency of judicious approaches to Spanish America's specific universalization. Moreover, his consciousness that identity formations are not mere givens but contested cultural composites that are intimately related to political power illustrates a critical understanding of the modernity of the region.

But there is still another "literary" and "empirical" reason that explains why Martí's critique of the rampant cosmopolitanism of his day does not exclude him from being considered a *modernista*. That Martí wrote "Our America" after attending the first Pan-American Conference (1889–90), where he had become disillusioned by both Latin American disunity and clear evidence of U.S. expansionism, is a well-known fact. However, a more uncommon perspective in the criticism on Martí is one that associates the poet's attitude toward politics with lyrical poetry. In *José Martí: La invención de Cuba*, Rafael Rojas illustrates how the tensions between the private and public became a central motif in the poetry of this intellectual and activist. According to Rojas, what distinguishes Martí's political discourse is his "invention of a moral community, from the foundational impulse of a civic-republican imaginary" (89).[14] Indeed, Rojas argues that not only are Martí's poems in *Ismaelillo* (1882), *Versos libres* (c. 1882), and *Versos sencillos* (1891) constantly "invaded" by the Cuban intellectual's political life (90) but the latter, written in the Catskill Mountains of upstate New York after the political disenchantment of the Pan-American Conference, is a "solitary exercise that reconstructs the poet's emotional intimacy after intense public activity" (91). Interestingly, what Rojas identifies in this exercise as the lyricism that emerges from contact with politics is frequently designated by the *modernista* trope of the *reino interior* [interior realm], that private space of solitude and introspection—often represented as a salon, chamber, tower, or soul—through which the *modernistas* engaged with their societies.[15] In Rojas's analysis, when Martí writes in the first stanza of *Versos sencillos*,

Yo soy un hombre sincero	I am an honest man
De donde crece la palma,	From where the palm tree grows,
Y antes de morirme quiero	And I want, before I die,
Echar mis versos del alma.	To cast these verses from my soul.
	(272; 273)

the poet succeeds in presenting a moral imaginary in which his stoicism (that republican code of self-discipline for the greater good of the community) is privately dismantled for the reader or listener in a casting of verses from the soul (Rojas 92). Martí, in other words, conceptualizes his poetry as "a refuge where the political weakness that could endanger his republican mission remains morally sheltered" (93). This reading reveals the appropriateness of the *reino interior* as a rhetorical means for separating Latin America's geopolitical weakness from the republicanism that informs his struggle for Cuban independence. In order to return to his activism, it

was crucial for Martí to distinguish between an ugly cosmopolitanism—
whereby, far from the sophisticated flair with which images and ideas
crossed oceans and national borders in *modernista* texts, he witnessed the
crude geopolitical realities of U.S. hegemony—and the struggle for Cuba's
political autonomy. Even though the poet's critique of *modernista* cosmopolitanism is directed at the way it camouflages real power configurations,
this critique is nonetheless rendered by means of a frequently employed
modernista trope.

Martí's response to blind imitation in certain *modernista* cosmopolitanisms is to imagine and advocate the rise of a figure ("un hombre sincero /
De donde crece la palma") that would incarnate the ideals of local knowledge and governance. The "natural man," a virile and noble organic intellectual of autochthonous knowledge, would vanquish artificial intelligentsia by overthrowing the authority of books that do not correspond to
the needs of the country (291). It is significant that in arguing for a Spanish Americanist, transnational politics of knowledge, Martí identifies this
natural man with the "native *mestizo*" who triumphs over the "alien, pure-
blooded *criollo*" (290).[16] This racialization of the relationship that the Cuban intellectual establishes between epistemologies and leadership facilitates Martí's vision of "our *mestizo* America" (292) because it critiques the
dominant pan-Hispanic racial-cultural formation of his day on the basis of
its failure or refusal to incorporate ignored populations and cultural "fragments" into the transnational body. In contrast to the strategically abstract
racial formations that characterized late-nineteenth-century discourses on
raza, Martí proposes a specific universalization of Spanish Americanism
by incorporating racial diversity within a collective "we." Miscegenation
transcended biologism in his thinking. With respect to a number of nation-
building projects, the concept of miscegenation not only permits him to
denounce a hetero-referential racism that ascribed inferiority to "minority"
populations, even as these sectors sometimes constituted the majority in
some Spanish American countries. It also allows him to elucidate the economic inequities of a "*mestizo* America with its towns of bare legs and Parisian dress-coats" (292) and the error of not pairing "the Indian headband
and the judicial robe" (293) in the administration of justice. In essence,
Martí's racialization of his subject advances the need "to undam the Indian, make a place for the able black, and tailor liberty to the bodies of
those who rose up and triumphed in its name" (293). In contrast to *raza*'s
homogeneity—what David Theo Goldberg might call "heterogeneity in denial" or "at once repressed" (16)—Martí proffers a specific universalization
based on miscegenation.

Martí's assertion that racial hatred does not exist "because there are no
races" (295) does not contradict his own racialization of the epistemological-
pedagogical debate in "Our America." His assertion promotes a "universal" ideal that was meant to transcend the false ideologies of competing

fictive ethnicities. At the same time, Martí's natural man, the idealized and racialized embodiment of local knowledge, functions conceptually to remind leaders and intellectuals that racial-cultural formations must emerge from their own historical circumstances. Maintaining his focus on epistemological and pedagogical issues, Martí links the universal and the particular in this essay through a critique of intellectual practices. First, he attempts to steer clear—except for an unusual reference to the "sluggish blood of the Indian race" (290)—of the scientifically derived racist categories of his day. Second, in claiming that "sickly, lamp-lit minds" create "library-shelf races" and that these practices may be distinguished from those of the "honest traveler" and "cordial observer" (296), he illustrates the role that superficial or dishonest intellectual practices can play in the production of false racial-cultural ideologies. As Julio Ramos shows (22–24; 234), the Cuban intellectual was critical of the "false erudition" (290) that led Sarmiento to posit that Latin America's progress lay in the region's ability to choose "civilization" over "barbarism." Martí disqualifies the existence of such erroneously conceptualized races in favor of a nobler "universal identity of man" (296). The racialization of his subject, therefore, not only presents challenges to late-nineteenth-century racial theories. More precisely, it calls also for the positive valorization of an autochthonous diversity as a teleological prerequisite for the region's specific universalization and its place within an international "community of nations."

THE LIMITS OF MARTÍ'S CRITIQUE

Yet *mestizaje* is also an abstraction with its own set of political and cultural agendas. Having argued in "Our America" for an integration of racial differences that would more accurately represent the region's specific universalization, Martí then faced the ideological difficulty of conceptualizing that integration with respect to the Cuban struggle for independence. In "The Truth about the United States," a text that was published the year before he was killed in one of the first attacks in Cuba's final war of independence, Martí writes that "there are no races: there is nothing more than mankind's various modifications of habit and form in response to the conditions of climate and history in which he lives, which do not affect that which is identical and essential" (329). Not only does he reiterate the humanism that he described in "Our America," but he also insists on it at the same time that he analyzes the particularities of U.S. cultural hegemony or "Yankeemania" in Spanish America (331). Martí, in other words, continues to associate Spanish America's potential for attaining its place in "world history" with the willingness of the region's intellectual and political leadership to end its own "excessive faith in the virtue of others" (332). In practical terms, he writes this chronicle on the United States to denounce "the crude, unequal, and decadent character of the United States, and the continual existence within it of all the violence, discords, immoralities, and disorders of which Hispanoamerican peoples are accused" (333). For Martí, deconstructing "Yankeemania" is inseparable from reminding this leadership of its responsibilities to local circumstances and its own racially mixed origins (331–32).

Because of the consistency with which Martí links local intellectual practices to the formulation of specific universal discourses, it is appropriate to examine how the ideological necessity of antiracism for the struggle for Cuban independence might be related to the call for racial integration in "Our America." With its ideological demand for nuanced positions on race and racism, the Cuban struggle for autonomy would appear to facilitate a testing ground for the specificities for which Martí appealed in "Our America." Martí's insistence that races do not exist or that they should, in Cuba, through an ideologically constructed miscegenation nonetheless retains an instrumental abstraction that he requires for his patriotic cause.[17] In *Insurgent Cuba*, Ada Ferrer observes that a powerful language of antiracism emerged during Cuba's first war of independence (1868–78) and intensified during the years between the end of slavery in Cuba (1886) and the start of the final war of independence in 1895 (3). That "the impossibility of racial conflict" could be considered one of the legacies of the first war (124) is amply reflected in Martí's conviction that there was no fear of a race war in Cuba (319). Martí's claim had its ideological reasoning for, as Ferrer asserts, "by declaring that there were no races and by asserting that racism was an infraction against the nation as a whole, nationalist rhetoric helped defeat Spanish claims about the impossibility of Cuban nationhood" (9). As a response to the colonial government's scare tactic of suggesting that Cuban independence would risk the creation of another black republic like Haiti, this antiracism brought the discussion of race and racism into the open. An opportunity to examine some of the limits that Martí sets on the appeal for miscegenation that he makes in "Our America" can be found in "The Abolition of Slavery in Puerto Rico" (April 1, 1893) and "My Race" (April 16, 1893), articles that he published just over two weeks apart in *Patria*, the official organ of the Cuban Revolutionary Party, the party that he founded in New York in 1892.

In "The Abolition of Slavery in Puerto Rico," Martí describes the official liberation of slaves that took place on that island in 1873. His aim, in revisiting this historical moment, is to describe the island's preparedness for the liberation of its slaves and, by implication, for Puerto Rican and Cuban independence. The tone of the chronicle is festive and optimistic. Martí writes that, with the exception of the Spaniards who belonged to the Círculo Hispano Ultramarino and a few proslavery homes, "no one walked alone for all San Juan was a single family" (317). The description of the parade that filed through the streets of the capital gives the impression of a euphoric but orderly occasion. Nevertheless, apart from the obvious antagonism of proslavery quarters, the reader must still make sense of a tension between former slave owners and slaves that does not get resolved directly in the text. On the one hand, an abolitionist declares that the slaves "entered into their freedom without hatred"—this claim permits the reader to understand how "masters and slaves walked side by side" in celebration (316). On the other, the glimpse of varied reactions to the news of abolition among the newly freed contrasts with the elated tone that pervades the text: "To the master who told his Negro, 'Now you are free!' the Negro replied, 'I will never be free as long as my master exists.' One slave said, 'No! My *niña* [mistress], I'm staying with my *niña*!' Another slave, sitting in a doorway, was overcome by a great burst of weeping and cried without knowing why, gathering his sobs in the palms of his hands" (317). The difference between the abolitionist's certainty about the former slaves' freedom from hatred and the former slaves' varied and complex responses to the official declaration is not reconciled in the text except, indirectly, through the figure of Sotero Figueroa. In Martí's version of the events, the public celebration culminates in a series of speeches that evening at the Círculo Artístico y Literario. And it is through Figueroa, the Círculo's secretary—a Puerto Rican and "virtuous son of the two bloods"—that the governor would be informed of the island's "mettle and independence" and "aptness for liberty" (318). The article closes with a last look at the members of the Círculo and states that despite this fleeting hour of justice, "there are still many slaves, black and white, in Puerto Rico!" (318).

Suggesting that Puerto Ricans, regardless of their race, were still enslaved invites the reader to see the abolition of slavery as a rehearsal for political independence. In addition to the governor's act of addressing the crowd "as to a people at the moment of its birth" (316), and to the shout of "*¡Viva Puerto Rico libre!*" (317) during the official celebration of the end of slavery, the issue of Puerto Rican and Cuban independence frames the entire text. Martí begins his account of the event in Puerto Rico by referring to the slave owners' voluntary emancipation of slaves in Cuba as the act of colonial insubordination that launched this island's first war of independence. He writes that this emancipation, "the purest and most consequential fact of that revolution, saved the Negro from servitude once and for all and saved Cuba from violence and upheavals that the freed slaves, grateful rather than injured, would never instigate in the republic" (314). The suggestion that the former slaves welcomed their liberation with gratitude attempts to quell fears about postindependence racial antagonisms on both islands. In "Our America," the creation of unique, racially harmonious nations rests on the ability of leaders to incorporate disavowed sectors of the population into their respective national projects and imaginaries; similarly, the message in the later essay is that the success of Puerto Rican and Cuban political autonomy would depend on the successful transformation of slaves into citizens. Obviously, although the abolition of slavery in Cuba had occurred seven years before he wrote "The Abolition of Slavery in Puerto Rico" (and that of Puerto Rico even earlier), Martí was still addressing concerns about black citizenship in the context of the Cuban independence movement. In these circumstances, Martí's depiction of Figueroa appears to orchestrate several issues. The Puerto Rican, a product of miscegenation, figuratively incarnates the racial harmony that would be necessary for political autonomy. Figueroa is not only the virtuous citizen of a nation-to-be but already stands out for his leadership in a prestigious artistic and literary society. It is from this urbane platform that Figueroa speaks of Puerto Rican independence. Like Martí's "natural man," the Puerto Rican is clearly a privileged source of local knowledge and leadership. However, why does Martí represent Figueroa as only able to deliver his message with "simple loftiness" (318) despite his esteemed voice and talent for leadership, on the one hand, and the readiness with which the governor listens to him—his "eyes full of humanity"—on the other? What lies behind this restraint?

Briefly, I would argue that the equanimity that Martí ascribes to Figueroa hints at the position on racism that the Cuban intellectual would espouse two weeks later in "My Race." This brief chronicle attests to the care with which Martí takes the politically delicate discussion of race and racism into the public sphere prior to independence. According to him, the purpose of the text is to clarify the meaning of the word *racist*. The first rhetorical strategy that Martí takes is to establish the parameters of his discussion: "No man has any special rights because he belongs to one race or another: say 'man' and all rights have been stated" (318). At the same time, any attempt to create divisions among men, self-imposed or not, "is a sin against humanity" (318). Given this humanist stance, Martí's next step is to pose similar rhetorical questions to both blacks and whites, regardless of their social standing. "What do blacks think of a white man who is proud of being white . . . ?" and "What must whites think of a black man who grows conceited about his color?" he queries (318–19). Consistent with the appeal for integration in "Our America," his response is that any insistence upon racial divisions and differences obstructs individual and public happiness (319). At this point, however, the Cuban intellectual's subsequent move is to shift from a declaration of "universal truths" to the particularities of racism in Cuba:

> It is true that in the black man there is no original sin or virus that makes him incapable of developing his whole soul as a man, and this truth must be spoken and demonstrated, because the injustice of this world is great, as is the ignorance that passes for wisdom, and there are still those that believe in good faith that the black man is incapable of the intelligence and feelings of the white man. (319)

For Martí, the realities and injustice of racism arise from an "ignorance that passes for wisdom." In keeping with his practice of avoiding essentialisms, this antiracist statement does not accuse whites of racism but turns false knowledge about blacks into the culprit. From this position, the Cuban intellectual is able to argue for "good racism," which he calls "pure justice" and recognizes as the means by which the "ignorant white could shed his prejudices" (319). In a significant move at the end of this quotation, Martí identifies the ability of the ignorant white to shed prejudices with an assumption of "natural respect" for the black man; he then posits this ability as crucial for "the life and peace of the nation" (319). By the same token, this respect—from the perspective of the black man—should be nothing less than "the limit of just racism, which is the right of the black man to maintain and demonstrate that his color does not deprive him of any of the capacities and rights of the human race" (319).

In other words, if the nation must come into being, black and white racists must negotiate a mutual respect that would transcend the extremisms that endanger the independence movement. Significantly, in order to reinforce this antiracist appeal, Martí recommends an attitude that places his humanist concerns on the same plane as his patriotism: " 'Man' means more than white, more than mulatto, more than Negro. 'Cuban' means more than white, more than mulatto, more than Negro" (319). This conflation of a universalizing humanism and patriotism is meant to ready Cubans for the approaching anticolonial struggle on the basis of an antiracism that emerged during the first war: "On the battlefields, the souls of whites and blacks who died for Cuba have risen together through the air. In that daily life of defense, loyalty, brotherhood, and shrewdness, there was always a black man at the side of every white" (319). But what sort of integration is this? Ferrer's study shows that there were many depictions of black pro-independence insurgents in which the black did not fight in equal conditions or with similar aspirations. The slave fought on behalf of his Cuban liberators so that "his very participation in the separatist struggle, was not found in his political ambition or ideology but in the gratitude he felt toward the independence leaders who granted him his freedom" (119). (This insistence on gratitude is also the abolitionist's strategy in "The Abolition of Slavery in Puerto Rico.") In fact, Ferrer's evidence allows her to conclude that "Martí wrote about a *mestizo* America but not quite about a *mestizo* Cuba: For him, as for others, racial union in Cuba was less the product of miscegenation than of masculine heroism and will. ... [T]he vision of a transracial Cuba essentially left intact racial categories like white and black, even as it argued for their transcendence" (126–27). Despite his efforts at depicting racial equality in the struggle for independence, Martí's promotion of an ideal social relation between blacks and whites in "My Race" places a greater intellectual and ethical burden on black self-consciousness and agency. The white racist suffers from ignorance and must be informed that "blacks are too tired of slavery to enter voluntarily into the slavery of color" (320). However, not only must the black's just or "good racism" help the ignorant white to "shed his prejudices"; the black man must also be able to know and respect the "limit of just racism." When he predicts that "the word 'racist' will be gone from the lips of blacks who use it today in good faith" (320), Martí is clearly appealing to a black leadership. And because "My Race" justifies a very specific and limited use of the word by blacks, the opening sentence— "'Racist' is becoming a confusing word, and it must be clarified" (318)—is certainly meant, during this crucial pre-independence period, to outline the limits of their legitimate claims against white racism.

CONCLUSION

Martí's antiracist discourse in "The Abolition of Slavery in Puerto Rico" and "My Race" cannot be deduced seamlessly from his appeal for racial integration in "Our America." In the earlier essay, he tackles a "theoretical racism" (the strategic disavowal of racial difference in the construction of a racial-cultural identity) by critiquing certain discourses on *raza*. In carrying out this critique, he does not reject aspirations to define a transnational community. "Our America," therefore, serves as a corrective for malicious or misguided intellectual practices that sought to privilege cosmopolitan over local knowledge. In the subsequent texts, Martí again tackles racism (the racist's insistence on absolute and "natural" distinctions between races), but this time to promote Cuban political autonomy. Although Martí's patriotic antiracism—the notion of a raceless nation—can also be read as a disavowal of racial differences for the sake of the nation, neither the stakes nor the approaches to both appeals for integration can be considered the same. Martí's argument for integration in "Our America" is geared toward facilitating a "fitting" place for Spanish America among the "community of nations." The call for integration in the other essays is accompanied by the "necessity" of circumscribing the perils of separatist racial formations for a "patriotic" cause. It is in light of what Martí claims are the nation's ideological demands that his praise for Figueroa's "simple loftiness" and the limits that the Cuban intellectual sets on "just racism" can be understood.

The notion of a raceless society in contemporary Cuba is frequently attributed to Martí even though he was by no means the only intellectual to argue for this ideology during the struggle for Cuban independence. A famous, recent instance of the ideological use of Martí's ideas is Roberto Fernández Retamar's *Calibán* (1972), an essay that frequently recruits "Our America" in order to critique the production of literary and intellectual work in capitalist countries. Retamar's text clearly models itself on Martí's keen observation that racial-cultural formations are essentially discursive and need to be engaged through a battle of ideas about what constitutes good scholarship. Yet Retamar does not treat Martí's essay as a text that had the potential to revolutionize racial thinking not only in the Americas but also in Western intellectual circles during its time. This is not simply a question of readership—that is to say, who was reading Martí—but of evaluating the ways in which the specific universalization that Martí promoted for Spanish America differed from other ways of belonging to an international community of nations.

"Our America," "The Truth about the United States," and "My Race" argue from intriguing but different perspectives that races do not exist as biological facts. Such assertions have a contemporary ring to them because a great deal of liberal intellectual labor has been invested in refuting the vestiges of nineteenth-century scientific racisms more familiar to us today as biologism that simply will not go away. However, there are qualitative differences in the way Martí posits the nonexistence of races in these essays. As I have already mentioned, one of the most resounding challenges to racial thinking in the earlier essay is the assertion that racial-cultural formations are not givens but discourses for which intellectuals can be held responsible. Conceptualizing identities as a politics of knowledge—that is, information, epistemologies, and pedagogies that are defined, imposed, repressed, or disavowed—liberates battles in which intellectuals, as Martí had done, could also be activists. In this sense, Martí takes no prisoners when he suggests that certain "sickly, lamp-lit minds" had been responsible for creating "library-shelf races." The claim in "Our America" that there are no races was an attempt to uncover and dismantle a disavowal, a class-informed and strategic silence about highly visible racial subjects in Spanish America. With their penchant for fetishizing European "high culture," *modernista* cosmopolitanisms played a crucial role in buttressing this disavowal across Spanish America. For Martí, racial integration becomes the only way of imagining an intellectually and politically honest specificity that would reflect the region's unique place in the modern world.

In "My Race," the argument against the existence of races shifts the discussion of race away from universalizing schemes and places it in the context of Cuban nationalist ideologies at the turn of the century. It is evident that the Cuban intellectual was motivated by a political agenda that required the deconstruction of racial antagonisms that the colonial authorities disseminated as anti-Independence propaganda. In that light, any antiracist claim that became too vociferous by declaring its self-referentiality risked the kind of separatism that could obstruct the independence movement. Nonetheless, in "My Race," Martí places the burden of self-restraint on politically aware blacks who seemed to require clarification about the "just" limits of the term *racist* that they for the most part employed. Ultimately, the only race that the text promotes is a nationalistic, racially non-specific Cuban race—a new fictive ethnicity and abstraction in keeping with the struggle for nationhood. While *raza* functioned by blurring racial differences in order to foster socioeconomic exclusivity, Martí's *mestizo* America is distinguishable from *raza*'s ambiguities because this conceptual miscegenation promotes a patriotism that in theory is racially inclusive but in practice maintains racial antagonisms in abeyance.

NOTES

1. Martí wrote "Nuestra América" while he lived in exile in New York and first published the essay in Mexico City's *El Partido Liberal* on January 20, 1891.

2. In Hispanoamerica, *mestizo* refers to a racially mixed person, usually of Spanish and indigenous extractions. *Criollo* originally designated a Spaniard born in the Americas but, in some parts of Spanish America, subsequently came to suggest autochthonous precedence without a very strict regard for racial specificity. With the semantic weight now placed more heavily on culture than on race, the term remains extremely ambiguous.

3. In incorporating Hegel's teleological approach to world history, I am interested in his definitions of rationality, self-consciousness, and spirit in the process of world history. However, I agree with Beatriz González Stephan's critique of nineteenth-century liberal ideologies for their subscription to Hegel's location of the process of "world history" in Europe (88–92).

4. González Stephan argues that political independence permitted the conservative ruling oligarchies to consolidate economic power especially through the insertion of the region as a source of raw materials into the international market. For her, this insertion marked the beginning of Latin America's neocolonial underdevelopment (23–28). In this scenario, the bourgeoisie remained subservient to these oligarchies (29–30).

5. Despite the preciseness of this teleology, the mid- and late-nineteenth-century penchant for abstractions in racial thinking facilitated a range of rhetorical strategies. For instance, the Victorian poet and public intellectual, Matthew Arnold, was an important practitioner of what Anthony Appiah terms "literary racialism," and Arnold employed his philological work on Celtic literature to theorize abstractions such as biological inheritance and racial filiation for a mainly Anglo-Saxon reading public (55–60). Such racial abstractions abounded during the period and greatly influenced discourses on *raza* in Spain and Spanish America. In addition to being a measure of historical and cultural self-awareness, *raza* may usefully be considered both a "racial formation," which, according to Michael Omi and Howard Winant, is a process through which "racial categories are created, inhabited, transformed, and destroyed" (124), and a "racial project," by which they mean "the ideological work of linking structure and representation" (125). As such, *raza* can be seen as the promotion of a utopian racial formation—analogous, at the level of cultural ideology, to the U.S. concept of Manifest Destiny and its embedded but unmarked whiteness—and as an ideological agenda that linked formation, for instance, to policies such as white immigration.

6. Balibar defines "racism" not as the "ravings" of racist subjects but as a historically grounded "social relation" ("Racism and Nationalism" 41). He distinguishes between "spontaneous racism"—the racist prejudice that is stereotypi-

cally associated with such "ravings"—and the "theoretical (or doctrinal) racism" (38) that characterizes *raza* and other such nineteenth-century discourses. A racist posture is either "self-referential," in that the bearers of the prejudice "designate themselves as representative of a superior race," or "hetero-referential," when the "victims" of racialization are deemed "inferior or evil" (39). A significant point that Balibar makes is that doctrinal racisms have closely been tied to humanist-universalist ideologies for over two hundred years (58).

7. Balibar defines "fictive ethnicity" as the conceptual means by which the idealism of the national or transnational discourse is rendered less arbitrary ("The Nation Form" 96). My position is that the avoidance of ethnic content and specificity was internal to the development of the discourse on *raza*.

8. *Modernismo* in Hispanoamerican letters designates the literary activities of a number of poets, journalists, and intellectuals in cities such as Buenos Aires, Mexico City, Havana, Bogotá, and Caracas during the last two decades of the nineteenth century. The end of this literary phenomenon is frequently dated as 1916, the year that marks the death of the Nicaraguan-born *modernista* Rubén Darío. The bibliography on Spanish American modernismo is vast and cannot be reproduced here. Some of the most recent titles include Iris M. Zavala, *Colonialism and Culture: Hispanic Modernisms and the Social Imaginary* (Bloomington: Indiana University Press, 1992); Cathy Login Jrade, *Modernism, Modernity, and the Development of Spanish American Literature* (Austin: University of Texas Press, 1998); and my *The Politics of Spanish American* Modernismo (Cambridge: Cambridge University Press, 1997).

9. In contrast to Spanish Americanism, Pan-Hispanism is a racial-cultural formation that includes Spain.

10. For Roberto González Echevarría, Martí's poetry shares many of the same sensibilities as those of Baudelaire and Rimbaud, two of the poets in the *modernistas'* pantheon of European poets. See González Echevarría's "José Martí: An Introduction," in *José Martí: Selected Writings,* ed. and trans. Esther Allen (New York: Penguin Books, 2002), p. xxii. Ivan A. Schulman dates the assessment of Martí as an important initiator of *modernismo* with Roberto Fernández Retamar's interventions during the 1960s. See Schulman's "La modernización de los estudios martianos y el discurso crítico de Roberto Fernández Retamar," *Revista de Estudios Hispánicos* 36.3 (2002): 627–32.

11. The *modernistas'* aesthetic eclecticism included studied imitations of French Symbolism, Parnassianism, and Decadentism. Many of them were familiar with the major European Romantic figures as well as with the Hellenism that swept through intellectual and artistic circles on both sides of the Atlantic. Some were drawn to Baudelaire's and Rimbaud's appeals for modern art and literature, while others admired the solipsism of Huysman's *À Rebours* (1884). Almost all of them, as their introduction of French lyrical forms into Spanish-language poetry demonstrated, were avid readers of Mallarmé and Verlaine.

12. See Alonso's *The Spanish-American Regional Novel: Modernity and Autochthony* (Cambridge: Cambridge University Press, 1990).

13. Ramos writes that Martí exhibited a great fear of fragmentation (234). I would argue that many intellectuals and artists on both sides of the Atlantic were conscious that fragmentation characterized most aspects of modern urban life and that Martí's "Our America" attempts to distinguish the constructive use of cultural fragments from what he viewed as an imitative, cosmopolitan eclecticism that failed to contribute to nation building.

14. The translations of Rojas's text are mine.

15. As opposed to a more traditional criticism that views these private spaces as a flight or detachment from society, the work, for example, of Theodor W. Adorno in "On Lyric Poetry and Society," from *Notes to Literature* (New York: Columbia University Press, 1991), and Herbert Marcuse in "The Affirmative Charac-

ter of Culture" from *Negations: Essays in Critical Theory* (Boston: Beacon Press, 1968) illustrates the ways in which lyric poetry (Adorno) and the mental and spiritual world (Marcuse) are constituted through a dialectical relationship with modern, industrializing societies.

16. Three years later, in "The Truth about the United States," Martí wrote that the way to nationhood in Spanish America was still obstructed "with patricidal blindness, by the privileged caste that the European engendered" (329). In the same text, which he wrote in order to launch a series of reports on the United States that he hoped would arrest "Yankeemania" in Spanish America, Martí notes that the disdain for "all that is native" among some members of this caste sometimes takes the form of a "subtle aristocracy whereby, publicly loving all that is fair-skinned as if that were natural and proper, they try to cover over their own origin, which they see as *mestizo* and humble [. . .]" (332).

17. Although Nancy Leys Stepan associates the emergence of "constructive miscegenation" with Latin American eugenics just before the start of the First World War, the ideological and discursive practice had already been taking place in literature as early as the "social whitening" of the slave protagonist in Gertrudis Gómez de Avellaneda's novel *Sab* (1841). For more on "constructive miscegenation," consult Stepan's *"The Hour of Eugenics": Race, Gender, and Nation in Latin America* (Ithaca, N.Y.: Cornell University Press, 1991).

9 Modernist (Pre)Occupations: Haiti, Primitivism, and Anticolonial Nationalism

Patricia E. Chu

> But the young black who used to kneel in worship before the head-lights on explorers' cars is now driving a taxi in Paris and New York. We had best not lag behind this black.
> —Jean Epstein, *"Bonjour cinéma* and Other Writings" (1926)

Critics traditionally define the modernist "primitivism" of the 1920s and 1930s as a psychoanalytically influenced Western elite practice in which artists treat "natives" and native cultures as sources of rejuvenation in a rapidly modernizing world. Modernization and its accompanying social norms separate modern Western people from their authentic impulses: sexuality, physicality, violence, play. Rather than considering racially-othered natives as simply deficient in "civilization," the primitivists see them as conduits to their own unconscious or as alternatives to Western civilization's rationality, bureaucracy, and mechanization. Paradoxically, primitivist representations of natives are, as Elazar Barkan and Ronald Bush maintain, "a highly charged signal of otherness . . . that came to signify modernity" (*Prehistories* 3). In this dynamic, primitivists are modern while natives themselves are not. Natives are unaware of the significance of modernization or their relationship to it, but primitivists, as rebellious and alienated cultural relativists, understand both modern and primitive modes of thought and their significance to the history of world civilization.

But Jean Epstein's comments suggest other ways of understanding the significance of "natives" in twentieth-century Western culture. These lines expose the inaccuracy of the assumption that primitivism always puts "the native" outside history regardless of what she or he represents.[1] Epstein suggests that the native is the historical subject and that "we," presumably elite modernist subjects, may not understand modernity well enough. He emphasizes motion and location: from subjected and immobile worshiper the native has not only moved to the metropole and learned its routes but now manipulates the object he once worshipped. Epstein and his presumed audience "lag behind" native history: has the leading edge of modernity become postcolonial?

Perceiving the native as the leading edge of modernity allows us to understand modernists' affiliations with the primitive as stemming from political rather than metaphysical concerns. Modernists may have used "natives" or "primitive art" to invoke tangible remnants of "pre-history"— fragments to make modernity and modernization visible—but their materials always emerged as by-products of Western exploration, conquest, and territorial organization. In this chapter, I emphasize the geocultural and geopolitical aspects of modernism's natives and primitives.

Elite Westerners could see that the technological modernization of occupied territory—roads, schools, sanitation, commerce—had to be accompanied by governmental or administrative modernization. To Western democratic powers, government itself is akin to roads and hospitals. Britain and the United States offered to replace the "feudal" or "tribal" hierarchies of indigenous peoples with centralized representative government structures and national identities. This process involved, as many critics have documented, information gathering, policing, categorization, and the regulation of social life.

Consider, for instance, the U.S. government's Philippines census of 1903–1905. Conducted shortly after the U.S. Congress had forbidden a census unless the islands were completely pacified, the act of beginning the census declared victory for the United States. It also established the conditions for national elections of a U.S.-approved colonial legislature, which would further consolidate the counterrevolutionary nationalism the United States wanted to establish and gather data that the U.S. government and U.S. corporations needed for guiding their capital investments in the islands. But, Vincente Rafael argues, the census is also a discursive state practice that categorized its subjects, making them visible, quantifiable and, thus, governable. The U.S. government hired 7,502 Filipinos as census workers. Exemplifying the Filipinos' potential for eventual self-government, these workers demonstrated their ability to work as disciplined subjects within a state apparatus *and* their acceptance of the categories that modern states establish for the purpose of creating a proper national population out of heterogeneous colonial subjects.[2]

This process had a popular audience in the United States. Far from burying the census results in a government archive, William Howard Taft, U.S. Secretary of War and former Governor General of the Philippines, personally informed Gilbert Grosvenor, the editor of *National Geographic*, of its release. *National Geographic*'s issue of April 1905, the third to contain photographs, covered the census and brought in so many new subscribers that the publisher had to put it back on the press to meet the demand (Abramson 62). Founded in 1888, *National Geographic* was the most widely read source of general science information in America. By 1920 it was the publishing industry's major success story, having increased its circulation during the war to 650,000 (while other publications failed) and then to over 750,000 within the next two years (Pauly, "'The world'" 517; Abramson, *National Geographic* 119–20). *National Geographic*'s use of the Philippines census material indicates the social forces behind these numbers. The Spanish-American War spurred an interest in geography and *Our New Possessions* (as an early *National Geographic* book put it). *National Geographic*'s adoption of the conventions of photographic realism quickly gave the magazine a reputation as a reliable, objective, and up-to-the-minute source on American empire. In the Philippines census issue, *National Geographic* converted a government document into a mass cultural one in order to position readers so that they could enjoy pleasurable positions as surveyors of "the world and all that is in it," the theme of the magazine as described in 1900 by Alexander Graham Bell, the society's second president (Pauly, "'The world'" 523). But this position obviously depended on appreciating that power as embedded in surveillance, enumeration, and social control, even if *National Geographic* consistently emphasized the benefits of colonialism to its subjects.

If the imperial arena displayed the exertion of state power more starkly, it also provided the backdrop for imagining antistate activity. Epstein's lines on modernity should also remind us of the rise in anticolonial movements during the 1920s and 1930s and of C. L. R. James's claim in *The Black Jacobins* that the conditions of plantation production in the Caribbean produced proletarianized revolutionaries ahead of their time. I argue that modernist primitivists construct "natives"/nationalists as enviable for their "fortunate" position: able to see and thus actively fight subjection by the state. In making this argument, I am outlining a new critical understanding of primitivists' objects of desire, not realigning their cultural politics. In fact, criticisms of primitivists as inaccurate, appropriative, manipulative, and indifferent to the political and psychological price of their discourse for "natives" and racialized others still apply. The primitivism I describe involves envy of an imagined ability to rebel, projected onto a racial other. Primitivists were not necessarily anti-imperialists. But understanding primitivism as grounded in imperial governance rather than imperial locations or "race" recognizes one of the ways in which modernists engaged with state formations as they constructed their definitions of modernity and of themselves as "revolutionary" subjects of modernity.

Modernism's arena, then, is not merely the battlefields of Europe and the "men of 1914." The concept of a racially and nationally inflected "geomodernism" demands attention to the imperial land grabs of the 1880s and 1890s, the countries of the Monroe Doctrine, the great powers' remapping of the world post–World War I, and American areas of intervention. Wilsonian "national self-determination" was circulated popularly in the context of a war framed as the battle between free (national) peoples and illegitimate (state/imperial) conquest. Many critics have discussed the complexities of its application after the war; I will not attempt to summarize their work here. What I find significant about the popularization of "national self-determination" and its associated ideologies with regard to modernism is its contribution to defining the modern self as a national subject with a potentially problematic relationship to a state. Benedict Anderson describes the end of World War I as the historical moment when the "legitimate international norm" became the *nation*-state "so that in the League [of Nations] even the surviving imperial powers came dressed in national costume rather than in imperial uniform" (Benedict Anderson 113). State authority—centralization—is illegitimate unless it is "really" national.

Where a uniform signals the wearer's contemporary agreement to mask difference in subordination to centralized authority, a costume invokes a standard of historically grounded, affective identity that governing authorities must acknowledge. Governance will now be judged on whether it has converted national desire into state policy. The United States, rather than simply annexing Haiti, actively worked to maintain an appearance of Haitian independence and volition. For instance, Haiti was to have its own elected president, even if the United States selected him. Rather than setting aside the Haitian constitution and seizing land, the United States rewrote "Haiti's" constitution to allow foreign investment. To put down resistance by nationalist guerilla fighters, and to police the cities, the United States used the Haitian *gendarmerie,* a Haitian military force invented, trained, and officered by U.S. Marines in addition to the marines' expeditionary forces.[3] Wilson unwittingly outlined the (il)logic of this paradoxical commitment to imperial democracy when questioned by the British Foreign Office about his imperial policies in 1914: "I am going to teach the South American republics to elect good men" (Heater 19; Ninkovich 52). Wilson uses the *National Geographic* version of the United States as a world power. As was true of the Philippines census, Wilson's words underscore representative democracy's entanglements with domination. Occupations, interventions, spheres of influence, and the oppositions mobilized against them militarily and intellectually threw the condition of being subject to a state apparatus into sharp relief. Subjection took on the rhetoric of empowerment —the Filipinos prepare for independent nationhood by surveying their own country for U.S. occupation.

One gets a sense of U.S. popular unease about this aspect of modern U.S. empire from debates about the government's censorship of American news coverage of the Philippines War, and about restrictions placed on what U.S. soldiers could receive in the mail. On April 27, 1899, *The Nation* reported that the government had refused to deliver a telegram from an organized group of families and friends to the men of the Nebraska regi-

ment. The telegram read: "Boys, don't reenlist; insist upon immediate dis-
charge" (Foner and Winchester 386). The Postmaster General ordered the
removal of anti-imperial pamphlets from mails going to Manila. One significant category of public criticism included variations on the idea that
the government's control of the information U.S. soldiers were allowed to
have demonstrated that the kinds of authority and categorization colonial
rule necessitated would be applied to metropolitan subjects as well. Other
writers claimed that voters on U.S. soil had been treated like Russian, German, Turkish, and papal subjects when denied information (Foner and
Winchester 363–421).

The debate on the soldiers in the Philippines focused on whether their
standing as soldiers in time of war superseded their standing as voters
who were entitled to full access to national debates. The May 18, 1899 issue
of *The Nation* published a letter from a Civil War (Union) veteran who
wrote that during the 1864 presidential campaign "[N]othing was with-
held from the soldiers of that most bitter and critical period. . . . When our
lines were near together. . . . we exchanged our [news]papers . . . for the
[news]papers of rebeldom. We were, men who had minds of our own. . . .
and could draw our own conclusions" (Foner and Winchester 397). This
underscores the extent to which a colonial context triggered discussions
about state power rather than national identity. The ideal these writers articulate is that of an informed voting public—the stuff of a representative
democracy. And yet, the anxiety is that it is precisely their status as individual voters that allowed and encouraged the state bureaucracy to over-
ride them—were they being trained to elect good men? Some newspapers
asserted that the censorship order had originated not from the Postmaster
General, but from McKinley's administration.

The shift Anderson describes from imperial "uniform" to national "costume" also highlights another element crucial to my analysis: how the
world powers justified their rulings on the numerous sovereignty cases presented after the war. The Wilson administration's group "The Inquiry," for
instance, was charged with gathering geographical, historical, economic,
and legal data to support Wilson's recommendations on specific cases involving sovereignty during the post–World War I settlements (Heater 38).
Wilson's elaborations of what constituted a nation as a proper "self" were
imprecise and often contradictory. He claimed to give the most weight to
what he considered "organic" ethno-linguistic characteristics: commonality of language, longstanding borders, shared historical consciousness,
and "ethnographic affinities" (Heater 22–43; Ambrosius 125–29). But the
Filipinos did not qualify for national self-determination because they were
too "diverse and heterogeneous" and Wilson did not insist that national
self-determination required breaking up the Hapsburg Empire or freeing
Ireland, Egypt, or India (Ambrosius 128). Despite these inconsistencies,
and regardless of the reasons behind them, "national self-determination"

became an important part of the vocabulary anchoring an aspect of modern political identity in anthropology's redefinition of culture.

In this chapter I examine the importance of U.S. imperial action to modernist thought. I focus on how primitivists derived their "natives" out of a sense of the interrelatedness of the U.S. colonial "regime" and its metropolitan "administration." Matthew G. Hannah writes that on the structural level these governments share the epistemological elements of "rule from a distance." State power in both places requires surveying and classifying territory, people, and resources, acquiring this knowledge without consent, and using it for social control (114–15). Wilson's rhetoric about American domination in the Caribbean differed markedly from Roosevelt's or Taft's. Wilson specifically cited the need for domination for the purposes of bringing other countries constitutional democracy (Ninkovich 52). For primitivists, "natives" are those who can both recognize the dominating nature of liberal representative democracy and organize against it based on identitarian and culturalist politics—they turn the state's own categories against it. Thus, the primitivist fantasy is partly to understand how one is being ruled.

In his infamous film *The Birth of a Nation* (1915),[4] D. W. Griffith confronts this concept of American "democratic occupancy," creating a narrative in which white men must free themselves from the forms of U.S. representative democracy and black men have pathetically succumbed to the false agency of voting. Written nearly twenty years after *The Birth of a Nation,* in another medium, and, most people would assume, out of a different politic, Zora Neale Hurston's *Tell My Horse: Voodoo and Life in Haiti and Jamaica* (1938) is surprisingly and significantly shaped by the same discourse: the relation of cultural nationalism to modern forms of government in a newly postcolonial world. In both of these works, the investment of modernism in primitivism emerges as an engagement with a modern, centralizing, imperialist governance that is racially stratified.

Griffith's films are notable for, among other things, their "run to the rescue" sequences that exemplify the move from a "cinema of attractions" to one based on narrative integration. Tom Gunning explains that chase films introduce the idea of focusing on how individual shots are linked. As a result, "[t]he process of following a continuous action through a series of shots created new relations to the spectator, new approaches to space and time" (66). Griffith also contributed to the development of parallel and contrast editing, which allowed audiences to see simultaneous reactions to the same occurrence, to "stop" time, to show one event from several perspectives, or to unexpectedly and rapidly juxtapose different places and times. Although critics have not described "run to the rescue" sequences as themselves aesthetically "modernist," the editing techniques that create them are, of course, classic descriptions of how modernism altered not only perceptions of space and time but also understandings of the relationship between past and present. But, as Michael Rogin and Walter Benn Michaels have allowed us to see, Griffith's greatest "run to the rescue" did not take space in abstract space and time but in the space and time of America's empire.[5]

The nineteenth-century white supremacist solution to the end of slavery—violent social and economic subordination and political disenfranchisement—worked. But although Griffith casts political power based in representative government as effective enough to drive a plot necessitating violence against black men when they vote, he also characterizes the vote as pathetically inadequate—something only black men would be foolish enough to want. Griffith uses the myth of the powerful black voter/legislator as much as he does the myth of the black rapist. A narrative of an uncertain white masculinity that must be transformed and shored up by a massed Klan and its rituals intertwines with a narrative about a different kind of white power: electoral power. The film asks individual white men to re-empower white men as a group by relinquishing identities of their own to form the "brotherly horde" of the Klan (Rogin 223). Electoral politics works similarly; one must have faith in a mystified system of democratic representation in which one vote is worth both nothing and everything—and in which one is reduced to being a voter in a group. In well-known philosophical narratives of the origins of the state, the band of brothers goes on to form a state in which they agree to this kind of relinquishing of individual power. The mysticism of the imagined community of the nation yields to the mystification of the institutions of the state. Not so for Griffith—it is here that we see the degree to which twentieth-century concerns about the status of (white) (male) individual agency drive Griffith's representation of a nineteenth-century white man's problem.

When we examine *The Birth of a Nation* from this perspective, two of its interests emerge as particularly striking. First, confrontation with state bureaucracy produces a nation. Second, Griffith focuses intently and sometimes contradictorily on elections and enfranchisement. It is the way these two things affect his aesthetic techniques, rather than the techniques themselves, that should define Griffith's relation to history and his definition of subjectivity and agency as modernist. The enfranchisement of black people makes manifest how the state has come to stage political existence in a way that suggests the abstract interchangeability of white and black men as citizens. In the context of winner-take-all districting, citizenship is "the ultimate reflection of individual dignity and autonomy and . . . voting is the means for individual citizens to realize this personal and social standing. Under this theory, voters realize the fullest meaning of citizenship by the individual act of voting for representatives who, once elected, participate on the voter's behalf in the process of self-government" (Guinier 124). But since all representation is group rather than individual representation, this promise cannot be fulfilled.[6] By this logic, the black legislators technically represent the "helpless white minority," as Griffith calls them.[7]

Griffith reaches back to Reconstruction, when the problem for white men was that black men were (theoretically) being enfranchised. But he actually articulates and tries to solve a different problem: that enfranchisement didn't actually work in the way the liberal individualistic view of representative democracy claimed it would. His interest in grounding an elite individualist whiteness outside mass politics is a response to what he does not overtly acknowledge. Enfranchisement could be easily circumvented, suggesting that it was not the source of individual agency, responsibility, and identity it promised to be.

Griffith's depiction of African Americans as voters and legislators reiterates, if contradictorily, this sense of enfranchisement's power as illusory. After an election day on which "[a]ll the blacks are given the ballot, while the leading whites are disenfranchised" (107) we see a black man placing two ballots in the box, while black and white men (carpetbaggers and men aligned with the character meant to stand for Thaddeus Stevens) prevent white men from placing their ballots, either with shakes of the head or by physically shoving them away. The next title reads: "Receiving the returns: The negroes and carpetbaggers sweep the state" (107). The consequence of this sweep is a State House filled with black people who don't understand the point of being representatives: they eat peanuts and joints of meat, drink, laugh, and take off their shoes while in session. Their bill to allow intermarriage of blacks and whites goes up alongside bills such as "all whites must salute negro officers on the streets" (107). Griffith meant the reference to racial intermarriage to be incendiary. In this, his claim seems to be that franchise is powerful, and that black people can wield it effectively.

But Griffith also suggests that the franchise actually does not accomplish very much for black people in the long run. His depiction of the black State House shows the legislators to be petty and childish, rather than crafty and intelligent. They manage to pass the marriage bill only because it brings the same kind of childish satisfaction that requiring whites to salute them would. But Griffith also makes the point that white women don't want to marry black men—this is why Lynch must kidnap Elsie and Gus tries to rape Flora—so that bill is useless. The black legislators do not have the competence to create legislation with the potential to change their status as a group or legislation that recognizes their historical constitution as a group. The state legislature does not pass a bill for the "forty acres and a mule" that appears on a placard in an earlier scene of black protest. Griffith obscures this group constitution and links any remedy based on it to the close-up image of a black hand illegitimately putting in two ballots. Even more significantly, he portrays black people as uninterested in legitimate groupness, that is to say, their authenticity as justification for their claims. Instead, they are eager to merge with the federal government's institutions and to marry out of their group.

As Hunter points out in her analysis of George Orwell's doublethink novels, awareness of "the artificiality of the state and its public presence [leads to] the recognition that even in an empowered position the individual can do nothing to affect the workings of the state" (209). The places where the workings of the state are being most obviously contested are sites of imperialism, precisely those sites from which primitivist representations come. One of the ways in which *National Geographic* characterized populations or cultures as "native" (as opposed to "developed" or "modern") was in terms of their inability to understand or their unwillingness to accept modern systems of state management, that is, as Nicholas Thomas puts it, "government and its conceptual categories" (Thomas 106). Indeed, both Britain (in the Fiji Islands and India) and the United States (in the Philippines) imagined "pacification," "civilization," "benevolent assimilation," and eventual accession to self-government in the early twentieth century as dependent on natives performing the kinds of acts that demonstrated the development of a self-consciousness connected to state bureaucracy.[8] Griffith takes to heart Woodrow Wilson's assertion that "teaching" South American republics fair and free elections is the way to conquer them; this is why the film's determination to disenfranchise black people cannot follow its own logic and conclude with the enfranchisement of white people.

Although they succeed in first "Disarming the blacks" and in "The next election" prevent the blacks from voting entirely, the Klansmen do not themselves vote. Griffith presents whites who are unfairly denied admission to the bureaucracy of the state and its administration, but Ben's longing is for a nation, not a state. After having been denied the vote, forced to allow a black man to behave rudely to "his" women, and having learned that blacks will outnumber whites in the state legislature 101 to 23, Ben sits on a hill and gazes hopelessly down at the landscape. The medium shot here encompasses Ben's upper body and the valley. "Title: In agony of soul over the degradation and ruin of his people. MS: Ben enters left and stands on the riverbank looking out across the valley. He takes off his hat and sits on a rock, holds his clenched fists out in a gesture of helplessness, then gestures sweepingly with his left hand and bows his head" (114). The more expansive angle and gesture in this shot directly contrast the narrowness of the entry into participation in the bureaucratic state as represented by the hole in the top of the ballot box with the kinds of affective linking of the land with the patriot we find in nationalism. Those who corrupt the balloting process by slipping in double ballots or depriving white men of their votes are aesthetically and visually "smaller" in close-up shots without the comprehensive sweep of Ben's gaze. The ballot box becomes a space of forced social association where Ben would be reduced to fit into the tiny state-allotted civic space of the black ballot-caster. According to Griffith's logic, Ben must refuse the limited comprehension of the black voter who thinks the franchise is something material handed out by the Freedman's Bureau.[9] Instead, he embraces the potentially limitless imagined expanse of the nation.

Griffith depicts Ben's defiance of the legislation of civil equality as post-colonial. He constructs him as a native complete with tribal dress that (unlike a modern Western uniform) robes his horse as well as himself, and is exotically effeminate in that it is a robe rather than trousers. He participates in rituals using blood, and in ritual murder. After Flora kills herself, Ben exhorts the men to go after Gus:

> MS: Ben holds up Flora's little Confederate flag and looks away as he dips it twice in a basin of water held by a fellow Clansman. He wrings it out and holds it aloft again. Title: Brethren, this flag bears the red stain of the life of a Southern woman, a priceless sacrifice on the alter of an outraged civilization. MS: . . . Ben takes a burning cross from a Clansman behind him and holds it and the flag aloft. . . . Title: Here I raise the ancient symbol of an unconquered race of men. . . . I quench its flames in the sweetest blood that ever stained the sands of Time. MS: . . . Ben quenches the fiery cross in the basin. (128–29)

Klan robes make of their wearers an ethnic group. The hallmark of "looking ethnic," after all, emphasizes how much each member of a group looks like the others. The Klan is even more of a racial group because, as Michaels puts it, the whiteness of Klan robes makes their wearers more white than they could ever really be (Michaels, *Our America* 121). To weight whiteness with its own ethnicity through the idea of the native authenticates it as an identity in a way particular to Griffith's own era rather than to the one he depicts.

Griffith's imagery follows the early-twentieth-century redefinition of the term *culture*. From *civilization,* it came to encompass the professionalizing American anthropological discipline's sense of a collection of recognizable, autonomous, and consistent ways of thinking and acting that made a group of people distinguishable as a group—a way of life that was a "conceptual whole" (Hegeman 64; Stocking 212–20). Michaels argues that after World War I, American discourse on racial and national identity took the form of a pluralism that shifted from justifying a group's practices based on its degree of deviation from a universal standard to making "the identity of the group . . . grounds for the justification of the group's practices" (Michaels, *Our America* 14).

Griffith's white tribe, then, must mobilize against other tribes based on its "whole way of life" and avoid assimilation. Griffith refuses expanded political representation as a solution; in "culture's" terms this solution is unacceptable because it is inauthentic. It is not indigenous, so to speak, to the kind of (white) subjectivity he wants to endow with an unassailable right to exist. This conception of primitivism damns both the U.S. government and the black people, who are to his mind so pathetically without the "culture" that would cause them to demand authentic and particular political rights that they are willing to assimilate themselves to a centralized government.

Woodrow Wilson's *A History of the American People* explicitly frames Griffith's film;[10] the constitutional philosophy that supported his decisions about imperialism in the Caribbean and the Pacific *and* his arguments for national self-determination in the peace settlements after World War I runs through it implicitly. Whether or not national self-determination worked (most accounts of Wilson at the Peace Conference chronicle the many times he and other statesmen sacrificed the principle to protect the interests of great powers),[11] national groups who wanted to establish their own nation-states took up the succinctly articulated concept and developed it (Heater 46). The right to national self-determination required a collective identity, and it is identity that, as Pomerance puts it, is the central problem of the doctrine that was never solved: identifying the "self" which is to do the "determining" (Pomerance 16). Any debate about whether to grant a nation what was essentially an identity—a self—turned on questions of authenticity, whether the definition of the moment was about contiguous territory, community of speech, common disidentity from "alien" rule, or shared institutions. It required an assertion of a recognizable, collective "whole way of life."

Hurston's and Griffith's impulses toward ethnographic and cinematic genres create the intense "locality" of the native other (Hurston creates "the Haitian" and Griffith "the Southerner/American") to express desire for/wonder about the native mind not in terms of his or her presumed psyche but as a political-historical way of understanding and acting in the world. Using the context of a newly enfranchised population that throws into question the definition of what it means to have a vote, Griffith creates a character who rejects "enfranchised subjectivity,"[12] that is, an understanding that his agency in the nation will be mediated by representation. Ben is "local" or "native" in contrast to the "cosmopolitan" colonial and federal powers. Griffith uses his character's gaze to suggest that the primary object of public nostalgia in his movie is not only slavery or the unburned South but is also a particular mode of visualizing the relationship between subject and state.

This is why, although one might think that this interest would inhere in the newly enfranchised group forging a new relationship with its nation, the focus is still on Ben and the Klan. Griffith makes sure black voters cannot be an object of interest because they are not local or native. Irrevocably yoked to the U.S. federals by their willingness to wear uniforms and require salutes from whites, consenting to corruptible systems of representative democracy without having strong beliefs in them, black voters in Griffith's film are (degraded) state subjects. Griffith reverses actual power relations to make a claim for the oppressed status of southern whites relative to those newly (and, one might argue, barely) enfranchised. This is consistent with primitivism: the primitivist envies people who are materially or politically disempowered based on their supposedly more meaningful connection with intangible spiritual or sensual capacities. Ben's appropriations of the signs of tribal ritual are similarly constructed. "Natives" are in a position to have a greater capacity for understanding the agency and freedom of being more than a voter. Griffith here makes *native* a positive term and then appropriates it for white supremacy. In the process, he denies that black people have their own whole culture. Making the "problem" with the black voters a matter of inauthenticity implies that if the real (white) citizens of America do not resist state subjectivity, they will be colonized as black voters have allowed themselves to be.

Hurston is explicitly writing ethnography, a genre with the goal of producing and presenting a group by organizing an understanding of them through a defining cultural practice. But Hurston, like Griffith, creates her natives and their culture in terms of political theory. *Tell My Horse* first stages Haitian cultural practice as incompatible with modern state practices but then proceeds to find the practices themselves political, in a deliberate "use and abuse" of ethnographic conventions of the time. She begins with a claim that "lying" is a cultural practice:

> It is safe to say that this art, pastime expedient or whatever one wishes to call it, is more than any other factor responsible for Haiti's tragic history. Certain people in the early days of the Republic took to deceiving first themselves and then others to keep from looking at the dismal picture before them. . . . They were trying to make a government of the wreck of a colony. . . . They were trying to make a nation out of very diffident material. . . . It must have been a terrible hour for each of the three actual liberators of Haiti, when, having driven the last of the Frenchmen from their shores, they came at last face to face with the people for whom they had fought so ferociously and so long. . . . Perhaps it was in this way that Haitians began to deceive themselves about actualities and to throw a gloss over facts. Certainly at the present time the art of saying what one would like to be believed instead of the glaring fact is highly developed in Haiti. . . . This lying habit goes from the thatched hut to the mansion. (81–82)

This analysis locates the origins of a culture's defining characteristic not in "traditional" practices independent of history but in the birth of the Haitian nation through revolution in 1804, the present economic problems of the country, and its recent occupation by United States.[13]

The lies of the hut and the mansion are different: "The upper class lie about the things for the most part that touch their pride. The peasant lies about things that affect his well-being, like work, food and small change" (81–82). The peasant, unlike the upper-class Haitian, will answer her questions about voodoo frankly, but not return with the change if paid to run an errand. The upper-class Haitian may be "the type of politician who does everything to benefit himself and nothing to benefit his country but who is the first to rush to press to 'defend' Haiti from criticism" (80). These people lie about the existence of voodoo "under the very sound of the drums," claiming that all that has been written about it is nothing but the malicious lies of foreigners. . . . Even if he is not an adept himself he sees it about him every day and takes it for a matter of course, but he lies to save his own and the national pride" (83). And finally, there are Haitians who "lie" to Hurston or to their fellow citizens about American involvement: why Americans invaded, how much money Haiti owed to foreign countries, and who was responsible for the end of the American occupation (84–85).

Although Hurston opens this section by structuring "lying" as an esoteric practice to be covered by ethnographic narrative as a "Haitian" thing to do, her descriptions of the lies she encounters are also always accounts of narrating the nation. "Culture" comes from the practices of nationhood rather than from practices existing independently and/or practices in danger from the modern world system. Lying is not a mode of narration incongruous with modernity, but is produced in response to the supposed "truths" of European colonization and American imperialism. After recounting an argument she has with a Haitian about whether America has taken advantage of Haiti or whether the Americans saved Haiti from having to immediately repay its debt to France, Hurston concludes:

> He was patently sorry for himself and all of the citizens who had suffered so much for love of country. If I did not know that every word of it was a lie, I would have been bound to believe him, his lies were that bold and brazen. His statements presupposed that I could not read and even if I could that there were no historical documents in existence that dealt with Haiti. . . . I soon learned to accept these insults to my intelligence without protest because they happened so often. (85–86)

Hurston imagines these "lies" as told by and on behalf of an imagined community of nationalized citizens. They are "lies" because the "historical documents" that would be consulted to settle their dispute would, she implies, take the American side. But in making a point of how often she must listen to these lies, Hurston underscores the solidarity of this man with "all of the citizens who had suffered so much for love of country" (103). This is a classic postcolonial moment—explicit contestation over which narratives are properly credentialed as "history" and "truth" and can therefore compel action or indemnity.[14] Given the centrality of national debt to Haiti's history and current situation,[15] these conversations are not simply bits of local color. The contrast between "lies" and "historical documents" serves to outline the process by which "all the citizens" come to assert a national narrative; this process creates them as subjects of history. At the same time, Hurston alleges the imagined community of the nation (as opposed to the national state) as the site of an authentic "people"—something it is the ethnographer's duty to find and describe.

In the twentieth century, both the ethnographer and the state have the same object. The chapter "Death of Leconte," about a presidential assassination, redefines ethnography's "people" in terms of the state's investment in creating its own subjects, often through the use of national narrative—a different version of "the people." As with the discussion of Haitian lying, credentialed history as opposed to people's narrative emerges:

> This is the story of the death of President Leconte the way the people tell it. The history books all say Cincinnatus Leconte died in the explosion that destroyed the palace, but the people do not tell it that way. Not one person, high or low, ever told me that Leconte was killed by the explosion. It is generally accepted that the destruction of the palace was to cover up the fact that the President was already dead by violence. (103)

Hurston's account of ethnography, by focusing on the interviews she had in order to be able to tell her story "the way the people tell it," suggests that for her, the ethnographical "primitive" is functionally antistate. The exotic beliefs of authentic natives center on modern political incidents. Like Griffith, Hurston paradoxically locates authenticity, or nativeness, as emerging from a hyperawareness of modernity, knowledge of the modern state's tricks, and, she hopes, the ability to challenge these tricks born out of a history of colonial revolt and oppression.

Hurston and Griffith articulate the same problem (even if Griffith willfully misperceives himself as its chief victim): the state deceptively promises the power to ensure one's own freedom. Haiti is supposedly a self-determined government, but this self-determination is constantly deformed by the need to defer to other countries' competing capital and foreign policy interests. Haiti's client presidents, U.S.-authored constitution, U.S.-controlled national budgets, and U.S.-established and -officered police highlight the development of a conceptual vocabulary that could maintain the existence of "a people" without ensuring that their government represented them.

Hurston sets government narrative against people's narrative. The government attempts to end "people's" narratives about Leconte. "When the daylight came they picked up something that nobody could say with any certainty was President Leconte and held a funeral. But then the way things were nobody could say the formless matter was not the late president either. So they held a state funeral and buried it" (110). Hurston's pronouns here indicate the flatness of the state narrative in comparison with the detail-packed, slightly folkish, "people's version" she herself uncovered. She sees these unofficial versions not as rational disagreements among citizens about official reports, but as manifestations of "the people" themselves. They establish themselves as a people by maintaining different stories about how the world works. In this description, the Haitians lose the kind of specificity normally assigned to analyzing political identities among elite Westerners. These natives are united across high and low classes, a factor that contradicts her earlier analyses of divisions by race, education, and class.

The Leconte chapter, moreover, reformulates "culture" around questions of political subjectivity. This may be where Franz Boas's influence shows itself despite their differences—Hegeman argues that Boas worked out his redefinitions of culture in political essays responding to World War I rather than in the scientific literature. Similarly, W. E. B. DuBois, well aware of the way "culture" anchored political categories in the twentieth century, published *The Negro* in 1915 partly in order to historicize Africa—to give it a "self" with a right to "determination"—in the face of a wave of colonization (Hegeman 50; Blight 52–53).

In other words, modernism's preoccupation with imagining the conscious self should be understood as entangled with the twentieth-century's consolidation of subjects and communities that would be free and authentic yet also both legible and malleable with regard to institutions that could coordinate, for instance, managed economies, migrant labor, the setting of international boundaries, and the interests of "the great powers."

Modernist criticism dealing with the construction of natives often examines the primitivist response to empire as a fascination with reconstructing the individual psyche. Racial and cultural otherness; different kinds of art, artifacts, and ritual; and the simultaneous threat and promise of "going native" stand in contrast to the internationalization, industrialization, commodification, homogenization, and rationalization perceived as characteristic of modernity. The shared political vocabularies of *The Birth of a Nation* and *Tell My Horse* suggest, however, that modernist primitivism's natives are, unlike their creators, potentially freer *citizens* than the state subjects elite modernists must remain. This (perverse) fantasy reveals the conditions of a politics of modernism that understands the problem of modernity as being that of governance and asks whether liberal democracy is compatible with the kinds of authority and subjectivity that modernity seems to demand.

NOTES

1. For a discussion of Epstein and primitivism see Rachel Moore, *Savage Theory*.

2. See Rafael, *White Love;* Anderson, "Census, Map, Museum" in *Imagined Communities;* and Hannah, "The Spatial Politics of Governmental Knowledge" in *Governmentality.*

3. See Renda, *Taking Haiti* for a recent account of the nineteen-year-long U.S. occupation.

4. Previewed as *The Clansman* on January 1–2, 1915, Riverside, California; first shown February 8, 1915, Los Angeles, California, as *The Clansman;* world premiere March 3, 1915, New York City, under the permanent title *The Birth of a Nation* (Lang 39). Quotations and descriptions from the film with page numbers are from the continuity script in Lang, ed., *Birth of a Nation.* Quotations and descriptions from the film that lack page numbers are from my viewing of the film on VHS.

5. See Michaels, "Anti-Imperial Americanism," Rogin, "'The Sword Become a Flashing Vision,'" and Kaplan, *The Anarchy of Empire in the Making of U.S. Culture* for readings of Thomas Dixon's Klan trilogy and Griffith's film as engagements of American empire.

6. Under a theory of liberal individualism, voting rights are assumed to belong to individuals and not to groups. But when opponents of race-conscious districting attack the idea of group representation using the liberal idea(l) of one-man, one-vote, they ignore the fact that all representation is based on groups in a system of geographical districting (Guinier 121).

7. As Guinier points out, the right to representation is not the same as the right to vote. A voter does not actually have to vote in order to be represented; living in the district is sufficient (126).

8. See Thomas for a description of how the British attempted to institutionalize what they thought were recognizable hierarchical social institutions that could be turned into "government" in the Fiji Islands.

9. Following the titles "Enrolling the Negro vote" and "The franchise for all blacks," Griffith has an elderly black man refuse to register for the vote when he finds out what "franchise" means: "Ef I doan' get 'nuf franchise to fill mah bucket, I doan' want it nohow" (103–104).

10. See Rogin, "'Sword Become a Flashing Vision'" for an account of Griffith's use of Wilson's writing in the film's titles and of the connections among Dixon, Griffith, and Wilson.

11. While Wilson was negotiating at the Paris Peace Conference, the United States, as a result of its brutal forced labor regime, was fighting Caco soldiers rebelling against the occupation (Renda 139). Representatives of the Haitian opposition to the occupation went to Versailles to try to meet with Wilson as he advocated for the rights of small nations to self-determination, but to no avail. Haiti had consequences for Ireland and vice versa—Britain and the United States traded silence on each nation (Renda 33; Heater 75).

12. Hunter's phrase. See "Blood and Marmalade."

13. The occupation ended three years before Hurston's trip.

14. Hurston's politics in *Tell My Horse* are, as in nearly all her works, difficult to track. She is not, unlike James Weldon Johnson, Langston Hughes, and C. L. R.

James (whose *Black Jacobin* was published the same year), openly critical of the U.S. occupation. See Carby, "The Politics of Fiction," on Hurston's ethnographical approach as imperial vision.

15. After the revolution, the Republic of Haiti was founded in 1804. Most nations refused to recognize Haiti as a nation until 1825, when France agreed to recognize Haiti upon payment of an indemnity of 150 million francs to the French planters who had lost "their" land. With little export income and low credit, Haiti had to borrow this money from France, which led to European and then to American intervention in and control of Haiti's finances and economy (Renda 50–53, 99).

10   Gadže Modernism

Janet Lyon

In April 1908, not long before his career-ending breakdown, the British Symbolist poet and critic Arthur Symons published a brief notice in the *Journal of the Gypsy Lore Society* titled "In Praise of Gypsies." Brimming with the exoticism that characterized most gypsophilia at the time, the essay was an emotional response to the impending passage of the Moveable Dwellings Bill, which aimed to register, regulate, and provide for the sanitary inspection of the vans and tents of British Gypsies and Travellers, and to mandate education for their children. Symons's indignation in the face of this proposed legislation, which, he claims, will "shuffle [the 'Gypsies'] right off the very earth to which they have the universal human right," is largely disconnected from the actual social conditions of Gypsy populations in England and Wales.[1] Instead, it springs mainly from Symons's investment in the fictional romantic figure of the "Gypsy," a "natural man" whose instinctive drive for freedom leads him away from civilization's gatekeepers along a secret and infinitely receding path at the outer reaches of modernity.

Symons repeats all of the nineteenth-century orientalist tropes of mysticism and ahistoricity: "Gypsies" "live by rote and by faith and by tradition which is part of their blood"; they are "our only link with the East, with mystery, with magic"; they possess the "lawlessness, the abandonment, the natural physical grace in form and gesture, of animals; only a stealthy and wary something in their eyes makes them human" (Symons, "PG" 295–96). They are an atavistic trace of the rural, pre-modern world, which will survive after "cities and nations have vanished, as the dust vanishes before the wind."[2] Even the well-known "Gypsy faults" of "secrecy," "lying," and "thieving" can be lessons in antimodern resistance for those perceptive enough to recognize them (Symons, "PG" 297–98). Thus Symons replicates one vector of the multivalent figure of the *gadže* (non-Romani) creation called the "Gypsy." This is the celebrated Romani "Gypsy," an emblem of natural liberty, unencumbered mobility, and communal loyalty and harmony, admirably impervious to manipulation by the state and everywhere subverting the disciplinarity of evolving modern institutions.

But of course there were other more dominant and historically entrenched vectors of representation, lingering on from pre-romantic policies of xenophobia and mid-empire racial sciences, heightened by the coalescence of wage labor after the major phase of the industrial revolution, and disseminated in the parallel nineteenth-century discourses of national character and social control. According to these, the perceived freedoms of the "Gypsy" were in fact manifestations of congenital lawlessness, habitual restlessness, a perversely arrested form of domesticity, and, perhaps most dangerously, a resolute unwillingness to settle and perform "honest" wage labor. The fabled insularity of "Gypsy" communities was proof of a radical alterity that might be antistatist or anti-Christian or just plain criminal in origin; in any case, it was seen to shelter illiteracy and uncleanliness, and to perpetuate itinerant poverty.

Both the celebratory and suspicious views of the "Gypsy" shared important assumptions, as they were largely flip sides of the same representational coin: the British "Gypsy" was "foreign" (in spite of five hundred years of Gypsy-Traveller populations in England), or at least fundamentally not-English; he was also, for all of his proud self-sufficiency, notably, even recidivistically, primitive. For both champions and detractors, the figure of the "Gypsy" seemed to reveal something about the leaky valves of modernity: living in a country of "progress," where the institutions of modernity had been established especially early, the "Gypsy" somehow—actively—avoided modernity's ineluctable telos. Thus the "Gypsy's" "exemplary autonomy [and] feared alterity"[3] were discursively taken up by proponents of social control *and* dissenters from liberal reform, in a contradiction that points to the status of "the Gypsy" as an ideological sign and a sociological aporia. The "Gypsy" is in most usages a figure of the European imagination bearing little resemblance to—and indeed, often forcibly deforming—the historical lives and material conditions of the Romanichal, Lovari, Kalderash, Sinti, Coppersmith, and Gitano populations of Europe.[4] Symons's florid use of the "Gypsy" is no different. But when he links his praise of "Gypsy" groups' alterity to a critique of "the tyranny of law" and the "heavy wheel" of "progress" (Symons, "PG" 296), he follows a pattern elaborated simultaneously in modernist sociology and modernism, which opposes unregulated forms of sociality against a depersonalizing instrumental modernity.

1

With the title of this essay I mean to suggest a fundamental relation between modernism and the continuously evolving *gadže* constructions of the "Gypsy." More specifically, I wish to argue that modernism, and in particular several threads of British modernism, take for a covert model of communality and subjectivity the peripatetic, ahistorical "Gypsy," whose actual historical counterparts filled contemporary newspapers in stories of forced mass evictions and county council Acts. Deborah Nord, George Behlmer, and Katie Trumpener have explored various aspects of the cultural work done by the figure of the "Gypsy" in nineteenth-century literature; Trumpener, for example, has argued convincingly that, over the course of the century, the "Gypsy" increasingly becomes a textual device which on the one hand disrupts cultural memory and temporality, and on the other hand, as a result of the heightened stylization of "Gypsy" characters, acts as a marker of the shifting uses of literary genres.[5]

It is certainly possible to extend these lines of argument into a reading of the cultural products of modernism, showing how the "Gypsy" figure persists as an operative element in many works of modernist literature and as a popular model for the "modern" lifestyle. Not only do "Gypsies" appear in numerous poems and novels of the modern period—one has only to think of the parodic Madame Sosostris to recognize the hinge between modernism's fascination with occult divination and the long-established trope of "Gypsy" fortune-telling—but the imagined culture of the "Gypsy" appears persistently in some of the most important modernist social formations. The Bohemian salon is one of these, wherein occurs, as I have argued elsewhere, a cultivation of sociability modeled in part on an aesthetic of intransigence and antimodern insularity.[6] In its more popular manifestations, the vaunted "freedom" of modern life finds its correlatives in "free dance" and "free love," which were widely (though falsely) reputed to be practices in "Gypsy" camps. "Gypsy" costumes (Mabel Dodge in her turban, Augustus John in his high leather boots), "Gypsy" music (played, for example, in the London avant-garde cabarets detailed by Laura Winkiel in the next chapter of this volume), and the famous "Gypsy" restlessness of writers as diverse as Arthur Symons, D. H. Lawrence, and John Reed all contributed to a cultural matrix that, though fictional in its origins, nevertheless anchored a divergent community of self-identified moderns.

But such an approach to cultural representations of "Gypsies" has its limits, at least from a certain perspective within modernist studies. One could justifiably claim, for example, that British modernism cannot be adequately understood without some recognition of its co-optation of popular *gadže* narratives of "Gypsy" culture (which, it must be stressed, bore almost no resemblance to the complex and heterogeneous lives of English Gypsy-Travellers throughout British history). But this approach would need to go further than the tidy conclusion that, since "Gypsy" culture is a *gadže* construction, modernism's putatively rebellious co-optation of the "Gypsy" is in fact little more than a new adaptation of a dominant cultural myth. On this view, modernism that deals implicitly or explicitly with "Gypsy" themes and figurations is a *gadže* modernism to be denounced on the grounds of its inauthenticity and racism. In the end, such an approach to *gadže* modernism tells us very little about Gypsies or modernism. So while I believe it is valid and instructive to pursue the textual record of *gadže* constructions into the field of modernist literature, my aims here are rather different. I intend to explore the problematic generated by the idea of the "Gypsy" as a putative subject of modernity, girded as that idea is by the historical forces exerted in the opaque relations between *gadže* and Romanies; and I want to suggest how these relations inform some of the problematics of modernism.

Modernism attends to the paradoxical incompleteness of modern subjectivity, which is on the one hand self-conscious, rational, and poised to interpret the world-as-representation, and on the other hand riven by gaps in consciousness that are increasingly illuminated by modern epistemologies.[7] Modernist sociologists—in particular, Émile Durkheim, Georg Simmel, and Max Weber—tend to approach modern subjectivity as a symptomatic effect of fragmenting historical-economic forces. They point to rationalism's detachment from value (which is effaced through modern disenchantment) and its ungrounded proliferation within increasingly dissociated systems (functionalist social formations, bureaucracies) which take as their ends the reproduction of rationalism. Less starkly, though no less insistently, modernist aestheticians, ranging through a variegated spectrum that includes Virginia Woolf, W. B. Yeats, Mary Butts, James Weldon Johnson, Mina Loy, Melvin Tolson, and Djuna Barnes, view the self-reflexivity of modern subjectivity as both the figure and ground of the modern art problematic. On the one hand, the representation of consciousness becomes the utterly impossible as well as the only task for artists who must reject epistemological realism. On the other hand, the task of representing positively the modern community against and through which modern consciousness takes its shape becomes equally compelling, since the accelerated diversification of modern social structures ensures that there can be no fit between an individual and any one community. Identity is necessarily striated across a series of function groups (economic, social, sexual, national, and so forth), and this process reveals retroactively the absence of organic or originary communities through which the *I* of the artist secures value and ground in modernity. Within the field of recognizably modernist aesthetic practices, literary experimentation takes as one of its objects the portrayal of subjectivity not simply as consciousness, but rather as consciousness being made and unmade in its relation to others. The rendering of individualism within sociality entails, for modernists, an avoidance of the ideals associated with "possessive individualism," which depend upon regulated economic and political relations and guarantee in advance the easy substitution of heteronomy for autonomy. Instead, what modernists across a whole political range aim to explore are the shifting connections between the labile structures of consciousness and labile forms of community, in order to reveal both the depersonalizing forces inherent in "modern" society and the creative possibilities for counter-modern forms of sociability.

When community is placed front and center in an analysis of modernism's projects, the attraction for modernists of the lives of Romanichals in Britain becomes clearer. Up until the modernist period, the historical record of the Romani diaspora was minimally elaborated and poorly understood by the dominant culture, to say the least. Whatever discontinuous narratives floated in the European imagination tended to be characterological in nature: a mysterious "race" had simply appeared in Europe "quite suddenly one day, without anyone being able to say exactly where it had sprung from," in Franz Liszt's influential words (Liszt 8). The striking characteristics of these people, for Europeans invested in the establishment and proliferation of settled nation-states, were related to their perceived intransigence and willful unassimilability. Confusion about origins (registered, for example, in the Egipcion/Gypsy lexicon that prevailed in England until 1715)[8] transmuted easily into a teleology of uncertainty: not only was their sociological role in the narrative of modern progress unreadable, given the anachronism of their migratory tendencies, but the very character ascribed to them reflected nothing so much as uncertainty within the dominant culture. So the characterological properties of secrecy, insularity, cultural autonomy, inscrutability (or lack of transparency), and detachment, all imposed from without, were, properly speaking, the negative markers of the failure of discursivity. What *could* be "known" through the most superficial contact could not be made to fit within the burgeoning narratives of nineteenth-century modernity. Self-employment, for example, read (perforce negatively) as a resistance to wage labor, could only be interpreted as an exceptionalist fluke, a pocket of sluggish impermeability in the dominant economic system. And the persistence, in Romani social structures, of what looked to be an aberrant *Gemeinschaft* was rarely received on its own terms, and instead bent against an ideological model of house-centered domesticity.

What I am thinking of as an aberrant *Gemeinschaft* requires a brief elaboration here. In Ferdinand Tönnies's original (nostalgic, modernist) sociological formulation, *Gemeinschaft* describes a rural, organic community "ennobled," in his words, by tradition and religion and bound by positive or extrinsic law, which regulates the necessary harmony of wills within the traditional community. Implicit in this conception of tradition, and explicit in the projected geographical model of *Gemeinschaft*, is the dictum that it centers on the home, "has its roots in family life and is based on land ownership" (Tönnies 223). Tönnies's 1887 description of *Gemeinschaft* had became a founding tenet of German sociology by the turn of the century;[9] it referenced a social structure that could be articulated easily to the nostalgic image of an enduring rural English life that both grounded and helped to offset the cultural anxieties attending the explosive urban growth within Great Britain. But the constitutive link between rural stability, land ownership (or even landed sedentariness), and religious tradition disables this *volk* concept as an explanatory model for Gypsy cultures within modern England, since "Gypsies" were held to be largely areligious and unlanded. So that in spite of the long tradition of migratory work in English agricultural systems (within which temporary Gypsy-Traveller labor was a stable fixture), "Gypsy" culture was seen to deviate in materially and symbolically important ways from both the community-based emblem of rural England and the vocational traditions of agricultural employment. All of which is to say that Gypsy cultures, which could not be made to fit into existing or imagined sociological models, exceeded the empirical categories through which England took stock of itself as a modern nation-state.

This "unmanageable excess"[10] held obvious attractions for modernists, who sought to create communities in opposition to bourgeois models. Precisely because Gypsy communities were rooted neither in orthodox religion nor in bourgeois domesticity they instantiated a seemingly extramodern alternative to the suffocating familial configurations against which so many modernists, from Lawrence to Marinetti, directed their polemic. At once organic and without a delimited territorial space, unrooted and yet hardly deracinated, devoid of written history and therefore in some sense a spoiler of the dialectic, and, especially, resistant (though certainly not immune) to the codifying forces of bureaucratic modernity, the "Gypsy" community held out to some few antibourgeois *gadže* the promise of a proximate countermodernity: not an anti- or pre-modernity existing beyond modernity in some mythic or romantic dimension, but, rather, a countermodernity, thoroughly imbricated in modernity.[11]

2

"The policeman, the social reformer, and the man of the school board, all have their eye on the Gypsy; and the best way of 'raising him to our level' is sapiently discussed on platforms and in the newspapers" (21) wrote David MacRitchie, a founding member of the Gypsy Lore Society, in 1908. This was a year of increasingly intricate elaborations of what was variously called the "Gypsy Nuisance," the "Gypsy Problem," and the "Gypsy Menace."[12] While explicitly corporeal anti-Gypsy measures, including execution, flogging, banishment, or deportation, had largely been phased out in England by around 1815, these punishments were replaced by networks of social control that intensified during and after the 1870s.[13] The trend was accelerated by the manic efforts of the anti-"Gypsy" "reformer" George Smith, whose speeches and screeds read like the script of a Foucauldian nightmare: in 1883 he observed bitterly that "By travelling in vans, carts, and tents," Gypsies unfairly "escape the school boards, sanitary officers, rent and rate collectors; and today they are—unthinkingly, no doubt— undermining all our social privileges, civil rights, and religious advan- tages, and will, if encouraged by us, bring decay to the roots" (qtd. in May- all 90–91). Proliferating legislation broadened the ambit of existing Acts, so that, for example, earlier Vagrancy Acts, which outlawed fortune-telling and wandering, were enhanced by the Pedlars and Hawkers Acts. The ear- lier Turnpike Roads Act and Highway Act (against roadside camping) were complemented by the Commons Acts and Local Government Acts, which allowed local authorities to close commons to Gypsies.[14] The Housing of the Working Classes (HWC) Act of 1885 contained clauses that had been outlined by Smith in his ultimately unsuccessful Moveable Dwellings Bill, which mandated compulsory education for traveling children, and ad- dressed into the bargain a laundry list of related social concerns: sanita- tion, registration, tax collection, sex separation, and perceived indolence. Smith relentlessly followed up with versions of his bill each year from 1886–89, all with an eye to "redeeming the Gypsy and Van children from their sad condition" (qtd. in Acton 112). Reintroduced again in 1908 (the year of Symons's brief, agitated essay), it was powerfully resisted by the Showman's Guild, who used it to "establish 'Gypsies' as their scapegoats" (Acton 121) by arguing that it would punish respectable show people for the crimes of antisocial Gypsies. Provisions for the compulsory education of Gypsy children came in through the Children's Act, passed in that same year. But the combined effects of the HWC Act and the Moveable Dwell- ings discussions had already begun to issue in a series of forcible, violent evictions of long-standing Gypsy encampments, from, for example, Ep- ping Forest in 1894, Black Patch in Birmingham between 1904 and 1905, and South Shore, Blackpool between 1908 and 1910 (Mayall 175–78). This latter group had been established for more than eighty years, and, accord- ing to a plaintive letter to the king written by a Gypsy on behalf of her community, regularly paid rent, rates, and taxes. "We are English gipsies," Mrs. Franklin wrote, "and we look to our King for justice" (qtd. in Thomas William Thompson 116).

These and other evictions, and the local agitation leading up to them, were welded into national consciousness through wide reportage in local and national papers.[15] Stories tended to portray Gypsies as rural itinerants who resisted education, hygiene, and meaningful labor, thereby further ho- mogenizing the figure of the "Gypsy" as a national object even as it ob- scured the widely heterogeneous lives of British Gypsies. And of course, most of these redactions were fictions. As David Mayall and Angus Fraser have emphasized, Gypsies in England in those years were both sedentary and mobile, rural and urban. Some practiced patterned forms of migra- tion based loosely on agricultural cycles; some moved seasonally from rural encampments in summer to urban encampments in winter. Some movement was necessitated by local harassment, and some by the shifting or shrinking markets for the goods and services sold to sedentary populations, both rural and urban.[16] All movement and cessation of movement, whether temporary or permanent, whether around London or towns or between villages, ultimately stemmed from economic relations with settled society.[17] And those relations figured heavily in the Romani pollution taboos (largely unintelligible to the dominant culture) that guarded against, among other things, specific forms of *gadže* contact.[18]

Education, too, was controversial from both directions. Reformers saw the regulated education of children as the only antidote to what might now be called the "cycle of poverty" ascribed to Gypsy populations. According to this way of thinking, Gypsies' ignorance about ignorance prevented them from understanding both their own "poverty" and its cure. But of course this diagnostic approach, so characteristic of a social control discourse modeled on epidemiology, missed a much more fundamental dynamic, since Gypsy children took their education from a variety of sources, principally the closely knit family group and wider kinship networks, but also from local schools (as Mrs. Franklin's letter to the king suggests when she avers that "most of our children have been born, christened, and educated" at Blackpool). And the state educational project itself faced resistance from schoolteachers who, according to Smith's biographer, "protested that it would be a great moral wrong to flood their schools [with] the contaminating influence of Gypsy children ... the very scum of the earth" (qtd. in Acton 127). Above all, the issues of mobility and labor practices were especially thorny in the early modernist period. Mayall has suggested that the "*nature* of [Gypsy] work, more readily identifiable with preindustrial than industrial formations" (Mayall 59) was the source of the dominant culture's hostility, and I would add that this problem is inseparable from the perceived problem of mobility, which was understood to exist in a sharp and sometimes threatening opposition to industrial society. No matter that Gypsy mobility was always already encumbered by economic considerations and existed across a continuum that included varieties of sedentariness. The bottom line was that even the most concretely domiciled sedentariness among Gypsy groups rarely coincided with cultural assimilation, which would have been marked by a majoritarian acceptance of, among other things, orthodox Christianity, wage labor, bureaucratic interpellation, and transparent practices of sociability. Gypsy mobility could not be categorized as migrancy, which entails a fixed and regulated territorial trajectory; instead, the very flexibility of Gypsy mobility resembled a kind of deterritorialization that was produced moment to moment by local conditions. Nor did this movement, which inexorably brings to mind Deleuze and Guattari's discussions of nomadology, allow for an easy equation of Gypsy mobility with nomadism.

Indeed, in spite of the seeming applicability of the concept of nomadic deterritorialization to Gypsy mobility, Deleuze and Guattari's meditations are, on the whole, unsuited to it. Situated in 1227, their "Treatise on Nomadology" precedes the development of Western modernity, and hence the figure of the modern nomad, so that the effortless agency they accord the nomad (who "occupies," "inhabits," "holds," and "distributes himself in" space) is largely unavailable to the Gypsy, who lives in an increasingly reactive relation to settled, industrial society (Deleuze and Guattari 381). Their (heroized) nomad, who is going, precisely, *nowhere,* is pitted on the one hand against the migrant, who is always going *somewhere,* from one point to another, along a "striated" or settled trajectory, and on the other against the sedentary, who is always already *somewhere.* I am suggesting that modern Gypsies cannot be assigned a stable place in this uncharacteristically stable triad.

Where Deleuze and Guattari may be of use here is in their observation of a constitutive antipathy of a developing State to unstructured nomadic movement within its margins, which interferes with "large-scale projects, the constitution of surpluses, and the organization of the corresponding public functions" (Deleuze and Guattari 358). And while the modern British State apparatus may not have been critically aggrieved by the "Gypsy Problem," considering the miners' strikes, suffrage activism, and Home Rule agitation taking place in these same years, it is nevertheless significant that the State's functions enumerated here by Deleuze and Guattari were all refused *a priori* in the established practices of Gypsy populations. Surplus, especially, found no place in Gypsy economies, which operated on principles of barter, the recycling of goods through repair, the crafting of goods from immediately available and largely gleaned materials, and the rendering of services on an as-needed, local basis. Nor could Gypsy activity be aggregated into State-building projects, which in these years had begun to interpellate the poor *as* working class by way of Liberal legislation formalizing workers' rights, pensions, minimum wage, and industrial unemployment. Moreover, at a time when social harmony and cohesion were actively fostered as decoys for the alarming increase in poverty rates at the turn of the century, as well as for the cracks in empire wrought by the Boer War, the specter of "the Gypsy" as recalcitrant other became somewhat starker.

Attempts to colonize these internal others, whether through missionary work or through coerced sedentarization, were, by any measure, unsuccessful. Whatever cultural anxiety attended these failures can be seen partly as an extension of the more general anxieties embedded in nationalist discourse with regard to alien groups: nation building must view nonassimilation as a problem, since it depends for its coherence upon an appearance of shared (not to say unified) heritage. An example of the fantasy of Gypsies' extranational loyalties can be found in Bram Stoker's *Dracula*

(1897), which has been read by contemporary critics as a gothic allegorization of, among other things, racial theory, reverse colonization, the Irish question, the invention of the homosexual, and degeneration.[19] But I would suggest that Stoker's representation of the Szgany Gypsies who "attach themselves" to Count Dracula is precisely *non*-allegorical. Jonathan Harker's diary entry, which notes that "They are peculiar to this part of the world, though allied to the ordinary gipsies all the world over. There are thousands of them in Hungary and Transylvania" (Stoker 50), reflects not only the statistics of the 1890 census that counted 275,000 Romanies living in the Hungarian territories,[20] but also points to a perceived intraracial alliance among Gypsies everywhere—and everywhere they "are almost outside all law . . . fearless and without religion, save superstition." Jonathan drops letters with a piece of gold into the Szganies' courtyard encampment, hoping that they will post them and effect his escape from Dracula's castle; their leader "press[es the letters] to his heart and bow[s]," but betrays him immediately (Stoker 50). The Gypsies' loyalties lie with the vampire, not the English representative of enlightened modernity;[21] and indeed, it is a Szgany who stabs and kills the American Morris in the final struggle to save the unholy master.

The undecidable loyalties of groups who could not be assimilated to the modern project of nation building comprised an important theme in another, more prominent coeval debate about racial difference, the Jewish Question. According to Amanda Anderson's penetrating account of the wide-ranging intellectual debates about Judaism, "the Jewish race" was seen by many to manifest "a recalcitrant separatist character that rendered it unequal to the tasks of modern citizenship, which required identifying oneself with humanity in general and the interests of the state in particular. . . . [T]he judgment that Jews were particularistic rather than universal, tradition-bound rather than modern, effectively wrote them out of the modern project" (Amanda Anderson 126). I would argue that in this and in many other respects, the arguments surrounding the Jewish Question were reflected in the construction of the "Gypsy Problem." Both groups were diasporic; both were deemed to follow the laws of insular culture rather than the civil laws of a self-reflexive polity; and both were seen to exist in a state of internal exile and to present drains on local resources and potential threats to national character. Indeed, the frequency with which the two groups are linked throughout the nineteenth century in casual comparisons or as mutually illuminating cases is quite striking, especially in view of the actual differences between them. The nineteenth-century narrative of Jewish diaspora, for example, is teleological in nature, depending upon centuries of written history, saturated with cultural memory and following a futural arc toward an endpoint of collective settlement. By contrast, the (*gadže*) narrative of Romani diaspora involves uncertain origins and an equally uncertain telos. Where Jewish law is based upon a strict codification of religious faith, the structures of Romani self-regulation, most notably through antipollution laws, cannot be understood as a derivation of institutional religious dicta.

Nevertheless, the pairing of Jews and Gypsies as exceptionalist challenges to universalist principles of political philosophy occurs regularly, and it is interesting to note that it often takes the form of a binarism within antisemitic discourse, according to which a romantic celebration of the "Gypsy" is propped on the denigration of the "Jew."[22] In this configuration, for which I take as a (particularly noxious) example Franz Liszt's *The Gipsy in Music,* Jews are portrayed as having prospered unethically, in spite of their hardships, through usury, obsequious accommodations, cowardly assimilation, or vicious insularity. Liszt spends four early chapters in this spiteful vein in order to dilate by comparison on the mystery of "Gypsy" endurance and the genius of "Gypsy" music. "Gypsies" have "consistently resisted all temptation to participate in the prosperity of the favoured nations," and, unlike converted Jews, never "ostentatiously deny their own [identities] . . . in order to partake of prosperity, vilely acquired" (Liszt 18). "Gypsy" music reflects this resolute self-determination: it is, in Liszt's account, a literal transmission of unmediated relations with nature and inseparable from the communities that create it: its eerie key changes and collaborative rhythmic patterns simply cannot be reproduced by the *gadžo.* For Liszt, "Gypsy" music is, like its musician-channelers, *sui generis.*

3

The fascination of a *sui generic* "Gypsy culture" for modernists like Symons, D. H. Lawrence, and Augustus John, the latter of whom spent a considerable amount of time learning Romani dialects and camping with Romanichals in southern England, cannot be extrapolated into a general claim about a constitutive indebtedness of British modernism to "the Gypsy." Such an effort would in any case depend upon a speciously homogeneous understanding of both cultures. What may be teased out instead, as I have suggested, is the significance of the parallels between the countermodern social formations understood by interested *gadže* to be intrinsic to "Gypsy culture" on the one hand and the sociological ideals underpinning modernist social formations on the other. What British modernism takes from "Gypsy culture," I would propose, can only be seen from a perspective that recognizes within modernism a painfully contradictory set of relations to modernity that seek palliation in flexible forms of sociability. Particularly disruptive for the British modernist generation was the recognition that it was itself a product of the liberal traditions through which the projects of modernity were conveyed, which is to say that while modernism was always already a product of modernity, it struggled with, reacted to, and aimed to escape this tautological conundrum.[23]

Sociability, or what modernist sociologists called communality, provided one way of mediating the conundrum. The sheer variety of the forms of sociability connected to modernism helps to focus this point: the workshops, art centers, salons, moveable feasts, hostess parties, gallery groups, poetry clubs, house parties, pageants, pub crawls, cruising grounds, and "Evenings" where modernists gathered were inseparable from the transmission and production of modernist aesthetics. The Poet's Club meetings at a Soho restaurant and an ABC tea room produced Imagism; dada emerged from a free-wheeling Zurich café; Saturday nights in the rue de Fleurus created a vocabulary for the reception of Cubism. The very flexibility of these social forms was in some sense engineered as a challenge to what was, in the modernist imaginary, the fixed architecture of bourgeois associations. In the best of circumstances, such social formations could provide spaces of un-becoming (of the "self") and becoming (into otherness), and could themselves fluctuate into spaces of living art. It is no accident that sites of sociability are featured so prominently in modernist fiction precisely *as* spaces of living art;[24] indeed, this is the role assigned to sociability by Georg Simmel, who understood it to be an artistic practice through which kaleidoscopic forms were made and unmade from fragments of personalities in recombinant relations. Of great value to Simmel was the role that modern sociability played in allaying the excesses of instrumental rationalism. True sociability, in his view, could not be harnessed to expediency or acquisition, but was an end in itself, a source of frictionless pleasure.[25]

The search for (and spontaneous creation of) alternative forms of sociability by modernists was, on this reading, a pursuit of a modality of art that could resist assimilation into the teleological projects of modernity. "Gypsy culture" offered a ready-to-hand example of this kind of minority form, especially for British modernists, whose national literary culture included, not incidentally, an abiding strand of nativism. What was seen by the dominant culture as an inscrutably archaic insularity could also be (and indeed was, correctly) interpreted as a surface dimensionality beyond which a shifting and variable sociability flourished. Gypsy groups shared a bond of protective self-differentiation from *gadže* culture even as they met with and departed from other Gypsy groups, linking up for carnivals and fairs, working in coalitions and small groups, and meeting on roads and in towns. The lure of this sub-rosa sociability, the frisson of a thriving world beyond the veil of *gadže* intelligibility, exerted a strong pull on many modernists. In 1907 Arthur Ransome, a self-styled "Bohemian," writes with awe about a "gipsy poet," a quiet boy who strays into Ransome's London café group, produces a slim volume of strange, good poetry (written with "the real blood and spirit of the country" [Ransome 268]), and disappears forever one night with a Gypsy couple who have subtly hailed him on Battersea Bridge. Ransome's physiogamous approach to "Gypsy" sociability, which reads the richness of its internal systems off of its subtle extrusions, can rightly be dismissed as another instance of romantic gypsophilia. Even so, it points to what I think was of interest to a number of modern-identified writers in these years, including Symons: the possibilities for forms of sociability issuing from encounters in heterotopic spaces that are, by definition, "outside."

The painter Augustus John, who was soon to become a well-known protagonist of "Gypsy culture," made unusual efforts to involve himself in the lives of Gypsies, not as a *gadže* ethnographer, chronicler, or philologist, but as an affiliate of sorts, a sympathetic carouser and frequent participatory guest of the camps. His biographer ascribes to John the usual thrills that such contact brought to the would-be insider, but what is of interest to me may be found in John's autobiographical accounts of a seemingly endless series of chance encounters with Gypsies in "outside" spaces. One of the many encounters chronicled in his memoir *Chiaroscuro* occurs in an open square in Marseilles, where John is sitting in a bar watching "the comings and goings of Spanish gypsies" when he sees a Coppersmith Rom in magnificent dress striding across the *place*. Addressing him in the correct dialect, John shares a bottle of wine with him, is invited to the encampment (a group of "single-roomed huts"), dines, listens to music and dancing, stays the night, which eventually becomes a week, and finally goes on his way (John 109–10).

In John's accounts, his serial, unplanned, and often intense contacts with Gypsies bear a strong resemblance to the forms of sociability associated with cruising practices. The "impersonal intimacy," as it has been called by Bersani and others, that informs this kind of contact involves a relinquishing of practical goals and a disavowal of bourgeois emphases on the "character" or "personality" that ground modern possessive individualism.[26] Impersonal intimacy is a strange intimacy arising purely out of the phenomenon of unfamiliar contact. And while it is probably too much to say that John is cruising Gypsies—even the observation runs the risk of reifying a traveling Coppersmith family as non-agentic "Gypsies" (since it is most unlikely that Gypsies are cruising John, or any other *gadže*, for that matter)—I nevertheless make the connection to suggest the value for modernists of an abstracted version of what we know as cruising's brand of ungrounded, unpredictable, anonymous, or at least impersonal, sociability. It offers a model for a living art that evades Weber's iron cage of rationalism and revalues the modern, fragmented identity lamented by Durkheim.

A more direct account of this abstracted sociability occurs in D. H. Lawrence's modernist novella, *The Virgin and the Gipsy*, written in 1925, but published in 1930 upon his death. It is the usual Lawrencian story about the awakening of desire, the primacy of the body, the deathly grip of bourgeois community and religion, the magnetism of true masculinity. A doe-like virgin, Yvette, imprisoned in her father's stifling rectory by his oppressive family, comes to some kind of blood-consciousness after a series of brief encounters with a handsome, virile "Gypsy." She first happens upon him by chance in his family's secluded winter camp, where she and her friends agree to have their fortunes told by the "Gypsy's" wife. His impersonal, level gaze—a typical "Gypsy" trait—ignites a sexual spark in Yvette, which persists through the winter and is fanned higher by a second chance encounter on the road. Twice he visits the rectory to sell his beautiful handmade brooms and copperware; once she revisits the camp for a trancelike meal at the fire. This latter event is interrupted by a bubbly tourist, significantly, a "little Jewess" whose wealth (figured as an enormous fur coat) encases and obscures her body, and the interruption diverts Yvette from what might have been a sexual consummation. Yvette's final encounter with the "Gypsy" is rather different: he and his family have just broken their winter camp and are traveling north when he realizes that Yvette and her rectory are in danger of being destroyed by the flood waters of a nearby ruptured dam. He reaches the rectory in time to save Yvette (though not, thankfully, her hated "fungoid" grandmother), frantically dragging her to the top floor of the flooded house, taking off her clothes and rubbing her freezing body, and disappearing before she regains consciousness in the morning. Her suffocating bourgeois life, we understand, is forever changed.

The "Gypsy" plot of *The Virgin and the Gipsy* has either typically been dismissed as one more instance of overbearing *gadže* romanticism, or read by Lawrence scholars as another allotropic version of the author's "sexual awakening" plot devices. An exception to this trend is John Turner's reading, which takes seriously Lawrence's portrayal of economic and social relations between *gadže* and Gypsy in the story. Yes, the "Gypsy" is arrestingly handsome, loose in his limbs, a master of horses, taciturn yet meaningful, potently sexual (he has "say, five" children, he tells Yvette), which is to say that he is always on the verge of stereotype. But I would suggest that he also holds out the promise of a subjectivity and a sociability that are sovereign and modern—or perhaps, more properly, countermodern. Lawrence supplies details that anchor him in the striated world of modernity. One of the most striking of these is the fact of his conscription and service in the war: "He had been through the war. He had been enslaved against his will" (Lawrence 236), as Lawrence puts it, and we learn that pneumonia in the trenches nearly killed him. To go "through the war," means, for Lawrence, to be broken on the rack of modernity: the "Gypsy's disillusion in hostility, which belongs to after the war" (Lawrence 237) is the psychic price exacted by modernity's irrational and relentless trajectory. And the "Gypsy" pays twice over: he is a Gypsy-"Tommy" (Lawrence 228), cannon fodder for a culture bent on his disappearance.

The narrative delicately reveals his complex double-consciousness as outsider-Gypsy and as a reluctant subject of modernity. His name—Joe Boswell—is given only in the penultimate line of the novella, at the end of a note he writes to Yvette after reading in the newspaper that she has survived the flood. This delayed disclosure, not only of his name but also of his literacy and compassion, and Yvette's surprise that "only then she realized that he had a name" (Lawrence 252) retroactively light up her primitivist ignorance. She had idly imagined herself living in the Gypsy's camp: "Just to be where he was, that was to be at home. The caravans, the brats, the other women: everything was natural to her, her home, as if she had been born there" (Lawrence 241). But the camp is the site of a sociability that can never be appropriated or even duplicated, least of all by gadže. And a Gypsy with a name, who reads the papers and writes letters, is not part of Yvette's fantasy: thus Lawrence establishes that Yvette is too far "inside the pale" (Lawrence 237) to fully enter the Gypsies' complex world of sociability. Boswell himself suspects as much: he hews to his position "on an old, old warpath against such as herself" (Lawrence 236) even as he recognizes her struggle against gadže confinement. These thoughts are delivered through wisps of free indirect discourse, by means of which Lawrence frankly accords Boswell narrative subjectivity; at the same time, Lawrence does not presume to focalize the narrative through Boswell. He instead marks Boswell's "ever-unyielding outsideness" as riven by "the vast and gruesome clutch of our law" (Lawrence 236), gadže law. Such double-consciousness is constitutive of subjectivity in modernity, as modernists from Baudelaire to DuBois will attest, and I would suggest that Lawrence's assignment of unstable but sovereign subjectivity to Boswell by means of this developed characterization should be read not as an example of exoticism but rather as an exploration of a model of modernist subjectivity.

There are other reasons to read the Gypsy plot from this angle. Boswell's craftsmanship, for example, and especially his sanctified relation to the objects of his craft are portrayed as conduits through which modern reification is resisted.[27] More to my purposes, the story's triangulation of domestic sites, which pits the clean, essential, transient camp of the Gypsies against both the physically disgusting rectory with its mushroomlike inhabitants and the "little Jewess's" faux-Bohemian (and terribly cluttered) domestic arrangements with her lover, helps to focus on the conditions of possibility for an alternative "smooth" sociality, to use Deleuze's term, beyond the colonizing grasp of settled society and law. Though familial in structure, the "Gypsy" camp in this story displays a constitutive flexibility that Lawrence clearly admires but with which he assumes no easy familiarity. We never see the insides of the caravans, nor do we hear or understand what is said among "Gypsies." What we do see, I would suggest, is a portrait of social alterity that recognizes the historical contingencies of its subjects.

More than this, Lawrence's story points to the wider modernist problematic with which I began this essay. Like so much modernist work, the
narrative imagines alternative social forms through which it explores and
performs and even attempts to ameliorate modern consciousness in sociality. Here Romani sociality is rendered, however minimally, as a form that
resists *gadže* territorializing, in stark contrast to the popular nineteenth-
century genre of Romany Rye texts that purport to lay bare the secret romantic core of "Gypsy" life. By making this comparison I do not mean to
suggest that Lawrence's, or indeed any, modernist treatment of Romanies
is more "legitimate" or less appropriative than nonmodernist representations of "Gypsies." Instead I am calling attention to the sociohistorical
problematic that undergirds modernist representation. As the incommensurability between *gadžikane* and Romani cultures was increasingly elaborated and codified through the discourses of social control, British modernism took incommensurability itself as a site of aesthetic investigation.
Wyndham Lewis's despotic individualism, Charlotte Mew's queer indirec-
tion, E. M. Forster's forced symbolism, and any number of other formal
strategies yielded a modernism characterized precisely by its own alterity
to alterity, its unwilling and unwitting and yet inevitable otherness to the
otherness it pursued. Like consciousness itself, in which alterity is embedded, alterity cannot be directly rendered, as modernists well knew. But in
the process of mapping strange social relations that resisted assimilation
or transparent intelligibility, some modernists aimed for a point of intersection between alterity and sociality, somewhere off the grid of instrumental modernity. The struggles of Gypsies in Britain in the modern period form the conditions of possibility for this *gadže* modernism. Taking
for an implicit model the movement of "the Gypsy" *and* Gypsies in modernity, *gadže* modernism pursues an infinitely receding community.

NOTES

A longer version of this essay appeared as "Gadže Modernism," *Modernism/Modernity*
11:3 (2004), 517–38. © The Johns Hopkins University Press. Reprinted with permis-
sion of The Johns Hopkins University Press.
   1. Symons, "In Praise of Gypsies," 298, hereafter cited as "PG." Though the
Bill had passed its second reading in the House of Lords at the time of Symons's
intervention, it was eventually withdrawn because it partially duplicated existing
bills under discussion. See Mayall, 166–74. For outsider-describers writing about
Romani peoples, lexical decisions are especially fraught. One preeminent Romani scholar, Ian Hancock, recommends that "Romani" be used to reference all
groups of Romanies everywhere, since, as he says, "*all* groups use the adjective
Romani to describe themselves" (xx). (As an activist, Hancock hopes to "instill a
sense of historical unity among the different groups" [xxi], and an umbrella name
is useful for this kind of identitarian project.) But Fraser points out that *Romani*
does not work particularly well in Britain, "because of the very considerable non-

Romani element in the ancestry of the British Gypsy population and the long [overlapping] history of other traveling groups" (7). He uses both *Gypsy* and *Romanichal* when referencing denizens of Britain (though not Ireland, for which he uses "Traveller"). Acton uses *Gypsy* but grounds that usage with a lexical discussion of eighteen different terms used to denote Romani populations (60–80); Okely uses both *Gypsy* and *Traveller*, Lee uses *Romani*, and Mayall uses both *Gypsy* and *Gypsy-traveller*. I have used *Gypsy* in scare quotes to denote the cultural constructions of *gadže* cultures, and *Gypsy*, *Romanichal*, or *Romani*, depending on context, to denote the Romani populations under discussion.

2. Symons, "Sir Thomas Browne on the Gypsies," 113.

3. Trumpener, 857.

4. This untenable ideological relation between the *gadže* construction of the "Gypsy" on the one hand, and Romani people on the other, has been discussed forcefully and at length by, among others, Acton (*passim*) and Mayall (esp. Chapters 3 and 4). Hancock also addresses stereotypes and misleading images. Behlmer concentrates on Victorian England and Mayall concentrates on turn-of-the-century Britain; Acton's sociological and Trumpener's cultural readings extend into the contemporary Romani civil rights movement. Social anthropologist Judith Okely's work offers detailed historical accounts of European Romanies with an analysis of her 1970s fieldwork in southern England.

5. Trumpener locates the bifurcation of this "social allegory" in Jane Austen's *Emma* and Sir Walter Scott's *Guy Mannering*; I am indebted to the extensive scholarship in this article.

6. See Lyon on the sociological and historical indebtedness of the concept and practices of Bohemia to both the Romani and the "Gypsy" cultural record.

7. Subjectivity in modernity is a vast philosophical problem that I do not aim to address here except in passing. Cascardi and Jameson—to take but two theorists of modernity who sustain a focus on subjectivity in late modernity—both make use of Heidegger's use of Descartes to launch their own (quite different) arguments about modern subjectivity, and between them provide some sense of the outline of this discussion and its significance for modernism. Cascardi, for whom modernity and subjectivity are mutually constitutive, writes that in Heidegger's theory of representation (which "has since provided the accepted interpretation of the relationship between the subject and the modern age"), "the position of transcendental reflection as established in the philosophy of Descartes marks the transformation of the world from an all-embracing cosmos into an objective representation, picture, or 'view,'" and "the fact that the world becomes a picture at all is what defines subjectivity and distinguishes modernity as an historical paradigm" (125). In a not-dissimilar vein, Jameson writes that, for Heidegger, modernity "is the word for a new arrangement of subject and object in a specific relationship of knowledge (and even domination) towards each other: the object coming to be only as it is known or represented, the subject only as it becomes the locus and the vehicle for such representation"; however, for Jameson, since consciousness itself cannot be represented, nor can the "lived experience of subjectivity itself," "no theory of modernity in terms of subjectivity can be accepted." Indeed, for this very reason, "Modernity is not a concept, but rather a narrative category" (Jameson, *Singular* 52–53, 94).

8. Fraser (130–42) reports that in the history of the numerous and variously brutal statutes passed against Romanies in England (beginning in 1530), the 1713 Act was the first to employ "Gypsy" instead of "Egyptian," a name which reflected early beliefs that Romanies had migrated from or through Egypt.

9. *Gemeinschaft und Gesellschaft*'s nationalist sentimentalism, put to use in the antimodern arsenal of the Third Reich, was thoroughly repudiated in the 1940s.

Brint has recently set out to update and reconstruct the sociological concept of community, for which project he is explicitly indebted to the concept of *Gemeinschaft*. Tönnies opposed *Gemeinschaft* (community) to *Gesellschaft* (society); the latter is based on rational association and agreement and its topos is the city and/or the state.

10. Chakrabarty coins this phrase in his study of Bengali colonial modernity; he argues that some cultural practices and especially practices of the self "always leave an intellectually unmanageable excess when translated into the politics and language of [the European colonizers'] political philosophies" (148).

11. Okely has long argued that the Romani "have never been an isolate but are a group which is perpetually created in opposition to the dominant and surrounding societies which they inhabit and from which they are partly created" ("Constructing Difference" 62). This nonracial view differs controversially from scholars such as Fraser, Hancock, and Acton, who agree with nineteenth-century philologists that a "nucleus" group began their migration from northwestern India around the year 1000.

12. This latter term was the subject of a conference rumored to be held in Berne in 1908 to discuss a European "solution" (Mayall 5; see also MacRitchie's bitter reference to "the sages who propose to meet at Berne this summer [i.e., 1908]" [MacRitchie 299]). Hitler's "solution" to the "Gypsy Plague" eventuated in the murder of up to 1.5 million European Romanies between 1940 and 1945.

13. The last Gypsy execution in England took place in 1650; in Scotland it was in 1714 (Fraser 140).

14. See Mayall's "Appendix I," which lists "major legislation relating to Gypsies, 1530–1908" (189–92).

15. See the *London Times* (e.g., January 30, 1909, 4; February 20, 1909, 8; May 22, 1909, 9), as well as coverage in the *Daily News, Manchester Guardian, Surrey Mirror, Surrey Times, Morning Leader,* and the news clippings reviewed regularly in the *Journal of the Gypsy Lore Society.*

16. Goods were small items that could be transported easily, such as handmade brooms and baskets, pots and pans (Mayall 58–59); services included the mending of tin, copper, and brass articles; umbrella repair, chair-bottoming, and knife-grinding; as well as musical entertainment, fortune-telling, and horse trading.

17. Georg Simmel's plangent meditation on "the stranger" is relevant to the overdetermined relations between Gypsy-Traveller cultures and settled society. The stranger, he writes, is "the person who comes today and stays tomorrow. He is, so to speak, the *potential* wanderer: although he has not moved on, he has not quite overcome the freedom of coming and going" ("The Stranger" 402). Like the Traveller groups living among but not within settled society, "strangers are not really conceived as individuals, but as strangers of a particular type" (407). While Simmel adduces the Jew as the example of the stranger, his observation that the stranger "often receives the most surprising openness—confidences that sometimes have the character of a confessional" applies as well to the intimate situation of Gypsy palmistry, where the *gadže* pays to be read.

18. See Okely, *Traveller-Gypsies*, 77–104; Hancock discusses pollution and purity much more generally (75–76; 80–83; 88–90).

19. The most recent of these is Joseph Valente's *tour de force* reading of the novel as a cautionary tale against racialized anxiety itself. See 145, fn. 2, for a review of the scholarship that Valente's work synthesizes and supersedes.

20. See Fraser 211. Stoker's placement of the Szygany in Transylvania effectively identifies them as second-generation descendants of the vast numbers of Roma emancipated from slavery in this region between 1842 and 1856. See Fraser 57–59, 222–28. Stoker's choice of the Szygany may have been influenced by Liszt's discussion of Zingani musicians in Hungary.

21. Affinities between Gypsies and vampires are hinted at throughout the novel. Van Helsing says of the vampire precisely what had been said throughout the century by gypsylorists about the "Gypsy": "He is known everywhere that man has been" (Stoker 245). The vampire traits of cannibalism, child stealing, restless wandering, and the ability to "vanish" were all ascribed to "the Gypsy" in nineteenth-century *gadže* myth.

22. A notable exception to this trend occurs in criminology, which is often equally antisemitic and anti-Gypsy. See for example Lombroso's notorious categorization of Jews and Gypsies, the latter of whom constitute "an entire race of criminals with all the passions and vices common to delinquent types: idleness, ignorance, impetuous fury, vanity, love of orgies, and ferocity" (140).

23. This formulation revisits Jameson's seminal argument about reification (*Political Unconscious* 236–42).

24. For example, *To the Lighthouse* and *Mrs. Dalloway* (Woolf), *Nightwood* (Barnes), "Scylla and Charybdis" and "The House Party" (Mary Butts), *Quartet* (Rhys), *Infants of the Spring* (Wallace Thurman), *Women in Love* (Lawrence), *The Ambassadors* (James), and *Parade's End* (Ford).

25. See, for example, Simmel, "The Sociology of Sociability." See also Lyon, "Sociability in the Metropole," for a broader discussion of modernist sociology's reaction to the alienating forces of modernity.

26. See, for example, Ricco, 8–10, and Bersani, *passim.*

27. Here I am indebted to Rochelle Rives's unpublished chapter on *Sons and Lovers,* which explores Lawrence's valorization of an impersonal ethos in handiwork.

11   Cabaret Modernism: Vorticism and Racial Spectacle

Laura Winkiel

> In the state of degeneracy, in which we live, it is through the skin
> that metaphysics will be made to reenter our minds.
> —Antonin Artaud, "The Theater of Cruelty" (1932)

In 1881, Rodolphe Salis opened the longest-running and most famous avant-garde cabaret in Europe, *Le Chat Noir*. By the end of the Great War, cabarets flourished throughout Europe. From *Die Elf Scharfrichter* and *Fledermaus* to *Els Quatre Gats* and *The Cabaret Voltaire*, cabarets gathered together groups of avant-garde artists who were dedicated to breaking from traditional art forms and challenging their aesthetic assumptions. These semiprivate spaces—usually publicized only through word of mouth—served as sanctuaries where artists could experiment freely with new art forms and anti-bourgeois attitudes away from the glare of the public eye. Participants presented modern dance routines, manifestos, poetry and stories, comic theatrical skits, and puppet shows; they also offered visual art as startling backdrops. These kaleidoscopic sequences of acts were loosely modeled after circus and variety shows (Segel xiv).

In adopting popular entertainment formats that staged sensational encounters with racialized subjects, the cabaret theater, in turn, aestheticized those encounters.[1] That is to say, cabaret by definition wrests people and things from their historical contexts and presents a varied series of absurd and often racialized spectacles to mark the historical interruptions and social transgressions of avant-garde art.[2] These racialized identities are lifted from their association with colonization and float in the semiotic context of cabaret and aesthetic masquerade. The deterritorialized space of the avant-garde cabaret uproots and challenges organic forms of nationalism and race. In this setting, the avant-garde's cabaret performances in Europe sought to make art "amid a mess of confusion, indeterminacy, paradoxes and constant change" (Sheppard 188).

Cabaret craze arrived in England in 1912 and by 1914 fostered the creation of the short-lived English avant-garde group, the vorticists. Their work, as I will show, is symptomatic of a crisis of the place of art in a world of rising mass democracy and anticolonialist movements. I will demonstrate that the deterritorialized, ahistorical space of vorticism created by the English avant-garde in their little magazine *Blast* enacts what I call *cabaret modernism*, a heterotopia where essentialized categories of race are called into question.[3] Thus, the avant-garde's participation in various forms of racial masquerade and their spectacularization of racial identities signal a shift in the categories of race themselves. Yet my contention in this essay is that though this cosmopolitan mixing suggests the avant-garde's need to rewrite representations of Eurocentric modernity and racial difference, these representations, rather than dissolve racial difference, continue to maintain hierarchies of race and thus demonstrate the unwillingness of the avant-garde to seize the possibilities of the heterotopic space imagined in their literary magazine *Blast*.

THE CAVE OF THE GOLDEN CALF

In June 1912, the first English avant-garde cabaret, "The Cave of the Golden Calf," opened its doors. Its owner and hostess was Frida Strindberg, former wife of August Strindberg and later the poet, dramatist, and cabaretist Frank Wedekind's lover. "The Cave of the Golden Calf" and its nightclub counterpart, "The Cabaret Theatre Club," served as a gathering place for bohemian artists and writers and provided, in the words of its promotional brochure, "a gaiety stimulating thought, rather than crushing it." Promising to mix Continental cuisine with "the picturesque dances of the South, its fervid melodies, Parisian wit, [and] English humor," the brochure expressed the hope that the cabaret "will create a surrounding, which, if it has no other merit, will at least endeavor to limit emigration" (Wees 50). The wish was that English art and literature might be rejuvenated by an infusion of Continental avant-garde activity. Wyndham Lewis, freshly arrived from the Continent after eight years of studying art abroad, was a central figure in the formation of the cabaret.

The fault lines of modernism—between dissolving categories of self and other and reinscriptions of them in new hierarchies—appear in stark contrast in Wyndham Lewis's vorticist work. Lewis, a prolific artist, essayist, and novelist, is far and away the least-read, least-loved "men of 1914" within the Anglo-American modernist canon. Called by Paul Edwards "a one-man Frankfurt school of the right," his bad-tempered rants against modernity and modernists alike and disastrous support of Hitler in the 1930s earned him a dubious place within the histories of modernism (ABR 441). But Lewis's critique of mass society, in which publicity and images can be manipulated at will in order to distract public attention from in-

creasingly consolidated economic and political power, continues to resonate powerfully. Lewis's solution to the herdlike conformity and standardi-
zation he saw in modern democracies was to present an aesthetic array of
shifting, indeterminate, contradictory forms and meanings that he believed might destabilize a consensus of opinion about the world.

To challenge mass culture conformism and to eschew what E. M. Forster called the "pinko-grey" tones of racial mixing that he and other modernists such as Lewis believed modernization ineluctably wrought, Lewis
imagines an avant-garde heterotopia that could yoke together the disparate
categories of formalist aesthetics, popular culture, and the antimodern violence of Anglo-Saxonism.[4] Out of this unsynthesized mélange of cultural
and racial positions, Lewis, in the vorticist manifesto published in the
founding issue of *Blast*, demands that the English avant-garde should engage in both the illusory and compensatory aspects of heterotopic space.
This space was first simulated by England's earliest art cabaret, "The Cave
of the Golden Calf."

With great press fanfare, the basement cabaret at 9 Heddon Street com-
menced and featured Lewis's oversized oil painting *Kermesse*, Jacob Epstein's white plaster caryatids, and Eric Gill's golden calf sculpture. In
the style of European avant-garde cabaret, various forms of *kleinkunst*, or
little art, were performed. Cuthbert Hamilton and Lewis prepared shadow
plays; others staged extemporaneous theatrical skits; poets delivered their
verse; and Lillian Shelley—"a perfect model of an Egyptian goddess"—
sang there and later took Madame Strindberg's monkeys to the Savoy Hotel for a late-night supper. The Italian futurist F. T. Marinetti appeared
and "declaimed some peculiarly blood-thirsty concoctions with great dramatic force," as Lewis reported to a friend (Wees 50). Osbert Sitwell, a frequent visitor to the cave, recounts its character in his autobiographical
Great Morning!:

> The Cabaret Club, where the lesser artists of the theatre, as well as the
> greater, mixed with painters, writers, and their opposite, officers in the Bri-
> gade of Guards. This low-ceilinged night club, appropriately sunk below
> the pavement of Beak Street, and hideously but relevantly frescoed by the
> then mature Wyndham Lewis, appeared in the small hours to be a super-
> heated vorticist garden of gesticulating figures, dancing and talking, while
> the rhythm of the primitive forms of ragtime throbbed through the wide
> room. . . . Dancing more than conversation was the art which occupied the
> young men of the time in the Cabaret Club. (229)

The moneyed revelers and less-moneyed artists of various categories freely
mixed. Strindberg hired Gypsy and Negro jazz bands to play to the crowd,
music hall girls sang, and everyone danced the Turkey Trot and the Bunny
Hug (Wees 50). The first English avant-garde club staged its aesthetic en-

counter with modernity in terms of primitivism: wild dancing, ragtime, jazz, Egyptian-style hairdos and jewelry, folk art, geometrical sculpture and paintings. Such styles and activities served as both a transgressive identification with the "primitive" and as an appropriation and erasure of racialized subjects.

The cabaret-goers performed aspects of what signified as African American, Gypsy, and other folk art forms, and they viewed modern renditions of ancient Egyptian and Greek arts. Joining these varied forms as part of its heterotopia, the cabaret collapsed distinctions between time, place, and otherness, rendering them fodder for the stage. Yet the cabaret disturbed as well: Osbert Sitwell's remembrance of the cabaret describes it as a subterranean attack on spectators' visual and auditory realms. It was "sunk" below street level, "hideously" frescoed. He added that "gesticulating figures" whirled around to the primitive music which "throbbed." The monstrous mixing of crowds was viscerally experienced as nondiscursive and visually indistinct, as individual outlines among the crowd were not discernible. Its misshapen form—the amorphous nature of all urban crowds—suggested to writers from Gustave Le Bon and Nietzsche to Lewis a crisis of individual autonomy in the face of growing urbanization, racial mixing, and mass forms of democracy.

Transforming these modern mass conditions as part of avant-garde art, the cabaret produced a disruptive setting for the production and reception of art. It brought together artists, their works of art, and the audience's response that broke aesthetic rules concerning the autonomy of art. The theatricality of cabaret performance estranged art from itself through its irreverent stagings. It recontextualized its production and reception within the rowdy, distracted domain of live entertainment. Art was no longer contemplated with calm detachment; instead, paintings and sculptures served as casual stage drops to theatrical declamations, dancing, conversation, and music. Verbal and musical forms were improvised in ways that suggested spontaneous, instinctual activity rather than reflective rationality. The improvised performances at the cabaret also added to the heterotopia of new art, language, and style.

Foucault's term *heterotopia*, introduced in *The Order of Things*, suggests both a disparate mingling of unrelated people and places as well as an underlying disturbance in language and meaning that comes from a taxonomic disorder. Foucault illustrates this term by means of Borges's reference to a Chinese encyclopedia in which a "wild profusion of existing things"—embalmed, tame, drawn with a camelhair brush, etc.—"disturb and threaten with collapse our age-old distinction between the Same and the Other" (xv). Foucault suggests that the monstrous quality of this list occurs because all common ground has been destroyed, even at the level of representation and being (i.e., the state of being dead, alive, or drawn by a brush). These disparate qualities are held together only in the non-place of language, an "unthinkable space." This space destroys the syntax that causes words and things to hold together. Heterotopias "shatter . . . common names" and "make it impossible to name this *and* that [. . .] they desiccate speech, stop words in their tracks, contest the very possibility of grammar at its source; they dissolve our myths and sterilize the lyricism of our sentences" (xvii–xviii). Heterotopias undermine received forms of sense and meaning and disturb rationality. Foucault's concept has been criticized for its lack of historical specificity and its placement outside power structures which render the concept banal and over-generalized.[5] To address these concerns, I situate the English avant-garde and its aesthetic forms within late imperial London and the power of state-sponsored racism.

As part of a profusion of new spaces in England, the cabaret stood both within the London public and outside it. It took its place among the counter-public spheres of the women's suffrage movement with its meeting halls, shops, and presses; union trade halls, and the consumer-oriented tea shops, department stores, and entertainment halls. The latter mass culture spaces were offset by an increasingly militant and racialized East End London, which by 1913 resembled a besieged territory that was hostile to police, armed, and comprised of Irish nationalists, Jewish immigrants fleeing pogroms, Asian and African migrants, working-class women suffragists, and radicals. The influx of immigrants arriving between 1870 and 1914 united an unholy alliance of Tory MPs, socialists, trade union leaders, and members of the proto-fascist British Brothers League. They lobbied for an end to the flood of immigrants and, in 1905, the Aliens Act was passed which subjected all non-British subjects to immigration control for the first time.[6] The spatial confrontation enacted in East End London and elsewhere testified to the proliferation of politically unruly groups within the metropolis. While the historical specificity of these conflicts may not have been specifically alluded to in the Cabaret Theatre Club, the random, often absurd, juxtapositions of persons and acts suggest this violent underside of modernity.[7]

In Foucault's 1986 reassessment of heterotopia, he suggests that it unfolds within two extreme poles of functionality. The first, which corresponds to the Cabaret, he calls a space of illusion that "exposes every real space . . . as still more illusory." For instance, the women's enfranchisement struggle contested gender-segregated spaces to show their artificial nature. The second, the space of compensation, is "as perfect, as meticulous, as well arranged as ours [Western metropolitan space] is messy, ill constructed and jumbled." Foucault likens the functioning of fixed, compensatory spaces to certain colonies ("Of Other Spaces" 27). Here Foucault indirectly suggests the relation of racism and the "statization" of biology, what Ann Stoler reads in Foucault within a different context as "the anatomy of state power and the murderous capacities within it" and, she adds, "the fact that state racism and European imperial expansion" occurred together (61–62). We shall investigate in the remaining sections the uneasy combination of both heterotopic functions, dissolving racial categories as illusory and re-writing them via fixed, statist notions of Anglo-Saxon superiority, as they are precariously presented in the vorticist journal *Blast*.

BLAST AS THEATER

The vorticist journal *Blast* provided a published, public forum in print analogous to what the Cabaret enacted nightly.[8] The collective presentation of contributors' work, witty social commentary, and aesthetic doctrine was striking and disparate. It included a variety of art forms: reproductions of paintings and sculptures, poetry, short stories by Rebecca West and Ford Madox Ford, a closet drama, and a twenty-page manifesto. It celebrated a wild and artificial heterotopia; but, as we shall see, it also worked to contain and recolonize its energies. Its intended effect was to galvanize England with new, vigorous art and a monstrous mixing of forms. The reviewers interpreted it accordingly. The *Little Review*'s critic Eunice Tietjins ironically announced *Blast*'s arrival: "the typical gamin, the street urchin with his tongue in his cheek . . . has at last invaded the quarterlies" (33). Meanwhile, the *New York Times* called vorticism "the last phase of the ridiculous rebellion which has given the world the 'Portrait of a Nude Descending the Stairs' and the writings of Gertrude Stein. It is the *reductio ad absurdum* of a mad modernity . . . a development of Futurism to its ultimate absurdity" (August 9, 1914, sec. 5, 10). Richard Aldington, who favorably reviewed the journal (he was a co-signer of the manifesto), said: "Quite naturally it was energetic, tremendously energetic" (272). *Blast* injected energized disorder and absurdity into the English art scene.

The vorticist manifesto—written by Wyndham Lewis in collaboration with Ezra Pound—sets the tone for the art work to follow. Its irreverent, impatient satire of modern culture and rowdy, hilarious language theatricalizes the manifesto's solemn intention of declaring a break from the past and offering a new aesthetic program. *Blast* is not pure theater; however, as a text, it circulates beyond the confines of a singular, immediate performance. The reception of its performance may be anywhere and anytime, which disqualifies it as a performance *tout court*.[9] Yet within the mise-en-scène of its covers, the twenty-page manifesto emphasizes the immediacy and urgency of creating a new aesthetic sensibility through its shocking proclamations and the visual display of its innovative graphic layouts and reproduced art.

Like the variety theater's commère and compère (mistress and master of ceremonies), the manifesto addresses its audience directly as though they are present. Unlike variety theater, its self-reflexive language places this "live" scene in the future: "CURSE those who will hang over this Manifesto with SILLY CANINES exposed" (Lewis, B1, 17; caps in original). As such, it may go further than live entertainments to present an illusory and heterotopic "non-place of language" that is both abstract and concrete, performative and representational. The twenty-page manifesto enacts a baffling struggle between opposing as well as complementary dualities. In the manner of Apollinaire's 1913 "L'antitradition futuriste" manifesto, with its lists headed "merde aux" and "rose aux," it begins with long lists of things and people to be "blasted" and "blessed." After cursing England, France, the Britannic Aesthete, professionals, amateurs, humor, sport, cod-liver oil, the British Academy, the Bishop of London and all his posterity, Beecham (Pills, Opera, and Thomas), the Victorian period, and luminaries of middle-class culture, the manifesto blesses England, France, humor, ports, the hairdresser, castor oil, 33 Church Street, the Salvation Army, the Commercial Process Company, those attached to the vorticist circle, aviators, music hall performers, boxers, cabaret and opera singers, militant suffragettes and Ulsterites, and James Joyce (B1, 11–28). The manifesto both blesses and curses humor, France, and England, and advocates working-class over middle-class entertainments. Its satirical targets include locations, companies, medicinal oils, and "posterity" to disturb epistemological and ontological categories. The parataxis of list-making, both pro and con, random and trivial, assails the reader from both directions. It offers the taxonomic disorder of heterotopic space.

Though Lewis's manifesto questions the stability and transparency of representational systems, it also asserts Foucault's second heterotopia of compensation, the fixed space of state-imposed colonial order based on a metaphysics of race.[10] Lewis voiced repeatedly fears that the erosion of cultural and racial distinction and division through modernization would yield an undifferentiated, mechanical society and a degraded, commodified mass culture. To recuperate the full presence of art within the imperial metropolis, the vorticist manifesto asserts an Anglo-Saxon nativism whose racial purity and rigid boundaries provide a universalizing authority for art. It is "permanently primitive" (B1, 33) and set apart from history, yet it also reasserts the dichotomized spatial divisions of modern/colonial world history. Lewis claims that this detachment is the result *and* source of imperialism. The English "genius" originated its imperial dominance and, conversely, imperialism justifies the authority of English artists. For instance, the manifesto states: "6) The English Character is based on the Sea. 7) The particular qualities and characteristics that the sea always engenders in men are those that are among the many diagnostics of our race, the most fundamentally English. 8) That unexpected universality as well, found in the completest English artist, is due to this" (B1, 33). English imperialism—as expressed through its seafaring activity—forms the geopolitical rationale for national and nativist identity and its link to universality.

Reversing causality—effectively giving birth to itself—the vorticist manifesto proclaims that Anglo-Saxon identity gave rise *to* England as a world colonial power. It proclaims the Anglo-Saxon genius to be the source of capitalist expansion and demands a new form of national art based on and justified by this invention. It argues that as this new mode of economic production spreads across the world—colonizing at will—it modernizes old modes of representation. Modern machinery "sweeps away the doctrines of a narrow and pedantic Realism at one stroke" (B1, 39). Furthermore, as this mechanical inventiveness spreads all over the Earth, it, in turn, brings "all the hemispheres" back to England, not as "Jungle," "dramatic tropic growths," or the "vastness of American trees," but as artificial and "wilder intricacies than those of Nature" (B1, 36). This artifice of wilderness checks an unqualified celebration of modernity by positing its return to the industrial center. The manifesto proclaims Anglo-Saxons' nativist superiority as the founders of the industrial revolution. This superiority claims the authority to halt the unchecked spread of modernity in favor of the formal stillness and central artifice of vorticist art. Not merely breaking from the past, the manifesto rewrites national history in racial terms to authorize the present geopolitical and aesthetic dominance in modernist, self-generating, and self-legitimizing terms.

Performing his dominance, Lewis imagines the nativist artist as a gladiator who wages war with modern life. Violently detaching from modernity's multiple assaults waged both at home and abroad, he remarks later in *Blast* on what the modern town dweller sees:

> the frontier's interpenetrate [*sic*], individual demarcations are confused and interests dispersed.... We all to-day (possibly with the coldness reminiscent of the insect-world) are in each other's vitals—overlap, intersect, and are Siamese to any extent.... All clean, clear cut emotions depend on the element of strangeness, and surprise and primitive detachment. (B1, 141)

Lewis deploys "strange" to denote a non-organic, non-kinship relation between city dwellers. The denizens of the modern metropolis, coming from all frontiers, conjoin promiscuously and sometimes violently, as Lewis likens these encounters to boxing matches or duels. Modernity dissolves individual "demarcations" and disperses autonomous interests: an urban subject perceives him or herself to be situated in proximate, multiple encounters. These absurd, mechanical, violent interpenetrations of disparate people and things, however, may be superseded by an indifferent artist whose "clean, clear cut emotions" are based on detachment from "the interstices of a human world." Extending this indifference to English culture to critique their sentimental and provincial nationalism, the manifesto asserts that the English people, as the source of this raw form of brutal art, "should be the great enemies of Romance" (B1, 41). The vorticist manifesto presents a taxonomic disorder in the heart of empire but ultimately preserves the unquestioned racial superiority of Anglo-Saxon artists.

REBECCA WEST AND THE IMPERIAL EXOTIC

In contrast to Lewis's manifesto that champions Anglo-Saxon superiority, Rebecca West's story "Indissoluble Matrimony," also published in *Blast*, first appears to embrace taxonomic disorder through racial mixing. As an antiromance romance, "Indissoluble Matrimony" parodies the racial dangers believed to arise from colonial mixing. It presents a violent encounter within a lower-middle-class London home between a mixed-race singer and her white husband and parodies the sensationalized dangers of the weakening of the white race due to overcivilization. Adapting the romance genre for her tale of a suburban encounter with otherness, West transforms romance narratives that relate how dependency, intimacy, and estrangement between colonizer and colonized occur. She demonstrates how geographical and racial interpenetration threaten to displace fixed categories of race and nation, particularly as these displacements are felt in the imperial metropolis. Because of the story's narrative form and realist language, it has been excluded by critics from discussions of vorticism. But West's contribution in *Blast* provides a further instance of the categorical mixing of heterotopia, with its disparity of avant-garde aesthetics and popular narrative fiction. West's story also provides evidence of vorticism's ambivalent (and failed) attempt to attract a wide public audience. Furthermore, as a colonial allegory, its subject matter parallels vorticist concerns as it expresses an erosion of autonomy that results from England's dependency and intimacy with its colonial subjects.

The conventional narrative, when seen as part of *Blast*'s heterotopic arena, becomes just one discourse and style among the wide range of disparate forms presented in *Blast*. In terms of content, it remains perfectly in line with Lewis's apocalyptic vision of frontiers interpenetrating and antagonistic, violent duos exchanging blows. In fact, Lewis's "War Crowds" story published in the second issue of *Blast* compares the crowd to a married man. The domesticated man brings a crowd into being "in the bowels of his wife." For Lewis, married life is a metaphor for the phenomenon of proliferating, amorphous masses of people, the "black London warcrowds" (B2, 79). Romantic intimacy symbolizes modernity's dangers, the promiscuous sexual and racial mixing within the metropolis that erodes individual autonomy and freedom.

In West's story, George Silverton, a solicitor's clerk, marries a passionate, sensual singer of mixed race, Evadne, who reads widely and, later in their married life, becomes a socialist speaker. The story is narrated from George's perspective as he nurses his grudges toward his wife and reflects on their courtship and their marriage of ten years. Evadne is more interested in workers' struggles than in cleaning the house and caring for her husband. When George sees his wife's name advertised as a socialist speaker at an upcoming event, he flies into a rage and forbids her to go. She refuses and begins to practice her speech. They fight and she leaves the house, shattering the glass in the front door and signaling a breakdown of private, domestic space. George, in a state of paranoid delusion, follows her, expecting to catch her in an adulterous rendezvous. She merely goes to a pond for a swim. They physically attack each other and he attempts to drown her. Walking back home in the belief that he has drowned his wife, George fantasizes that he is Napoleon, a fantasy that allows West to satirize imperial militarism. Idealizing his act of ridding the world of Evadne, George decides to make the ultimate self-sacrifice, suicide. When he returns home, however, he finds Evadne asleep, having escaped his murderous intentions by plunging deeper into the water and swimming away from him. Before going to sleep, she turned off the gas at the main, preventing George's suicide attempt. The story ends as Evadne embraces George in her sleep, suggesting that the conflict has been resolved in favor of Evadne's stronger role within the marriage and George's continued dependency.

Though it is problematically primitivist, West's story places imperial critique within the affective, generative center of English nationalism, the home. By so doing, it effectively displaces imperial and domestic delineations of space. It opens with a cutting jab at imperialism: "When George Silverton opened the front door he found that the house was not empty for all its darkness" (West 98). West rewrites *Heart of Darkness* by locating "the horror" not in the depths of Africa but within the heart of the metropolis, in an ordinary London home.[11] Marlow's romantic lie in the home of the Intended covers over "the horror" with a hollow nod to conventions in much the same way that the Silvertons initially conform to the conventions of marriage. West's story, however, confronts the lie of colonial desire, allowing George's egocentric, dismissive judgments of Evadne and his insecure overcompensations to become satire. Moreover, she refuses the existential emptiness in which Kurtz's "horror" is allowed to reverberate. West's colonial subject is a modern, ordinary person. Evadne Silverton inhabits the darkness of the house and is, in fact, struggling to light the lamp when George enters the house. The banality of her everyday life undercuts race as spectacle. Indeed, West's story exposes the fantasmatic nature of race and desire, specifically, that raced subjects serve as an empty marker onto which the colonizer's ghostly imaginings of the racialized other are projected: "There was something about the fantastic figure that made him feel as though they were not properly married" (99). Imperial romance procures much of its political love from colonial encounters replete with phantasmatic imaginings, unfulfilled longings, and nostalgic reminiscences.

As a colonial allegory, West makes clear how colonial partnership produces an intimacy of economic and social dependence that is based, not on mutuality, but on fantasy and mis-remembered history. What West's story suggests is that once colonization takes effect, and "vows" are exchanged— that is, once economic and cultural interdependence forms—there is no escape from what Robert Young calls the ambivalence of colonial desire. As Evadne is presented through George's point of view, he is both attracted and repulsed by her: "She was one of those women who create an illusion alternately of extreme beauty and extreme ugliness." She is both modern as she "unwind[s] her orange motor-veil" (98) and primitive; intellectual and sensual; weak and strong; chaste and promiscuous, though the omniscient narration undercuts George's dramatic views of her alterity in favor of Evadne's ordinariness. Nonetheless, Evadne is presented as contradictory and fragmented, largely through the dislocating effects of colonization.[12] She is caught between modernity's promised freedoms and a raced and sexed position that is constructed as elsewhere and prior to the modern.[13]

Even while presenting an anti-imperial perspective, West reimposes hierarchies of racial difference. She achieves this through the couple's violent confrontation, a climax that closely resembles an avant-garde event, though their sublime hatred for one another replaces vorticist indifference. The couple argue over Evadne's public speaking engagement, breaking from their ten-year pattern of interaction. The marital conflict between Evadne and George generates heightened energy that overshadows the past. The ten years of their marriage disappear behind this "intense event" like "the pale hair trails behind the burning comet" (109). This moment of reckoning produces a warlike hostility where the past dissolves before the intensity of the moment: "A sublime loathing was between them. . . . For the first time they were possessed by a supreme emotion and they felt a glad desire to strip away, [*sic*] restraint and express it nakedly. It was ecstasy; they felt tall and full of blood" (110). The ordinary language of domestic fiction is subsumed by the metaphysical register of their passion as the characters experience an intense urge to kill each other. History and mimetic representation fall away before dissolving, violent action. This sublime desire is described as a magnetic current which decomposes the electrolyte, a burning comet, and "stars [that] trembled overhead with wrath" (110). The couple's crisis takes on cosmic, absolute proportions: "with an uplifting sense of responsibility they realized that they must kill each other" (110).

This moment of freedom to act regardless of social implications suggests the effects of manifesto-like speech act declarations: the couple's cursing and painful truth-telling sever marital bonds and enact a break in their relationship. Their accusations involve the memory of Evadne's mother, who in George's words is "that weird half-black woman from the back of beyond" (109), a phrase that, for him, consolidates a chasm of racial difference and spatial dislocation. However, this moment of marital liberation falters, stopping short of its most far-reaching implications of racial struggle and domestic dispute. It preserves, in one essentializing moment, racial and gender hierarchies. For the first time, the narrator presents Evadne's thoughts:

> These things were so strange that her civilized self shrank back appalled. There entered into her the primitive woman who is the curse to all women: a creature of the most utter femaleness, useless, save for childbirth, with no strong brain to make her physical weakness a light accident, abjectly and corruptingly afraid of man. A squaw, she dared not strike her lord. (111)

Though this moment passes quickly and Evadne regains her sense of intellectual superiority, her virtue—as the narrator puts it—lies in her desire for meek surrender. West's reluctance to present Evadne on absolutely equal grounds with George at the moment of crisis suggests that the metaphysics of race persists. Evadne's subordinate hesitation allows George to strike the first blow. Even though George ultimately loses the battle, Evadne's racial difference excludes her at a crucial moment from access to full subjecthood. Her decision to remain married to George—the story circles back to their domestic abode and ingrained patterns of behavior—suggests West's need to contain Evadne's difference through an assimilative—and sterile—marriage even while George's hypocritical Victorian moral codes are exposed and critiqued. In effect, West unsettles spatial demarcations and racial classifications from within the metropolis but carefully recontains such critique within a Eurocentric, liberal framework. For the most part, Evadne remembers to enact her modern, cosmopolitan self. But the essentialist difference she carries in her blood will, in West's estimation, always exclude her from becoming a full subject of modernity. Preserving such hierarchies, West's story contributes to *Blast*'s heterotopia because it stands in formal contradiction to the innovative aesthetic of vorticism and, in the end, upholds Lewis's reclamation of Englishness by showing it to be, underneath the satire, ultimately superior in racial conflict.

ENEMY OF THE STARS

The third and final instance of heterotopic juxtaposition in *Blast* is Lewis's experimental closet drama *Enemy of the Stars*. The drama attempts to put into practice the aesthetic positioning Lewis calls for in his manifesto. It represents the interpenetrating geopolitical spaces of nation and world while pursuing the possibility of universal aesthetic judgment that depends upon an autonomous subject. Lewis wrote *Enemy of the Stars* for the first issue of *Blast* in an effort, as he remarks in his autobiography *Rude Assignment,* "to show the way" to his literary contemporaries whom he "looked upon as too bookish and not keeping the pace with the visual revolution" (RA 139). Lewis's paintings redeploy space, flattening and fragmenting it, and foreground abstract, geometrical designs. So, too, the play's temporal unfolding in abstract space is disrupted. Its action and dialogue are presented as a series of surreal images and episodic fragments. A synopsis (this need was anticipated by Lewis and parodied within the play) for the uninitiated goes something like this: the artist-protagonist, Arghol, retreats from Berlin, "in immense collapse of chronic philosophy" in order to purify his soul, feeling ascetic revulsion toward the world. He travels to Siberia, seeking escape from metropolitan art scenes, and finds work at his uncle's wheelwright shop. Arghol, whose name may be a reference to "Algol," the double star, is shadowed by Hanp, a fellow worker who represents the philistine audience. Arghol is violently mistreated by his uncle and Hanp continues this abuse. Arghol passively submits to Hanp's blows until, at last, he turns with equally violent disgust to Hanp. He kicks Hanp out of the hut and falls asleep, dreaming of his untidy student years in which he rejects the solipsistic thinking of Max Stirner's 1844 philosophy of egoism. Meanwhile Hanp's hatred of Arghol increases. The play ends as Hanp kills Arghol while he sleeps and then Hanp commits suicide by drowning. If the vulgar audience is represented by Hanp, Lewis suggests that the integrity of the artist was never pure and detached but always dependent upon—and in relation to—his despised audience. By the same token, when the philistine kills the artist, he discovers that his life becomes unlivable; he is further enslaved and commits suicide.

The play is set in a "non-place of language" that transforms linguistic categories of meaning, including subject and object positions that become radically intersubjective. As a closet drama, it blends performative mimesis with narrative diegesis to transform both categories of representation.[14] Though the plot may be summarized, its episodic form, stuttering language, and phantasmagoric setting enact a doomed confrontation between the artist and his modern audiences and between the text and the production of meaning.

The play demonstrates the illusory space of philistine conformity and crass commercialization. It begins as a circus spectacle, deploying block typography of poster art and "advertising" the opening scene: "some bleak circus, uncovered, carefully-chosen [*sic*], vivid night. It is packed with posterity, silent and expectant. Posterity is silent, like the dead, but more pathetic." Moreover, it is "very well acted by you and me" (B1, 55). Lewis sets the drama near the Arctic Circle, a place where, at the time, it was widely believed the "Aryan" race originated: "Type of characters taken from broad faces where Europe goes arctic, intense, human and universal" (B1, 59).[15] Then Lewis punctures that originating myth and primitive setting by positing a very particular and bourgeois audience reacting within and without this (falsely) universal setting: "'Yet you and me: why not from the English metropolis?'" Lewis situates "our intimate ceremonious acquaintance" (B1, 59) of writer and audience who gather for the drama as neither here (the English metropolis) nor there (Siberia) but in a phantasmagoric conflation of space and time, where whiteness nonetheless remains paramount.

The circus arena presents an intensely focused, but imaginary, space holding together different representational registers and allowing Lewis to experiment with nonmimetic language. The circus may suggest classical Greek and Roman theater but it also overlays that space with references to modern spectacle: electric lights and box office success. Though the text is privately read, it insists on its status as performance by declaring to its readers that it is "very well acted by you and me." However, if the projected audience is posterity, then the text must circulate as a literary work, not only as performance. This textual instability challenges a knowable locus of enunciation: who and where are these characters? David Graver argues that "the closest physical corollary to the performative display of this text would be a multi-ring circus" (204). Just as the instabilities of heterotopia shatter language, syntax and taxonomies, "the groundlessness of Lewis's theatrical display is achieved not by dissolving particularities of place but, rather, by multiplying them" and by "placing the drama in a bewildering array of conceptually disparate milieux" (204). The ontological turbulence, moreover, exceeds the montage effect of fragmented forms that is often taken to be the central point of vorticism (Edwards, "Afterward" 459). It destabilizes the very ground on which such fragmented representation occurs.

Indeed, sentence structure, grammar, and generic form are so altered that Fredric Jameson calls the textual world Lewis creates one of *hypallage:* "a world in which the old-fashioned substances, like marbles in a box, have been rattled so furiously together that their 'properties' come loose and stick together" (*Fables* 27). This form is a continuously transformative, asymmetrical, destructive, and kinetic structure that refuses closure. The performance space is unfixed; it opens boundaries simultaneously to abstract and particular spaces. Metropolis and Siberian wheelwright's shop blend into each other in a dubiously unstable performance space. We are never quite sure where we are: in Siberia or in a distorted, dangerous shifting artscape that forcefully unsettles any conventions for representation and any possibility of a fixed meaning.

Taxonomic disorder extends to the level of syntax and grammatical structure as Lewis creates a linguistic and discursive conception of unstable polarities. The text is so volatile we are not sure how to read it; at points it resembles narrative fiction, and, at other points, it oscillates between circus spectacle, metaphysical allegory, and science fiction. Subject and object are at times indistinguishable and its ontology is obscure. For instance, Arghol "lay silent, his hands a thick shell fitting back of head, his face grey vegetable cave" (B1, 65). Eluding personification, Arghol is composed of disparate items, organic and otherwise. Syntax is broken, injecting spatial disjunction into the temporal unfolding of meaning. The presence of meaning is also frustrated as the play's sentence structure drags against its forward momentum. Active verbs and clausal subordination are eliminated as much as possible. Often Lewis presents phrases that are strung loosely together: "Bastard violence of his half-disciple, métis of apache of the icy steppe, sleek citizen and his own dumbfounding soul" (B1, 100). This description of Hanp renders the character ontologically incomprehensible. He is primitive, modern, and a metaphysical projection of Arghol simultaneously.

The unsynthesized dualism between Arghol and Hanp underscores the influence of Nietzsche on Lewis. Like Nietzsche, Lewis problematizes language and foregrounds Nietzsche's claim that representation is always mis-representation, even at the level of subjectivity. The dilemma for Lewis, then, is that representations of race are emptied of meaning and yet impossible to transcend. In a contradictory both/and formulation, which both dissolves racial categories and reinscribes them, Lewis shows in *Enemy of the Stars* the impossibility of preserving aesthetic and individual autonomy within the "non-place of language."

To explain how the meanings of identity categories are broken down in this shifting non-place, Lewis wrote an explanatory essay of this play called "Physics of the Not-Self." The exercise of the Not-Self, represented by Arghol as that which can rise above the self, is that of a "breaker-down of walls, a dissolvent of nations, factions, and protective free-masonries" ("Physics" 198). He calls the not-self an inhuman force. It is both a devil and a force of love: "there is something indefinably *disreputable* about it. It is not 'clean.' It cannot be described confidently as 'white' . . . It is unquestionably not 'top drawer.' It is irreparably 'un-pukka'" (198). Breaking down walls and categories, the artist is "both a devil and a force of love," neither one nation nor another, one political faction nor another, not quite white, neither morally nor socially reputable, and imperially suspect, "un-pukka." Lewis defines the artist's universality in contrast to his disparate and encyclopedic lexicon of terms: "un-pukka" coming from the Raj; and "top-drawer" coming from English high society. The artist shatters commonplace expressions, identity categories, and the meanings and values that arise from them.

Though Lewis celebrates the artist's ability to wage war on hardened meanings and values, he demonstrates in *Enemy of the Stars* how this ability is fatally compromised. The artist-protagonist, Arghol, cannot achieve aesthetic or individual autonomy. He is described as a "statue-mirage of Liberty in the great desert" (B1, 59). The narrator describes Arghol's difficulty: "When mankind cannot overcome a personality. . . . It becomes it. It imitates and assimilates the Ego until it is no longer one" (B1, 66). Hanp is this imitative force. He is a "black bourgeois" which suggests Lewis's 1916 description of the London (pro)war crowds as "black," and stands as a metaphor for conformity, imitation, and the dissolution of the clear subject boundaries. But Lewis also means *black* literally as modernization spreads to the colonies and produces black bourgeois subjects. Art's emancipatory potential is further compromised as the artist contributes ineluctably to the spread of art as bourgeois spectacle. Arghol attempts to "liberate" his philistine audience, Hanp, by assisting in the process of making him into a projection of himself. He realizes, however, that this vanguard position would merely spread a different sort of conformity, a false copy of himself: "I find I wanted to make a naïf yapping Poodle-parasite of you. —I shall always be a prostitute. I wanted to make you myself; you understand?" (B1, 73).

Unable to break from this cycle of conformity, Arghol depends on Hanp, his vulgar double, to make his idealist aspirations known at all. The imitation-self is approximate and imprecise, but it is perceived by the world as real in its particularities. Lewis's "not-self," the artist, transcends racial categories (though, according to Lewis in his manifesto and his play, only the Aryan race can ever become universal). Once this transcendence is achieved through art, it can still only be conveyed through the distorting and fragmenting lens of his imitation-self/double, Hanp. As Hanp and Arghol pummel each other, the recognition of their mutually constitutive relation blocks the possibility of an autonomous ground for judging and creating art. This problematic dualism plays itself out in racial terms as a reactionary antimodernism that ominously predicts the death of art and the end of Western civilization.

Enemy of the Stars presents the failure of the avant-garde artist. As Arghol prepares to die, he imagines himself trading blows with Hanp as a: "clown in the circus . . . with obsequious dignity down gangway" (B1, 82). The artist becomes a gladiator, his life and dignity sacrificed for the audience's pleasure. What is left is modernity's expansionary drive where all is grist for the commodifying mill, including humanity itself. The play closes as the audience slowly sinks into the "hypnotic trance of art": "THEY BREATHE IN CLOSE ATMOSPHERE OF TERROR AND NECESSITY TIL THE EXECUTION IS OVER" (B1, 61; caps in original). With this conclusion, Lewis suggests that the danger of mass forms of popular entertainment is that they allow for a mechanical perpetuation of the present, a grinning unreality that lures the masses into happy forgetfulness and totalitarianism. *Enemy of the Stars* suggests that the fashionable primitivism of racial spectacle, celebrated by moderns in cabarets for awakening spectators through shocking and sensational performances, distracts society from modernity's dehumanizing effects. And yet, the artist who would warn spectators of these consequences is compromised by this very spectacle.

As *Blast's* contributors Wyndham Lewis and Rebecca West demonstrate, modernists deploy the spectacle of racialized performance to suggest the movement's transgressive and transformative nature, but, in so doing, they reveal a new dilemma. Racial spectacle calls racial essentialism into question and inadvertently adds to the crisis of authority and legitimacy faced by metropolitan writers in the face of expanding mass culture at home and in the colonies. Though Lewis redeploys race as nativism, he recognizes that the double movement of modernity back to the metropolis (and, in his eyes, back to the future) deterritorializes and dehistoricizes race. It thereby interrupts the production of racialized subjects and potentially undermines racial categories. Race, for both West and Lewis, is fodder for modernity's assimilative mill and yet, conversely, delineates the disruptive, discontinuous forms of geomodernisms.

NOTES

1. See Urmilla Seshagiri's excellent essay that shows how Roger Fry and Virginia Woolf participate in the modernist project of achieving "aesthetic purity through racial difference" (75). Discussing Fry's prewar Postimpressionist art exhibits, his Omega (arts and crafts) workshops (with which Lewis was briefly affiliated), and his fetishization of "primitive" art objects, Seshagiri shows how they "add[ed] very specific cultural associations to [Clive] Bell's rhetoric of formal aesthetic purity" (72). She demonstrates that "Omega art embodies the belief that non-Western art is shaped by purer, more direct vision than Western art, and that nonwhite racial otherness floats freely, infinitely interchangeable and adaptable" (74–75). See also Simon Gikandi's essay in this volume.
2. See Janet Lyon, "Josephine Baker's Hothouse," for a trenchant analysis of the Parisian cabaret *Chez Josephine* and how it negotiates avant-garde aesthetics, race, and nationalism. There, Lyon argues, "the cultural multiplicity experienced . . . took the form of embodied identification. . . . [in which] otherness . . . was comprised of both the dancer and her audience, bound together in a historical moment" (42). Moreover, this "improvisational participation," Lyon asserts, "seems to have created a path of intimacy that largely evaded the double threat of political relativism and racialist essentialism" (42). While this evasion may indeed have been achieved in avant-garde cabarets, I will show in this essay how racial categories are both unsettled and re-encoded as essentialist in vorticist texts.
3. Paul Peppis argues that Lewis presents racial categories in transition, between Victorian typologies and individualized, primitivist attributes, what Peppis calls "[a] peculiar blending of conceptual rigidity and fluidity" ("Thinking Race" 372). Furthermore, in his outstanding monograph on the prewar English avantgarde, Peppis situates Lewis's both/and mapping of racial characterization in terms of scientific and anthropological debates: "Lewis's stories toy with the con-

temporaneous anthropological dilemma of how to reconcile evidence of individual human variation with the 'scientifically' validated stereotypes of race and nationality" (*Literature* 41–42). While I agree with Peppis's delineations of Lewis's contradictory stance toward racial categories, I take issue with such a progressivist linearity, from Victorian typology to modern individuality. In my reading of Lewis, individuality is only ever available, even provisionally, for white metropolitan subjects. Racial otherness forecloses autonomy, even when taken on an individual basis.

4. Lewis hated how European culture and ideology was disseminated throughout its colonized territories. In 1927, he wrote that instead of missionary Bibles distributed around the globe, Europe exports "white magic," science, and socialism, so that Everyman, "Black, White, and Yellow—becomes a leisured gentleman; with the aid of machinery (the good God Science) he only needs to work two hours a day. All the rest of the time he sits in a velvet jacket and paints a field of buttercups, one eye on a copy of the 'Idylls of the King,' while his mate feeds his ear with Puccini and Offenbach." This "white magic," Lewis ominously predicts, turns the white populations "into not an irresistible race of supermen, but a horde of particularly helpless children" (TWM 294–95). The chief danger, for Lewis, is the disappearance of great art in the face of a racially blended tide of mediocrity.

5. David Harvey has recently discussed the political possibilities and drawbacks of Foucault's concept of heterotopia: "The formulation is surficially attractive. It allows us to think of the potential for coexistence in the multiple utopian schemes—feminist, anarchist, ecological, and socialist—that have come down to us from history. It encourages the idea of . . . 'spatial plays' to highlight choice, diversity, difference, incongruity, and incommensurability" ("Cosmopolitanism" 537). Importantly, these spaces of difference are places of contact with social processes already in motion. But, Harvey warns, Foucault assumes that such spaces are outside the dominant social order and the workings of power/knowledge. So, too, at times, Foucault speaks about such spaces as escape, such as, Harvey notes, "'the ship is the heterotopia par excellence'" (538). Harvey's critical challenge is to link such local spaces with the globalizing forces of modernity.

6. Francesca Klug writes that "between 1870 and 1914 about 120,000 Jews came to Britain to escape persecution and massacres in tsarist Russia and the surrounding countries. The Jewish refugees met with hostility and discrimination when they arrived" (17). From 1912–14, Sylvia Pankhurst, in alliance with working-class women activists, organized the East London Federation of Suffragettes (ELFS) that was allied with local labor organizations, including dockers who were especially vulnerable to extremes of economic fluctuations in global trade. The ELFS was committed to the redistribution of wealth, Irish Home Rule, and the Dublin General Strike. The women's army (which at its peak numbered seven hundred) was trained in self-defense and carried India rubber batons to defend themselves against police brutality, a force seen as an external occupying army (see Winslow).

7. Lisa Tickner has examined the symbolic significance of the Parisian underclass called "apaches" who were "unemployed, violent, criminal hooligans" (72). They were called by the press at the time "the native scum of our civilization" (qtd. in Tickner 72). Their imagined social practices were choreographed to wildly popular effect on the Paris and London stage. According to Tickner, the apache dance condensed anxieties concerning twentieth-century modernity. Sexually explicit, vengeful, illicit, and wildly disruptive, the apache was the antithesis of the bourgeois subject (73).

8. When Madame Strindberg closed the Cabaret Theatre Club in February 1914 due to financial difficulties, she promised that it would reopen as the Blast Club (Wees 50). See also Martin Puchner's critical investigations of the re-

lation between avant-garde manifestos and theater, "Screeching Voices" and "Manifesto=Theater."

9. David Graver writes that "three elements are required to make an action a performance: (1) an audience (either real or imagined), (2) a formalized setting in space and time that separates the performance from other objects and activities, and (3) a consciously performing agent, that is, someone engaged in an activity for a particular audience in a particular setting. Literary texts cannot normally be considered performances for a number of reasons. First, the reader is not always constituted as an audience. . . . [Second] texts do not generally occupy particular settings in the way performances do. . . . Taken autonomously, the [literary] text is a disembodied series of gestures and movements within a particular (literary) space. . . . [Finally] the major difference between literature and performance is that literature creates the parameters of its aesthetic space and performance fills an aesthetic space with its activity" (206–207).

10. Paul Peppis also discusses the unresolved contradictions animating vorticist modern aesthetics and antimodern political aims: "BLAST aggravates the contradictions between Vorticism's agenda of social transformation and cultural elitism and its effort to win support for national consolidation. . . . they placed the competing claims of avant-gardism and nationalism at the core of Vorticist theory and practice, making BLAST an arena of confrontation" (*Literature* 93).

11. John McClure argues that imperial stories of the early twentieth century (*Heart of Darkness, Kim, A Passage to India*) "sharply interrogate the popular romance of civilizing mission or 'development' and relate in its stead a counter-romance of descent into realms of stubborn strangeness and enchantment. . . . It invites the audience to enter a spectacularly unrationalized zone, to participate in pleasures abolished by rationalization" (8–18). Sarah Cole's reading of *Heart of Darkness* in terms of alienation and intimacy anatomizes imperial romance in terms of a crisis of narrative and language: "This moment of linguistic saturation and indeterminacy—so central to the notion of Conradian modernism—is brought on by the inefficacy and incompleteness of the over-charged imperial encounter between Marlow and Kurtz" (260).

12. Robert J. C. Young locates the antimodern need to fix identity as part of rapid modernization: "In the nineteenth century, the very notion of a fixed English identity was doubtless a product of, and reaction to, the rapid change and transformation of both metropolitan and colonial societies which meant that, with nationalism, such identities needed to be constructed to counter schisms, friction and dissent. . . . The need for organic metaphors of identity or society implies a counter-sense of fragmentation and dispersion" (3–4).

13. See Laura Doyle's essay in this volume for a genealogy of modernity's double bind of race and liberty.

14. See Martin Puchner's *Stage Fright* for his analysis on modernist closet drama and its transforming effect on representational practices.

15. The belief that humankind originated near the Arctic Circle is discussed by Paul Edwards, *Wyndham Lewis: Painter and Writer*, p. 164.

PART THREE

Modernisms' Imagined Geographies

12   Township Modernism

Ian Baucom

THE COURTESAN'S GAZE

About midway through the assortment of notes and quotations that comprise his convolute on Baudelaire in *The Arcades Project*, Walter Benjamin offers the following somewhat surprising suggestion:

> From the argument of the Guys essay, it would appear that Baudelaire's fascination with this artist was connected above all with his handling of backgrounds, which differ little from the handling of backgrounds in the theater. But because these pictures, unlike scenery on the stage, are to be viewed from close up, the magic of distance is cancelled for the viewer without his having to renounce the judgment of distance. In the essay on Guys, Baudelaire has characterized the gaze which here *and in other places* he himself turns toward the distance. Baudelaire dwells on the expression of the oriental courtesan: "She directs her gaze at the horizon, like a beast of prey; the same wildness, the same indolent distraction, and also at times the same fixity of attention."[1]

I say that Benjamin's argument is somewhat surprising because in the essay on Guys that Benjamin has in mind ("The Painter of Modern Life") Baudelaire gives little mention to the problem of backgrounds, nor does he take up at any great length the question of distance, its magic, or what Benjamin here calls its mode of "judgment." The essay is more famously concerned with the crowd, fashion, the "shock" of metropolitan experience, the importance of the "transitory" and the "fugitive" as indexical modern forms, and the fate of an array of social types, most notably the flaneur, the dandy, and the prostitute.

Benjamin, to be sure, may simply be conflating "The Painter of Modern Life" with another essay, the "Salon of 1859," in which Baudelaire does take up the question of backgrounds, distance, "magic," and stage scenery ("I long for the return of the dioramas whose enormous, crude magic subjects me to the spell of a useful illusion. I prefer looking at the backdrop paintings of the stage where I find my dreams treated with consummate skill and tragic concision. Those things, so completely false, are for that very reason much closer to the truth.")[2] It is worth noting that in the essay on Baudelaire that Benjamin worked up from the *Arcades Project*'s material, it is the "Salon," rather than "The Painter of Modern Life" that he draws on in discussing Baudelaire's willed tendency to "pierce" the "magic of distance."[3] It is also true that Benjamin quite clearly indicates that his comments on distance are not limited to the "Painter" essay but, more significantly, engage "the gaze which here *and in other places* he himself [i.e., Baudelaire] turns to the distance." That gaze, which somehow manages to cancel the *magic* without renouncing the *judgment* of distance, it thus turns out, is for Benjamin proper not only to Guys or his courtesans but to Baudelaire himself. Description here, Benjamin thus argues, is also a form of Baudelairian self-description, as it is a way of typifying the gaze of the modern subject on modernity itself: a modernity "viewed from close up," with the magic of its distance pierced.

It is, then, not so much Guys but his courtesan that provides the Benjaminian link between the concerns of "The Painter of Modern Life" and the problem of a modernity conceived as canceled or no-longer-magical distance, or, as Baudelaire puts it in the fuller passage from which Benjamin is drawing, a modernity figured as a "horizon" toward which the courtesan directs an alternately absentminded and fixed attention, "tinged with a weariness which imitates true melancholy." And it is this simultaneously weary, disillusioned, and melancholy experience of apprehending "modernity" as a distant "horizon" whose distance has been canceled that I want to suggest characterizes the modernity not only of Baudelaire's Parisian demi-monde but of the colonial and postcolonial township, as it further characterizes the *modernism* that both township and demi-monde produce. Or let me put it this way. "Modernity," Fredric Jameson has argued in his recent *A Singular Modernity,* is not so much a thing as a narrative convention, a trope or figure for telling a "break" and reimagining that "break" as a period. More vexingly, he contends, it is a narrative with which we are not yet done, a figure still in global circulation. My intention here is to examine some aspects of the imperial and postimperial circulation of that figure, particularly as it is deployed in the quasi-Baudelairean demi-monde of the colonial and postcolonial township, and in the literatures that trope a set of Fanonian "native-quarters" as a dispersed global region of modernity discourse and modernist narrativity. As a scattered region of modernism/modernity discourse, I want to suggest, the global township grounds a melancholy rereading of what Ayi Kwei Armah calls the "capricious gleam" of modernity, a rereading in productive tension with Benjamin's (Baudelairean) counterallegory of modernity as that "canceled distance" across which the gaze of the "oriental" courtesan plays, "tinged with a weariness which imitates true melancholy."

But what, on Benjamin's terms, is this "canceled distance"? Modernity itself, I have suggested, and in so doing depart from the more explicit definition of modernity Baudelaire provides in "The Painter of Modern Life." "By modernity," as Baudelaire there directly states, "I mean the ephemeral, the fugitive, the contingent, the half of art whose other half is the eternal and the immutable . . . [the] transitory, fugitive element, whose metamorphoses are so rapid, [and which] must on no account be despised or dispensed with."[4] Shock, intensity, the ephemeral, the fugitive: these are what Foucault and others have taught us to expect of Baudelaire's theory of modernity. What, then, does such a modernity have to do with "the judgment of distance," with distance pierced, distance canceled, distance demystified, or with the melancholy horizon across which the courtesan's distracted/fixed gaze plays? By way of preliminary answer let me simply indicate that as Benjamin's backward-glancing angel is to his quasi-modernist philosophy of history, so is this horizon-gazing courtesan to my understanding of a demi-urban or township modernism "tinged with a weariness which imitates true melancholy" as it absentmindedly *and* fixedly regards, "from close up," a modernity made to appear like an enormous crude and magic diorama on the fringes of the imperial metropolis.

I will develop these arguments in what follows. But first, since I began with him, let me put the question back to Benjamin. What is this "gaze in which the magic of distance is extinguished"? A type of blasé cosmopolitanism surely, to borrow one term from Baudelaire and one from current theories of distance and detachment.[5] Cosmopolitan, blasé, dandyish, brothel-wise, the gaze of detached, extinguished distance is also, for Benjamin, something else. "Relevant here," as he notes in the *Arcades*: "my definition of the aura as the aura of distance opened up with the look that awakens in an object perceived."[6] This, like so much else in the *Arcades*, is generically cryptic, but a little less so if we follow the comment through to its explication in "Some Motifs in Baudelaire." Aura, as Benjamin makes clear in that essay, is intimately related to an almost Hegelian play of recognition across a distance:

> Looking at someone carries the implicit expectation that our look will be returned by the object of our gaze. Where this expectation is met . . . there is an experience of the aura to the fullest extent. . . . To perceive the aura of an object we look at means to invest it with the ability to look at us in return. This experience corresponds to the data of the *memoire involontaire*. (These data, incidentally are unique: they are lost to the memory that seeks to retain them. Thus they lend support to a concept of the aura that comprises

"the unique manifestation of a distance." The essentially distant is the in-approachable: inapproachability is in fact a primary quality of the ceremo-nial image.)[7]

This is dense, too dense for satisfactory explication in a brief essay. So let me note just a few things. Aura, Benjamin argues, adheres to an object "awakened" by a gaze, an object held to return our look from a distance. As such, the auratic object is not merely something we recognize: it is something that recognizes us as proper to it, as privy to its domain. It incorporates us within its sphere. That sphere, however, is distant. The auratic object recognizes us from afar, whether across a distance of time or of space, in either case from across a space the gaze traverses but which it does not, therefore, cancel. The distance remains even as it is crossed, and is, indeed, made more fully evident by being crossed. Without this double movement—of traversing and marking the distance between ourselves and the auratic object our gaze has awakened—the aura is pierced as its dis-tance is canceled.

Schematically, then, for Benjamin the pre-modern is that which pre-serves the magic of distance in the objects it perceives and the modern is that which, while preserving the judgment of distance, finds that distance canceled or pierced. This, Benjamin suggests, was Baudelaire's experience of the world, and his modern genius was not to lament but to force such an extinguishing of distance. The fugitive and the transitory may then be intense, but they cannot be auratic. They have been stripped of their magic. They fail to acknowledge us, refuse an organic awakening in our gaze. We regard them as the courtesan regards the things of her world, as the "data" of a no-longer inapproachable horizon of experience, as that which induces no true moment of recognition, only a weariness tinged with melancholy. This, for Benjamin, is Baudelairean modernity: a giant and crude diorama of life, a no-longer distant and magical horizon of experience, a fixated *and* detached way of regarding a set of impressions so obviously false they can only provide the *useful* pleasure of the obvious lie. And this, I want to suggest, is one of the ways in which "modernity" renders itself globally visible on the fringes of the imperial metropolis (on the border of Fanon's Algerian medina; at the edge of the abject neighborhoods of Ayi Kwei Ar-mah's urban postcolony; across the color line of South Africa's Sophiatown throughout the 1950s as the bulldozers of the apartheid state rolled in). This is the guise "modernity" so frequently takes on the border of the township, native quarter, and shantytown. Which is, perhaps, another way of saying that it is to such spaces that we should look if we are to under-stand the untimely workings, imperial and postimperial wanderings, and uncanny persistence of what, following the unlikely lead of Jameson, Ha-bermas, and Appadurai, we might think of as an unfinished modernity, at large.

THE VIEW FROM THE TOWNSHIP

To read or discuss Benjamin is perhaps always to risk an allegorizing of thought. So let me turn from the allegory of the courtesan's gaze to something more bitterly and more literally observed: Frantz Fanon's description of colonial topography in *The Wretched of the Earth:*

> The colonial world is a world cut in two. . . . The zone where the natives live is not complementary to the zone inhabited by the settlers. The two zones are opposed, but not in the service of a higher unity. No conciliation is possible, for of the two terms one is superfluous. The settler's town is a strongly built town, all made of stone and steel. It is a brightly lit town, the streets are covered with asphalt, and the garbage cans swallow all the leavings, seen and unseen, unknown and hardly thought about. . . . The town belonging to the colonized people, or at least the native town, the Negro village, the medina, the reservation, is a place of ill fame, peopled by men of evil repute. They are born there, it matters little where or how; they die there, it matters not where, nor how.[8]

The sardonic anger of Fanon's final sentences is evident, as is his determination, throughout the body of his work, to make a lie of these ventriloquized sentiments, to reveal not only the fundamental centrality of the "native town" to the colonial and postcolonial worlds but, as importantly, to demonstrate the paradigmatic *modernity* of "the native town, the Negro village, the medina, the reservation." For it is, Fanon argues, in precisely such abject spaces that a colonial culture comes to "modernize" itself (240). If modernism, by one definition, reflects a thoroughgoing determination to "make it new," then, Fanon argues, in the colonial world that determination is never more evident than in the "native town" and the medina, in "the fluctuating movement" which the struggling people of the township "are just giving a shape to and which, as soon as it has started, will be the signal for everything to be called into question" (226). "Let there be no mistake about it," Fanon admonishes his readers, "it is to this zone of occult instability where the people dwell that we must come" (226).

Fanon's comments are drawn from the essay "On National Culture," in *The Wretched of the Earth,* and they are generally, and accurately, read as an exhortation to reject both nativist nostalgia and a habit of Eurocentric mimicry, and as reflecting his assumption that to the extent that it can be wielded as a weapon of anticolonial struggle, culture is, and must be recognized as, national. What is often missed in the ensuing debates regarding Fanon's commitment to the nation form, however, is what I can only think of as the radical, demi-urban modernism of his conception of the nation and of national culture. It is not only the intellectual who must "come" to "the zone of occult instability where the people dwell." The national culture (and the nation) those intellectuals are charged with helping to "assemble" (243) must also come from these wretched dwelling places, and coming from the medina, national culture, Fanon argues, will be, and must be, one whose "traditions are fundamentally unstable . . . shot through by centrifugal tendencies." The nation, for Fanon as for Benedict Anderson, may be of the present, but the present to which it commits itself is recognizably modernist (in the aesthetic and cultural sense): an experimental, transitory, centrifugal present the nation encounters not as empty simultaneity but in the densely fugitive streets and experimental cultural practices of its ghettos, reservations, and townships.

As a discourse on the transitory, the experimental, and the new, cultural modernism has been understood as serving any number of ideological purposes. But Fanon, I believe, is almost unique in so directly allying a modernist commitment to the new with the cause of a radical, anti-imperial nationalism or in imagining that the centrifugal and the experimental, and the subaltern ghettos that are home to such forms of cultural newness could provide the basis for a national culture he evokes in a continuing series of comments on the modernizing impulses of the artists and storytellers of the native town which read, collectively, not merely like a nationalist, but like a modernist manifesto, or perhaps a manifesto for an alternative cultural modernism, a medina—or township—modernism charged with the task of formally assembling a nation around its own disassembling of tradition and inherited form.[9]

To speak of an "alternative modernism," is, of course, to allude to Dilip Gaonkar's recent theorization of alternative modernities, and so also to imply that the colonial townships in which Fanon detects the fluctuating movements of the new are not only zones of an alternative *modernism* in cultural practice but also the zones of an alternative social *modernity*, sites in which, as Gaonkar suggests, a globalizing and Western-style pattern of social modernization (the paradigm of convergence theories of modernity) finds itself diverged as it encounters the cultural multiplicity of the globally modern.[10] And that is, indeed, part of what I want to suggest. But if Gaonkar's "alternative modernities" might thus find their conceptual precursors in Fanon's zones of occult instability, then they also find a source in another, pre-Fanonian, theorist of the modern: unsurprisingly, perhaps, in Baudelaire, and that "attitude to the present" in which Foucault suggests Baudelaire demonstrates the essential character of modernity. But while Baudelaire's modernity, like Fanon's native town, like any one of Gaonkar's "alternative modernities," is indissociable from an attitude to a fugitive, transitory, unstable present, Fanon's conception of the modernity of the colonial township does differ from Baudelaire's theory of the modern metropolis in at least two crucial respects. However unstable, however centrifugal, however experimental, modernity, in the Fanonian township, is still occult, still magical. And it is, simultaneously, distant: distant both from the reader whom Fanon enjoins to "come" to this *not-yet-approached* zone of fugitive instability; *and*, perhaps more vexingly for Fanon, too-often perceived as distant from the point of view of the medina itself, mis-identified with the "brightly lit" habitus of the settler, held inapproachably apart from the native town, a stone's throw and a revolution in conscious-ness away. Pressing up against the edge of the colonial reservation, the set-tler "zone," Fanon understands, remains separated from the township by a colonial color-line (and anger-line, and poverty-line) masquerading (and too often mistaken) as the border, the boundary, the uncrossable "horizon" of modernity.

Fanon, I am suggesting, understands himself to know and to see that the *modernist* zone of the present from which colonial societies will refash-ion themselves *is* the zone of the township, but he also understands that colonial society often fails to share that vision. And indeed this should come as no surprise, either to Fanon or to us. For as an analyst not only of society but of desire, Fanon recognizes throughout his work that desire is predicated not on arrival, not on what is, in fact, already present, but on lack, or the perception of lack, on what is denied or unheld, on what is not here, but there . . . beyond the color line, on the horizon, in the brightly lit colonist's cities: modernity, or at least the illusion of modernity.

Let me put this another way. The colonial world, Fanon suggests, is a world cut in two but jammed together. Modernity, Reinhart Koselleck argues, is a world equally predicated on an enjambed division, a world made out of the collapsed partition between what he calls a "space of ex-perience" and a "horizon of expectation."[11] For Koselleck, that is, moder-nity makes its appearance when the gap between a collectivity's historical space of experience and its horizon of expectation simultaneously widens and collapses; when, that is, a collective anticipates that a radically novel future is rushing in on it, has, indeed, already begun to arrive. Settler co-lonialism, Fanon's work suggests, also embeds just such a structure—such a simultaneously widened and collapsed distinction between a received "space of experience" and a novel "horizon of expectation"—in its organi-zation of everyday social life and space, particularly in the colonial town-ships, those demi-urban spaces in which a received structure of cultural experience finds itself doubly confronted by a novel horizon of expectation: one proper to the township itself, within which antecedent cultural prac-tices and forms are so evidently shot through with a set of emergent, cen-trifugal tendencies, and one identified with the colonial color-line and with the unapproachable but brightly lit zones of settler life which the wretched of the earth expect, one day, to make their own.

While the virtue of Koselleck's model, in other words, is to empty "modernity" of any normative content, to alienate it from the exclusive property claim of any particular cultural formation, to prevent it from functioning as no more than a codeword, variously, for "Europe," "America," or "the West," "modernity," thus construed, is still susceptible to normalization if one half of its structure (the approach and part arrival of a novel horizon of expectation) is taken for the whole (the entanglement of a novel horizon of expectation and a received space of experience) *and that half is then further given a single, universal ("Western") content.* "Modernity" then becomes merely what is expected (seen, glimpsed, partially approached, but still "distant"); while what is expected is the "West" (brightly lit but held apart, on the far side of the color-, poverty-, anger-line). And this is how modernity, to Fanon's considerable frustration, all too often appears to the colonial subject, not only to the colonizers but to the colonized, particularly a nascent intelligentsia trained by colonial ideology and the colonial educational system to mistake the color-line for the border (the horizon) of modernity. Alternately put, this is what happens when Koselleck's fraught, dialectical, two-part modernity is filtered through the simplifying optic of a modernist historiography that expects a common modernity as the universal future of global history and so holds out modernity to the un- or underdeveloped world as no more than a distant promise, a not-yet-crossed horizon.

And this, the cultural anthropologist James Ferguson has argued in his important study *Expectations of Modernity: Myths and Meanings of Urban Life on the Zambian Copperbelt,* is precisely how modernity appears not only in the colonial shantytown, but in the cities and townships of postindependence Africa. In the townships and cities of the Zambian Copperbelt in particular, he indicates, urbanization has frequently "seemed to be a teleological process, a movement toward a known endpoint that would be nothing less than a western-style industrial modernity."[12] Over the last quarter of the twentieth century in particular, Ferguson further suggests, "urban workers' conceptions of town and country, and of the cultural differences among urbanites were . . . not simply *compatible* with the modernist metanarratives of social science; they were a local version of them. Modernization theory had become a local tongue" (84). And perhaps unsurprisingly so, at least in the Zambian instance. Because, for a while, that anticipated, coming modernity seemed to be in the process of constituting itself on Zambian soil as, by another of the code switchings common to the global transition from colony to postcolony, colonization and independence alike came to signify urbanization, and urbanization to signify modernity. To cross through the old colonial color-line thus came to be equated with the crossing into postcoloniality, while the postcolonial event horizon came to be coded, in its turn, as the passage into modernity. However parsed, the postcolonial processes Ferguson describes preserve the basic Fanonian structure of colonial misrecognition and desire, yet again equating modernity not with the dialectical enjambment of a differential structure of experience and horizon of expectation but with lack: an exclusive turn to a horizon perhaps less distant than it had earlier appeared, perhaps even partially crossed, but always defined from (a Western) elsewhere.

But this, while central to Ferguson's argument, is not his major concern. His problem, rather, is more Baudelairean than Fanonian. For Ferguson, the problem of "modernity" in the postindependence urban quarters of southern Africa is not, primarily, the problem of an overtly auraticized, not-yet-approached object of desire, but of an object whose aura has been pierced, of an extrinsic "modernity" that has been experienced as no longer entirely distant but viewed (however briefly) "from up close," with the magic of its distance canceled, and the obvious lie of its pleasing illusions revealed. The problem of "modernity" in the townships of the Zambian Copperbelt, in other words, is not that it remained forever distant but that something posing as modernity appeared to have arrived, sometime in the 1960s to be precise, when the lucrative mining and export of copper seemed to have drawn Zambia into partnership with the industrial West. Zambia, however, was unable to retain its newly significant place in the world copper market. By the end of the 1980s, the flow of foreign investment and capital dried up. Europe and America moved decisively on, not only forgetting Zambia but, as Ferguson demonstrates, actively abandoning it, barring it from future capital investment, rewriting the old color-, poverty-, anger-line as a world-banker's redline. His comments on this subject bear citing at some length:

When the color bar cut across colonial Africa, it fell with a special force upon the "Westernized Africans" . . . It was they—the "not quite/not white"—whose uncanny presence destabilized and menaced the racial hierarchy of the colonial order. And it was they who experienced the sting not just of exclusion but of abjection—of being pushed back across a boundary that they had been led to believe they might successfully cross. In a similar way, when the juncture between Africa and the industrialized world that had been presented as a stairway (leading from the "developing" world to the "developed") revealed itself instead as a wall (separating the "first world" from the "third"), it was the Copperbelt and places like it—proud examples of just how modern, urban, and prosperous an emerging Africa could be—that experienced this boundary-fixing process most acutely, as a kind of abjection. The experience of abjection here was not a matter of being merely *excluded* from a status to which one had never had a claim but of being *expelled,* cast out-and-down from that status by the formation of a new (or newly impermeable) boundary. It is an experience that has left in its wake both a profound feeling of loss as well as the gnawing sense of a continuing affective attachment to that which lies on the other side of the boundary. (236–38)

And what then, Ferguson asks? How is life experienced on the other side (rather than the near side) of "modernity's" boundary line? What happens when "modernity," misidentified with a distinct, normative horizon of capital and cultural expectation, approaches, collapses its distance, and then departs, actively distances itself once again? What happens when this spectacle of modernity has been viewed not only from close up but from its far side; from backstage, if you will; from the wings to which the idled stagehands of imperial history have been exiled to no more than watch the main actors on the stage?

The question is not only Ferguson's, not only the question from the townships of the Zambian Copperbelt. It is also, I have been suggesting, the question from the brothels of Baudelaire's Paris. As it is the question Ayi Kwei Armah poses from the abject urban neighborhoods of post-independence Ghana. Certainly this is the question of Armah's novel *The Beautyful Ones Are Not Yet Born*, in which "the gleam" of a simultaneously grasped and withdrawn/withheld modernity serves as one of the text's organizing ways of invoking the object of the postcolony's weary, melancholy, disillusioned, and angry structure of desire. The figure of "the gleam" appears throughout the text; uncoincidentally, however, it makes its first appearance as the protagonist of the novel (simply, almost Kafkaesquely, identified as "the man") looks from the squalid quarter of the city in which he lives and works to the still surviving and still brightly lit settler's zone, now occupied by the postcolonial elite:

> On top of the hill, commanding it just as it commanded the scene below, its sheer, flat, multistoried side an insulting white in the concentrated gleam of the hotel's spotlights, towered the useless structure of the Atlantic-Caprice. Sometimes it seemed as if the huge building had been put there for a purpose, like that of attracting to itself all the massive anger of a people in pain. But then, if there were any angry ones at all these days, they were most certainly feeling the loneliness of mourners at a festival of crazy joy. Perhaps then the purpose of this white thing was to draw onto itself the love of a people hungry for something just such as this. The gleam, in moments of honesty, had a power to produce a disturbing ambiguity within. And something terrible was happening as time went on. It was getting harder to tell whether the gleam repelled more than it attracted, attracted more than it repelled, or just did both at once in one disgustedly confused feeling all the time these heavy days.[13]

Anger, desire, repulsion, attraction—all attached to a capricious spectacle of simultaneously unapproached and captured whiteness: Armah's "gleam" is a virtually complete Baudelairean emblem of the pleasingly false, so obviously duplicitous illusion of modernity that Fanon, Ferguson, and Armah himself understand to be the poisoned (and withdrawn) gift of empire to colony and postcolony alike. But however obviously false, that illusion nevertheless has the power to fix attention, to capture the gaze (no matter how melancholy). The man's gaze, the gaze from the township, the gaze from the Copperbelt, the gaze from the medina, I am thus suggesting, are all, also, formal, global, ex-centric analogues of the courtesan's gaze on modernity (all, like hers, directed "at the horizon, like a beast of prey, the same lazy absent mindedness, and also, at times, the same fixity of attention"); as the colonial and postcolonial township repeats, extends, and continues Baudelaire's Parisian brothel, Joyce's "Nightown," and Fanon's neighborhood of "ill-fame." The inhabitant of one is like the denizen of the other: "a sort of gypsy" as Baudelaire has it, "wandering on the fringes of a regular society."

But—and this is the fundamental point I have been trying to make—that subject, that space, and that look, are not, in fact, the subjects modernity leaves out, the spaces modernity leaves behind, the viewpoints on modernity from outside its blessed sphere. Rather, as Benjamin's reading of Baudelaire would suggest, these are the subjects, spaces, and looks *of* modernity from within and on itself, the immanent actors, zones, and views on and of a global modernity whose magic and whose distance have been pierced. Modernity, however much it has been presented as such, is not a white thing somewhere out there on the abandoned "third world's" or abject city dweller's horizon of expectation and desire. Modernity, rather, is the experience, the dialectic, of engaging such a capricious, illusory spectacle of desire from a weary/angry/hungry space of experience actively distanced *and* no longer distant from a "white thing" seemingly lit up for the dual purpose "of attracting to itself all the massive anger of a people in pain" and compelling "all the love of a people hungry for something just such as this." Or let me put it this way: if modernity is not Armah's gleaming "white thing," it is because it is, instead, his "man," standing in the abject squalor of his global ghetto, wearily, angrily, fixedly studying this caprice of history. Modernity is not the gleam. It is the view from the township.

THE LITTLE PARIS OF THE TRANSVAAL

Well enough. But what does this suggest? More things than I am competent to answer or have the space to address. So, in concluding, let me suggest just three: one drawn from the realm of global economy, one from geopolitics, one touching more closely on the question of modernism. On the question of economics I want simply to underline one of Ferguson's arguments. Urban life in the Zambian Copperbelt—and the many, many places structurally like it—is not outside modernity because modernity is not a thing but a system, a system of connections and active disconnections, of accumulation and exploitation, of development and abjection. In all cases, modernity encompasses both terms in the binary or, indeed, exists in and as their dialectic. On geopolitics: one of the greater intellectual errors to emerge from the tragedy of September 11 and, now, the occupation of Iraq has been the suggestion that the task of a post 9/11 "West" is to engage an Islamic "third world" humiliated by its exclusion from modernity; to, in effect, usher the medina into a modernity it has failed to enter. It is my sense that this suggestion is fundamentally and comprehensively wrong. Modernity, here, is not the solution; it is the problem. The angry look in question here is not a look from without but from within modernity, the look from within a global system of modernity at a "huge building [that seemed to have] been put there for a purpose, like that of attracting to itself all the massive anger of a people in pain." To say this is not to justify the atrocity of a mass murder. The 9/11 act was an atrocity and should be named as such. But its atrocity was not that of an assault committed *against* modernity. It was an assault *of* modernity.

And then there is the question of a township geomodernism, though this is a question that is again indissociable from anger, from crumbling buildings, active disconnection, canceled distance. I am speaking now not of New York but of Sophiatown, the South African township that first provoked the questions raised in this essay. A full account of Sophiatown's history (it was one of the few multiethnic urban communities in twentieth-century South Africa), of its "glorious decade" of cultural production (the 1950s), and of its brutal demolition by the apartheid state are outside the purview of this essay, so let me close by briefly discussing just three short essays by Can Themba, one of the leading figures of the "Sophiatown Renaissance" of the 1950s.[14]

Situated immediately adjacent to a white Johannesburg suburb (West-dene), Sophiatown was under assault by the apartheid state for virtually all of its great decade of literary, musical, and theatrical production and ferment. The South African Defense Force and the government's bulldozers completed the leveling of Sophiatown in 1962 (the white suburb of Triompf, "Triumph," was erected on its ruins) but they had been actively at work since 1954, gradually pecking away at the corners of the township, razing houses, shebeens, community halls, and shops one by one and then separating and trucking the newly homeless residents off to one or other government-designated ethnic "homeland." Yet for all the pressure the state was exerting on Sophiatown throughout the 1950s, Themba and the other writers and artists who helped make the Sophiatown Renaissance were not, in any straightforward sense, a politically committed intelligent-sia. By which I mean that they were not, on the whole, committed to the African National Congress or to an activist, mass, or underground politics of defiance. What they were committed to, instead, was Sophiatown, its jazz, its illicit drinking clubs, its American gangster fashions, its general air of cosmopolitanism. "Somewhere here, and among a thousand more individualistic things is the magic of Sophiatown," as Themba noted in his "Requiem for Sophiatown" (an essay—written at the very tail end of the demolitions—in which he attempts to account for the apparently apolitical cast of the "glorious decade"): "It is different and itself. You don't just find your place here, you make it and you find yourself. There's a tang about it. You might now and then have to give way to others making their ways of life by methods not in the book. But you can't be bored. You have the right to listen to the latest jazz records at Ah Sing's over the road. You can walk a coloured girl of an evening down to the Odin Cinema, and no questions asked. You can try out Rhugubar's curry with your bare fingers without embarrassment. All this with no sense of heresy."[15]

Jazz, cinema, the delight of nonindigenous tastes, sexual freedom, the liberty to fashion a unique self, the pleasure of the unexpected and the new ("we were cavaliers of the evanescent," he earlier indicates): these, for Themba, are the constituent elements of Sophiatown's "magic" and the source of his commitment to the township. That these are all also readily consistent with what we generally understand to constitute a set of modern, modernist, or cosmopolitan pleasures is obvious enough. But what I want to stress is that in each case the "magic" Themba finds and commits to in Sophiatown is an enjambed or dialectical magic, a pleasure that comes not only from some or other habit or thing (listening to jazz records, walking to the cinema) but in what that habit or thing is set off against and manages, in this place, simultaneously to evoke and to escape: questioning, embarrassment, heresy. Magical it may have been, but while it lasted Sophiatown's magic, as Themba describes it, was of a distinctly negative modern sort, a positional magic, the magic of the "brazen" lived experience of a dialectical enjambment (the magic of "a swart jowel," as Themba later notes, pressed "against the rosy cheek of Westdene") enriched rather than confused by the fact that the boundary Themba's township pleasures pressed up against, so frequently trespassed, but could never avoid registering, was a dual boundary, a boundary marked by a perceived indigenous "traditionalism" on the one side and a minatory, brightly lit white settler zone on the other.[16]

But while Themba, like Fanon, thus figures the modernity of the township as a type of precariously snatched magic (an "occult instability"), modern magic, however tenuous, is the one thing the Baudelairean side of the model I have been working with seems actively to deny. And if this appears to imply the need, in the last instance, to choose between Baudelaire and Fanon, to side either with a Fanonian conception of the township as positively modern because still magical or with a Baudelairean understanding of the township as inauthentically modern because not yet invested in its own disillusionment, that is precisely the choice that I want to suggest need not be made. Baudelaire, we remember, even when splenetically canceling the magic of metropolitan modernity, yearns for it

("I long for the return of the dioramas whose enormous, crude magic subjects me to the spell of a useful illusion. . . . Those things, so completely false, are for that very reason much closer to the truth."). Recognized as illusion, magic, Baudelaire here allows, is the very ground of an angry, almost Fanonian truth: the truth that comes from holding in concert the allure of the painted diorama and the disillusioning knowledge of what it looks like from behind. This, we might say, is the dialectical key Baudelaire and Fanon collectively offer to the melancholy truth of modernity. And Themba? Does he share that bifurcated gaze? Does he surrender to the pleasure of the modern spectacle and then look angrily, wearily, behind the curtain? Does he venture across that horizon to discover in the very modernity of the township he loved, mourned, and eulogized something more desperate, something angrier and more abject, something, thus, more typically, dialectically, and globally modern than the gleam of an auratic modernity-at-a-distance? Does he find in this dialectic of modernity the material for an experimental, fugitive, modernist aesthetic of township life?

By way of answer, let me close with two brief pieces from the archive of Themba's writings as journalist and social essayist. Both pieces, though in quite different ways, assume as their object the reconstruction of received gender roles in the township and both discover in the figure of the township courtesan (or coquette) something of the secret of the "modern." Themba, in one of the frequent asides in the "Requiem" essay, refers to Sophiatown as "the little Paris of the Transvaal." There are any number of reasons why that comparison is both as desperate and not as strained as it seems. The likeness of Themba's courtesan to Baudelaire's is only one of them: a likeness strongly linking one crowd-jostled, shock-ridden, fugitive demi-monde to another.

But if Themba's "Modern African Miss," as he facetiously calls her in the first of the two essays ("Girls in High Heel Shoes"), is the product of a quasi-Baudelairean image of modern urban life, then she first appears on Themba's stage very much as a piece of scenery, a pleasing stock emblem and human façade of the modern:

> The Modern African Miss. She's city slick and sophisticated. She's smart. She's delicate and unselfconscious in the way she handles men, the home, and life. . . . At first she was gaudy and brash, and flourished her newly-won freedom and funds in the manner of the prostitute and the brazen flirt. . . . But soon she learned grace and poise. True this brought brand-new problems for her man. This creature was talking back, was catty and gossipy. . . . She's a woman of the world. Whereas in days gone by she didn't think much beyond the kraal walls, she now imagines herself as a Lena Horne, a Vijayalakshmi Pandit, or a Madame Chiang Kai-Shek. . . . But we're not go-

ing to make it sociological. We're going to grin at the tricky packet of femininity, while we try to solve it.[17]

This, by all appearances, is mere knock-off commentary, and not just because Themba's language here seems so prepackaged but because his "modern miss" is so equally a copy—though less, perhaps, a copy of Lena Horne than, as he elsewhere allows, of "the delightful things they put in magazines." Which magazines Themba doesn't say, but his writings as a whole strongly indicate that what he has in mind are the American magazines (and movies, and advertisements) that so vitally constituted Sophiatown's cosmopolitan "mediascape," its fantasy of a "modernity," in Arjun Appadurai's terms, "at large."[18]

If this were all that Themba had to say about the type of the township coquette, his work might be understood to illuminate the powerful "gleam" of such a modernity-at-a-distance, but it would cast little light on the anguished dialectical experience of the modern that I have been attempting to sketch. But this is not his only word on this subject. In the essay that immediately follows "Girls in High Heel Shoes" in Essop Patel's anthology of Themba's writings, another, strikingly different and stylistically more experimental view emerges: an offset image that in its relation to the sketch that has just preceded it has something of the effect of the image/negative-image prose diptychs of Adorno's *Minima Moralia*. I will quote that second piece (whose very title, "Russian Famo Sesh!" signals something of its modernist departure from the caricature realism of "Girls in High Heel Shoes") at length, beginning with the opening sentences and omitting just a few lines from the middle:

A dark figure swathed in a coloured blanket swerved from the muddy pavement into the dark yard of a house. Soon familiar figures appeared, men and women, the men looking ferocious and carrying sticks, the women lascivious with blue artificial pimples or 'beauty' lines painted on their faces. Now and then a giggle would come from the dark, and straining eyes would discern two dark forms clinging to each other. From the house came the music of an organ, harmonicas, the shrieking of voices, the stomping of feet. That is Famo, the famous sex dance of the Russians, Basotho gangsters of the Reef. The place was Germiston Location. We slid out of the car and went in. It was a stunning scene, so crammed with swarming life and sweating bodies. There were long wooden benches along the walls, and Russian men and women had filled them in the order of man and woman, man and woman, man and woman right around the room. In the center were sweating dancers yelling their heads and the roof off. The men just swayed. The women were the stars. They danced a primitive thing that looked strangely like jive. Now and again, at little climaxes in the song and the dance, the women kicked up their legs to show panties, and with some of them, no panties. The men ogled and goggled. But in their ogling and goggling they were secretly choosing the women who seemed to promise them most. . . . The organ went groaning again, harmonicas wailed, human voices took up the lament and the crowd started dancing. I watched a young woman near me. She was dancing a dance all on her own. She stood in one spot, but her body was darting back and forth like a cobra preparing for an attack. Suddenly she kicked up her leg. A flash of petticoat, a dash of panties. Not content with that attack on my modesty, she whirled around, stopped before me, and yanked her dress up over her head in a swift movement so that I saw knees, thighs, black panties, belly and a navel. She threw out a leg clean over my head. I bought more hooch. As the night wore on I noticed that the crowd was thinning. I went out of the stuffy room into the night air. I noticed that some of the girls who had been dancing were walking off arm in arm with blanket-robed Russian men. I went to the yard. I hurried back. I had seen enough. In the open couples were making love.[19]

Toulouse-Lautrec's posters for the Moulin Rouge ghost this scene, as, perhaps, does the Nightown episode of *Ulysses*. But those comparisons are not what make this short essay, in the terms I have been trying to establish, either modern or modernist. Sophiatown's modernity, and the experimental, modernist richness of Themba's prose here are not borrowed. They are, rather, paradigmatic; paradigmatic of a global modernity and a global (geo)modernism harried into existence by the step Themba proves himself willing to take, the step behind the packaged façade of the African Miss (that "tricky packet of femininity," and tricky, generic, prepackaged emblem of an approaching, but still extrinsic, modernity-at-large). Stepping behind the scenes, what Themba finds in this now ambiguous, dialectical survey of his neighborhood of ill-repute is what Baudelaire found in his: a canceled magic, a weariness tinged with melancholy, a cosmopolitanism blasé by policy and for survival. But he also discovers in this, in exactly this, the secret Fanonian life of the globally modern; its detached anger, centrifugal countertraditionality, and occult instability; its little, ephemeral, climaxes; its "transitory, fugitive element . . . [which] must on no account be despised or dispensed with."

NOTES

1. Walter Benjamin, *The Arcades Project*, trans. Howard Eiland and Kevin Mclaughlin (Cambridge, Mass.: Harvard University Press, 1999), 314.
2. Charles Baudelaire, "The Salon of 1859," cited in Walter Benjamin, *Illuminations*, trans. Harry Zohn (New York: Schocken Books, 1968), 191.
3. Benjamin, *Illuminations*, 191.
4. Baudelaire, "The Painter of Modern Life," in *The Painter of Modern Life and Other Essays*, trans. Jonathan Mayne (London: Phaidon, 1964).

5. Baudelaire, "The Painter of Modern Life," 9. See Amanda Anderson, *The Powers of Distance: Cosmopolitanism and the Cultivation of Detachment* (Princeton, N.J.: Princeton University Press, 2001).

6. Benjamin, *Arcades Project*, 314.

7. Benjamin, *Arcades Project*, 188.

8. Frantz Fanon, *The Wretched of the Earth*, trans. Constance Farrington (New York: Grove Press, 1963), 38–39.

9. The following comments, all drawn from Fanon's essay on "National Culture" in *The Wretched of the Earth*, provide a fair sample of his conception of the modernizing impulses of the artists and storytellers of the medina: "On another level, the oral tradition—stories, epics, and songs of the people—which were formerly filed away as set pieces are now beginning to change. . . . The contact of the people with the new movement gives rise to a new rhythm of life and to forgotten muscular tensions and develops the imagination. Every time the storyteller relates a fresh episode to his public, he presides over a real invocation. The existence of a new type of man is revealed to the public. The present is no longer turned in upon itself but spread out for all to see. . . . The storyteller replies to the expectant people by successive approximations and makes his way, apparently alone but in fact helped on by his public, toward the seeking out of new patterns, that is to say national patterns" (240–41). "Where handicrafts are concerned, the forms of expression which formerly were the dregs of art, surviving as if in a daze, now begin to reach out. Woodwork for example, which formerly turned out certain faces and attitudes by the million, begins to be differentiated. The inexpressive or overwrought mask comes to life. . . . This new vigor in this sector of cultural life very often passes unseen; and yet its contribution to the national effort is of capital importance" (241–42). "If we study the repercussions of the awakening of national consciousness in the domains of ceramics and pottery-making, the same observations may be drawn. . . . Jugs, jars, and trays are modified, at first imperceptibly, then almost savagely. The colors, of which formerly there were but few and which obeyed the traditional rules of harmony, increase in number and are influenced by the repercussion of the rising revolution. Certain ochres and blues, which seemed forbidden to all eternity in a given cultural area, now assert themselves" (242). "We might in the same way seek and find in dancing, singing, and traditional rites and ceremonies the same upward-springing trend, and make out the same changes and the same impatience in this field. Well before the political or fighting phase of the national movement, an attentive spectator can thus feel and see the manifestation of new vigor and feel the approaching conflict. He will note unusual forms of expression and themes which are fresh and imbued with a power that is no longer that of invocation but rather that of the assembling of the people, a summoning together for a precise purpose" (243).

10. See Dilip Gaonkar, "On Alternative Modernities," in Goankar, ed., *Alternative Modernities* (Durham, N.C.: Duke University Press, 2001), 1–23.

11. See Reinhart Koselleck, *Futures Past: On the Semantics of Historical Time*, trans. Keith Tribe (Cambridge, Mass.: MIT Press, 1985).

12. James Ferguson, *Expectations of Modernity: Myths and Meanings of Urban Life on the Zambian Copperbelt* (Berkeley: University of California Press, 1999).

13. Ayi Kwei Armah, *The Beautyful Ones Are Not Yet Born: A Novel* (Boston: Houghton Mifflin, 1968).

14. See, among others, Don Mattera, *Gone with the Twilight: A Story of Sophiatown* (London: Zed Books, 1987) and Rob Nixon, "Harlem, Hollywood, and the Sophiatown Renaissance," in *Homelands, Harlem, and Hollywood: South African Culture and the World Beyond*, ed. Rob Nixon (New York: Routledge, 1994).

15. Can Themba, "Requiem for Sophiatown," in *The World of Can Themba: Se-*

lected Writings of the Late Can Themba, ed. Essop Patel (Braamfontein, South Africa: Ravan Press, 1985).

16. I borrow James Ferguson's sense of "traditionalism" as a deliberate urban style adopted to establish a form of cultural authority rather than a type of cultural given.

17. Can Themba, "Modern African Miss," in *The World of Can Themba,* 130–32.

18. See Arjun Appadurai, *Modernity at Large: Cultural Dimensions of Globalization* (Minneapolis: University of Minnesota Press, 1996).

19. Can Themba, "Russian Famo Sesh!" in *World of Can Themba,* 133–35.

13   Paranoia, Pollution, and Sexuality: Affiliations between E. M. Forster's *A Passage to India* and Arundhati Roy's *The God of Small Things*

Susan Stanford Friedman

This volume's neologism—*geomodernisms*—invites a spatial approach to the history of multiple modernities and modernisms enmeshed in the consciousness and conditions of rapid change and rupture around the globe. An internationalist approach to the study of modernism in the West is nothing new, of course—Picasso's appropriation of African masks, Pound's and Eliot's turn to the East have been thoroughly explored and often critiqued. But what is needed now, in my view, is a more systematically intercultural, comparative, and transnational framework for modernist studies, one that breaks with the conventional chronotopes of modernism that bound the field historically and geographically within a Eurocentric, center-periphery model of metropolitan modernity.

To develop a new kind of transnational approach, I propose a reading strategy I call *cultural parataxis,* by which I mean a juxtaposition of texts from different times and places for the new light this geopolitical conjuncture sheds on each.[1] I am borrowing the term *parataxis* from modernist poetics, where it means a formal strategy of radical rupture and nonhierarchical juxtaposition, with connections suppressed and imagined by the reader looking for possible correspondences between the disjunct and the fragmentary. Cultural parataxis invites a new form of comparativism, one not based solely on analysis of similarities and differences or tracing the itineraries of influence often from a presumed Western center to non-Western peripheries.

In modernist studies, cultural parataxis can foster a spatial orientation that decenters the West and foregrounds a geography of intercultural encounters in contact zones shaped by the historical conditions of modernity, colonialism, and postcolonialism. By *space,* I mean not a site of static emptiness outside time, but rather space as the location of multiple cultural constructions and historical overdeterminations. Temporality has typically dominated approaches to modernity—whether positing modernity as progress or as the shattering of the illusion of progression. Cultural parataxis *spatializes* modernity as a historical phenomenon emergent around the globe at different times in history. Such a compensatory emphasis on space allows for what geographer Edward Soja calls in *Postmodern Geographies* a "creative commingling . . . a triple dialectic of space, time, and social being; a transformative retheorization of the relations between history, geography, and modernity" (12). For the modernisms formed in the wake of the European Enlightenment, cultural parataxis involves examining colonial and postcolonial forms of modernism in juxtaposition, not from a premise of the Western metropole as center and the colonized as periphery. Rather, it means examining writers from different nodal points of modernity, recognizing the heterogeneity and stratifications of many centers around the globe as well as the reciprocal influences and cultural mimesis that result from transnational cultural traffic and intercultural contact zones.

Cultural parataxis can also borrow from psychoanalytic hermeneutics, looking for ways in which texts exhibit the symptomology of displacement, condensation, and symbolization in psychodynamic patterns of repression and return around issues of race, gender, sexuality, class, religion, and national origin. The textual and political unconscious of modernity in texts from different times and places comes into clearer focus through the radical juxtapositions of cultural parataxis. What can remain covert in texts read in relation to a single national tradition and period can potentially become overt through comparative readings based on juxtaposition. A psychoanalytic hermeneutic in particular facilitates the analysis of complex power relations in circuits of desire in transgressions of borders established by the social order. I work here, of course, in the wake of Frantz Fanon, who pioneered a form of cultural-political psychoanalysis to explore the psychopathology of race in *Black Skin, White Masks*. Reflecting more recent feminist, gender, and queer uses of psychoanalysis, however, I look for the clash and blend of race with other cultural systems and psychological effects.

For colonial and postcolonial modernities, cultural parataxis can foster intersectional and relational readings of racialized geographies and geopolitics. With its emphasis on imperialism, racism, and emergent nationalism, postcolonial studies has at times established a rhetoric of fixed oppositions between the imperial gaze of Western modernity and revolutionary resistance of resistant others. Cultural theorists such as Paul Gilroy, Simon Gikandi, Homi Bhaba, Mary Layoun, and Uma Narayan (to name a few) have done much to unravel such binarist approaches. But for (post)colonial modernisms, more needs to be done to bring into greater visibility the complex interplay of different systems of stratification *within* emergent nations as they interact with structures of power *across* national borders. In this context, cultural parataxis helps bring to light how colonial and postcolonial contact zones produce not just racial oppositions but also forms of biological, linguistic, and cultural hybridity, particularly among colonial rulers and indigenous elites. It helps as well to reveal how each location of modernity contains its own heterogeneity and structures of power that interact with geopolitical ones on the (post)colonial landscape.

By way of example, I will set E. M. Forster's *A Passage to India* (1924) and Arundhati Roy's *The God of Small Things* (1997) in dialogue with each other as narratives that engage with a traveling, transnational modernity in which the stories of race endorse the discourses of nation and empire, while the rhetorics of gender, caste, and sexuality challenge them. I regard each as a modernist text in its own right, reflecting the modernity of its time and place, as well as the textual and political unconscious of its distinctive geomodernism. Both narrativize the psychologically damaging effects of colonial and postcolonial race relations at the same time that they explore how race is mediated by other systems of power. What this "conversation" between novels shows is that across space, time, and the power relations of (post)colonialism, Forster and Roy do not stand in fixed opposition to each other—the one, reflecting the standpoint of the colonial power; the other, expressing the resistance of the formerly colonized. Rather, their novels read paratactically disclose some unexpected lines of affiliation and cultural mimesis.

THE PLACE OF RACE IN *A PASSAGE TO INDIA*

In *The Rhetoric of English Empire,* Sara Suleri reads *A Passage to India* as an Orientalist fantasy of cross-cultural, erotic congress that reveals "the anus of imperialism" and adolescent rhetoric of colonialism (132).[2] And yet the novel uses a form of irony familiar to the English novel of manners epitomized by Jane Austen to satirize a spectrum of British racist attitudes—from the outright assertion of English/white superiority among the Anglo-Indians, to the paternalism and ignorance of the seemingly more tolerant, to the ignorant curiosity of those who travel to see the "real India." One of the marks of the novel's modernist indeterminacy is its simultaneous critique of and participation in a colonial standpoint. As a liberal with scathing contempt for British racism and yet a lingering Orientalist attachment to the British Empire, Forster understood that the jewel in Victoria's crown was shattering under the sheer weight of imperial blundering and bullying. Forster's residence in India in the employ of an Indian prince in 1921–22 following the shocking events of the bloody Amritsar Massacre of 1919 and the accelerated rise of Indian nationalism had a deep impact on his rendering of imperial rule in India (Furbank 2: 68–70). While the novel famously closes with the assertion that cross-racial friendship is not yet possible, it nonetheless presents an anatomy of the colonial racism that was endemic to the rise of the Raj and that was hastening its demise.

For all its ties to the realist tradition in the English novel of manners, however, *A Passage to India* goes well beyond satire in its depiction of colonial racism. The novel's fusion of realism with symbolist, religious, and mystical dimensions creates a hybrid text that, while not "high modernist" in formal terms, nonetheless departs significantly from the conventions of realism and introduces an unsettlingly indeterminate dimension to the story of many passages to and within India. As a particular marker of the novel's modernist dimension, a space of absence governs the narrative. What happened in the Marabar cave is unnarrated and unnarratable, left in the blank space between Chapters 15 and 16, as Brenda Silver and many others have observed.[3] This gap operates as the narrative's pivotal point—everything before leads up to it; everything that happens afterwards results from it. It is the narrative's "black hole," a source of enormous power into which traumas, forbidden desires, and crimes have been drawn and disappeared from view. Forster is not known as a writer who admired or read Freud; nor is he usually read as someone who anticipated the kind of revolutionary use of psychoanalysis evident in Fanon. Nonetheless, I would suggest that the novel's colonial modernity centers on that black hole. It is the heart of colonial darkness repressing the psychopathology of race that returns symptomatically evident in the paranoia, hysteria, and desire of cross-racial relations in the context of empire. As Jenny Sharpe has shown in *Allegories of Empire,* Forster's plotting of colonial racial psychology revolves around the fear of racial pollution through sexual contact between "black" men and "white" women, a fear that had taken the form among the tiny but powerful population of Anglo-Indians of extreme paranoia, beginning especially with the Sepoy Rebellion of 1857 and then reawakened in the wake of the Amritsar Massacre of 1919. Stories of Indian men attacking white women circulated widely throughout the Raj and were used as the justification for the imposition of martial law (Sharpe 113–17).

Forster's psychological study of white paranoia takes an ironic form that has the effect of heightening his racial critique. The woman at the center of the paranoia seems the least likely candidate for it. Adela is an outsider to the Anglo-Indian culture of the Raj and most unsympathetic to the forms of racism she observes. As Dr. Aziz observes, Adela, like Mrs. Moore, "had no race-consciousness" (129). Nonetheless, it is Adela's accusation of assault that upends his life. Having set Mrs. Moore and Adela up as lacking "race-consciousness" in Part I: Mosque, Forster smashes the illusion by having the plot of colonial paranoia return with a vengeance in Part II: Caves. The elaborate trip to the Marabar Caves that Aziz arranges to fulfill Adela's desire to see the "real" India removes the veil of racial tolerance from the English women to reveal another kind of reality: the "real" of

English racism, all the more virulent because originally unconscious prior to its powerful return. Mrs. Moore becomes unhinged in some sort of unspecified way, resulting in a profound and nihilist indifference to everyone. Like instances of trauma as theorized by Freud, her horror and despair set in after the experience itself, as a sort of secondary event signified by the symptomatic and hysterical echo that never leaves her head.

Mrs. Moore's hysterical symptom foreshadows Adela's pathological response. Of the many ways in which the cave episode can be read, the experience of the two "liberal" Englishwomen signifies their confrontation with the primitive and primeval Other, for which an ancient formation in the Indian landscape serves as a convenient symbol. Racialized in the utter blackness inside the caves, "India" surrealistically externalizes and projects a darkness within English identity that the concept of Englishness suppresses. For the women, the caves embody what anthropologist Michel-Rolph Trouillot calls "the savage slot" of Western consciousness, the repressed, dystopic side of white subjectivity (17–44). Repressed beneath the Englishwomen's patina of racial tolerance and sensitivity is the fear of the racial Other as an unacknowledged part of the self and as evidence of how the English concept of English racial superiority is based in utopian fantasy.

The effect of the caves on Adela makes even more explicit the relationship between "the savage slot" and racial paranoia in the colonial context. What the narrator calls Adela's "intellectualism" leaves her unprepared for the return of her own repressed racial and sexual fears. Having scorned the overt racism of the Anglo-Indians, she ironically ends up repeating the paranoia of the whole community as a form of repetition compulsion. Her disclaimers of the event—"He never actually touched me once" (193)— would lead to tears and "then she would break down utterly" (193), weeping as "the echo flourished, raging up and down like a nerve in the faculty of her hearing" (194). The crime becomes in the minds of all, including Adela's, what might have happened, not what did not happen. Adela's hysteria snowballs into communal hysteria as the repressed script of blackman-rapes-white-woman comes fully into play. As the choric voice of the community, the narrator reports: "Each felt that all he loved best in the world was at stake, demanded revenge, and was filled with a not unpleasing glow, in which the chilly and half-known features of Miss Quested vanished, and were replaced by all that is sweetest and warmest in the private life. 'But it's the women and children,' they repeated" (183). The effect of this racial fear for which the purity of white womanhood serves as the touchstone is the justification of the Raj in the eyes of the community.

Adela's retraction in the midst of the trial functions as a kind of "talking cure" that releases her from the echo, from the symptom of her own hysteria (229, 239). The witness box is an unlikely scene of psychoanalytic transference, but for Adela, the act of having to retell what happened—

rather, what did not happen—in the cave allows her to move beyond the repetition compulsion of neurotic symptom into the act of remembering what has been repressed. In a series of "numerous curious conversations" with Fielding (238), Adela continues the talking cure, attempting to figure out why she behaved as she did, playing out the script of the frightened white woman who imagines an attack by a black man.

Exhibiting a characteristically modernist indeterminacy, the novel covertly suggests multiple overdeterminations for Adela's behavior, refusing to authorize any single cause and thus spawning differing critical interpretations that run the gamut from colonial racism, to Anglo over-intellectualism, sexual repression, hysterical neurosis, Orientalist homoeroticism, mysticism, misogyny, feminism, and so forth. For my purposes, Forster's examination of white paranoia and hysteria is especially interesting for the way he explores the role of eroticism in white colonial racism. Fear of the racial Other is the countercoin side of desire for the racial Other, Forster shows. Adela's experience in the cave, which leads to hysteria, is immediately preceded by her sad thoughts about her loveless marriage and her repressed desire for "the handsome little Oriental" (153), the sexualized Other who fills "the savage slot" in Adela's imaginary as a projection of the Other within herself that she has repressed and must repudiate by invoking the myth of the black rapist.

Forster's powerful critique of colonialist racism and the psychopathology it induces in the English does not, of course, free the novel from its own forms of colonial racism. Another level of the novel reflects how Forster's position as a member of the British elite that he himself criticizes bleeds into his portrait of Indians. Indians remain in some ways forever a heterogeneous but nonetheless racialized Other to him, at times all the more desirable because foreign (e.g., Aziz) and at times, just inscrutable (e.g., Godbole). Forster's discomfort with the Indian nationalist movement and his at-best ambivalent attitude toward the British Empire and Indian nationalism raise inevitable questions about ways in which his novel perpetuates the racism that underlay the British Empire even as he attacked the racism that upheld it.

RACE RELATIONS IN ROY'S POSTCOLONIAL MODERNISM

Modernity in Roy's *The God of Small Things* centers in the shattering of the Raj at Independence in 1947 and the struggles of the new nation to make that independence real in the context of the ongoing aftereffects of colonialism. Like Forster, she is most interested in the psychological effects of colonial racism, but where he focused primarily on the racial paranoia of the English, she examines the psychopathology of racism in those who were colonized and their descendants, no doubt reflecting Fanon's psychoanalysis of internalized racism in *Black Skin, White Masks*. In its ruptures of language, narrative chronology, and voice, *The God of Small Things* shares more with the "high modernist" form of writers like Joyce and Woolf than with the more conventionally realist narrative of Forster. Repression of traumatic events and their symptomatic return govern the novel's reliance on a textual fabric of interlocking motifs and fragmentary memory to tell the story of what happened during the novel's two narrated time periods: the thirteen disastrous days in 1969 and the aftereffects of those events on one day in 1992. Echoing and rewriting *A Passage to India* and Conrad's *Heart of Darkness*, Roy explores colonial and postcolonial forms of Anglo-phobia and -philia, adding to this concern with empire the meanings of American hegemony at the end of the twentieth century.[4]

The novel takes place in Kerala, an atypical Indian state on the south-west coast. Twenty percent of the population are Syrian Christians whose conversion to Christianity goes back two thousand years. The catastrophes in 1969 bring about the collapse of the Syrian Christian Ipe family, initi-ated by the visit of Chacko Ipe's former English wife Margaret and daugh-ter Sophie, whom he has never seen. Sophie's accidental death by drown-ing is entangled with the sudden affair of Ammu, Chacko's divorced sister, and Velutha, for whom Gandhian "affirmative action" programs allowed the talented Untouchable to become foreman over lower caste workers in the Ipe family's Paradise Pickles and Preserves Factory. To cover up the disgrace of the affair, Ammu's aunt and mother charge Velutha with kid-napping Ammu's twins and raping Ammu, an accusation that leads the police to beat him nearly to death in front of the horrified eyes of the hid-ing twins. Estha, one of the twins, is convinced that he must lie about Velutha, whom he has loved for years as a surrogate father, in order to save his mother from prison. Velutha dies after watching Estha betray him, and Ammu is banished from the family home and later dies alone in poverty. The twins are separated, leaving Chacko in charge of his mother's success-ful pickle factory that he destroys by importing Western business practices before he eventually emigrates.

In 1992, Rahel, the other twin, returns from the United States to her decaying home in Kerala, finding her recently returned brother mute and shut off from life and her aunt fixated on American TV shows. Like the children of Salman Rushdie's *Midnight's Children*, the twins are allego-ries of India's past and future. But unlike the children in Rushdie's novel, the twins are emblems of pathological hysteria, reversing conventional gender patterns of traumatic effects: for twenty-three years, Estha has been obedient, silent, neat, and housebound; Rahel has been rebellious, loud, messy, and world-traveling. Symptomatically opposites, they both remain frozen in past time, metonymically signaled by the motif of the child's watch stuck at 2:15 lost at the site where they watched Velutha. With Rahel's return, they attend scenes from the great national epic of royal family strife, the *Mahabharata,* after which they lie down together, breaking another of the novel's many "Love Laws," leaving readers with an open question. Does the incest presage a decadent and ingrown paralysis (a frequent charge against the Syrian Christian elite) or a rebellious new beginning based in a transgression enacted for love that holds out the possibility of healing?

As avatar of a postcolonial love–hate relation with the former colonizers, Chacko informs the seven-year-old twins that the Ipes "were a *family* of Anglophiles. Pointed in the wrong direction, trapped outside their own history and unable to retrace their steps because their footprints had been swept away" (51). Chacko is himself a specimen of the germ he despises. He was a Rhodes Scholar whose degree from Oxford and acquisition of a white wife raised his status in the family and community. This family context explains the twins' sense of inferiority before the "clean white children" in *The Sound of Music* and their related belief that Sophie's whiteness made her the favored grandchild.

Echoing *A Passage to India,* Margaret and Sophie naïvely embark on their own passage to India, unaware of the internalized racism that awaits them, ignorant of the privileged position they occupy in the Ipe family's imaginary as a result of colonial racism. Margaret has something of Adela's curiosity about foreign India. "How marvelous!" she exclaims when Chacko explains that the cook raised Sophie's hands to her face and inhaled deeply as a "way of kissing you." "It's a sort of sniffing!" she continues and asks inappropriately, "Do Men and Women do it to each other too?" (170). Realizing her mistake, she blushes, not preventing, however, Ammu's cynical outburst: "Must we behave like some damn godforsaken tribe that's just been discovered?" (171). Like Adela, the contact zone between Margaret and India had led to an awakening: "Being with Chacko made Margaret Kochamma feel as though her soul had escaped from the narrow confines of her island country into the vast, extravagant spaces of his" (233).

After the death of Sophie, Margaret's behavior sharpens Roy's echoes of *A Passage to India.* Adela's unjustified accusation of Aziz reappears in Margaret's "irrational rage" at the twins, particularly Estha, whom "in her fevered mind" she blames for the accident and slaps in one of her moments of "sharp, steely slashes of hysteria" (249–50). Like Adela, she recants and apologizes, too late to help the one she accused, who had already been sent away. "*'I can't imagine what came over me,'* she wrote. *'I can only put it down to the effect of the tranquilizers. I had no right to behave the way I did, and want you to know that I am ashamed and terribly, terribly sorry'*" (250). Like Forster, Roy points to the particular futility of English apology that cannot undue the harm done across racial lines in either a colonial or postcolonial context.

Chacko's metaphor for the inevitability of the racial chasm is to imagine the forces of history in architectural and spatial terms: "history was like an old house at night. With all the lamps lit. And ancestors whispering inside" (52). "To understand history," Chacko tells the twins, "we have to go inside and listen to what they're saying." This project is doomed to failure because the "post" in "postcolonial" is only an illusion that covers up the ongoing presence of the colonial past in the present:

> "But we can't go in," Chacko explained. "because we've been locked out. And when we look in through the windows, all we see are shadows. And when we try and listen, all we hear is a whispering. And we cannot understand the whispering, because our minds have been invaded by a war. A war that we have won and lost. The very worst sort of war. A war that captures dreams and re-dreams them. A war that has made us adore our conquerors and despise ourselves." (52)

Chacko represents the view that the postcolonial condition of modernity provides no radical rupture from the colonial past but only a paralyzing return of the repressed. The twins literalize his metaphor by associating the "history house" with Akkara, the abandoned manor house of the rubber plantation across the river. The narrator blends the imaginary of Chacko and the twins to trope it repeatedly as the "History House," the "Heart of Darkness," and the site of the novel's most intense transgressions of the laws of touch.

The History House is a space that contains the palimpsestic layering of time within it, embedding Roy's scathing critique of racism in the context of colonial and postcolonial modernity. Here, in the colonial period, lived Kari Saipu, "The Black Sahib. The Englishman who had 'gone native.' Who spoke Malayalem and wore mundus. Ayemenem's own Kurtz. Ayemenem his private Heart of Darkness" (51). Roy weaves together echoes of Conrad and Forster to allegorize the postcolonial modernity of India. In 1959, the Anglo-Indian shot himself when the parents of his young lover took the boy away, leaving his cook and secretary to bicker about ownership of the house (an allusion, perhaps, to Forster's racialized homosexuality). By 1969, the History House was abandoned, the site of the children's escapades, Ammu and Velutha's affair, and the police beating of Velutha. In 1992, when Rahel returns to Ayemenem, the History House has become the Heritage Hotel, a tourist site owned by a multinational chain of five-star hotels. Giving its franchise a "regional flavor," the Heritage Hotel packages the "real" India in bite-sized pieces: "So there it was then, History and Literature enlisted by commerce. Kurtz and Karl Marx joining palms to greet rich guests as they stepped off the boat" (120). Allegorizing the power of global forces of history to shape the lives of people in local places, the History House represents the structures of European imperialism and American economic and cultural hegemony that link Kerala—and by extension—all of India with the West in the twentieth century.

DOMESTIC AFFAIRS IN *THE GOD OF SMALL THINGS*

The cultural parataxis of *The God of Small Things* and *A Passage to India* helps to emphasize how each addresses the psychopathology of (post)colonial racism on both sides of the racial divide. But it also brings more sharply into view additional affiliations between the fictional projects of the two novels, as well as with *Heart of Darkness*, Roy's other colonial intertext. No doubt Roy's novel "writes back" to the Empire from the standpoint of postcolonial subjects. But even more radically, Roy's novel identifies with the projects of her colonialist precursors. Like them, she forces readers "at home," in her case, India, to confront what she calls the "dark of heartness" within home itself—"home" as the space of intimacy and family, and "home" as nation. For all their own reification of colonial racism (Conrad more than Forster, in my view), *Passage* and *Heart of Darkness* turn the gaze of the English traveler back onto European imperialism itself, calling into question the ideology of empire and Western racial superiority that underlie the contact zones between Britain and India, Europe and Africa. But unlike them, Roy borrows their project—the critique of "home" by travel to the "other"—to move from considerations of race to explicit questions of gender, sexuality, and caste. In addition to attacking the racism of postcolonial relations between "West" and "East," Roy writes a political allegory of both Kerala and the nation to challenge Chacko's view that all India's current problems stem from British imperialism. The events of 1969 in the novel expose the violence of the state and the family based in reactionary Indian institutions of caste, sexuality, and gender that cling to past traditions, refuse an Indian modernity, and threaten to paralyze the future.

Like *A Passage to India*, the plot of *The God of Small Things* turns around a false accusation of rape. Roy borrows the emotional charge from the colonial racial plot that Forster used to heighten the significance of a false charge against the outcast Untouchable, Velutha. Here, the accuser is the Ipe family itself, specifically Ammu's mother and aunt, who cry rape to cover their shame at Ammu's affair with an Untouchable. The Ipe family closes ranks to protect its reputation, preventing Ammu from telling the truth in time. Lies, secrets, and silence propel the cover-up, making the children's acts of forgetting and memory a kind of allegory for a nation which, in Roy's view, has not sufficiently "remembered" its own complicity in the suffering of its people.

Roy's rewriting of the false accusation rape plot—so resonant in the history of the Raj—forces attention to the violence of the caste system that Chacko ignores in his analysis of India's problems. In so doing, she addresses both the specific situation in Kerala and by extension political debates about India as a whole. In being touted as the miracle model for India and the developing world in general, Kerala does not come to terms with the suffering that its social conservatism causes for women and Dalits (Untouchables), Roy suggests. Kerala has the highest literacy rate for women in all of India, along with a generally better "safety net" and many other indicators of a higher status for women than in other parts of the country. However, compared to the cosmopolitan cities of New Delhi, Bombay, and Calcutta, Kerala is a gender backwater, where women have little choice about marriage and property and where being divorced is a major family disgrace. Moreover, Kerala has the worst record in all India for land reform for the Dalits. The Communist Party, which has been elected to govern Kerala for most of the post-Independence period, won the loyalty of the lower caste workers and unions by playing the "caste card" and blocking the advancement of the Dalits.[5]

The novel sets up Ammu and Chacko, sister and brother, to highlight the double standard for men and women in socially conservative Kerala around issues of marriage, divorce, sexuality, education, caste, and property. Each chooses a mate instead of accepting a parentally arranged marriage; each marries outside the family religion; each divorces and returns home. But the status of each is diametrically opposed. The family's money sends Chacko to Oxford, while Ammu's only escape from Kerala is to marry. Chacko's marriage to a white woman raises his status while Ammu's marriage to a Hindu lowers hers. Chacko's divorce is ignored, and his mother arranges a private entrance to the house so that "a Man's Needs" can be discreetly taken care of (160). Ammu, on the other hand, lives out a "modern" form of *sati*, like that of widows, a sexual status of living death. As for the caste laws, Chacko does not upset the family by having sex with lower caste women from the factory, even in his own house (160). Ammu's breaking of the love laws governing touch, however, brings punishment, exile in penury, and death whereas Chacko takes over the family home and business and then opts to emigrate. Roy's exposure of the sexual double standard in Kerala charges the state with hypocrisy in touting its progressive stand on gender.

The inequities of the gender system mingle with the injustice of the caste system as the bodies of Ammu and Velutha ecstatically meet in the dangerous waters of the Menachal River, a scene not fully narrated until the final chapter of the novel. Roy's attack on the persistence of caste politics in Kerala begins in the irony of the Syrian Christian family's outraged response to the violation of the Hindu caste laws. As Christians, they should not share in the Hindu prohibition against touch. But as descendants of the original Brahmin converts, Syrian Christians in Kerala retain the aura of the upper castes and assume the prohibitions against caste pollution as their own. "Pappachi," we learn, "would not allow Paravans [Dalits] into the house. Nobody would. They were not allowed to touch anything that Touchables touched. Caste Hindus and Caste Christians"

(71). Once Velutha and Ammu touched each other in all the forbidden ways, both families were scandalized as the fabric of tradition ruptured in their blasphemous break with the past.

Roy's exposure of Syrian Christian hypocrisy is matched by her scathing portrait of the caste politics of the Keralan Communist government. Comrade Pillai is a contemptible character, in bed with the Syrian Christian elite as well as the lower caste unions in order to maintain his own power. He sells out Velutha, a rising member of his own party, to please both constituencies. His eventual success—evident in the striking prosperity of his family in 1992—rests upon the crime of his betrayal of Velutha to the police, who "in the Heart of Darkness . . . acted with economy, not frenzy. Efficiency, not anarchy. Responsibility, not hysteria. . . . merely inoculating a community against an outbreak" (293).

Like Forster and Conrad, Roy tells a tale of many passages and travel in the contact zones of (neo)imperialism to encourage her readers "at home"—in this case, India—to look within the heart of its own civilization for the darkness within. Roy's anger at the West is evident enough in her more recent writings about the World Trade Center attacks and political activism both within and outside India. But in *The God of Small Things*, she refuses to ignore the violence *within* the nation at the same time that she attacks the evils of colonialism and the multinational corporations of the global age. Reading Roy in the context of Forster highlights the way she borrows his racial plot in order to interrogate questions of gender and caste at home.

LOVE, RAPE, HYSTERIA IN FORSTER'S QUEER PLOT

Returning to *A Passage to India* after reading *The God of Small Things* helps bring into focus the ways in which issues of sexuality and gender that Roy explicitly explores exist in more covert forms in Forster's novel. Roy's narrativization of cultural paranoia about the pollution of forbidden touch suggests yet another partial affiliation between the colonial English and the postcolonial Indian writers. *A Passage to India* also contains a much less explicit story about forbidden touching, in this case cross-racial homosexuality. The taboo desire of intercaste eroticism acted out by Ammu and Velutha has an analog in the unconsummated cross-gender homoeroticism thinly disguised in Forster's rendering of the "friendship" between Fielding and Aziz and in the more deeply suppressed story of Adela's desire for Aziz.

For Suleri, Forster's use of the false rape accusation to attack British racism diverts attention from the "real" subject of the novel, the homoeroticism of empire that covertly underlies the relationship between Aziz and

Fielding, with cross-racial sex diluted into the more palatable question of cross-racial friendship. She regards the novel's homoeroticism as a symptom of imperialism and Forster's own racism, evident in his propensity to fall in love with "dark" men of the British colonies—first, his friend Syed Ross Masood, the man who inspired the characterization of Aziz and appeared in the novel's dedication; and then Mohammed el Adl, the Egyptian with whom Forster had his first consummated affair in Alexandria during World War I. But read paratactically in the context of *The God of Small Things,* Forster's covert homosexual plot shares with Roy's project the insistence upon the multiple constituents of identity on both sides of the (post)colonial racial divide. The complex intersections of race, sexuality, caste, and gender that Roy explicitly examines (re)appear in Forster's novel in more repressed and displaced forms, a largely hidden dimension of the novel that exposes the effects of heterosexism.

To explore this effect, I suggest that we regard Adela as Forster's fictionalized queer persona instead of reading her merely as a misogynistically imagined, sexually repressed female hysteric. In this context, Adela's accusation of rape and subsequent hysteria are vital parts of the repressed homoerotic plot and introduce issues of external and internalized homophobia. Evidence for such a reading lies in Forster's closeted homosexuality, the composition history of *Passage,* and the novel's intertextual relationship with the overtly homosexual narrative of *Maurice.*

Encouraged by Masood to write a novel about English-Indian relations, Forster first drafted Part I: Mosque of *Passage* before his trip to India in 1912–13 and then set the novel aside until 1922. Right after his return from India in 1913, he visited Edward Carpenter, the well-known theorist of love between members of the "third sex," where an unexpected erotic touch led him to realize incontrovertibly his own homosexual orientation. The writing of *Maurice* followed quickly on the heels of this revelation in 1913, narrating the awakening of the upper-middle-class Maurice to homosexual desire and consummation through the touch of the charismatic gamekeeper. Short stories openly exploring homosexuality followed, but Forster refused to publish either *Maurice* or the stories in his own lifetime.[6] Perhaps silenced by the need for secrecy, Forster abandoned the novel form, turning instead to memoir and essay. Grief-stricken and paralyzed by the death of Mohammed, he returned to his drafts of *A Passage to India* in 1922, taking up the story with Part II: Caves and Part III: Temple, but never again writing a novel.[7] Thereafter, Forster's closeted affairs were either with men of different races or different classes, men who filled "the savage slot" in the psychosexual circuits of forbidden desire. For Foster, the transgression of sexual mores went hand in hand with crossing racial or class boundaries. The entanglements of race, class, sexuality, and self-censorship in the context of empire and British laws against homosexuality underwrite both

Maurice and *A Passage to India*—not just as instances of Orientalist racism but also as explorations of internalized homophobia mediated by race or class.

Certain aspects of Adela's story resonate strongly with Forster's closeted homosexuality—namely, the uncanny erotic awakening that Adela experiences in the accidental touch of hands during the car accident (87–88); Adela's preoccupation with love, marriage, and the physical beauty of Aziz's body just before she enters the cave (153); the echo as symptomatic hysteria and sign of repressed and forbidden desire; and her conclusion in her talks with Fielding that she hallucinated the touch in the cave after a period of nervous illness (238–43). The implication of cross-racial rape underneath Adela's accusation of an inappropriate touch and struggle over her field glasses takes on additional resonances in the context of Forster's hidden homosexuality. What Forster does is introduce the complications of race and colonialism into the etiology of hysteria that Freud postulated in *Dora*. As an instance of queer displacement, Adela represents a case study for someone who imagines what she (he) desires and thereby creates social havoc and personal catastrophe in her (his) neurotic confusion of hallucination with reality. She figures in fictional form a displaced form of Forster's own repressed sexuality and cross-racial desire. She acts out, perhaps, his sense that catastrophe lurks in the open expression of these wishes and the consequent need for silence.

Forster's earlier drafts of the novel support such a reading. The gap between Chapters 15 and 16 in the published novel—what happens in the Marabar cave—is the story of desire that dares not speak its name, but did in fact do so in displaced form in earlier versions of the novel. In the earliest fragment, Forster planned a doomed love affair between Aziz and Janet, the English protagonist. As Forster's brief outline makes clear, the relationship breaks taboos of interracial sex, love, and marriage in colonial India. Each of the lovers has mixed feelings based on some combination of moral repugnance, pragmatic assessment of public consequences, and concern about "purity of blood," a fear of pollution that itself picks up on India's caste system and Britain's racial imaginary (Forster, *Manuscripts* 580). In this case, the impossibilities of interracial marriage substitute for homosexuality, and the fear of moral transgression takes the place of internalized homophobia.[8]

Forster's second and more substantial draft of *A Passage to India* changes the story of an affair into a tale of sexual assault. In this version, Forster directly narrates what happens in the cave, leaving ambiguous only the identity of the assailant, whom Adela assumes to be Aziz. The scene is a violent one, stopping just short of rape when Adela manages to fight off the attack with her field glasses. To quote in part: "She struck out and he got hold of her other hand and forced her against the wall, he got both her hands in one of his, and then felt at her <dress> \breasts/. 'Mrs. Moore,' she yelled. 'Ronny—don't let him, save me.' The strap of her Field Glasses, tugged suddenly, was drawn across her throat. She understood—it was to be passed once round her neck, <it was to> she was to be throttled as far as necessary and then..." (Forster, *Manuscripts* 243; ellipsis in original).

The change from love to assault in the first two versions of the novel is itself a form of symptomatic condensation that resides in the textual and political unconscious of the published version of the novel. This change could signify how a desire that is forbidden expression in a relationship of love can be turned into a fantasy of being raped to bring about what cannot be consciously chosen. Heterosexual rape fantasies in women are sometimes interpreted in this way: sexual repression can lead to dreams of "being taken" by force. Alternatively, the two early versions together suggest another kind of love, a form of sadomasochistic blending of *eros* and *thanatos*.

As the novel that stands in between Forster's composition of the early and final versions of *Passage, Maurice* supports particularly the latter reading. A sadomasochistic mix of tenderness and incipient, phallic violence characterizes the first sexual meeting between Maurice and Scudder, the gamekeeper. Filled with an unnamed desire, Maurice stands at the window of his own bedroom, saying "Come" into the darkness, a call that brings Scudder climbing up a ladder into Maurice's room: "The head and shoulders of a man rose up, paused, a gun was leant against the window sill very carefully, and someone he scarcely knew moved towards him and knelt beside him and whispered, 'sir, was you calling out for me?... Sir, I know.... I know,' and touched him" (Forster, *Maurice* 192; ellipses in text). The intimacy of Scudder's touch is nothing like the attack Adela faces in the second version of *Passage*, but the gun he carries symbolically links the homosexual phallus with violence. Maurice's fear of homosexuality has its parallel in Adela's terror of cross-racial, heterosexual attack. Like the final version of *Passage*, what happens next in *Maurice* is left unnarrated in the gap between chapters. But unlike the published version of *Passage*, there is no ambiguity about what happens. *Maurice* is a utopic coming-out *Bildungsroman*, a narrative *rite de passage* that ushers in fulfilled love. As such, Forster would not allow its publication in his lifetime, accomplishing in its publication history the sexual repression that Maurice gives up. The published version of *Passage to India*, in contrast, leaves Adela in a state of neurosis and sexual repression that brings about disaster for both Aziz and herself.

In moving from the story of homoerotic relations across class lines to the narrative of interracial relations in the colonial context, Forster engages in a complex transposition. He encodes the homoerotic story in his queer protagonist Adela, whose unresolved neurotic fear of and desire for black men stands in for Maurice's fear of his own homosexual desire for working-class men and perhaps Forster's own anxiety about his unfilled desire for Masood, his grief for Mohammed, and the needs and psychology of the closet. Though much less directly than Roy, Forster "echoes" Roy's project by bringing readers of colonial modernism "back home" to the homophobia and heterosexism that can paralyze desire and forbid love in Britain as well as its colonies.

Reading into the gap in Forster's novel—what happened in the cave—raises the question of how gaps function in Roy's novel. *The God of Small Things* is a novel whose narrative strategies depend upon elision, fragmentation, and displacement—the very symptomology of hysteria produced by trauma according to Joseph Breuer and Freud in their 1895 *Studies in Hysteria*. The readers must piece together into a coherent narrative the fragments of the twins' childhood perceptions and adult memories. But where Forster excised from the final version of the novel the secret events in the cave that drive the whole narrative, Roy finally fills the gaps in memory by directly narrating in the novel's concluding chapters the beating of Velutha, the twins' incest, and most taboo of all, the ecstatic cross-caste touches of Velutha and Ammu. More attuned to high modernist narrative strategies, *The God of Small Things* is paradoxically less indeterminate than Forster's novel, which only hints at and hides its subterranean desires.

CONCLUSION

A reading strategy based in a psychoanalytically informed cultural parataxis in the case of *A Passage to India* and *The God of Small Things* helps to remove the reading of race in (post)colonial geomodernisms from fixed binaries of colonizer/colonized, white/black. The stories of race and racism still have a central but not exclusive role to play in narratives of modernity and nation. This cultural parataxis also suggests a complex pattern of relations that encourages porous boundaries around the categories of modernism and modernity instead of fixed historical periodization and assumed geographical locations. Rather than a diffusionist model of modernism/modernity that privileges the West, the cultural parataxis of Forster and Roy suggests an intercultural and interactive paradigm attuned to the mutually constitutive nature of a modernism/modernity in which each text is its own nodal center of a modernity in tune with its particular space and time.

Rather than assuming a plurality of isolated modernisms around the globe, cultural parataxis helps track the web of relations between them, to see how each local formation evolves through its interactions with others. The concept of geomodernism spatializes modernism and foregrounds the issues of borders, in-betweens, contact zones, and connections in the interplay of modernity and tradition in each locality. It needs to be attuned not only to the oppositional consciousness around issues of race that often characterizes (post)coloniality but also to the possibility of unexpected affiliations, hybridity, and cultural mimesis across lines of difference.

Roy's transposition of the plot of false rape accusation to challenge gender and caste oppression highlights the ways in which positionality across racial lines is not inevitably and fixedly oppositional. As Edward Said writes in *Culture and Imperialism* about postcolonial studies in the wake of Arab feminist scholarship, "Gone are the binary oppositions dear to the nationalist and imperialist enterprise. Instead we begin to sense that old authority cannot simply be replaced by new authority, but that new alignments made across borders, types, nations, and essences are rapidly coming into view, and it is those new alignments that now provoke and challenge the fundamentally static notion of *identity* that has been the core of cultural thought during the era of imperialism" (xxv). I question Said's insistence on such alignments only being possible *after* the era of European imperialism, especially since Forster's novel brings these borders well into view. What the cultural parataxis of *A Passage to India* and *The God of Small Things* helps us to see is that such affiliations have always existed alongside the oppositional in the geomodern landscape. Geomodernity's contact zones make for violent clashes, but they also bring complex connections and intersections based on multiple hegemonies both within and across national boundaries.

NOTES

1. For my earlier discussions of cultural parataxis and transnational modernism, see "Modernism in a Transnational Landscape," "Definitional Excursions," and *Mappings*, 107–31.

2. On homoerotic Orientalism, see also Boone; for a more sympathetic treatment of Forster's liberalism, see Parry, 260–320.

3. See for example Silver; Moran; Restuccia.

4. For other discussions of Roy, see my "Feminism"; Dhawan.

5. See Franke.

6. For discussions of Forster's homosexuality, see especially Martin and Piggford, *Queer Forster*.

7. See Furbank, vol. 1: 255–60, vol. 2: 106–20; Forster, *The Manuscripts*; Harrison; Levine.

8. In the outline, the Englishwoman is assaulted in a cave, but not by Aziz, with whom she is in love. See alternative discussions of the manuscript versions in Levine; Harrison; and Sharpe.

14   Unreal City and Dream Deferred: Psychogeographies of Modernism in T. S. Eliot and Langston Hughes

Eluned Summers-Bremner

"Haunted places are the only ones people can live in," Michel de Certeau writes in *The Practice of Everyday Life* (108), in what is still one of the most compelling takes on modern metropolitan habitation. De Certeau's claim that "places are fragmentary and inward-turning histories" that remain enigmatic, "encysted in the pain or pleasure of the body," reminds us that all geographies are psychogeographies, changefully interactive settings fortified by the cultural myths and communal memories that ground them (108). But a culture's mythical rallying points are no less changeful for the place-sustaining labor they expend, as Langston Hughes, who made a career out of bringing place, race, and political and artistic endeavor together in an often contrapuntal colloquy, well knew. "America is a dream," he wrote in 1943, "[t]he poet says it was promises. / The people say it *is* promises—that will come true" (267). Hughes's self-imposed vocation as a poetic voice for the African American people acknowledges the tension between poetry and democratic politics, but insists that the latter no less than the former is a matter of symbolic and imaginative effort. And while the poet, like any artist, is attuned to a temporality more volatile and retrospective than that of the larger mass of people, his or her interventions into the politics of place—in Hughes, America, and more specifically, Harlem—accrue value only to the extent that they converse with the quotidian workings of its inhabitants' means.

The bebop- and blues-influenced work of Hughes is often read as poetry specific to a time, place, and racialized identity—namely "the Harlem Renaissance"—while T. S. Eliot's characterization of London, in *The Waste Land,* as an "unreal city" whose harried postwar crowds flow through a foggy winter dawn has become the text of urban disaffection in modernist poetry par excellence. How did Eliot's poem, arguably arising from its author's ambivalent feelings about his native country and his desire to find materials in the literary past with which to furnish a future transatlantic home, come to represent the losses and longings of an entire post–World War One generation? What light might be shed on the process by which Eliot's metropolitan lament journeyed in the public imagination from specific city site to modernist exemplar if we compare its fortunes with those of Hughes's Harlem-centered output in the period between the wars?

In raising these questions, my essay attempts to engage larger ones central to our understanding of modernism. For at the same time as modernism as a trans- and supranational phenomenon—a placeless place—is coming under question, so has the experience and role of memory and nostalgia in modern life. As a growing number of scholars of the period between the two European world wars have begun to note, *modernism* is the name for the modern as a retrospective movement, a becoming-aware on the artistic level of what industrial expansion, international war, and metropolitan experience render lost. The temporally and spatially disjunctive or post-traumatic character of those works we call modernist—arising from "the shock of the new" in specifically located yet essentially disorienting experience—is repeated in the encryptionary workings of literary scholarship. Canonical modernism becomes knowledge enshrined, achieved after the fact of loss, an aesthetic and academic labor or compensation that is permanently behind itself or temporally deferred. Canons are monumental in this sense, inviting later readers to an experience of funereal communality where anxiety about origin is soothed by an apparently transcultural cohesion.

The sense of spatial and temporal dislocation that characterizes the modern metropolis and that is evident in both Eliot's *The Waste Land* and Hughes's *Montage of a Dream Deferred* registers in literary critical terms as nostalgia, then, as cover for a highly conflictual set of responses to the modern moment. America was arguably the cathexis of this conflict. As Jani Scandura and Michael Thurston note, "'America' occupies a privileged position within the discourses of modernity. More than simply referring to a nation-state or geological formation, America may be seen as an allegory for a 'disenchanted modernity' serving elsewhere—for instance in Europe—as 'a catalyst for [twentieth-century debates] on modernity and modernization'" (Hansen 367, cited in Scandura and Thurston 4).

Hughes's Harlem and Eliot's London seem, on the surface, as different as the poets' texts: Eliot is overtly learned, taciturn, retiring; Hughes is resolutely popular, often rebellious, clearly passionate always. Yet both write poetry and criticism across the divide created by their exile from America as mythical site of democratic freedom, artistic opportunity, and personal advancement. In what follows, I consider Eliot's *The Waste Land* and Hughes's *Montage of a Dream Deferred* as post-traumatic poems memorializing the losses entailed in modernity, in which the central lacuna or generative question—posed within the theatricalized topos of the city—is one of race.

Race, as Laura Doyle suggests in a recent essay, is "a narrative concept," and yet "within both narrative and the notions of race as they have developed in the West there lies a sharp tension, or paradox, between pastness and futureness, history and progress" ("The Flat" 250). This tension was literalized by Eliot's transplantation from America to England. While Eliot's distinguished family was traceable to America's first settlers, it was his desire to escape the melting pot that early-twentieth-century America had become that led him to the famed meeting with Ezra Pound in Oxford in 1914, when Pound enthused over early poems and urged his compatriot to escape academia and the law and settle in England (Zwerdling 269).

Eliot's debt to Pound for the final, pared-down version of *The Waste Land* is well known. Pound internationalized and Europeanized the poem by de-emphasizing its American references and, through compression, highlighting the textual echoes of its times and places. The poem's cast of theatrical international characters, and its theme of urban hallucination and decontextualized linguistic play produce a London far stranger than the historical London of the century's early years. Yet the substitution of the city for a larger sense of cultural malaise is presaged in Eliot's past, where the Boston in which he lived and studied from the age of sixteen until twenty-two was perceived as a distinguished world in decline, temporally and geographically under siege.

Between 1880 and 1924 the United States was radically altered due to the "influx of some 25 million immigrants," contributing to what Eliot, with Pound, regarded as a loss of Anglo-Saxon primacy (Barrett 163, cited in Scandura and Thurston 7; Eliot, "President Wilson" 140; "War-Paint" 1036, cited in Zwerdling 275). But it is the inability of his Boston confraternity to resist this process of national alteration that earns the early Eliot's disgust and fuels his search for a home that would be his elsewhere, first in Paris, for which he departed in 1910, and then in England. "A society 'quite uncivilized,'" Eliot called the Boston of his youth, "'but refined beyond the point of civilization'" ("Henry James" 860, qtd. in Gordon, *Eliot's Early Years* 18). This early source for the characteristic masklike quality of Eliot's verse, where the trappings of civilization, emphasized, belie a hollowness within, suggests that the conspicuous absence at the heart of *The Waste Land*'s global reach is that of America. Indeed, we might well regard the London of *The Waste Land*, the poetic paradigm of the city as unreal, fascinated and appalled by turns at its rapidly changing composition, as the displaced version of Eliot's own fears about cultural displacement in the early twentieth century.

But it would be misleading to claim that *The Waste Land* is nothing more than the rhythmical grumbling of Eliot's own unhappy history in personal or private terms. Eliot's depiction of early-twentieth-century Boston as a world uncivilized and yet refined beyond the point of civilization is a racial indictment of his people. The charge is effectively that of being immigrants who have not succeeded in making America their own. Mass immigration and commercial expansion thus only exacerbate an already existing problem. The characteristic "gap between his outward and his private life" that Eliot's biographer Lyndall Gordon notes is thus not only spatial and geographical in kind, but also temporal and historical (*Eliot's Early Years* 1). Finding little to identify with at home, Eliot departs for Europe in search of a richer sense of cultural belonging. But because his own identity is forged in the time and place of England's own departure for American shores—the immigrant experience of the founding fathers—this sense of racial dislocation travels with him.

Where Hughes's *Montage* showcases the question of deferral of an African American future, Eliot's *The Waste Land* recreates the inadequately buried trauma of his dislocated origins between two worlds. And where Hughes's poetic sequence is defiantly future-oriented, Eliot's is obsessively backward-looking. Gordon observes that to an extent, Eliot "mastered Boston by understanding it. . . . He took upon himself . . . the character of late nineteenth-century Boston," including "its rigid manners, its loss of vigour, its estrangement from so many areas of life, its painful self-consciousness" (*Eliot's Early Years* 18). Eliot's own sense of racial dislocation, moreover, is imbricated with the history of slavery that is more obviously irreducible in Hughes. As Michael North's landmark research into the function of dialect in modernist literature has shown, Pound's and Eliot's communication in an intimate code of mock African American speech is one means by which both poets mask and assuage their lack of national belonging, borrowing from America's racist history the means of renewal of a literary English they feel they have outgrown.

But while Pound's appropriation of black speech reads as a self-conscious resistance to linguistic convention, Eliot's relation to it is more tortured. In a letter to Herbert Read, Eliot describes himself as "an American who wasn't an American, because he was born in the South and went to school in New England as a small boy with a nigger drawl, but who wasn't a southerner in the South because his people were northerners in a border state and looked down on all southerners and Virginians, and who so was never anything anywhere" (Read: 15, qtd. in North 78). As North puts it, "for Eliot, black dialect is a flaw, a kind of speech impediment, a remnant of the inarticulate that clogs his language and stands in the way as he attempts to link his own individual talent with tradition" (78).

Race as an inarticulate remnant that stands in one's way, simultaneously impelling and disrupting a revisionist history, is very close to a definition of trauma, a rubric that Scandura and Thurston associate with the Euro-American modernist moment of rapid, postwar social change whose outcome, particularly as regards the mythical shape of nationality, could not be foreseen. Tim Dean observes that "trauma gives rise to historically specific material effects whose cause remains elusive because resistant to symbolization," or in Cathy Caruth's now well known version, "since the traumatic event is not experienced as it occurs, it is fully evident only in connection with another place, and in another time" (Dean 309; Caruth 8). As Aldon Nielsen notes in his essay in this volume, African American modernity is articulated in precisely these belated terms. Like the maternal body's appearance as a loss for the speaking subject that is only experienced as a loss at the point of its linguistic incorporation—as suggested by the phrase "mother tongue"—African American modernity inhabits the New World in the performative mode in which a fetishized past is the material means of modernization. Its bodies are simultaneously the basal matter of the burgeoning economy and the sign of what American modernity claims to have left behind: the pre-modern.

But this incorporation will not lie down. In persisting as the vexed point of origin that is continually dehistoricized and rehistoricized in commodification and which troubles not only the distinction between past and present but also that between private and public, American modernity's racist origins reverberate throughout *The Waste Land*. Mass immigration is experienced by Eliot as a threat to American identity not only because of his connections with the early settlers but also because of the interimbrication of settler identity with the history and economy of slavery, a connection whose anxious, detemporalizing effects persist. "A society 'quite uncivilized,' but refined beyond the point of civilization," as Eliot depicts his Boston compatriots, is a society that has reverted to barbarism, where outward manners serve only to display the lack of groundedness within. As the progeny of two differently placed American nationals, both of whom sought to reawaken the English literary future by selective plundering of the past, *The Waste Land* crosses the Atlantic from America to England as Eliot's ancestors did in reverse centuries before, but in the multitude of other crossings and hauntings to which it refers, suggests that this past is far from happily settled.

The Waste Land is fascinated by liminal states of all kinds, including seasonal ones conveyed by rain, frost, and lack of water. But just as significantly, it is compelled by what these liminal states, taken more broadly as cultural markers or movements of unbelonging, make possible or what exceeds them, as though in an attempt to cover over a wound within language, and history, that is still burning. The oft-cited Chaucerian reference of the opening lines

> April is the cruellest month, breeding
> Lilacs out of the dead land, mixing
> Memory and desire, stirring
> Dull roots with spring rain (61; lines 1–4)

makes this a pilgrimage that resists transcendental comforts. Growth depends upon death as desire is bound up with memory, bondage to the past, whose roots nonetheless are "dull," insufficiently nourished and grounded to allow new life.

The corpse figured in *The Waste Land*'s opening section, "The Burial of the Dead," is identified by many scholars as representative of Europe's post–World War One loss of population, under cover of allusion to Dante's "abject neutrals" or insufficiently devilish citizens who are condemned to "the outskirts of hell" (Gordon, *Eliot's Early Years* 111) as to English suburbia. But these dead are also legible, through the American reference to "Stetson!" and the fraught but emotionally purposeless journeying of Canterbury pilgrims, European aristocrats, and London workers, as Boston's "alive but dead" intelligentsia and, reaching further back, to America's pilgrim fathers and to the alive-in-chains bodies of slavery. The invocation of America via "Stetson!," widely recognized as a reference to Pound, is swiftly qualified by the Baudelairean one in French:

> "That corpse you planted last year in your garden,
> "Has it begun to sprout? Will it bloom this year?
> "Or has the sudden frost disturbed its bed?
> "O keep the Dog far hence, that's friend to men,
> "Or with his nails he'll dig it up again!
> "You! hypocrite lecteur!—mon semblable,—mon frère!" (63; lines 71–75)

The emphasis, however, is on corpses that refuse to stay dead, on the annihilation of nature by a culture whose signs revert to natural ones again but with displacing force, as the nails of a coffin become the scrabbling nails of the Dog, worrying in the dirt, and the sudden change of season functions obversely to treat the buried corpse as premature bloom.

The poem does not, as Maud Ellmann notes, "fear the dead themselves so much as their invasion of the living; for it is the collapse of boundaries that centrally disturbs the text, be they sexual, national, linguistic or authorial, and the hybrid origins their collapsing fails to hide" (94). What Gordon characterizes as the Eliotic choice between "the sordid city street and the transcendental silence" (Gordon, *Eliot's Early Years* 108) may just as well be read, with Eliot's fraught Americanness in mind, as the relentless opening up of an urban environment—earlier, Boston, later, London—to a national trauma that predates and is never completely assuaged by it, a national guilt for which a transcendental silence may be the only cure, if it could be found or mastered.

In fact, while bemoaning the dullness of the present, the poem performs a sensuous memorializing—appearing as compulsion—of bodily crimes. The corpse in Section One is followed by the rape of Philomel in Section Two, and the return of Lil's husband Albert from the killing fields of war which prompts Lil's abortion is another tale with death-ridden origins. Section Two also contains an echo of earlier versions of the poem's more obvious use of minstrel reference, allied to an existential question:

O O O O that Shakespeherian Rag—
It's so elegant
So intelligent
"What shall I do now? What shall I do?
I shall rush out as I am, and walk the street
With my hair down, so. What shall we do tomorrow?
What shall we ever do?" (65; lines 128–34)

Typically, the impulsive act is feminized ("I shall rush out . . . and walk the street / With my hair down") and contained within the detemporalizing question ("What shall we ever do?"), just as the passion attributed to the African American minstrel rag with its repeated "O" mocks the barrenness of feeling of the more privileged male and female speakers, while staying allied with the allegedly timeless reference to Shakespeare:

"What is that noise?"
 . . .
            Nothing again nothing.
                            "Do
You know nothing? Do you see nothing? Do you remember
Nothing?" (65; lines 120–23)

As the publication of the manuscripts has shown, the opening scene of the poem was originally to have featured a group of Boston partygoers, their movements backgrounded by popular songs, at least one of which derived from the minstrel show (Eliot, *The Waste Land* 5, 125n, cited in North 85). The "Shakespeherian Rag" refers to the common practice in minstrelsy of introducing fragments of famous "classic" texts whose effect was both to mock the original context and to emphasize the ignorance of the Negro figure from whom the quotation came (North 85; McElderry 185–86, cited in North 223n). Eliot originally considered naming the poem "He Do the Police in Different Voices," which contains the same mix of mockery and acknowledgment of authority fueling minstrelsy while at the same time gesturing to something uncontainable whose workings estrange both body and language: the voice (Eliot, *The Waste Land* 5).

Cities are zones within nations where questions of home and belonging become particularly charged, as the languages and customs of different races and cultures are brought into dynamic proximity with each other. Perhaps the most ungovernable instance of this cultural mixing is that of the voice, precisely because it is both local—that is, physical in origin—and communal, inseparable from other sounds that animate the metropolis, giving it its own peculiar mix of dynamism and ephemerality. The London of *The Waste Land*, however, while recognizable as London by its reference to certain landmarks and kinds of speech (London Bridge and St. Mary Woolnoth; the cockney slang of Lil and friends), contains a relative lack of

London voices, as well as of social and historical detail relating to the city. Instead, we find a montage of references to other cities, cultures, and languages: Russian, German, French, Spanish, Indian, and Greek. The combined effect is to displace and perplex the reader, an effect that renders the poem almost cinematic in its reproduction of the confusion and sensory multiplicity of urban life.

In evoking the media while replacing the content of mass cultural forms—the cinema, the gramophone, the radio—with complex literary and cultural allusions, the poem reveals its ambivalence about the new media and a related anxiety about the emancipatory possibilities for non-Europeans (as well as for women and the lower classes) represented by the modern city. So while the reader is waylaid by the poem's cryptic references to other times, languages, and cultures, she or he is also borne along on a rhythmical mimicry of the machinery of modern life. The silent encounter between the typist and the young man carbuncular, for instance, is specified as mechanical itself by the regular rhyme scheme (Jay 238), the typist's "half-formed thought" and the "automatic" placement of a record on the gramophone suggesting a commodification of experience (69; lines 251, 255).

Pound's cutting of the poem emphasizes the cinematic effect, and it is here where the apparent continuities of history—including the history of race as a narrative, particularly its American version—are edited out that the poem's ambivalence about blackness may paradoxically be seen. The cinema, which the poem's colorful characters, appearing without context, and its general sense of disorientation evoke, is the heir to English vaudeville and American minstrelsy. Like these theatrical forms, cinema is a technology of masking where its double-edged function—to hide and to show—depends upon borrowings from black and working-class culture which are then diffused through the secondary medium of the screen and the circulation of monetary capital to which the new technology is bound.

The poem is, moreover, engaged in its own kind of commodification of the world's cultures, and the process of abstraction by which its wide-ranging cultural references appear as fragments has a correlative in Eliot's own well-attested performance of Englishness, which may have served as a cover for ambivalence about his American origins. Unlike Pound, Eliot kept a daytime banking job distinct from his poetry and literary critical work. Gordon notes the extreme care, bordering on excess, with which Eliot cultivated the appearance of an English gentleman, of "a face to meet the faces that you meet," in Prufrock terms, "the voice so measured as to sound almost dead-pan" (*Collected Poems* 14; Gordon, "Eliot's New Life" 5; quoted in Zwerdling 302). In *The Waste Land* we find this same careful cultivation applied to the representation of the city, as a superficial Englishness—a city originally recognizable as London, if only dimly, by the poem's end becomes any city, every city ("Jerusalem Athens Alexandria /

Vienna London / Unreal" [73; lines 374–76])—fails to mask a distinctively American attitude to investment.

As Zwerdling notes, "Eliot frequently refers to his poems as assets" and uses the language of business to describe them (Eliot, *Letters* 105, 362, 383, cited in Zwerdling 297). The allusive framework of the Grail myth enables a syncretism that gives seemingly disparate terms and languages the suggestion of commonality, although the responsibility for its discovery is deferred to the reader as seeker or consumer. In this way, the poem operates as a kind of bank vault, the city a tomb or Dantescan inferno in which ancient debts shape the present, and where "the cultural capital of each country is simply currency to be used, exchanged, accumulated" (298). Pound's collusion in the erasure of American reference from the poem reinstates local color via expatriate investment in other cultures. In *The Waste Land*'s case, the process of capitalization is taken one step further as the poem becomes central to the emerging mid-century discipline of English studies and as academics set to work deciphering and restoring to it a sense of pre-modern coherence (Middleton; Bowen 42).

Central here is the fact that, as Peter Brooker notes, "the term 'modernist'" in the sense in which it became associated with Eliot as an attempt at artistic salvaging of or resistance to the modern, mechanized world, "was a construction after the event" (Brooker, "Reconstructions" 6). This makes Eliot's passage from the American South via Harvard to literary London the pre-eminent case of a racialized history erasing its origins to become a literary critical institution. Identifying London as the place in which to forge a new identity for himself, Eliot leaves behind the life of an American poet—which for reasons of familial expectation and financial indebtedness was deemed impossible at home—but also that of an academic, feared as equally stultifying. In England he develops a mode of literary criticism that stakes out a territory between academia and journalism, that of the professional specialist he is electing to become.

Such new professionals are to be the middlemen between the challenging poetry of the present and the new reader to which it gives rise. The difficulties readers find in poetry like Eliot's—and *The Waste Land* is to become the paradigmatic case of this difficulty—"produce a new opening for academics" in the form of the New Criticism, "the discipline of close reading" (Zwerdling 282). In this way, *The Waste Land* becomes the quintessential challenge whose surmounting confirms the value of the new literary criticism—in which "the poem is traced back to its sources and is brought forward into an extrapolated wholeness" (Middleton 159)—while the excavatory method of reading, in turn, justifies the apparent difficulty of the poem. Middleton observes that Eliot's "anglicization" functions to allay anxieties in British academia about the place and influence of American popular culture between the 1930s and the 1960s, the period in which

"English" as a discipline was seeking status and autonomy. Eliot's well-known efforts to become "more English than the English"

> represented a significant countermovement to the growing American cultural hegemony that was felt by intellectuals in Britain during the thirties, forties, and fifties. Films, popular music, and popular fiction seemed to dominate cultural production. . . . Eliot's repudiation of America by taking up English citizenship could be understood as a triumph, and the inclusion of his work on the syllabuses of English literature courses was then a strategic demonstration of the force of English culture, whose hegemony had been challenged throughout the twentieth century not only by the United States but also and almost as powerfully by Scotland and Ireland. (155)

Perhaps the most interesting feature of the poem's incorporation into the literary academy is the way its American history—its origin in Eliot's racial anxiety, his identification of and with the inarticulate remnant that haunts his poetic labors—is so readily accommodated as an instance of *English* uncertainty about the modern. This displacement may have as much to do with the way England's national composition was originally bound to America as one of England's first colonial outposts (as Laura Doyle's essay in this collection suggests) as it does with Eliot's historically vexed return journey. It is as though, in the emergent discipline of English, the question of the relation of the real, physical England to the literary canon depends upon the invisible but historically central third term of American capital and culture.

Zwerdling notes the way Eliot's poetry and critical prose work against, fail to meet, or compensate for each other (296), which creates space for the academic labor of poetic elaboration. *The Waste Land* is the poetic instance of the role Eliot has unwittingly created for academics, who, like him, are seeking a new mythos of home in response to the perceived onslaught of American populism. In this sense, the imagined community of literary English is enabled by Eliot's poem that could only have been written by someone to whom a nostalgic elaboration of European tradition serves as placeholder for less articulable anxieties about his own racial belonging. If, as Benedict Anderson suggests, "the nation . . . as imagined community comes into existence thanks to a death it cannot mourn, a corpse it cannot bury" (cited in Redfield 68), then the absence of American reference in *The Waste Land* prolongs the poem's afterlife as the contestable ground of cultural legitimation.

In the work of Langston Hughes, by contrast, the residue of American racial anxiety and oppression that animates the city is of necessity taken seriously. "What happens when a dream of equality is perpetually deferred?" Hughes's *Montage* asks, in the style and manner of African American musical invention that, far from eulogizing, is still engaged in the work of enabling survival. If Eliot's Boston compatriots are charged with insufficient feeling, Hughes's problem is the opposite. African Americans are credited with too much feeling, and the commodification of this feeling by white America displaces them from ready access to their history. In *Montage,* Hughes faces the paradox of being without a representational history that is not bound up with the market, and by white America's appropriation of African American roots. This means that while *Montage,* like *The Waste Land,* is a poetry of fragments, the silences that animate the poetry are differently inflected. Where Eliot moves back across the Atlantic to a London of resident aliens, his Poundian collaboration enabling an assault upon literary sensibilities, Hughes navigates the minefield of white patronage on which Harlem's celebration of black artistry depends. And while Eliot bemoans cosmopolitan modernity, looking to the European past for renewal, Hughes cannot afford to ignore the opportunities—albeit fraught with obligation—offered by the city. Where Eliot's London suffers from a postwar loss of fervor, Hughes's Harlem signifies a modernity African Americans have yet to claim.

This makes the black sensibility of *Montage,* like the European sensibility of *The Waste Land,* both forward- and backward-looking. The two poems differ not only in the orientations of their present moments, but in the relation of the fragmentary poetics they employ to the traumatic absences that drive modern, and modernist, history. For Eliot, the past, present, and future aspire toward a timeless standard to which the critic holds the key, a culturally prescriptive forward looking in the guise of looking back, where nostalgia for a mythically coherent past is the central impulse. For Hughes, the task of representing loss is more complex and conflicted. Eliot effectively uses black unbelonging within American culture to capitalize on his own (American) lostness. In comparison with this, Hughes's poetics has the task of giving voice to black dissatisfaction—itself represented by its absence within European modernism and American history—and indicating, through poetic play with gaps and elisions, that the source of this dissatisfaction has been borrowed by European modernism ahead of time.

So where Eliot, with Pound, edits out the minstrel show sources of *The Waste Land,* in *Montage* poems such as "Parade," "Juke Box Love Song," "Not a Movie," "Neon Signs," and "Jam Session" indicate the dynamic functions of masking and performance that served as the lexicon of black modernity. For Hughes, this includes the performance of writing poetry. Where Eliot takes fragments from many cultures to express postwar urban desolation, Hughes takes the Harlem streets, with the chief difference that for Eliot, the page and the act of constructing poetry, a scholarly endeavor, is masked or taken for granted. For Hughes, the life of the street *is* the poetic medium, and he presents it in its living complexity as he does the act of writing poetry through emphasizing the politics of the page. Hughes highlights what in Eliot is invisible: the complexly mediated nature of the relationship between street life and literary modernism as tradition. Thus the most oft-cited poem in the sequence, "Theme for English B," refuses to allow the material medium of the page to serve as transparent conveyer of meaning—whiteness as absence or available space—and insists that artistic sensibility is enmeshed with the structures of racialized subjectivity, including those of tutelage:

> The instructor said,
> *Go home and write*
> *a page tonight.*
> *And let that page come out of you—*
> *then, it will be true.*
> I wonder if it's that simple? (409)

Among several factors complicating the presence of colored marks on a white page as the means of artistic expression is the illiteracy of many of Harlem's blacks, newly arrived from the American South in the period memorialized by the poem. Harlem in the 1920s undoubtedly functioned as a hopeful dream space for blacks, including Hughes, a "migrant Mecca" full of opportunity and home to a vibrant remixing of black diasporic culture. Yet from the start, two very different temporalities or sets of historical conditions jostled for expression in one urban space. Euro-American artists and enthusiasts of African culture, seeking evidence of cultural renewal in the period following on World War I, flowed into the city by night to attend the clubs and dance halls celebrating black music and movement (Brooker, "Modernism" 234–35). By contrast, the largely black population of lower Manhattan, impelled by the Great Migration of people of African descent from the newly emancipated South to the North, itself moved north into Harlem where in this everyday reality of black occupation poverty and discrimination were rife.

Like whites, "the élite blacks of the literary and artistic intelligentsia . . . came and went . . . on different terms and even at different times of the day" from those who lived in Harlem, as Brooker notes. As such, "the dynamic physical site of Harlem itself expressed the very "twoness" of the American Negro as famously described by W. E. B. DuBois; embodying in its spatial relations the paradox and hope of being at once black and American" (Brooker, "Modernism" 235, 237; see also Mulvey). It is this contradiction that *Montage* consistently raises, refusing the American dream of individual and social betterment the neutrality it claims by emphasizing the racial politics of the transposition of life on Harlem streets into poetry:

> Being me, [my page] will not be white.
> But it will be

a part of you, instructor.
You are white—
Yet a part of me, as I am a part of you.
That's American. (410; lines 28–33)

Hughes's *Montage* thus situates itself in the space of deferral that drives the modernist intelligentsia's desire for black culture. At the same time, it expresses the longing by black residents of Harlem for the conditions in which dreams of professional success and domestic security could grow. This space is clearly overdetermined. We should recall the tensions of timely patronage and debates about the validity of using black folk traditions of music and song to give voice to a people who sought to move forward with the new century that, by 1951, when *Montage* was published, had become literalized in race riots and the failure of belief in urban democracy (de Jongh 135–36).[1]

As a signifier for blackness and a space of democratic dream deferral, Harlem is rendered unpredictable and uncontained by its incorporation of the structurally improvisational forms of black music, the sonic equivalent of, but also a form of dynamic challenge to, primitivist modernism's minstrel mask. "The modernist moment of jazz composition," as Brooker terms it, comes in the late 1930s through the 1940s, chronologically after the time of New York as "race capital" of the world, the canonically termed Harlem Renaissance, as of European literary modernism (Brooker, "Modernism" 243). This is also the time of bebop, in which "traditional lyrics" are replaced by "a language of sound often without apparent sense," epitomizing, as Hughes's biographer notes, "the new fragmentation of black cultural consciousness," and a possible form for retrospective modernism moving back in time to a distinctively African American beat (Brooker, "Modernism" 243; Rampersad 151).[2]

Adding bebop to this mix accentuates the third term that gives meaning to any performance, the unprecedented and opaque encounter between performer—or writer—and audience, which by definition is never the same twice. Bebop gives new currency to this encounter precisely as absence, for, as Robert O'Brien Hokanson points out, its musicians took "the jazz tradition of devising variations on standard tunes to lengths that tested the limits of what other musicians and jazz audiences would accept" (65). Citing jazz critic Marshall Stearns, Hokanson explains that while "the new music's harmonies sounded like mistakes to a typical Dixieland jazz musician," many bebop numbers were "based on the chord progressions of standard jazz tunes," so that "the piano, guitar and bass would play the accompaniment to a known tune" like "I've Got Rhythm," and "the soloist would improvise as usual—but nobody would play the tune," thus producing a variation on a melody that remained unstated (Stearns 229, quoted in Hokanson 65–66).

This refractory opacity may also be read as a means of paying homage to the materially changeful and phantasmatically future-oriented space of the city. The allusive gaps in *The Waste Land* require academic labor for understanding, and justify English as a discipline through the expression of what I have argued is a specifically American anxiety about tradition and racial composition. But Hughes knows that the actuality of community is always deferred because of the way in which European modernity is built on the labor—physical and artistic—of black bodies, meaning that black modernity inhabits European modernity from within, but must also inflect this absent origin differently, to different ends.

Thus *Montage* emphasizes the poetry of lives that must quickly take advantage of the privilege of black visibility offered by the Renaissance, and the sequence is impoverished without some understanding of the visual and musical forms—montage and bebop—on which it draws. In evoking these forms to remark what cannot appear within the poem's text but contributes to poetic meaning precisely through its absence, Hughes returns written poetry to its material origins as a dialogue with the losses and aspirations of its community. Thus, in "Parade," the second poem in the sequence, the sense of forward progress, both literal as marching and figurative as an increase in black visibility on the street, is refracted as black-white imagery is used to convey the relation of black-white presence to larger, hegemonic presence and absence. The "Grand Marshal in his white suit," who leads the parade, and the "Cadillacs with dignitaries" (lines 5, 7) to follow are themselves followed by a black presence invisible except as the movement of bodies marching, conveying at once white anxiety regarding a mass of blackness in public space and the invisibility of those bodies except as members of the category "black":

> And behind will come
> with band and drum
> on foot . . . on foot . . .
> on foot . . . (389, lines 9–12)

Yet through this combination of rhythm and typography Hughes also imparts a sense of the history of black struggles for equality as they are echoed in the musical march through Harlem streets. The representation is complex and includes the way this history is bound up with the elision of the black viewpoint that underwrites the spectacular commodification of blackness on which the occasion of the march depends. Black bodies in motion, conveyed through syncopation and rhythm break, almost disappear from the page, but their presence is noted not just by the uniform dots of a largely white-authored typography but in the absent sounds of their bodies' feet, whose "natural" propensity for rhythm is routed ironically by Hughes through the artifice of its commodified and legally cir-cumscribed presence:

> Motorcycle cops,
> white,
> will speed it
> out of sight
> if they can:
> Solid black,
> can't be right.
>
> Marching . . . marching . . .
> marching . . .
> noon till night . . . (389; lines 14–23)

However, always attuned to the situation on the street, Hughes knows that looking too far back is not a productive option for African Americans. Black marchers and musicians here inhabit the present moment, which exceeds both the history of black oppression to which it refers and the con-fines of the terms of modernist poetics, in which fragmentation and nos-talgia signify high art. Where Eliot's modernist poetics aspires to the time-less expression of ruination through the juxtaposition of textual fragments from many cultures, Hughes expresses African American aspiration to the category of universal—here represented through the near-universal marks of absence, typographical ellipsis—in the context of the historical forms of black expression: activist protest (marching), music, dance, and, in Harlem, the physical celebration of life on the street.

The uniform black marks that also signal the reader's pause for breath and capitulation to the poem's rhythm, then, stand in for the absent black bodies of the text. But just as important, they represent the imbrication of this absence with white presence in the poetics of high literary modernism that frame the sequence, and thence to a historical structure in which black lives subsidize, from the first, the poetic expression of cultural trauma. In drawing attention to the poem's material layout on the page in the context of the bodies whose artful rhythms it borrows, Hughes makes clear the temporal and spatial double bind in which Harlem's blacks find them-selves, where blackness is simultaneously remarked, for whites, as spectacle, a spatial problematic, and threat—a temporal one, where America's racist history makes African American ambitions threatening in their vaguest in-timation for many whites. The punctuated, lively absence represents Har-lem, thus, not only as a geographical region, but as a modernist psycho-geography, a contested terrain for the artistic expression of at least two historically divergent trajectories of aspiration and loss: the European and the African American. In this way, "Parade" makes of the Harlem streets what "Theme for English B" makes of the supposedly blank page, a space uncannily inhabited by dual aspirations—black and white—that, while moving in opposite directions, are unavoidably implicated in each other.

The lines that follow the second set of dots, indicating marching, above, dramatically express this opaque overdetermination of meaning by deliberately clouding the issue of whence the voice, in subjunctive mode, proceeds:

> *I never knew*
> *that many Negroes*
> *were on earth*
> *did you?*
>
> *I never knew!* (389, lines 23–27)

An instance of Hughes's admirable poetic economy and canniness with regard to the spectacular conditions under which Harlem's blacks accessed a form of public subjectivity, the dreamlike phrase might have been uttered by a white onlooker of the twenties previously blind to black cultural presence, or a black spectator identifying the happy reality of being surrounded by others of his or her race. The lines do, in fact, strongly echo Hughes's own rendition of his reaction on arrival in Harlem in 1921 ("Hundreds of colored people!" [*The Big Sea* 81]). But in their imbrication with the white viewpoint, and with the knowledge that the lines are being penned much later, after black Harlem's dreams have turned sour, they also function as a belated recognition that black access to Harlem's urban subjectivity depended on whites having effectively borrowed the meaning of that presence in advance (where "*I never knew*" might carry the meaning: "if I'd only known then what I know now . . ."). The final lines of the poem ironically refuse to clarify whether it is a genuine joy or sorrow that is expressed here, where the mask ("PARADE!") is overplayed in order to convey the complexity of the black visibility it borrows and, in doing so, also hides:

> A chance to let
>   PARADE!
> the whole world see
>   PARADE!
> old black me! (389, lines 29–33)

Cinematic montage, a "method of breaking up and slowing down" action by splicing in "similar but unrelated images" (Shoptaw 118), is the visual equivalent of bebop's runs and breaks, shifts and distortions, but it is also the means by which the poems comprising *Montage* yield to the reader's comprehension of Harlem as a place whose history is overwritten by unconscious conflicts that make every rendition of "blackness's American signifier" peculiarly charged, and where nothing is what it initially seems (Jarraway 826). In "Neon Signs," cinematic montage becomes legible in the way capitalized words are laid out like street signs on the page. As in "Parade," physical movement between spectacular places is signified by a starburst of black dots indicating vibrant nightlife, as the splicing of film in montage can alert the viewer to the representational gap of the splice or cover it over, depending on how it is done:

WONDER BAR

·

· ·

·

WISHING WELL

·

· ·

·

MONTEREY

·

· ·

·

MINTON's
(ancient altar of Thelonious)

·

· ·

·

MANDALAY
Spots where the booted
and unbooted play

· · ·

Mirror-go-round
where a broken glass
in the early bright
smears re-bop
sound (397; lines 1–12, 36–40)

Highlighted is the capitalist circuit that habitually masks its workings in advertising signs, the same logic that fueled black minstrelsy as an art form for white consumption and jazz as something whites could listen to without awareness of its traumatic, postemancipation roots (Shoptaw; Patterson 682).

While the method is the opposite of Eliot's overt erudition, the ambivalence toward the commodification of experience is similar, although it is not populism per se that bothers Hughes. As John Shoptaw notes, Hughes was well acquainted with the European "avant-garde and ideological history of montage," as Hughes had visited the Soviet Union in 1932 with other black artists to work on a cinematic venture for which Sergei Eisenstein gave the opening party in the guests' honor (Berry 159, cited in Shoptaw 118). Here, it is the cryptic qualities of the form that are to the fore. In this move away from realism, *Montage* earns its orthodox modernist credentials (Patterson 680). Yet it also pushes the cool detachment of the poetic persona of an Eliot back toward its roots in the South whose postemancipation violence pushed African Americans northwards and produced such scenes as the one, also headlined, in "Ballad of the Landlord":

MAN THREATENS LANDLORD

TENANT HELD NO BAIL

JUDGE GIVES NEGRO 90 DAYS IN COUNTY JAIL.
(403, lines 31–37)

In a compelling reading, Shoptaw emphasizes how the "smear" in the final lines of "Neon Signs" echoes the red-baiting of the politically narrowing 1940s, as in "smear-sheet," an expression coined around this time. In jazz terminology, smearing also refers to the "sliding or slurring" of "one note into another," making Hughes's "word-smearing . . . his variation on cryptography" or secret movement, "playing off-beat and sometimes dissonant harmonies over continuous melodies" in order to complicate the state of play (119). The smearing of bebop into "re-bop" in the poem's penultimate line suggests other shifts: where the broken glass of a mirror ball becomes the broken glass of violence and the "bright and early" of the imminent day becomes the early escape of music into the street (120). The smearing or borrowing of bebop—in the defamatory sense—by white capital investment that underwrites the problems black Harlem residents faced from the region's heyday on, may be referred to here. But just as important is the way the smearing of "re-bop" emphasizes the inventive nature of black movement, musical and quotidian. As in "Parade," this movement resists a smeared reduction by being earlier remarked in its absence through the star-shaped layout of the dots representing signs, just as black bodies are the signs on which white Harlem capitalized but was unable to subdue completely, and which reappear in "Harlem [2]," for instance, as the unanticipated material response to the question: "What happens to a dream deferred?"

Maybe it just sags
like a heavy load.

Or does it explode? (426, lines 9–11)

The post-traumatic aesthetics displayed in both *The Waste Land* and *Montage of a Dream Deferred* may, ultimately, have more in common than has been thought by virtue of the shared irreducibility of Anglo-American and African American history which turns around issues of loss, appropriation, past violence, and the problematic relation to compromised roots. And yet it seems that it is what is not historically transmittable, or, at least, what is transmittable only as a question to existing, white-authored accounts of modernity that *Montage* returns to in the repeated refrain: "have you heard?" and its companion phrase: "What happens / to a dream deferred?," phrases that pull and push the question of black history and its future back and forth (414, line 53; 426–27, line 1).

In emphasizing and unsettling the relation of the demand for self-expression to the writing medium ("will my page be colored that I write?" [410]), Hughes complicates the injunction to express an interior impulse in exterior form, or the seeming self-sufficiency of European modernism, what Raymond Williams calls "the metropolitan interpretation of its own processes as universals" ("Metropolis" 93) that is rendered by the canonical history of Eliot's poem. Yet in highlighting, instead, the way Harlem as the signifier for black Americanness produces subjectivity in the mode of haunting, a historically overloaded yet nondivisible speaking space, *Montage* equally resists the relegation of black American history to one imaginary location, either in the past or future. In this regard, the sequence insists on the mixed and detemporalized origins of African American subjectivity, where a political moving forward staked on publicly articulable claims has to accommodate the nostalgic looking back of an Anglo-American modernity that is beginning to realize the costs of expanding beyond its means. Insofar as the "city within a city" that is Hughes's Harlem becomes the ongoing means of expression of this difficulty, it shares with the London of *The Waste Land*, but also enlarges upon, an unfinished history whose parameters stretch forward and backward in time.

NOTES

1. Hughes broke in 1930 with his white patron, the wealthy Mrs. Charlotte (Osgood) Mason, who had financed his college tuition and travels from 1928, over the issue of black self-definition. See Hughes (*Big Sea* 325), Brooker ("Modernism" 239–40).

2. Brooker makes a strong case for reading *Montage* as a modernist poem while admitting that 1951 seems late for canonical modernism's terms. "The point," he argues, "is that 'canonic' modernism was engaged in a process of renewal and consolidation; indeed, that both cultures were involved at this moment, as earlier, in the process of cultural re-definition" (246).

15   Modernism's Possible Geographies

Jessica Berman

John Joyce once said of his son James, "If that fellow was dropped in the middle of the Sahara, he'd sit, be God, and make a map of it" (Richard Ellmann 28). While this statement may come as no surprise to Joyce scholars, its significance as commentary about the profound geographical impulses of modernism writ large is only beginning to be explored. Recent theory has moved the spatiality of texts to the forefront, asking us to consider place or location along with history or genealogy as crucial to textual study. But what often emerges instead is a contest for critical attention, or a claim for the priority of space over the often vexed relationship between modernism and history.

For example, Soja claims that cultural geography was eclipsed in the early to middle years of the twentieth century by critical theory's focus on historicism. He calls for "an appropriate interpretive balance between space, time, and social being or what may now more explicitly be termed the creation of human geographies, the making of history, and the constitution of society" (Soja 23). But what is often forgotten in the recent turn to questions of space is that human or cultural geography flourished as a discipline in the early years of the twentieth century. Further, the new human geography that was being devised in this period often emphasized its connection to history and to questions of time, and sought to revise Darwinian principles of evolution that were often too simply imported from the biological sciences. After the nineteenth century's rush of exploration and mapmaking, early- to mid-twentieth-century geography increasingly engaged with the problems of human–landscape interaction, migration, and the relationship among human developments over time, all of which made geography into a science of both temporal and spatial dimensions. Thus if we take seriously Joyce's mapmaking—or indeed the clear and deep-seated concern with geography that we can see in the work of other modernists such as Virginia Woolf, Jean Rhys, and Gertrude Stein— we must consider it in light of the concerted effort of geographers of the time period to remake their discipline as a new science of ongoing human–landscape relations.

It is no coincidence, then, I will argue, that the development of cultural geography in Europe and the United States coincides with the height of literary modernism. The same struggle between simple evolutionism and its deterministic racial categories and a more nuanced model of human-landscape interaction that preoccupies geographers of the period, such as Ellen Churchill Semple, Halford John Mackinder, and Paul Vidal de la Blache, also underlies much European modernism. Semple's emphasis on geography as relationship, Mackinder's focus on the "world island," and especially Vidal de la Blache's insistence on historical "possibilism" rather than strict determinism all provide crucial frameworks for understanding the geographical impulses of modernist writing. The geopolitics that begins to emerge from these modernist geographies, both scientific and literary, often rests on physically based notions of race and identity. Still, this essay will argue that the emphasis in these scientific and literary texts on geography as bidirectional, long-term and relational—that is: involving not only geographical causes of human development but also human effects on geography over the *longue durée*—can also serve to undermine the determinative power of the locations of identity.

As Stephen Kern points out, "Rivers of geopolitics coursed all over the European cultural terrain" (Kern 228) following the creation in the final years of the nineteenth century of geographical societies and journals in Germany, Britain, France, and the United States. While the military demands of the two world wars served to re-emphasize the importance of cartography at the expense of less practical study, cultural geography continued to grow in sophistication and importance throughout the first half of the twentieth century. Geography came increasingly to be predicated on the observable relationships between people and land and the multiple ways in which the two could be shown to interact over time. In 1903, the president of the newly founded Association of American Geographers wrote that "the essential in geography is a relation between the elements of terrestrial environment and the items of organic response" (William Davis 470). As one British geographer put it in 1911, "The geography of today is in the act of escaping from the matrix of mere facts in which it has been too long imprisoned" (Newbigin 13).

The essential key words in this new cultural geography were *relationship* and *change*, especially as applied to human existence in landscape over the long term. Importantly, cultural geography diverged from cartography and physical geography by focusing on the interaction between human communities and their natural contexts, and especially on the way in which this interaction always moves in both directions over the *longue durée*. Thus, for the theorizers of this discipline, such as the great French geographer Paul Vidal de la Blache, whose work led ultimately to the triumph of regional approaches to geography, the development of ecology and urban geography, and to new practices in other fields (such as the *an-*

nales school of history), geography was as much about how humans affect the landscape as about how a physically defined landscape affects humans. Easy models of evolutionary development or environmental determinism were increasingly put into question.

Nonetheless, geographers continued to appropriate simple Darwinism as a principle of scientific explanation. Environmental determinism can be seen in even the best writings of prominent American, British, and French geographers of the time, such as Ellen Churchill Semple, Halford John Mackinder, and to a lesser extent, Paul Vidal de la Blache. Its most notorious and influential expression appears in the work of Friederich Ratzel in the 1880s and 1890s (Glassner 332–33), whose term *Lebensraum* was appropriated by Hitler to justify his geopolitical program of national expansion.[1] But in the introduction to her version of Ratzel's *Anthropogeologie,* Ellen Churchill Semple distances herself from Ratzel's most extreme determinism, from his racialism, and most importantly from his organic view of the state.[2] She "shuns the word geographic determinant, and speaks with extreme caution of geographic control" (Semple, *Influences* vii). In this way she denies the determining power of race:

> If . . . peoples of different ethnic stocks but similar environments manifested similar or related social, economic or historical development, it was reasonable to infer that such similarities were due to environment and not race. Thus by extensive comparison, the race factor in these problems of two unknown quantities was eliminated for certain large classes of social and historical phenomena. (Semple, *Influences* vii)

For Semple, adaptation is an ongoing issue of environment, not an embodied trait that characterizes a specific people. Geography is important because it marks the constant in "the long history of human development" and contrasts with "shifting, plastic, progressive, retrogressive man" (Semple, *American* 2). Though still prey to organicism, Semple's geography avoids the pitfalls of simple evolutionism, as it emphasizes the interaction of geography and human history.

In Great Britain by the end of the nineteenth century, debate at the Royal Geographical Society also concerned the distinction between study of the physical aspects of regions, as opposed to the historical and political development of human societies within landscape (Goldsmid, qtd. in Crone 38). In a series of lectures, Halford John Mackinder insisted on the interconnection between the physical or "scientific" efforts of geography and its interest in human society. Importantly, he pointed out that the physical environment is not a static element in the equation; thus, its power to determine can never be established: "Man alters his environment, and the action of that environment on his posterity is changed in consequence" (Mackinder, "Scope" 236). In much the same way as Semple, Mackinder sought to create British geography as a question of human–environment interactions *over time* and to move it away from the more purely descriptive project of straightforward cartography or from a set of location-based races.

Mackinder develops a notion of what he calls the "world island" that seeks to explain the interrelated histories of Europe and Asia. While compelling in its ability to transcend geographical nationalism and to connect the development of empire to geographical forces, this model also ultimately invited arguments of geographical necessity in Nazi expansionism and encouraged the view of the Eurasian "World Island" as the "center," with all other regions moving to the periphery. Further, Mackinder assumes that each national region on the map corresponds to a particular "people" and he does not hesitate to refer to the English as a "race" whose differentiation may be followed as it encounters different environments (Mackinder, "Scope" 235). The movement away from descriptive geography at the turn of the century to the concern with human–landscape relations was thus fraught, here as elsewhere in the literature, with the complicated question of how to describe those relations over time, and during movements of populations, without resorting to suspect claims of physical causality and presumptuous ideas about the various "qualities" of peoples.

Vidal de la Blache avoids such racial thinking by developing a model that has been called geographical "possibilism" (Dickinson 209). Vidal maintained from the 1890s that environment did not function in a simple determining fashion but rather that humans also greatly affect the landscape in which they develop. "The physical (natural) environment provides a range of possibilities which Man turns to his use according to his needs, wishes and capacities, in creating his habitat. . . . Hence, as opposed to . . . 'environmental determinism' . . . , [Vidal] established a conceptual framework of 'possibilism'" (Dickinson 209). This is the crucial distinction of the French school, a distinction that became important not only for the development of French and American geography,[3] but also for the historians Lucian Febvre and Fernand Braudel.[4] Vidalian "possibilism" carried with it clear implications about the connection between history and geography as disciplines and its divergence from biological racialism.

Three important aspects of Vidal's thought set it apart from the Anglo-American geographical practice of the time and make it resistant to both oversimplified evolutionism and suspect geopolitics. Like most geographers of his age, Vidal focused on the earth as the context for human activity, but for Vidal as opposed to Mackinder the unity of the earth and the relative insignificance of national or even regional boundaries was the key to modern geography: "The dominant idea in all geographical progress is that of terrestrial unity" (Vidal 6). Conceiving of the earth as a whole "whose parts are coordinated," Vidal sought to describe the environment as a "composite, capable of grouping and holding together heterogeneous beings in mutual vital relationships" (Vidal 6, 20). Thus large regions and even the entire globe may come to function as one "world island" rather than being divided into central and peripheral parts. Further, Vidal emphasized again and again in his writings that we cannot know the basic determining geographical conditions of human development, since years of historical life and of human/landscape adaptation intervene. Thus geographical and human history, seen as one, become the study of influence, adaptation, and effect, rather than clear predictive causality. Finally, in examining human adaptations to geography over time, Vidal de la Blache discovers complexity that belies any attempt to rationalize human populations into homogeneous racial groupings. "When an attempt is made . . . to discover the elements of the population, not only of a large region but even of a small one, lack of homogeneity is found to be the rule almost without exception" (Vidal 16). Adaptation is an ongoing process of coalescence and blending which makes the description of "races" nearly impossible.

All of these early-twentieth-century geographic texts revolve in some crucial sense around the question of time–space interrelations and the challenge that these pose to static models of either place or human society. If Soja sees critical theory as neglecting space, and Anthony Giddens hinges his theory of modernity on the disjuncture of time and space (Giddens, *Consequences* 16), these key texts of cultural geography, on the other hand, require us to understand place as a crucial component of the time–space matrix of human society. In Semple, Mackinder, and especially Vidal de la Blache, we find a more complex notion of human–landscape interaction than Giddens or Soja describe—as well as, in Vidal's "possibilism," a direct challenge to the assumption that early-twentieth-century geography tacitly promotes both reductive models of race and the geopolitics that accompanies them.

MODERNIST GEOGRAPHIES

In the high modernist fiction of the years between 1910 and World War II, we encounter everywhere the same concerns about location, mapping, center and periphery, and race and its relationship to identity that also dominate the cultural geography of Semple, Mackinder, and Vidal de la Blache. If Joyce provides little description of natural locations, *Dubliners* nonetheless situates its characters in a particular time–space nexus where human–landscape relations may be seen as among the most determinative relations that exist. So too we find in Jean Rhys's work an effort to redraw the map of the colonies in close juxtaposition to the centers of empire. If Woolf severs Orlando from the determinates of national and gender identities, she ultimately constructs landscape as one of the key fluctuating forces in her development over what we might easily call the *"longue durée."* Finally, if Stein abandons realistic narrative settings and characters rooted in a single specific location, she nonetheless refers constantly to geography and its principles, adopting what we might call a map-based model of narration.

In this sense, I want to argue that many modernist texts are engaged with the concerns of cultural geography in the period from the turn of the century to World War II, and that the ideas of human–landscape interrelations, "possibilism," and the time frame of the *longue durée* lurk beneath constructions of social identity, race, and political belonging in much literary modernism. This is a different claim than that put forward by Stephen Kern, who draws an abstract "culture of space" from the geographical connections of modernism and modernity, as well as from that advanced by Susan Stanford Friedman in *Mappings,* which describes a geopolitical critical method. Nor do I claim that these writers had read geographical theory or were consciously replying to it. Rather, I want to argue that the geographical concerns that arise in modernist fiction form part of a complex interdisciplinary conversation about human–landscape relations. Describing geography as relational, ongoing, and a science of possibilism rather than simple determinism, as these writers all do, complicates the mapping of social and racial identity in modernism.

LOCATIONS: THE WORLD AS ISLAND

At first glance, the location of Joyce's work seems little occupied with the broad questions of landscape and the development of human populations over time that concern cultural geography. Indeed, natural Ireland makes very little appearance in Joyce's work, entering for example in "The Dead" as Seamus Dean points out, as the imagined place of liberation in the west, "a phantasmal place," one that, in contradistinction to Dublin itself, seems to belong to pre-modernity. Recent critical works on Joyce by Emer Nolan, Enda Duffy, Vincent Cheng, and Joseph Valente, to name a few, all question the easy critical assumption of Joyce's ambiguous relation to Irish nationalism and empire, but rarely turn to the specific geography evoked in the texts. But the west country is nonetheless "a geographical reality as well as a symbolic region" (Seamus Dean 1997: 95) in *Dubliners,* just as the concatenation of east and west in *Ulysses* forces a complex interrelationship between the Greek past and the Irish present that Michael Seidel has termed "epic geography." The west becomes a location that Joyce uses to establish the stereotyped and sentimentalized notion of rural Ireland in *Dubliners.* But the west also stands for Ireland as the source of ancient knowledge, the home of learned Celtic voyagers, and the locus of the amalgamation of races that is the legacy of centuries of migration and conquest (Joyce, "Ireland"). For Joyce, treating the "unity of the earth," as Vidal would put it, means rediscovering the relationship between these geographical spaces and any renewed historical or geopolitical identity that might emerge.

Famously, Miss Ivors in "The Dead" extols the virtues of traveling west and condemns Gabriel for "being sick of [his] own country" (Joyce, *Dubliners* 243). For her, there is a marked difference between the modernity of Dublin and the essential Irish culture represented by Aughrim or the Irish-speaking Aran Islands. "Renewal," if one occurs, will come out of the past, the land of the dead, and the geographical history that has preserved the west from alien modernity. Along these lines one might then be tempted to read Gabriel's shift at the end of the story, and the oft-remarked statement, "The time had come for him to set out on his journey westward" (Joyce, *Dubliners* 287) with Ellmann, as a "concession, a relinquishment" of his Continental tastes and "eastward" habits of mind (Richard Ellmann 249).

But what does it mean to go west? To begin, it must evoke the adage about the "westward march of empire" and its implications not only for Joyce's still-colonial Ireland but also for more general European conceptions of the west. *A propos* here is Miss Ivor's taunt, "West Briton," which she whispers to Gabriel to accuse him of collaboration with the empire. Within the geographical history of Europe, the west evokes the age of exploration in which westward voyages meant voyages of discovery. But as Mackinder, like Vidal, claims, "the opening of the twentieth century is appropriate as the end of a great historic epoch . . . the world, in its remoter borders, has hardly been revealed before we must chronicle its complete . . . appropriation" (Mackinder, "Pivot" 241). There are no longer any gaps in the political or cultural possession of the earth's surface; henceforth, "every explosion of social forces, instead of being dissipated in a surrounding circuit of unknown space . . . will be sharply re-echoed from around the globe" (Mackinder, "Pivot" 242). Thus the twentieth century has a new relationship to the west, as all social forces must be seen in global focus.

This way of understanding the crucial shift in geography at the turn of the century also opens up an alternate way of reading the much-analyzed ending of "The Dead." If we have understood Gabriel to have recognized his need to "go west" and reconnect with the Irish national past, while renouncing his Continental sympathies, then the beginning of snow that softly blankets all of Ireland at the end of the story shows his new openness to physical, rural Ireland and all that it symbolizes for Miss Ivors. On the other hand, this passage is clear in its insistence that Gabriel witnesses a particular kind of snowfall: "Snow was general over *all* of Ireland. It was falling on every part of the dark central plain, on the treeless hills, falling softly upon the bog of Allen and, farther westward, softly falling into the dark mutinous Shannon waves" (Joyce, *Dubliners* 288, my emphasis). It is not often that snow falls over all of Ireland, uniting it in a single climate. This unification is crucial for Gabriel in this story because it means that Gabriel's going west does not require him to leave Dublin—or modernity and the Continent—behind. Rather, he has come to the realization that one cannot be splintered from the other, that climate as a force disregards the gaps between locations. The possibility that either he can leave his country behind and escape to the Continent, or Miss Ivor's false assumption that "his country" lies discoverable there in the west, both succumb to the new twentieth-century geography of a "unified earth." At the same time, it challenges Giddens's notion that the separation of time and space is a crucial element of modernity, since space serves here to bring past and present, the western land of the dead and the eastern scene of modernity, into direct relationship.

This same concatenation of time and space lies behind the geographical complexity of *Ulysses*. As critics have long pointed out, *Ulysses* represents the "layering of Irish and Mediterranean spaces" (Seidel xiii) that gives sense to the Joycean phrase "Jewgreek is greekjew" (Joyce, *Ulysses* 411) to Bloom's musings about Turkish farmland (Joyce, *Ulysses* 49–50), as well as to Stephen's constant reference to both Greece and Italy. This layering defines what Seidel calls epic geography, "which depends upon the principle of extension of the old or the familiar. Time extends space" (Seidel xi). But given the context of early-twentieth-century cultural geography, we might just as easily term this *modernist geography*, which defines landscape as an ongoing time–space matrix.

When Stephen walks over Sandymount Strand, pondering the significance of the beach and the history of invasion it has witnessed, we may see very clearly the geopolitical implications of the terrain as inseparable from its relationship with human society over time. Thinking of his own past, Stephen's thoughts turn to the characterization of Ireland as "isle of saints" and sages, a popular comment that, as Joyce puts it in his essay of the same name, "goes back to the most ancient times, when the island was a true focus of sanctity and intellect, spreading throughout the continent a culture and a vitalizing energy" (Joyce, "Ireland" 154). The beach would then represent Irish openness to the sea, to travel, and to dissemination of knowledge (an aspect also especially appealing to Stephen and to Joyce himself). On the same page, however, reference to the crackling of what Stephen calls "human shells" underfoot (34) and later "bones for my steppingstones" (37) makes clear that the "Sands and stones. Heavy of the past" (37), under the watchful eye of the Martello tower, are heavy with the history of loss of life in conquest. The strand's very material is composed of the crushed Irish, its landscape inseparable from its human history. Further, as Emer Nolan points out, the episode on the strand also contributes to the complicated notion of race and its relation to geography in Joyce's writings. Stephen "believes himself to be involved in this history of his ancestors not merely imaginatively, but . . . by means of his blood-inheritance: . . . 'their blood is in me, their lusts my waves' (*Ulysses* 38)" (Nolan 74). The crucial issue in this early-twentieth-century text, then, is the impossibility of geographical isolationism and the ongoing amalgamative force of place.

If for Stephen it is the strand that brings him into contact with geography, for Bloom it is the water. Much has been said about Bloom's symbolic connection to water throughout *Ulysses*, from his bath in the morning to his hand washing at the end of his journey. But beyond its epic importance, water connects Bloom to island life, and to the global oceanic and climatic systems that surround it. For example, in the Ithaca chapter, as Bloom turns on the faucet to fill his kettle, we learn the complex trajectory of the water as it flows from the Roundwood reservoir in county Wicklow to Dublin. "What then did Bloom, waterlover . . . admire?" the text asks. Answer: "Its universality . . . its vastness in the ocean of Mercator's projection . . . its preponderance of 3 to 1 over the dry land of the globe, its indisputable hegemony . . . its persevering penetrativeness . . . its metamorphoses as vapour, mist, cloud, rain, sleet, snow, hail . . . its ubiquity," etc. (549). Remarkable for its depth of geographical knowledge and detail, this passage also marks the geography of water as a global phenomenon, one that makes distinctions between landmasses, or between center and periphery, moot. If both Mackinder and Vidal highlight geographic forces beyond the regional or national borders of human construction, this passage makes these forces crucial to day-to-day human life. Like the snow falling over all of Ireland in "The Dead," the water that flows from the world into Bloom's faucet demonstrates the possible coalescing and aggregating function of geography.

In the work of Jean Rhys, the question of isolation versus amalgamation as a function of human–landscape relations becomes still more salient. While in the twenties and thirties Rhys wrote from a position of exile not unlike Joyce's, her work from this period takes place mainly in Europe. It is imbued with a feeling of dislocation and dispossession; Rhys's sense of nationality or belonging is difficult to pin down: "I don't belong to anywhere but I get very worked up about the West Indies" (qtd. in Gregg 2). In her early stories, Rhys seems to shun West Indian themes and settings, developing an abbreviated style of writing and a disdain for description that makes the characters appear to drift in the modern metropolis. This perhaps explains why Ford Maddox Ford claimed that "Rhys's business was with passion, hardship, emotions: 'The locality in which these things are endured is immaterial'" (Gregg 2).

At the same time, it is clear that location did matter increasingly for Rhys, especially as it brought to the fore questions of the interrelationship between metropolis and colonial outpost, central and marginal island. Rhys's writings from the twenties and the thirties, and *Voyage in the Dark* in particular, often force the two topographies together in a strikingly unusual and original manner. In a letter dated 1959, Rhys writes "there are two places for me. Paris . . . and Dominica . . . both of these places or the thought of them make me want to write . . . the West Indies started knock-ing at my heart. So—'Voyage in the Dark'" (Rhys, *Letters* 171). In an earlier letter, Rhys claims that in *Voyage in the Dark* she was trying to present the character's past in the West Indies as vividly as the present (in Britain) and to show them "side by side" (Rhys, *Letters* 24). The novel's landscape is per-petually bifurcated at the same time, as its parts are shown to matter only in relationship to each other. In a more extreme manner than in Joyce's work, time and space are manipulated so as to force not a disjuncture but a hyperconnectivity, whereby the place of the past is made modern by be-ing ceaselessly brought into the present.

The descriptions of Dominica then become fully realized only as they are part of the British landscape lived by Anna Morgan as she begins her downward spiral to death.[5] What might seem to be signs of her growing madness in the context of this narrative become indications of the reality of the topography that she inhabits. If Gabriel in Joyce's story is at pains to bring west and east together, Anna can find no rational model that can help her unite the two. Thus the very first page begins with a confusion of landscape and climate: "Sometimes I would shut my eyes and pretend that the heat of the fire, or the bed-clothes drawn around me, was sun-heat; or I would pretend that I was standing outside the house at home looking down Market Street to the Bay. When there was a breeze the sea was mil-lions of spangles; and on still days it was purple" (Rhys, *Voyage* 7).

This same kind of climate or landscape confusion occurs again and again in *Voyage*. For example, since England is almost always associated with cold in the novel, when Anna becomes feverish her thoughts are in-stantly transported back to Dominica and to her home life there (31). Flow-ers at Savernake Forest remind her of flowers in the Caribbean, and a dreamlike state makes her unable to make sense of their differences. Col-ors, smells, and even bends in the road can trigger a connection to her past home. The road to Constance Estates, Dominica, which she vividly remem-bers, is like none of the roads she has traveled since. Yet its memory is trig-gered by thoughts of English travel and comes to stand for her entire life's journey. "That's how the road to Constance is. . . . It was as long as a life sometimes" (151). It is as though Anna expects to zigzag around another bend in an English lane and encounter this road and the terrain where the fragmenting experiences of her life will suddenly coalesce.

On the other hand, when Anna repeatedly tells her lover, Walter, "I'm a real West Indian. . . . I'm the fifth generation on my mother's side" (55), she tries to establish "West Indian" as a positive category of difference tied to a specific and racialized time–space position. Instead, Walter is amused by the depth of her concern about her identity, as though not only can he not see her exoticism as a real difference, but he also can't imagine why she would have use for an identity. Anna tries to tell him more about her past, linking the description of its topography to identity through her frequently spoken desire to be black (which to her implies more authentically Dominican), but Walter's response once again elides any positive difference in her identity or its landscape: "Everybody thinks the place where he was born is lovely" (55). Unlike her stepmother, or the schoolgirls (who in not only racial but geographical confusion call Anna "The Hottentot"), Walter is not shocked by the notion that she might wish to be black; for him, in her generalized colonial exoticism and her sexual availability, it is almost as though she already is.

Thus the question of describing human–landscape relations is not a purely topographical one here, and is deeply racialized at its core. Indeed, the entire novel may be seen as an extended rumination on the inadequacy of the reference-book description of Dominica: "Lying between 15°10' and 15°40' N and 61°14' and 61°30'W. A goodly island and something highland, but all overgrown with wood" (17). Conceptions of centrality or marginality here do not follow the lines of latitude and longitude increasingly made rational in the first decades of the twentieth century. Nor, as Mackinder would have it, do racialized identities stay attached to the specific groups or the particular geographical situations they were meant to describe. That Anna as a young girl wishes she could have been born into a black Dominican identity, with its seemingly more full and more rooted traditions and culture, implies not only her (and Rhys's) acceptance of a sentimentalized notion of black experiences in the colonies, but also an understanding of her unmapped position as a Creole, West Indian but not black, and as such, to white English eyes, without any acknowledged identity at all.

Further, that Hottentot was a specific term meant to apply to Khoikhoi women from South Africa enters not at all into the fact that the girls call Anna "Hottentot." The epithet *Hottentot*, in the white imagination, clearly implies hypersexuality of the sort attributed to Sara Baartman, who was labeled the "Hottentot Venus" and displayed, studied, and paraded around Europe in the early nineteenth century. The comment is thus proleptic; Anna in her youth is neither black nor sexualized. But in her abusive relationships with Walter and other men, and in her entrapment in Europe, Anna comes more and more to resemble the Hottentot Venus. The geographical and historical irony that attaches blackness to Caribbean and not African identity here becomes even more pronounced by the connection of blackness to the imprisoned and abused white courtesan. Geographical markers of difference that are tied to a specific space–time nexus are thus destroyed. The play of identities, and in particular racialized identities in Rhys's novel, demonstrates the profound disruption to the ongoing human–landscape relationship posed by colonialism. Rhys's bifurcated geography marks not only the colonial subject's desire to move from periphery to center, but also her need to remake the disrupted geography of her situation.

GEOGRAPHY, TIME, AND THE *LONGUE DURÉE*

If the time–space continuum dominates cultural identity in Joyce and Rhys, in Woolf's *Orlando* duration stretches to its fantastical limits. Not a novel concerned on its surface with the presentation of a particular region qua region, *Orlando* nonetheless presents us with an immense amount of data about landscape change over time and the degree to which human occupation of the landscape can be seen to effect transformation over the *longue durée*. Thus at the beginning of the novel

> [Orlando] walked very quickly uphill through ferns and hawthorn bushes, startling deer and wild birds, to a place crowned by a single oak tree. It was very high, so high indeed that nineteen English counties could be seen beneath, and on clear days thirty, or forty perhaps, if the weather was very fine. Sometimes one could see the English Channel, wave reiterating upon wave. Rovers could be seen and pleasure boats gliding on them; and galleons setting out to sea.... To the east there were the spires of London ... and perhaps on the very sky line, when the wind was in the right quarter, the craggy top and serrated edge of Snowdon herself showed mountainous among the clouds. (Woolf, *Orlando* 18)

We know this view is fantastical: there is no possible way that both the Channel and Mt. Snowdon, which is in Wales, can be seen from the same vantage point. Since Woolf patterned much of *Orlando* on Vita Sackville-West and her family's manor house, Knole, we can imagine this spot to be somewhere on its grounds. This passage is therefore meant to evoke a sense of English geography that parodies the importance attributed to the United Kingdom of England and Wales, and the possibility that they emerge from a self-evident geopolitics, or from the notion that the manor house forms the natural center of a kingdom. The old adage "I am the king of all I survey" is made a mockery here and Orlando's easy assumption of inheritance is also undermined.[6]

As many have remarked, the landscape in *Orlando* provides the primary means of indicating historical and technological change over the long period of Orlando's life. For example, the sky itself changes from the brightness of the eighteenth century to the damp heaviness of the nineteenth; the ivy grows faster for the Victorians, and by the twentieth century the view from the foot of the oak tree appears encumbered with "houses, castles, and woods" (326). Landscape here represents more than just the symbolic use of nature, or Woolf's paean to the romantic poets—it also represents Woolf's insistence on the principle of possibilism over the *longue durée*, which we might easily term Vidalian. Her discussion of geomorphology as conditioned by the close relationship between human populations and the landscape also has a Vidalian echo. Nothing takes place in this novel without its being written in some manner on the landscape; no climate change or vegetal shift occurs without repercussions for the development of society. Her depiction of London over the centuries must also be seen in the geographer's light: How does the rationalization of the roadways, where "even the cobbles in the streets showed distinct one from the other," change life in the eighteenth century? (224); how do we see the density of population in the twentieth century ("the old Kent Road was very crowded on Thursday the eleventh of October, 1928" [306]) as connected to Woolf's understanding of the pressures on British society in her own period? As with Braudel's celebrated study of the Mediterranean, Woolf shows the process whereby the changing characteristics of the region over a period of several hundred years may be seen to effect changes in human living patterns, and habits that help determine the history of England.

At the same time, much of the landscape displayed in *Orlando* is Turkish, not English, and from the moment Orlando departs for Constantinople, the Turkish countryside itself is contrasted with English culture and nationalism. Orlando as ambassador is, after all, a representative of imperial Britain; his displacement into the company of the Gypsies is not only a gender displacement but also a disruption of imperial power, coming as it does as a consequence of a revolution with which she appears to have colluded (141).[7] Orlando's decision to return home is prompted by her different sense of geography: the Gypsies do not love nature, they do not value large manor houses, and they consider private ownership of land to be thievery. "Looked at from the Gypsy point of view, a Duke, Orlando understood, was nothing but a profiteer or robber who snatched land . . . and could think of nothing better to do with it than to build three hundred and sixty-five bedrooms when one was enough" (148). The re-emergence of Orlando's national longing and her subsequent return home is occasioned by the reassertion of the English conception of "nature" as a realm of beauty and reverence and by the English habit of land use and development. Her idyllic vision of undulating hills, oak trees, and shade also contains "heavy carts coming along the roads laden with tree trunks, which they were taking, she knew, to be sawed for firewood" (151). English geography is not separate from development, and English national sentiment is closely bound with national habits of land use.

But this vision of the English countryside appears in the very middle of a description of a Turkish mountain landscape. The same kind of convergence of landscapes occurs again in reverse at the end of the novel, with Turkish elements appearing in the midst of the description of twentieth-century Britain: "Here the landscape . . . shook itself, heaped itself, let all this encumbrance of houses, castles, and woods slide off its tent-shaped sides. The bare mountains of Turkey were before her" (326). Night falls, and then even the Cape Horn becomes visible, collapsing map spaces much further than had that original fantasy view from Snowdon to the Channel, and implying the kind of imperial gaze that might imagine them all to be part of a future Britain. The sixteenth-century fantasy clearly had imperial intentions, even if mocked and even though Orlando throughout expresses deep English cultural nationalism. Yet around the time of the writing of *Orlando,* Woolf clearly derides both imperialism and nationalism in general, exclaiming to Harold Nicolson, "Can't you see that nationality is over? All divisions are now rubbed out" (Woolf, *Diary* 145). Thus what we must read here is not simply a reassertion of conventional imperialist nationalism but rather a different sort of integrative geography, not unlike that apparent in Joyce and Rhys. The concatenation of Britain and Turkey at the end of the novel implies Orlando's ultimate recognition of the commonalities between the Gypsy perspective on landscape and her own; the geography of exploration represented by Shel's travels around the Cape here jibes with her own renewed exploration of the natural (if fantasized) landscape. Geography over the *longue durée* thus gives rise to a Vidalian unity of terrestrial phenomena where landscapes and their morphologies are interconnected and mapping serves less as a means of defining borders or as a vehicle for the geopolitics of empire than as a representation of ongoing relationships.

MODERNIST MAPPING

Mapping emerges as key to Gertrude Stein's work, both in its spatial dimension and as a narrative principle, substituting geographical movement for conventional development or plot. Steinian geography works on two frontiers, as it were—to further define the relationships between people and land over time and to remake narrative along geographical principles.[8] When she claims that "America is my country; Paris is my hometown," she insists that national identity and community feeling are distinct though paired terms, and that they develop in conjunction with geography. For Stein, "geographical history" may bring both individual and national identities into being, but movement in space changes their *relation,* forcing us to seek community in the network of lines on a map, or in the juxtapositions inherent in landscape, or in the narrative extension of a shifting plural subject.

Stein's early novel *The Making of Americans* begins as an attempt to describe the relationship of Americans to their long history of movement and migration across the country. Though it begins with a genealogical conception of identity, the novel ultimately rejects the rule of biology, and substitutes instead a notion of affiliation rooted in place and experience, and inscribed within the play of "ones" who wander in the American landscape. Here it seems that Stein adopts Semple's kind of insistence on a geographically based understanding of the principles of human diffusion and differentiation.

In *The Geographical History of America,* the landscape and its social effects become even more specific. The fact that Stein chooses a title so close to that of Semple's *American History and Its Geographic Conditions* (1903) makes clear that she is in effect writing an alternative geographical treatise, and challenging current geographical practice by substituting her nonteleological, wandering history for the linear trajectories often implied by Semple and her fellow geographers. In Chapter 2 of *The Geographical History* (or, the first of its many versions in this very circular text), Stein writes of the slow geographical changes in the land, where the water has either receded or advanced. She refers to the age of the terrain as determined by the fossils buried in it. All of these elements contribute to human nature and human mind and ultimately to the place of "communism, individualism, propaganda" and war within that schema (Stein, *Geographical* 68). But what might seem like determinism here becomes limited because Stein's model not only minimizes the significance of these political systems, but also through her insistently recursive prose, minimizes any development toward them. The American landscape becomes only a variety of mapped spaces—the open sky of the prairies or the intersecting roads that wander endlessly in and around them. The only space that can be claimed for living in this geographical history of America is one with an "open sky" mentality and a network of wandering paths as its location. Stein insists that we see the importance of geography—be it flat-land mentality or having no sky—as a broader question of the ever-shifting recursive location of being.

What is intriguing about the concern with landscape and nationality that emerges in Stein's late texts is the evolution of this recursive idea of landscape into a focus on the map as a principle of narration. If, as Stein claims, the American landscape must be named to be delimited, then naming is mapping. Yet as we know from so many Stein texts, naming not only calls up the question of multiplicity but makes of it a principle of narration, substituting for conventional plot the endless repetition of names and their qualities. This connection from mapping to narration emerges as a direct mode of narration in the geographical texts of the late twenties and the thirties and in such late texts as *Ida: A Novel.* In *Ida,* Stein creates a subject who is protean, plural, and on the move from place to place, almost a nomadic American Everywoman. She creates Ida through her traveling. "Was she on a train or an automobile, an airplane or just walking. . . . She was saying, yes yes I like to be sitting. Yes I like to be moving" (Stein, *Ida* 34). It is the intersection of wandering and belonging that marks her, but the location makes very little difference. "Ida did not go directly anywhere. She went all around the world. It did not take her long and everything she saw interested her" (51). In these texts mapping becomes a dynamic process that generates movement in time and space. The bidirectional human–landscape relationship described by the geographers becomes a multitudinous array of intersecting vectors that undermine the determinative power of any one set of borders or identities.

Thus these experimental narratives, like the other modernist texts that have been in question here, often use location and the habits of cultural geography to escape the constraints of borders. Building on the same kinds of insights that led early-twentieth-century geographers to stress the unity of global terrestrial phenomena, the dominance of broad regional rather than national features of landscape, and the ongoing interaction between diverse human populations and their environments over the long term, modernist fiction often gestures toward a new and profound cosmopolitan geography. The complex relationship between time and space, which dominates early-twentieth-century cultural geography, and clearly emerges as salient in the work of Joyce, Rhys, Woolf, and Stein, resists the pull of oversimplified biological determinism, and of static national or racial categories. Thus, rather than viewing modernism as characterized by its lack of concern with traditional habits of landscape, or by its seeming disjunction of time and space, we need to look to the new possible geographies emerging in its pages. In these texts, when restrictive models of identity encounter new notions of center and periphery, new emphasis on human–landscape relations over the *longue durée*, and new possibilities of narrative mapping, little, including race, remains fully determined.

NOTES

1. Ratzel never uses the term "geopolitics," which is distinct from the discipline of political geography.

2. Semple was, until 1984, the only woman ever to be president of the Association of American Geographers. Semple was Ratzel's only woman student and was forced to listen to his lectures from behind a partially closed door in an adjacent room (Wanklyn 23). The parallels between Semple's experience with Ratzel and Stein's experience as a "special student" of William James at the Harvard Annex for women would make an interesting study.

3. Vidal's influence on the famed mid-century American geographer Sauer has been credited for the development of ecology in the United States.

4. Though Febvre is most celebrated for his work on Renaissance France, and as a founder of the *Annales* school of historians, in the 1920s he authored *A Geographical Introduction to History*. Braudel's concept of the *"longue durée,"* it must be clear, is a notion developed directly out of Vidal's practice of geography.

5. See the original ending of the novel where Anna's death is made clear in Bonnie Kime Scott, ed.

6. Thanks to Catherine Dahlstrom for her suggestions regarding Orlando's situation in this passage.

7. See Jane Garrity for a discussion of the interconnection of gender and the geographies of empire here. I am indebted to her discussion of Woolf and geography.

8. See the chapter on Stein in my *Modernist Fiction*.

16 Modernism(s) Inside Out: History, Space, and Modern American Indian Subjectivity in *Cogewea, the Half-Blood*

Justine Dymond

Redefining the modern means rethinking our sense of history and time, continuity and rupture, revolution and tradition.
—Rita Felski, *Doing Time*

We must be insistently aware of how space can be made to hide consequences from us, how relations of power and discipline are inscribed into the apparently innocent spatiality of social life, how human geographies become filled with politics and ideology.
—Edward W. Soja, *Postmodern Geographies*

[T]he body is . . . fascinated by the unique occupation of floating in Being with another life, of making itself the outside of its inside and the inside of its outside. And henceforth, movement, touch, vision, applying themselves to the other and to themselves, return toward their source and, in the patient and silent labor of desire, begin the paradox of expression.
—Maurice Merleau-Ponty, *The Visible and the Invisible*

About a third of the way into Mourning Dove's[1] *Cogewea, the Half-Blood* (1927), the Okanogan ingenue Cogewea takes dictation from Alfred Densmore after he breaks his arm while bronco riding. The white "tenderfoot" owes his recent employment at Horseshoe Bend to Cogewea, who hired him as a prank to annoy her brother-in-law and owner of the Montana ranch, John Carter. The narrator reveals that Densmore is gold-digging, convinced that there are "mines of it among the Indians" (84), but his intentions are not as clear to Cogewea as they are to the novel's readers. As he dictates a letter to his mother, Cogewea effectively becomes his amanuensis, but the letter that forms under her pen is intended more for her eyes than for Densmore's mother, its duplicitous language ("My nurse, while not a professional, is one of the very best; kind and affectionate") meant to create an impression of Densmore's integrity as a suitor (85).

That Mourning Dove, the second female Native American novelist, is trying her hand at a genre traditionally written by white authors brings added import to this scene in which Cogewea stands in for a white man as the writing subject. For one, it speaks of Mourning Dove's self-consciousness at working in a genre in which, as Louis Owens describes it, we generally find

> a western ranch setting; a cast of rough-and-ready cowboys; a beautiful young woman who will conveniently become the necessary damsel in distress; a dastardly "easterner" who comes to plunder Eden; and a strong-and-silent, quick-triggered cowboy hero ready to save the hapless female. (65)

What will it mean that in *Cogewea, the Half-Blood: A Depiction of the Great Montana Cattle Range,* the "damsel in distress" is biracial and independently minded, the "cowboy hero" is a Flathead Indian "breed" determined to challenge racial discrimination, and the ranch's motley crew is made up of ranch hands "from nearly every state in the Union" (33), a "light-complexioned half-blood Cheyenne" (36), and a Parisian? That Mourning Dove intends to trouble the formula of the Western romance is also reflected in the amanuensis scene. As Cogewea becomes aware of Densmore's flirtatious intentions, she says angrily, "'Shall I add a post-script and say that your nurse wrote this and that she is an Injun squaw?'" (86).

In this moment, Cogewea reveals the racial politics of writing sentimental romance for a white audience, and Mourning Dove turns the genre inside out, deconstructing the marriage plot in the very act of writing it. What other kinds of duplicities will be exposed if the writer is revealed as an "Injun squaw"? For one, Mourning Dove's novel makes central to its narrative the history of colonization otherwise obscured by the Western romance genre and its precursors, the sentimental novel, the captivity narrative, and the frontier romance. Furthermore, as this essay argues, *Cogewea* can help us bring into sharper focus the racial ideologies not fully renounced by modernism's rejection of the sentimental tradition. Oddly enough, in its apparent conventionality, the novel obtains a dimension of experimentation "other" than, but tangential to, modernism's experiments in form. Both Mourning Dove and modernists share an impulse to critique the sentimental tradition, an impulse that shapes the form of their projects, though to different ends.

The flipside of this revision of the sentimental from the inside—the exposure of the racial politics of *reading* sentimental romance—is revealed in the very next scene. Here we see Cogewea reading *The Brand*, a Western romance written by a white woman who makes, in Cogewea's view, "an unjust presentation of Indian sentiment and racial traits" (90). Cogewea becomes so furious about *The Brand*'s portrayal of "a half-blood 'brave'" who falls in love with a white woman that she snaps at Jim LaGrinder, the "breed" hero of *Cogewea,* when he asks her a simple question. After Jim walks away, Cogewea throws the novel to the floor in disgust, regretting her rudeness. But she doesn't leave it there—instead, she picks it back up again and considers its narrative: The "brave" hesitates to express his affections to the white woman because "[h]e deems himself beneath her; not good enough for her. But to cap the absurdity of the story, he weds the white 'princess' and slaves for her the rest of his life" (91). In contemplating the implications of *The Brand*'s narrative, Cogewea offers an audience analysis of the "hateful volume" (90):

> "Bosh!" she mused half aloud. "Show me the Red 'buck' who would *slave* for the most exclusive white 'princess' that lives. Such hash may go with the whites, but the Indian, both full bloods and the despised *breeds* know differently. (91, emphasis in original)

That white and Indian audiences "know differently" has implications for *Cogewea*'s readers, making this intertextual moment effectively a meta-commentary on the racial subjectivity of reading practices. In the figure of Cogewea, we find a reader unanticipated by the culture of sentimental romance, a figure standing outside the tradition in a way both similar and different from, say, Virginia Woolf's Lily Briscoe or Jean Rhys's Antoinette Cosway. Mourning Dove thereby signals to *her* readers that she is familiar with the tradition of the romance novel and the racial ideology inscribed in the genre for its white readership. The romantic triangle of Cogewea, Jim, and Densmore is fraught in its narrative tensions by the same racial constructions Cogewea bemoans in *The Brand.* But by calling her reader's attention to these ideologies, Mourning Dove exposes the racial seams of the Western romance—and its literary heritage in the sentimental tradition—and produces a self-conscious reading practice, such that the careful (white) reader will, if not already, "know differently." This same readerly self-consciousness can turn inside out the racial seams that connect modernism and the sentimental tradition in ways made invisible by modernism's overt disdain for that literary tradition. A phenomenological reading of subjectivity enables us to see the effect of Mourning Dove's "experiments" on the representation of the American Indian subject. It also allows us to see the limitations of canonical modernists' reconfigurations of subjectivity when their texts write into being the racial "other."

EMBODYING THE SUBJECT OF THE SENTIMENTAL TRADITION

Recent criticism of popular fiction in the late eighteenth and the nineteenth century has acknowledged "the expansive, imperial project of sentimentalism."[2] The seduction and marriage plots, much like the earlier captivity narratives, promoted an image of a beautiful (read: fair), naïve, artless heroine seduced by the artful villain (or, in the captivity narrative, the "primitive"), away from her natural state of domesticity. Indeed, as Laura Wexler and others have shown, literary and cultural sentimental fictions went beyond inculcating middle-class virtues in white, female readers; they enacted racial violence by covering up "the deeper tracings of its terrorism against nonreaders and outsiders" (Wexler 37). In its reaction against the culture of sentimentality, Suzanne Clark has argued, modernism implicitly rejected femininity.[3] In critiquing nineteenth-century marriage plots and their narrative "trope for the sex-gender system as a whole," modernist women writers, according to Rachel Blau DuPlessis, revised the genre by "writing beyond the ending" (5). Literary modernism did not, however, similarly renounce the sentimental romance's construction of the racial other, and even appropriated from the Victorians the concept of the "primitive" as a means, paradoxically, to counter the Victorian project of keeping the English language pure.[4] One has only to think of Gertrude Stein's "Melanctha," for example, to understand how the voice and body of the racialized other provided the launching pad for her self-conscious linguistic play, the experimental texture of her modernism.

From this racial point of view on modernism's innovations, it becomes clear that the rejection of nineteenth-century sentimentalism prompting modernism was perhaps most readily pursued by those already positioned as sentimentalism's inheritors. For example, Virginia Woolf's position as cultural insider allowed her entry into modernism through the nineteenth-century sentimental tradition, and it is from this vantage point that she could critique the construction of femininity at the center of that tradition. In *To the Lighthouse* Woolf straddles the fence between a recuperation of the Victorian figure of the "Angel in the House" and a critique of the imperialist project in that same image. Woolf more overtly presents her concern with the intertwining narratives of imperialism and the sentimental in her first book-length work, *The Voyage Out*, which takes as its theme a young woman's voyage to love by way of South America. In her awakening sexuality, Rachel's unconscious is troubled by "barbarian men" (77), and her romance with Terence Hewet is interrupted by the stares of women with "long narrow eyes" in a South American village (284). While Woolf is consciously questioning the imperialist project of the British Empire, the novel's romance narrative still depends upon the othered bodies, "the senseless beasts," as Helen thinks of them (285), who do not occupy the position of subject. In the Oedipal reading of modernism's repudiation of its literary fathers, Woolf and other canonical modernists belonged to the literary family they rebelled against. How does a writer already positioned outside that tradition, by virtue of its construction of race and class difference, join modernism's departure from nineteenth-century forms?

For Mourning Dove, her critique of the romance plot means she must first find a way for her biracial heroine to inhabit its tradition. Mourning Dove endows Cogewea with the sympathetic physical qualities of a sentimental heroine: "Her eyes of the deepest jet, sparkled, when under excitement, like the ruby's fire. Hair of the same hue was as lustrous as the raven's wing, falling when loose, in great billowy folds, enveloping her entire form" (15). While modernists were rejecting sentimental subjectivity and its domestic enclosures through formal experimentation, Mourning Dove enters sentimental subjectivity in order to undo its racial and geographic enclosures. She reshapes Native American subjectivity that had been previously erased by modernity's imperialist projects and represented in its cultural productions as "savage," "primitive," or tragically vanished.

Michelle Burnham argues that the sentimentality of captivity narratives and frontier romances constructed an "imperialist audience."[5] In reading one particular frontier romance, Harriet Cheney's *A Peep at the Pilgrims*, Burnham writes that "the romance plot is forever eclipsing the historical narrative, distracting the imperialist audience away from the scene of violence. Romance alternately depends on and obscures history as both narratives move toward a teleological end of marital/national union" (98). Burnham's "imperialist audience" has by early twentieth century become a nostalgically nationalist audience,[6] belatedly mourning a romanticized American Indian past and concerned with the perceived invasion of immigrants on nativist spaces. *Cogewea* was published only three years after the 1924 Immigrant Act and, on the first page, boldly declares that Cogewea "proclaimed a proud descent from the only true American—the Indian" (15). In her creation of a sympathetic, educated, and articulate biracial protagonist, Mourning Dove uses *Cogewea*'s romance plot to consistently remind its audience of "the scene of violence" historically and geographically. The novel refuses to obscure the history of federal Indian policy and therefore exposes the conditions of modernity that produced captivity narratives and frontier romances. One effect of this reminder is to reverse, on multiple levels, the sense of who has invaded whose land in captivity narratives and frontier romances. In this sense, Mourning Dove positions herself and her heroine as readers of a sentimental yet racialized modernity that refuses to subordinate completely the effects of history to romance. She claims a stance "outside" and "other" that is both at odds with white modernism and akin to it by means of the deconstruction of the sentimental genre.

THE "NEW" AMERICAN INDIAN SUBJECT

The "scene" of that history is made explicit by Mourning Dove since it is in the very landscape that Cogewea reads the past, and this spatially rooted memory effects a subtle but profound reconfiguration of subjectivity for the novel's heroine. Cogewea's intersubjective relationship to the landscape, as produced by her knowledge of the violent past, creates a powerful polemic about integrationist pressures and the destruction of Native land and culture. It also argues for a new understanding of the American Indian subject as fragmented, or necessarily split, not only or not primarily as a result of "mixed race" identity but in response to land theft and federal Indian policy. Thus, Mourning Dove's novel reveals the very embodiment of spatiality, in Edward Soja's use of the term, that produces racialized subjects and the temporal dichotomization of primitive-modern cultures, showing, for example, the inevitability of Native American "extinction" in the path of modernization that, in turn, informs literary narrative. We can trace this gradual but radical shift in Cogewea's subjectivity over three mirrored scenes that are fairly evenly distributed over the course of the narrative.

In the novel's opening pages, Cogewea sees range riders in the distance and the sunset over the Pend d'Oreille where canoes "ruffled its bosom no more" (17) and whose banks would "never again . . . reflect gleam of signal or camp-fire. The buffalo no longer drank of its cooling flood, nor thundered over the echoing plain" (18). In this reminiscence of what has disappeared as a result of land theft, extermination, and relocation, the geography, specifically the Pend d'Oreille River, orients spatially Cogewea's memory of the Salish tribes' past abundance. Likewise, the *absence* of markers of American Indian settlement and activity *disorients:* "Cogewea imagined that the time-grizzled peak beckoned a parting farewell, and a chill of loneliness struck to her heart. The world was receding!—and she buried her face in her hands to suppress the sob which welled to her lips" (18). Cogewea's sentimental reading of the landscape—the play of light on a mountain at dusk—provokes a feeling of isolation in her, underscored by Mourning Dove's use of a sentimental prose style. The emotional response to Cogewea's imagined vision of the landscape's disappearing could imply an inextricable relationship between, or effectively a familiar conflation of, nature and American Indianness. Perhaps this moment's occurrence early in the narrative risks such an essentializing interpretation, one that parallels the anthropological sense of Native Americans as frozen in a past time, a pre-modern culture doomed to disappear under modernity's geographic advancement. But it is this passage's very essentializing sentimentalism that grounds the novel's later revision of American Indian subjectivity for a nostalgically nationalist audience. In other words, this sentimentality is Mourning Dove's entry point to critiquing modernity's construction of the American Indian "traditional self." Furthermore, it is important to notice in this textual moment that Cogewea's ontological being emerges from an intersubjective relationship with the landscape, such that orientation and disorientation are mapped onto each other simultaneously in time and space. As Cogewea's "world" recedes, so does her "traditional self" as phenomenologically felt. That the "world" is disappearing, not merely the land or territory, seems to support the conclusion that Cogewea's very being is at stake in U.S. westward expansion, both her ethnic belonging *and* her individual existence.

As the novel proceeds, however, Cogewea's subject position grows more complex. Next to her grandmother, the Stemteemä, who represents the "vanishing race" in her unwillingness to adapt to modernization, Cogewea appears quite modern. On the Montana ranch, the Stemteemä continues "some of the old-time customs—tepee and ground-couch—moccasins and ankle-wraps" (41), and recounts orally "many interesting tales of the past" (40).[7] By contrast, Cogewea's everyday clothing is more cowgirl than Okanogan; she easily moves between Salishan, "standard" English, and ranch slang; and she works as a rancher. Through Densmore's gaze she remains conflated with the natural world: "Her graceful form, bending slightly over the saddle bow, appeared an integral part of the flying steed" (138). But by this point in the novel the narration/narrator has distanced itself from this essentializing gaze and instead has associated that gaze primarily with Densmore. In the narrator's voice, she is not interchangeable with the landscape nor a "vanishing breed" to be nostalgically mourned. She is a part of the landscape in that it orients her interiority, *and*, as a rancher, she has agency in shaping the environment around her. To illustrate this shift in the narrative's representation of Cogewea, I will quote one particular passage at length to examine the movement in her subjectivity from the earlier passage and to give a sense of the weight the narrative gives to this shift. Cogewea has climbed Buffalo Butte once again to watch the sunset:

The glow of the setting sun lit the western sky with the ruddy sheen of a prairie fire. The splendid Flathead valley lay below, while the mighty Rockies, like Cyclopean battlements, towered in the east. Cogewea gazed enraptured. A vision of the dim misty past rose up before her. The stately buffalo roved in the distance, while the timid antelope stood sentinel on the neighboring heights. An Indian village on the move, wound its way like a great mottled serpent over the crest of the highest ridge. It reached the brow, where each separate horse and rider showed in sharp silhouette against the horizon, then vanished over the crest. The girl arose and stood as in a trance. Slowly, with outstretched arms she whispered.

"My beautiful Eden! I love you! My valley and mountains! It is too bad that you be redeemed from the wild, once the home of my vanishing race and where the buffalo roamed at will. Where hunting was a joy to the tribesmen, who communed with the Great Spirit. I would that I had lived in those days,—that the blood of the white man had not condemned me an outcast among my own people."

Cogewea sank down, burying her face in her hands. A half suppressed sob burst from her lips, convulsing her slender form. In silence she remained as the evening shadows deepened about her. She had often stood upon this butte at the close of the summer day in dreamy sadness, but never had she felt so lonely and forsaken. The form and face of the white man constantly intruded upon her vision. (109)

As in the earlier passage, Cogewea envisions what is absent from the landscape, an absence that is a marker of time, the "dim misty past." The view from Buffalo Butte is literally mesmerizing for Cogewea, as she looks on "enraptured" and "in a trance," as though, more than projecting her imagination onto the landscape, she is a medium for the ghostly presence of the past. (In her monologue addressing her "'beautiful Eden,'" she may also be a medium for Lucullus Virgil McWhorter's editorial commentary.) Also here, as earlier, she cries, "burying her face in her hands." This gesture on one level works as a sentimental device, but it is also significant that in both passages Cogewea covers her face, physically shielding her eyes from an imagined vision. Disconnecting her sight from the "flesh" of the landscape suggests more than mere melodrama. Philosopher Maurice Merleau-Ponty's "fundamental phenomenon of reversibility," the dynamic of perceiving simultaneously the subject-ness and object-ness of the other, necessitates grasping that reversibility in the self by way of the "flesh" of objects in the world.[8] Those very objects that constitute Cogewea's subject-ness, her American Indianness, are nonexistent except as she is able to imagine them—thus, her subject-ness depends upon a self-conscious recreation of absent objects in the world. And yet, this recreation means "the scene of violence" will also be recalled; Cogewea's "world" is thus both remembered by her and rendered by Mourning Dove through its violent erasure. This passage implies that Cogewea's vision is not completely in her power to recreate, since it "rose up" unbidden and leaves her "lonely and forsaken." Here, the narrative expresses a textual ambiguity about Cogewea's subjectivity (and, perhaps, Mourning Dove's position as the writing subject): Cogewea is at the same time agent of her envisioned surroundings and diminished by the spatial absence of her cultural "flesh."

This ontological ambiguity is further heightened, unlike in the earlier passage, by Cogewea's explicit articulation of the correspondence between the absence of the past's abundance and her "'vanishing race.'" She also makes a direct link between her biracial identity and her isolation, wishing "that the blood of the white man had not condemned me an outcast among my own people," a desire seemingly consistent with the "tragic mulatta" figure of literary imagination. The novel does not, however, "condemn" Cogewea to this "tragedy," and, particularly in references to the intrusion of the "white man," continues to remind its readers of white settlement practices that contributed to the construction of early-twentieth-century American Indian subjectivity. The generalized "white man" in the middle of the passage whose "blood" Cogewea shares seems to be the same "white man" who trespasses "upon her vision" at the end of the passage. But in the next sentence we discover that this second reference to "the white man" is specific to Densmore: "She had thought to ask Densmore to ride with her, but some impelling influence had deterred her" (109). On the next page, Jim LaGrinder complains to Cogewea that she only has time "'for that there white man'" (110). The repetition of the same words makes the seamless interchangeability of the history of the "white man" and a particular "white man" come across as quite purposeful on Mourning Dove's part. The "white man's" intrusions therefore occur on several levels: Densmore interrupts Cogewea's idyllic life on the ranch, and he intrudes on the affections Jim has for Cogewea; the "white man" has historically trespassed on and invaded Native land; and both Densmore and the "white man" in general intrude on Cogewea's interiorized reflections, her nostalgic reverie of a lost landscape. These trespasses take on even more significance in light of the actual editorial intrusions of McWhorter, which make it difficult to discern at times where we hear Mourning Dove's voice unadulterated by McWhorter's. Thus, the novel's subject and Cogewea's subject-ness are inextricably, and violently, altered by the "white man" and his legalized trespassing such that one cannot separate the encroachment of whites on "the dim misty past" from the onto-historical-legal legacy of genre production.

A more radical shift from a subject conflated with the natural landscape to a subject fragmented by the federal government's land usurpation emerges more clearly in the novel's climactic scenes and denouement. Intending to steal her land through marriage, Densmore has kidnapped Cogewea, but when he learns that she does not in fact own the ranch, he becomes enraged, takes her money, and ties her to a tree. Once rescued by Jim LaGrinder, Cogewea persuades her friends that "an appeal to the courts looking to justice, would be of little or no avail" (279). The penultimate chapter ends with another description of a sunset and a one-sentence paragraph:

> The sunset, glorious in its fiery splendors reflected from the snow-capped Rockies, held not its accustomed interest for her.
> To Cogewea, the world was dead! (279)

As in the earlier scene, a description of the landscape precedes an interiorization of the narration, though this time the "world" doesn't merely recede—it no longer exists for Cogewea. The landscape is still perceptible, it still exists in itself, but it no longer holds Cogewea in an intersubjective embrace. Since the one-sentence paragraph begins "*To* Cogewea" (my emphasis), it is in Cogewea's perception that her intercorporeal relationship to her surroundings withers. In the novel she enters "white" sentimental subjectivity, from within which she names and mourns that loss. For her, this assumed subjectivity *is* a fragmented subjectivity, despite its "flowery" language.

This world-diminishing perception does not by chance occur after Cogewea's argument about the powerlessness of American Indians before the law. The earlier scene where the "world recedes" also follows from Cogewea's consideration of the history of legalized white settlement on American Indian lands. Indeed, the dramatic tension of the kidnapping depends upon a perception of Cogewea's subject position as shaped by intrusive allotment policies. The General Allotment Act of 1887, or the Dawes Act as it was also known, reserved 160 acres for the head of each American Indian household, actively promoting a Euro-American concept of family structure. The ontological effect of allotment was to destroy a collective sense of self defined by communal land use, and allotment thereby fragmented Native American tribes into individual landowners. Even if the destruction of communal land ownership did not accomplish its cultural assimilation goals, it did spatially integrate American Indians with their white neighbors. The reservation land left over after allotments were made was sold to whites and the payment was held in trust. The Allotment Act was merely one step in the reduction of reservation lands during the time of mass land cessation by the U.S. government between 1880 and 1895, during which "tribes lost 60 percent of the amount that would be taken in the next century" (Hoxie 44). In the territory of Washington, where Mourning Dove comes from, white settlers clamored for diminishing Indian ownership of the Colville reservation. In 1892, the U.S. government allowed white settlement on the northern half of the reservation, "voting to reject payment negotiated with the Colville by the Indian office" (Batker 43). In 1896, the rest of the reservation was opened to mineral exploration, and then in 1906, the entire Colville Valley was made available for white settlement (Batker 43). Densmore's kidnapping of Cogewea re-enacts this history in a literal manner, but also metaphorically: Cogewea's traditional sense of "self" has already been stolen, at least the self as constituted by pre-contact Okanogan cultural practices and communal land ownership. The enforced individualism combined with gender-based inheritance laws make Cogewea, by virtue of her racial and gender subject position, vulnerable to Densmore's scheme.[9] The conflation of Densmore, the formulaic villainous figure of the narrative, with the larger cultural "bad guy" of U.S. federal Indian policy constitutes a radical inversion of the Western romance genre. Mourning Dove manipulates readers' affective reading practices such that to despise Densmore and hope for Cogewea's safety produces, consciously or unconsciously, an emotional rejection of U.S. colonialism's legacy. Thus to lose one's self in the narrative means that white readers who don't "know differently" risk disrupting their racial, cultural, and national loyalties.

But to end *Cogewea* with the death of her intercorporeal relationship to the world would enact the anthropological narrative of the inevitable demise of American Indians and their culture in the wake of modernity's advancement. Such an ending would, furthermore, drastically alter the romance plot that, as Burnham reminds us, "end[s] with the prospect of a future family" (99), though in the typical plot of the earlier frontier romance, this future family satisfied "the desire for marital, and American, union" (99). At the end of the novel, Cogewea and Jim do marry, producing the sentimental closure expected of a Western romance, but their union also brings the "world" back into an intersubjective configuration with Cogewea. In the last chapter, "A Voice from the Buffalo Skull," the material world speaks to Cogewea, encouraging her to recognize her love for the other "half-breed," Jim LaGrinder. In this scene, Jim is approaching Cogewea at the Buffalo Butte:

> Her eyes dropped to the old skull. She started visibly! *Could* she be deceived? A voice seemed to issue from its cavernous depths in the Indian tongue; a laudation of—
> *"The Man! The Man! The Man!"*
> Then it was accusing; a plea of pity that such deep and honorable love should be requited with nothing more than insipid friendship.
> The voice ceased as suddenly and as mysteriously as it came. (282, emphasis in original)

McWhorter footnotes this last sentence to give it anthropological context: "To hear voices from inanimate objects as intermediary to the Great Spirit or Great Maker, is not uncommon in Indian philosophy" (302, footnote 1). Though McWhorter's intrusive authentication of this fictional moment comes across as cumbersome and humorous (adding to the humor, perhaps, of the passage's melodramatic typography), the buffalo skull brings back "the dim misty past," still in the past—it is a skull, and not a live buffalo, but nonetheless a past that, as it were, speaks to Cogewea's present. It is the return of this "world" which effects and blesses her marriage with Jim, though it is not a return to an essentialized American Indian subject. Modernity has irreducibly changed, or "bred," American Indian subjectivity. And Mourning Dove has created a "breed" novel, because her heroine and her people cannot yet afford a "modernist" ending.

And yet it is also true that the novel's ending accommodates the new order: It is through marriage that Cogewea further assimilates to the dominant culture's family structure, and it is only by virtue of her marriage that she loses her legal vulnerability as a single "squaw" to land-scheming "Easterners." In these ways, by writing the conventional marriage plot, Mourning Dove is unable to transgress the genre's enforcement of gendered economies of racial modernity. But unlike the frontier romances that interwove national union with marital union at the narrative's closure, stabilizing national family descent and historical right to land usurpation from Mexico and Native Americans, *Cogewea's* marital union does not enforce legal land theft. Since *Cogewea* ends with Cogewea's marriage to Jim LaGrinder, the romance plot implies the failure of assimilationist land schemes and pressures. Jim says to Cogewea, " 'We despised *breeds* are in a zone of our own and when we break from the corral erected about us we meet up with trouble. I only wish that the fence could not be scaled by the soulless creatures who have ever preyed upon us' " (283, emphasis in original). A few paragraphs later, Jim refers again to the metaphor of the "corral": " 'S'pose we remain together in that there corral you spoke of as bein' built 'round us by the Shoyahpee?' " (283). This is a different "corralling" of the world. And even the "corral" Jim wants to keep as a border between the white world and the world of the "breeds" is not rigidly enforced in the novel because both of Cogewea's sisters voluntarily enter into interracial marriages. One marries "a polished and wealthy Parisian scholar" (285) and the other is the wife of the ranch owner, John Carter, a man of Scottish heritage. While stabilized by marriage, these racial crossings keep alive—and further embody—the novel's exposure of the exclusions of the sentimental plot.

Mourning Dove also incorporates a final plot twist that resonates with DuPlessis's "writing beyond the ending" and suggests multiple levels of ironic comment on Cogewea's position as a modern subject. Cogewea receives a telegram stating that her estranged father has died, and though he wrote a new will leaving his estate and wealth to his second wife, "a technical flaw" in the will means that Cogewea and her sisters will actually inherit "a quarter million dollars each" (284). A fairytale ending for sure, but one that makes the "Shoyahpee" the butt of his own joke. In the final paragraph, the narrative abruptly shifts into Densmore's perspective "[i]n a cheap boarding house in an eastern city," where he reads in a newspaper about Cogewea's inheritance and wedding to Jim (284–85). Ironically, the "law" does give Densmore his comeuppance, though clearly not in the way intended by its creators. While Cogewea does not inherit land from her remiss father/Fatherland, the money she does receive implies that she and Jim may be able to protect the borders of their "corral" from other Densmores. The novel's ending is therefore a usurpation of modernity's law by its victims and through their positioning as sentimental subjects.

Ultimately, the novel's reassertion of the polyglot space of the ranch against the criminally opportunistic "white man" strengthens Mourning Dove's argument for eschewing a nostalgic view of American Indian subjectivity as unified with the natural world. Such a conflation of the "primitive" with "nature" aids and abets the culture-exterminating practices of federal Indian policy and justifies the genocidal practices of the state. Instead, Mourning Dove presents us with a modern Native American subject, fragmented by modernity's spatial-legal configuration but not destroyed by it.

REREADING MODERNISM

Mourning Dove finds a powerful entry into the controversies of modernity and modernism through the back door of sentimentalism. To understand her appropriation of genre as *self-consciously critical,* without immediately dismissing it as antimodernist, gives us insight into the formal experimentation her novel undertakes. As Mourning Dove "invades" the literary space of white readers and writers, she enters as an already "bred" or sentimentalized figure. Her power to write a "radical" or "modernist" text is limited by this condition. Yet this entering, as it were, of the center by the already appropriated margin might also suggest another kind of displacement of the center, as Rita Felski acknowledges when she embraces a redefinition of the modern that reshapes "our sense of history and time, continuity and rupture, revolution and tradition" (61). Mourning Dove does more than merely remind us of modernism's repression of certain histories in its borrowing from the "primitive" to produce a revolutionary aesthetic. Mourning Dove forces us to confront the spatiality, to use Soja's term, of historical ruptures and the ontological *dis*location and *dis*ruption obtained by modernity and erased by modernism.

Accordingly, Mourning Dove's attempt to deconstruct and then reconstruct modern American Indian subjectivity through the historical and spatial matrix of racial embodiment may open up new readings of canonically modernist texts. Thus, we can see how novels such as *Cogewea* share a continuum, a history, and a critical project with modernism, and against it. It is in reading otherwise, from outside the enclaves of white modernism, that we see the radical break Mourning Dove makes with modernity's ontology of the colonized, the "primitive," and the racialized other. Seeing this "break" then allows us to reread canonical modernists such as Virginia Woolf and Gertrude Stein with an eye to the spatiality of race, subjectivity, and language that limits their experimentality.

Those few phenomenological moments in which we can trace *Cogewea*'s reconfiguration of modern Native American subjectivity resonate, retrospectively, with the intersubjective experiments of Woolf and Stein. Woolf deliberately orients her characters' subjective perception through spatial embodiment in *To the Lighthouse,* when the narrative weaves in and out of several perspectives in Part I, "The Window," as the characters circle around Mrs. Ramsay, the "Angel in the House." Famously, sometimes the shifts in perspective occur within a single sentence, as in the following:

She [Mrs. Ramsay] knitted with firm composure, slightly pursing her lips and, without being aware of it, so stiffened and composed the lines of her face in a habit of sternness that when her husband passed, though he was chuckling at the thought that Hume, the philosopher, grown enormously fat, had stuck in a bog, he could not help noting, as he passed, the sternness at the heart of her beauty. (64)

The consciousnesses of the characters interconnect within paragraphs and sentences, and in their spatial organization around the central figure of Mrs. Ramsay. Likewise, Woolf uses shared objects of perception[10] to orient her characters' subjectivity, as when Lily and Mr. Bankes watch the waves on the beach and "both felt a common hilarity, excited by the moving waves" (20). In summary, the narrator of "The Window" works to weave together the consciousnesses, the insides, of the novel's characters who otherwise stand at great distances from each other in the external world, literally, and metaphorically, since they occupy different subject positions.

In Stein's *Tender Buttons* the author/narrator introduces us to rooms where she is always "there behind the door" (64) but never revealed to us except indirectly through the language of her outside, that is, the objects in her house. The central reason why we enter these rooms and these pages, to find Stein *in* them, is then frustrated. She knows this and so orders us to "Act so that there is no use in a centre" (63). Stein's text circles around a *particular* absent body made present through the text's encoded language: the sexual other. But unlike other texts in which homosexuality is represented by silences or gaps in the narration, *Tender Buttons* transforms the signifieds represented by signifiers and encodes lesbian sexuality into things—red roses, hats, a feather, shudders, and so on. Stein thus inverts the usual mimetic function of language in orienting us spatially to represent lesbian sexuality.

In writing a novel about her characters' bodily orientation in space, Mourning Dove shares a project with these authors. Indeed, in doing so all of them expose the limits of the tradition of sentimental fiction, especially for representing the embodiment of women. Though Stein's and Woolf's projects more fundamentally rearrange the phenomenological landscape of language, perhaps they have more in common with Mourning Dove than it would seem at first glance. All three work to de-form and de-naturalize the reader's relationship to "traditional" textual bodies, as well as othered bodies. They create disorientation for readers who don't relinquish conventional, representational modes of reading. They respond to modernity's understanding of the subject by questioning the conventional boundaries of the self. They re-envision the temporal and spatial dimensions of intersubjectivity.

However, their projects and Mourning Dove's project diverge sharply when it comes to the permeation of space and body by race. Stein's word play encounters limits when language is so embedded in the materiality of the body that language replicates the very violence it signifies by fragmenting the image of the body into racialized parts. For example, in the "Food" section of *Tender Buttons*, Stein writes, "[N]eedless are niggers and

a sample sample set of old eaten butterflies with spoons" (55). Racialized language reinscribes the difference on which binary systems rest—
white–black, male–female, outside–inside—in its resistance to non-sense.
Stein's modernism, as I more thoroughly argue elsewhere,[11] positions itself against mimetic representation and yet has trouble *dis*locating the one-
to-one correspondence of the othered body and racialized language. In
Woolf's *To the Lighthouse,* the transition from the "Angel in the House"
figure of the nineteenth century to the "writing beyond the ending" of
the Modern Woman (i.e., Lily Briscoe) depends upon an "other." In "Time
Passes," the second section of the novel, Mrs. McNab "'works' structurally
at the center of the novel to reposition an ideological dichotomy of private
and public so that a new female subject may be negotiated in contest but
also in compromise with dominant representations of women's 'nature'"
(233).[12] And, as Patrick McGee has argued, Woolf's *The Waves* offers a critique of imperialism that nonetheless "depends on the ethnocentric mapping of the world into areas of light and areas of darkness" (645), a trope
that surfaces in colonial fiction no matter how self-reflexive.[13]

However, similar to canonical modernists like Woolf and Stein, form *is*
the substance of Mourning Dove's novel. And, in this sense, her novelistic
critiques of form are experimental. *Cogewea* thus challenges generic conventions and yet is *other than* exclusive understandings of formal experimentation in modernism. Aldon Lynn Nielsen argues in this collection that
positing an "alternative modernity" means "black writers have had to steal
past the disciplinary boundaries erected by whiteness around modernity,
to slip inside modernity to demonstrate that they had been there all along."
Similarly, by demonstrating that Mourning Dove engages in a critique of
modernity's practices, I argue that her innovations shaped emerging definitions of the modern subject. Moreover, instead of asking if Mourning
Dove and other non-canonical writers are modernists, we might ask how
writers such as Mourning Dove challenge the assumed dominant claim
modernism has on experimentality. An understanding of the legacy of modernity in the long view enables us to see a wider range of "innovations"
in the short view of early-twentieth-century fiction that are at once formal,
historical, and ontological.

NOTES

I am grateful to Laura Doyle and Ron Welburn for their advice on this essay.

    1. Mourning Dove is another name for Okanogan writer and activist
Christine Quintasket (1888–1936). *Cogewea* is the second published novel written
by a Native American woman. (S. Alice Callahan's *Wynema: A Child of the Forest*
was the first.) *Cogewea*'s original editor, Lucullus Virgil McWhorter, is a controversial figure because his editing went beyond including footnotes and other ex-
tratextual apparatus, to injecting an overt political and anthropological discourse

into Mourning Dove's narrative. A final edit he published was never approved by Mourning Dove before its publication. For a more complete history of Mourning Dove and McWhorter's collaboration, see the introduction by Dexter Fisher (a.k.a. Alice Poindexter Fisher) in the 1981 edition of *Cogewea* (Lincoln: University of Nebraska Press).

2. Laura Wexler, "Tender Violence: Literary Eavesdropping, Domestic Fiction, and Educational Reform," in *The Culture of Sentiment: Race, Gender, and Sentimentality in Nineteenth-Century America* (New York: Oxford University Press, 1992), p. 15. See also Glenn Hendler's *Structures of Feeling in Nineteenth-Century American Literature* (Chapel Hill: University of North Carolina Press, 2001).

3. *Sentimental Modernism: Women Writers and the Revolution of the Word* (Bloomington: Indiana University Press, 1991).

4. See Michael North, *The Dialect of Modernism: Race, Language, and Twentieth-Century Literature* (New York: Oxford University Press, 1994).

5. Burnham, *Captivity and Sentiment: Cultural Exchange in American Literature, 1682–1861* (Hanover, N.H.: Dartmouth College, 1997).

6. In *Playing Indian*, Philip J. Deloria examines the romanticized appropriation of white notions of authentic Indianness in the early twentieth century as a tonic for the artificiality of modern urban industrialization and mass-mediated culture. American Indians were not passive bystanders in this cultural kidnapping. As American Indians themselves participated as models and teachers in the youth cultures of Boy Scouts and Camp Fire Girls, they were attempting to control a "potential power in mediating between modern and primitive" (Deloria 122). This mediation on the part of real Indians involved "using antimodern primitivism to defend native cultures against the negative stereotypes left over from colonial conquest" (Deloria 122).

7. The Stemteemä's tales are integrated into the novel in several chapters as lessons or warnings to Cogewea about Densmore and the white man's historical perfidy. These chapters represent another way in which Mourning Dove revises generic conventions.

8. Merleau-Ponty, *The Visible and the Invisible* (Evanston, Ill.: Northwestern University Press, 1968).

9. In "Indian and White in the Inland Empire: The Contest for the Land, 1880–1912," Herman J. Deutsch provides evidence that would suggest Mourning Dove's plot line may have historical precedent. He describes newspaper ads and other accounts of active solicitation of American Indian wives by white men, and vice versa, as a way of taking advantage of allotment policies that benefited "squaw men" and "mixed bloods" (50). *Pacific Northwest Quarterly* 47.1 (April 1956).

10. In *Bordering on the Body* (New York: Oxford University Press, 1994), Laura Doyle uses the term "intercorporeal narrative practice" to describe the use of objects as pivots between consciousnesses in *To the Lighthouse*.

11. Justine Dymond, "'Mixing the Outside with the Inside': The Phenomenological Challenge to the Inside/Outside Dichotomy in *To the Lighthouse* and *Tender Buttons*," forthcoming in Gail Weiss, ed., *Intertwinings: Merleau-Pontian Reflections on Body, World, and Intersubjectivity*.

12. Mary Lou Emery, "'Robbed of Meaning': The Work at the Center of *To the Lighthouse*," *Modern Fiction Studies* 38.1 (Spring 1992): 217–34.

13. Patrick McGee, "The Politics of Modernist Form: Or, Who Rules *The Waves*?" *Modern Fiction Studies* 38.3 (Autumn 1992): 631–50.

WORKS CITED

Abramson, Howard S. *National Geographic: Behind America's Lens on the World*. New York: Crown Publishers, 1987.

Acton, Thomas. *Gypsy Politics and Social Change: The Development of Ethnic Ideology and Pressure Politics among British Gypsies from Victorian Reformism to Romany Nationalism*. London: Routledge and Kegan Paul, 1974.

Adams, Eleanor N. *Old English Scholarship in England from 1566–1880*. New Haven, Conn.: Yale University [dissertation], 1917.

Afsaruddin, Asma, and A. H. Mathias Zahniser, eds. *Humanism, Culture, and Language in the Near East: Studies in Honor of Georg Krotkoff*. Winona Lake, Ind.: Eisenbrauns, 1997.

Aghacy, Samira. "Domestic Spaces in Lebanese War Fiction: Entrapment or Liberation?" *Crisis and Memory: The Representation of Space in Modern Levantine Narrative*. Ed. Ken Seigneurie. Wiesbaden: Reichert Verlag, 2003. 83–100.

———. "To See with the Naked Eye: Problems of Vision in Hassan Daoud's *The Mathilde Building*." *Arabic and Middle Eastern Literatures* 3.2 (2000): 205–17.

Ahmad, Aijaz. "The Politics of Literary Postcoloniality." *Contemporary Postcolonial Theory: A Reader*. Ed. Mogia Padmini. Delhi: Oxford University Press, 1997. 276–93.

Aldington, Richard. "Blast." *Egoist* 1 (15 July 1914): 272.

Alonso, Carlos. *The Burden of Modernity: The Rhetoric of Cultural Discourse in Spanish America*. Oxford: Oxford University Press, 1998.

Althusser, Louis, and Balibar, Étienne. *Reading Capital*. New York: Verso, 1979.

Ambrosius, Lloyd E. *Wilsonianism: Woodrow Wilson and His Legacy in American Foreign Relations*. New York: Macmillan, 2002.

Anderson, Amanda. *The Powers of Distance: Cosmopolitanism and the Cultivation of Detachment*. Princeton, N.J.: Princeton University Press, 2001.

Anderson, Benedict. *Imagined Communities: Reflections on the Origin and Spread of Nationalism*. New York: Verso, 1991.

Andrade, Carlos Drummond. *Poesia completa e prosa*. Rio de Janeiro: Aguilar, 1973.

Andrade, Mário de. *Obra escogida. Novela cuento ensayo epistolario*. Caracas: Biblioteca Ayacucho, 1979.

———. *Poesias completas*. Belo Horizonte. Rio de Janeiro: Villa Rica, 1993.

Andrade, Oswald de. *Obra escogida*. Caracas: Biblioteca Ayacucho, 1981.

Appadurai, Arjun. *Modernity at Large: Cultural Dimensions of Globalization*. Minneapolis: University of Minnesota Press, 1996.

Appiah, Anthony. "Is the Post- in Postmodernism the Post- in Postcolonial?" *Critical Inquiry* 17 (1991): 336–57.

———. "Race, Culture, Identity: Misunderstood Connections." *Color Conscious: The Political Morality of Race*. Eds. K. Anthony Appiah and Amy Guttman. Princeton, N.J.: Princeton University Press, 1996. 30–105.

Archer-Straw, Patrine. *Negrophilia: Avant-Garde Paris and Black Culture in the 1920s*. London: Thames and Hudson, 2000.

Arkoun, Mohammad. *L'Humanisme arabe au IVe/IXe siècle: Miskawayh, philosophe et historien*. Paris: Vrin, 1982.

Armah, Ayi Kwei. *The Beautyful Ones Are Not Yet Born*. Boston: Houghton Mifflin, 1968.

Arnold, Guy. *Wars in the Third World since 1945*. London: Cassell, 1995.

Artaud, Antonin. "The Theater of Cruelty." *The Theater and its Double*. New York: Grove, 1958. 89–100.

Attiyeh, Ahmad Mohammad. *Al-Iltizam wa-al-Thawra fi al-A^ɔdab al-A^crabiyya al-Haditha* (Commitment and Revolution in Modern Arabic Literature). Beirut: Dar al-A^cwda, 1974.

Augstein, Hannah Franziska. 1996. "Introduction." *Race: The Origins of an Idea, 1760–1850*. Ed. Hannah Franziska Augstein. Bristol: Thoemmes Press, 1996. ix–xxxiii.

Backscheider, Paula. *Spectacular Politics: Theatrical Power and Mass Culture in Early Modern England*. Baltimore: Johns Hopkins University Press, 1993.

Badawi, M. M. "Commitment in Contemporary Arabic Literature." *Critical Perspectives on Modern Arabic Literature*. Ed. Issa J. Boullata. Boulder, Colo.: Three Continents Press, 1980. 23–44.

Bailyn, Bernard. *The Peopling of British America*. New York: Vintage Books, 1988 [1986].

Baker, Houston. *Modernism and the Harlem Renaissance*. Chicago: University of Chicago Press, 1987.

Balibar, Étienne. "Ambiguous Universality." *differences* 7.1 (1995): 48–74.

———. "The Nation Form: History and Ideology." *Race, Nation, Class: Ambiguous Identities*. Eds. Étienne Balibar and Immanuel Wallerstein. London: Verso, 1998. 86–106.

———. "Racism and Nationalism." *Race, Nation, Class: Ambiguous Identities*. Eds. Étienne Balibar and Immanuel Wallerstein. London: Verso, 1998. 37–67.

Baraka, Amiri. *Blues People*. New York: William Morrow and Company, 1963.

Barakat, Hoda. *Hajar al-Dahik*. London: Riad al-Rayyes, 1990. Translated by Sophie Bennett as *The Stone of Laughter*. London: Garnet, 1994.

Barbeito, Patricia Felisa. " 'Making Generations' in Jacobs, Larsen, and Hurston: A Genealogy of Black Women's Writing." *American Literature* 70.2 (June 1998): 365–95.

Barkan, Elazar, and Ronald Bush, eds. *Prehistories of the Future: The Primitivist Project and the Culture of Modernism*. Stanford, Calif.: Stanford University Press, 1995.

Barker-Benfield, G. J. *The Culture of Sensibility: Sex and Society in Eighteenth-Century Britain*. Chicago: University of Chicago Press, 1992.

Barrett, James R. "Americanization from the Bottom Up: Immigration and the Remaking of the Working Class in the United States, 1880–1930." *Discovering America: Essays on the Search for an Identity*. Eds. David Thelan and Frederick E. Hoxie. Urbana: University of Illinois Press, 1994. 162–86.

Batker, Carol J. *Reforming Fictions: Native, African and Jewish American Women's Literature and Journalism in the Progressive Era*. New York: Columbia University Press, 2000.

Baudelaire, Charles. "The Painter of Modern Life." *The Painter of Modern Life and Other Essays*. London: Phaidon, 1964. 1–40.

Baudrillard, Jean. *La Transparence du mal: Essai sur les phénomènes extrêmes*. Paris: Galilée, 1990.

Behlmer, George K. "The Gypsy Problem in Victorian England." *Victorian Studies* 28 (1985): 231–55.

Benítez-Rojo, Antonio. *The Repeating Island: The Caribbean and the Postmodern Perspec-

tive. 2nd ed. Translated by James E. Maraniss. Durham, N.C.: Duke University Press, 1996.

Benjamin, Walter. *The Arcades Project.* Cambridge, Mass.: Harvard University Press, 1999.

———. *Illuminations.* New York: Schocken Books, 1968.

Berman, Jessica. *Modernist Fiction, Cosmopolitanism and the Politics of Community.* Cambridge: Cambridge University Press, 2001.

Berman, Marshall. *All That Is Solid Melts into Air: The Experience of Modernity.* New York: Penguin, 1988.

Berry, Faith. *Langston Hughes: Before and Beyond Harlem.* New York: Citadel, 1992.

Bersani, Leo. "Sociability and Cruising." *Umbr(a)* (2002): 9–23.

Bhabha, Homi K. " 'Race,' Time and the Revision of Modernity." *Oxford Literary Review* 13 (1981): 193–219.

Blight, David W. "W. E. B. Du Bois and the Struggle for American Historical Memory." *History and Memory in African-American Culture.* Eds. Geneviève Fabre and Robert O'Meally. New York: Oxford University Press, 1994.

Bliss, Robert M. *Revolution and Empire: English Politics and the American Colonies in the Seventeenth Century.* New York: Manchester University Press, 1990.

Boone, Joseph. *Libidinal Currents: Sexuality and the Shaping of Modernism.* Chicago: University of Chicago Press, 1998.

Booth, Howard J., and Nigel Rigby, eds. *Modernism and Empire.* New York: Manchester University Press, 2000.

Boullata, Issa J., ed. *Critical Perspectives on Modern Arabic Literature.* Boulder, Colo.: Three Continents Press, 1980.

Bourdieu, Pierre. *The Field of Cultural Production: Essays on Art and Literature.* New York: Columbia University Press, 1993.

Bowen, John. "The Politics of Redemption: Eliot and Benjamin." *The Waste Land.* Eds. Tony Davies and Nigel Wood. Buckingham and Philadelphia: Open University Press, 1994. 29–54.

Brenner, Robert. *Merchants and Revolution: Commercial Change, Political Conflict, and London's Overseas Traders, 1550–1653.* Princeton, N.J.: Princeton University Press, 1993.

Brettell, Richard R. *Modern Art 1851–1929.* Oxford: Oxford University Press, 1999.

Breuer, Joseph, and Sigmund Freud. *Studies in Hysteria.* Trans. James Strachey. New York: Basic Books, 1957.

Brinkley, Roberta Florence. *Arthurian Legend in the Seventeenth Century.* Baltimore: Johns Hopkins University Press, 1932.

Brint, Steven. "*Gemeinschaft* Revisited: A Critique and Reconstruction of the Community Concept." *Sociological Theory* 19.1 (March 2001): 1–23.

Brooker, Peter. "Modernism Deferred: Langston Hughes, Harlem and Jazz Montage." *Locations of Literary Modernism: Region and Nation in British and American Modernist Poetry.* Eds. Alex Davis and Lee M. Jenkins. Cambridge: Cambridge University Press, 2000. 231–47.

———. "Reconstructions." *Modernism/Postmodernism.* Ed. Peter Brooker. New York: Longman, 1992. 1–33.

Brown, Bill. "How to Do Things with Things (A Toy Story)." *Critical Inquiry* 24 (1998): 935–64.

Burke, Edmund. *A Philosophical Enquiry into the Origin of Our Ideas of the Sublime and Beautiful.* Notre Dame, Ind.: University of Notre Dame Press, 1968.

Burnham, Michelle. *Captivity and Sentiment: Cultural Exchange in American Literature, 1682–1861.* Hanover, N.H.: Dartmouth College, 1997.

Butler, Christopher. *Early Modernism: Literature, Music and Painting in Europe 1900–1916.* Oxford: Clarendon Press, 1994.

Callinocos, Alex. *Against Postmodernism: A Marxist Critique*. Oxford: Polity Press, 1989.

Canclini, Néstor Garcia. *Hybrid Cultures: Strategies for Leaving and Entering Modernity*. Trans. Christopher L. Chiappari and Silvia L. López. Minneapolis: University of Minnesota Press, 1995.

Carby, Hazel. "The Politics of Fiction, Anthropology, and the Folk: Zora Neale Hurston." *History and Memory in African-American Culture*. Eds. Geneviève Fabre and Robert O'Meally. New York: Oxford University Press, 1994. 28–44.

———. *Reconstructing Womanhood: The Emergence of the Afro-American Woman Novelist*. New York: Oxford, 1987.

Carter, Michael G. "Humanism and the Language Sciences in Medieval Islam." *Humanism, Culture, and Language in the Near East: Studies in Honor of Georg Krotkoff*. Eds. Asma Afsaruddin and A. H. Mathias Zahniser. Winona Lake, Ind.: Eisenbrauns, 1997. 27–38.

Cartier-Bresson, Henri. *The Decisive Moment*. New York: Simon and Schuster, 1952.

———. *Henri Cartier-Bresson in India*. London: Thames and Hudson, 1987.

Caruth, Cathy. "Introduction." *Trauma: Explorations in Memory*. Ed. Cathy Caruth. Baltimore: Johns Hopkins University Press, 1995. 3–12.

Cascardi, Anthony J. *The Subject of Modernity*. Cambridge: Cambridge University Press, 1992.

Certeau, Michel de. *The Practice of Everyday Life*. Vol. 1. Trans. Steven Rendall. Berkeley: University of California Press, 1984.

Chakrabarty, Dipesh. *Provincializing Europe: Postcolonial Thought and Historical Difference*. Princeton, N.J.: Princeton University Press, 2000.

Chang, Sung-sheng Yvonne. *Literary Culture in Taiwan: Martial Law to Market Law*. New York: Columbia University Press, 2004.

———. *Modernism and the Nativist Resistance: Contemporary Chinese Fiction from Taiwan*. Durham, N.C.: Duke University Press, 1993.

———. "*The Terrorizer* and the 'Great Divide' in Contemporary Taiwan's Cultural Development." *Island on the Edge: Taiwan New Cinema and After*. Eds. Chris Berry and Feiyi Lu. Hong Kong: Hong Kong University Press, 2005. 13–25.

Chen, Letty Lingchei. "Reading between Chinese Modernism and Modernity: A Methodological Reflection." *Chinese Literature* 24 (2002): 175–88.

Clark, Suzanne. *Sentimental Modernism: Women Writers and the Revolution of the Word*. Bloomington: Indiana University Press, 1991.

Clemmen, Yves. "Nella Larsen's *Quicksand*: A Narrative of Difference." *CLA Journal* 40.4 (June 1997): 458–66.

Cole, Sarah. "Conradian Alienation and Imperial Intimacy." *Modern Fiction Studies* 44.2 (1998): 251–81.

Correa, Charles. 1999. "India Seminar." http://www.India-seminar.com/1999/481/481%20correa.htm

Crone, G. R. *Modern Geographers: An Outline of Progress in Geography Since AD 1800*. Rev. ed. London: The Royal Geographical Society, 1970.

Al-Daif, Rashid. "Al-Nitaj al-Riwaʾfi Lubnan: Tayyarat wa Ittijahat" (Novelistic Production in Lebanon: Currents and Trends). *Fusul* 16.4 (Spring 1998): 167–72.

———. *Fusha Mustahdafa Bayna al-Nu ʿas wa-al-Nawm*. Beirut: Mukhtarat, 1983. Translated by Nirvana Tanoukhi as *Passage to Dusk*. Austin: University of Texas Press, 2001.

———. *Nahiyat al-Baraʾa*. Beirut: al-Massar, 1997. Translated by Paula Haydar as *This Side of Innocence*. New York: Interlink, 2001.

———. *Taqniyyat al-Buʾs* (Techniques of Misery). Beirut: Dar Mukhtarat, 1989.

———. *ʿAzizi al-Sayyid Kawabata*. Beirut: Mukhtarat, 1995. Translated by Paul Starkey as *Dear Mr Kawabata*. London: Quartet, 1999.

Dallmayr, Fred. "The Discourse of Modernity: Hegel, Nietzsche, Heidegger and Habermas." *Habermas and the Unfinished Project of Modernity: Critical Essays on the Philosophical Discourse of Modernity.* Eds. Mauricio Passeria d'Entrèves and Seyla Benhabib. Cambridge, Mass.: MIT Press, 1997. 59–96.

Daoud, Hassan. *Binayat Mathilde.* Beirut: Dar al-Tanwir, 1983. Translated by Peter Theroux as *The House of Mathilde.* London: Granta, 1999.

Darío, Rubén. "Palabras liminares." *Prosas profanas.* Vol. 2 of *Obras completas.* Madrid: Mundo Latino, 1917.

Darwish, Mahmoud. *Shay ʾn ʿn al-Watan* (Something on the Nation). Beirut: Dar al-ʿwda, 1971.

Davidson, Cathy. *Revolution and the Word: The Rise of the Novel in America.* New York: Oxford, 1986.

Davis, Thadious M. *Nella Larsen, Novelist of the Harlem Renaissance: A Woman's Life Unveiled.* Baton Rouge: Louisiana State University Press, 1994.

Davis, William. "The Essential in Geography." *American Geographical Society of New York Bulletin* 36.8 (1904): 470–73.

Dean, Seamus. *Strange Country.* Oxford: Oxford University Press, 1997.

Dean, Tim. "The Germs of Empires: *Heart of Darkness*, Colonial Trauma, and the Historiography of AIDS." *The Psychoanalysis of Race.* Ed. Christopher Lane. New York: Columbia University Press, 1998. 305–29.

De Jongh, James L. "The Image of Black Harlem in Literature." *New York: City as Text.* Eds. Christopher Mulvey and John Simons. London: Macmillan, 1990. 131–46.

Deleuze, Gilles, and Félix Guattari. *A Thousand Plateaus: Capitalism and Schizophrenia* [1980]. Trans. Brian Massumi. Minneapolis: Minnesota University Press, 1987.

Deloria, Philip J. *Playing Indian.* New Haven, Conn.: Yale University Press, 1998.

Deutsch, Herman J. "Indian and White in the Inland Empire: The Contest for the Land, 1880–1912." *Pacific Northwest Quarterly* 47.1 (April 1956): 44–51.

Dhwan, R. K. *Arundhati Roy: The Novelist Extraordinary.* New Delhi: Prestige Books, 1999.

Dickinson, Robert E. *The Makers of Modern Geography.* London: Routledge, 1969.

Dirlik, Arif. "The Postcolonial Aura: Third World Criticism in the Age of Global Capitalism." *Critical Inquiry* 20.1 (1993): 328–56.

Dittmar, Linda. "When Privilege Is No Protection: The Woman Artist in *Quicksand* and *The House of Mirth.*" *Writing the Woman Artist: Essays on Poetics, Politics, and Portraiture.* Ed. Suzanne W. Jones. Philadelphia: University of Pennsylvania Press, 1991.

Douglas, Ann. "Periodizing the American Century: Modernism, Postmodernism, and Postcolonialism in the Cold War Context." *Modernism/ Modernity* 5.3 (1998): 71–98.

Douglas, Mary. *Purity and Danger: An Analysis of Concepts of Pollution and Taboo.* New York: Routledge, 1966.

Dove, Mourning. *Cogewea, the Half-Blood: A Depiction of the Great Montana Cattle Range* [1927]. Ed. Lucullus C. McWhorter. Lincoln: University of Nebraska Press, 1981.

Doyle, Laura. "The Body against Itself in Faulkner's Phenomenology of Race." *American Literature* 73.2 (June 2001): 339–64.

———. *Bordering on the Body: The Racial Matrix of Modern Fiction and Culture.* New York: Oxford University Press, 1994.

———. "The Flat, the Round, and Gertrude Stein: Race and the Shape of Modern(ist) History." *Modernism/Modernity* 7.2 (2000): 249–71.

D'Souza, Dinesh. *The End of Racism: Principles of a Multicultural Society.* New York: The Free Press, 1995.

DuBois, W. E. B. *The Autobiography of W. E. B. DuBois: A Soliloquy on Viewing My Life from the Last Decade of its First Century.* New York: International Publishers, 1968.

——. *Black Reconstruction in America 1860–1880* [1935]. New York: Atheneum, 1972.

——. *Darkwater: Voices from within the Veil* [1920]. New York: A.M.S. Press, 1969.

——. "The Realities in Africa." *The Oxford W. E. B. DuBois Reader.* Ed. Eric J. Sundquist. New York: Oxford University Press, 1996. 653–63.

——. *Voices of a Black Nation: Political Journalism in the Harlem Renaissance.* Ed. Theodore G. Vincent. San Francisco: Ramparts, 1973.

DuCille, Ann. *The Coupling Convention: Sex, Text, and Tradition in Black Women's Fiction.* New York: Oxford, 1993.

Duffy, Enda. "Disappearing Dublin: *Ulysses,* Postcoloniality and the Politics of Space." *Semicolonial Joyce.* Eds. Derek Attridge and Marjorie Howes. New York: Cambridge University Press, 2000. 37–58.

DuPlessis, Rachel Blau. *Writing beyond the Ending: Narrative Strategies of Twentieth-Century Women Writers.* Bloomington: Indiana University Press, 1985.

Dymond, Justine. "'Mixing the Outside with the Inside': The Phenomenological Challenge to the Inside/Outside Dichotomy in *To the Lighthouse* and *Tender Buttons.*" *Intertwinings: Merleau-Pontian Reflections on Body, World, and Intersubjectivity.* Ed. Gail Weiss. Forthcoming.

Eagleton, Terry. *The Idea of Culture.* Oxford: Blackwell, 1922.

Edwards, Paul. "Afterward." Wyndham Lewis. *Time and Western Man.* Santa Rosa: Black Sparrow, 1993. 455–508.

——. *Wyndham Lewis: Painter and Writer.* New Haven, Conn.: Yale University Press, 2000.

Eliot, T. S. "Henry James: The Hawthorne Aspect." *Little Review* August 1918. Rptd. in *The Shock of Recognition.* Ed. Edmund Wilson. New York: Random, 1955. 860.

——. *The Letters of T. S. Eliot.* Ed. Valerie Eliot. New York: Harcourt Brace, 1988.

——. "President Wilson." *New Statesman* 9 (1917): 140.

——. "The Use of Poetry and the Use of Criticism." *The Selected Prose of T. S. Eliot.* New York: Farrar, Strauss, 1975. 79–97.

——. "War-Paint and Feathers." *Athenaeum* 4688 (1919): 1036.

——. *The Waste Land: A Facsimile and Transcript of the Original Drafts Including the Annotations of Ezra Pound.* Ed. Valerie Eliot. New York: Harcourt Brace, 1971.

——. "The Waste Land" [1922]. *The Collected Poems and Plays.* London and Boston: Faber and Faber, 1985. 61–80.

Ellmann, Maud. *The Poetics of Impersonality: T. S. Eliot and Ezra Pound.* Brighton: Harvester Press, 1987.

Ellmann, Richard. *James Joyce* [1959]. Oxford: Oxford University Press, 1982.

Emery, Mary Lou. "'Robbed of Meaning': The Work at the Center of *To the Lighthouse.*" *Modern Fiction Studies* 38.1 (Spring 1992): 217–34.

Esteve, Mary. "Nella Larsen's 'Moving Mosaic': Harlem, Crowds, and Anonymity." *American Literary History* 9.2 (Summer 1997): 268–86.

Everett, Anna. *Returning the Gaze: A Genealogy of Black Film Criticism 1909–1949.* Durham, N.C.: Duke University Press, 2001.

Eysteinsson, Astradur. *The Concept of Modernism.* Ithaca, N.Y.: Cornell University Press, 1990.

Fanon, Frantz. *Black Skin, White Masks: The Experience of a Black Man in a White World.* New York: Grove Press, 1967.

——. *The Wretched of the Earth.* Trans. Constance Farrington. New York: Grove Press, 1963.

Felski, Rita. *Doing Time: Feminist Theory and Postmodern Culture.* New York: New York University Press, 2000.

Ferguson, James. *Expectations of Modernity: Myths and Meanings of Urban Life on the Zambian Copperbelt.* Berkeley: University of California Press, 1999.

Ferrer, Ada. 1999. *Insurgent Cuba: Race, Nation, and Revolution, 1868–1898.* Chapel Hill: University of North Carolina Press.

Fisher, Rudolf. "Miss Cynthie." *Classic Fiction of the Harlem Renaissance.* Ed. William L. Andrews. New York: Oxford University Press, 1994. 242–53.

Foner, Philip S., and Richard C. Winchester, eds. *The Anti-Imperialist Reader: A Documentary History of Anti-Imperialism in the United States.* New York: Holmes and Meier, 1984.

Forster, E. M. *The Manuscripts of* A Passage to India. Correlated with Forster's final version by Oliver Stallybrass. New York: Homes and Meier, 1978.

———. *Maurice.* New York: Norton, 1971.

———. *A Passage to India* [1924]. New York: Harcourt Brace, 1984.

Foucault, Michel. "Of Other Spaces." *Diacritics* 16.1 (1986): 22–27.

———. *The Order of Things.* New York: Random House, 1970.

Franke, R., et al. "The Kerala Model of Development: A Debate (Part 1)." *Bulletin of Concerned Asian Scholars* 30.3 (July–September 1998): 25–36.

Fraser, Angus. *The Gypsies.* Oxford: Blackwell, 1992.

Friedman, Susan Stanford. "Definitional Excursions: The Meanings of *Modern/Modernity/Modernism.*" *Modernism/Modernity* 8.3 (2001): 493–513.

———. "Feminism, State Fictions and Violence: Gender, Geopolitics and Transnationalism." *Communal/Plural* 9.1 (2001): 111–29.

———. *Mappings: Feminism and the Cultural Geographies of Encounter.* Princeton, N.J.: Princeton University Press, 1998.

———. "Modernism in a Transnational Landscape: Spatial Poetics, Postcolonialism, and Gender in Césaire's *Cahier/Notebook* and Cha's *Dictée.*" *Paideuma* 32: 1/2/3 (Spring/Fall/Winter 2003): 39–74.

Frobenius, Leo. *The Voice of Africa* [1913]. Trans. Rudolf Blind. New York: Arno Press, 1980.

Fry, Roger. *Vision and Design.* London: Chatto and Windus, 1925.

Furbank, P. N. *E. M. Forster: A Life.* New York: Harcourt Brace, 1981.

García Canclini, Néstor. "Memory and Innovation in the Theory of Art." *The South Atlantic Quarterly* 92.3 (1993): 423–43.

Garrity, Jane. *Step Daughters of England.* London: Macmillan, 2003.

Gaonkar, Dilip Parameshwar, ed. *Alternative Modernities.* Durham, N.C.: Duke University Press, 2001.

Gates, Henry Louis, Jr. "Planet Rap—Notes on the Globalization of Culture." *Field Work: Sites in Literary and Cultural Studies.* Eds. Marjorie Garber, Rebecca L. Walkowitz, Paul B. Franklin. New York: Routledge, 1996.

Ghosh, Amitav. *The Glass Palace.* Toronto: Viking, 2000.

———. Interview [online]. Tehelka.Com. August 7, 2000. http://www.tehelka.com/aspsite/lr080400ghose1.htm [Accessed 09/05/01; the link has since been removed.]

———. "The March of the Novel through History: The Testimony of My Grandfather's Bookcase." *Kenyon Review* 20.2 (Spring 1998): 13–24.

Giddens, Anthony. *The Consequences of Modernity.* Stanford, Calif.: Stanford University Press, 1990.

———. *Modernity and Self-Identity.* Stanford, Calif.: Stanford University Press, 1991.

Giest, Anthony L., and Monleón, José B., eds. *Modernism and Its Margins: Reinscribing Cultural Modernity from Spain and Latin America.* New York: Garland, 1999.

Gikandi, Simon. "Race and the Idea of the Aesthetic." *Michigan Quarterly Review* 40 (Spring 2000): 318–50.

Gilroy, Paul. *The Black Atlantic: Modernity and Double Consciousness.* Cambridge, Mass.: Harvard University Press, 1993.

Glassner, Martin Ira. *Political Geography.* 2nd ed. New York: John Wiley, 1996.

Goldberg, David Theo. *The Racial State.* Malden, Mass.: Blackwell, 2002.

Goldwater, Robert. *Primitivism in Modern Art* [1938]. Cambridge, Mass.: Harvard University Press, 1986.

González Stephan, Beatriz. *La historiografía literaria del liberalismo hispano-americano del siglo XIX.* La Habana: Casa de las Américas, 1987.

Gordon, Lyndall. *Eliot's Early Years.* New York: Oxford University Press, 1977.

———. *Eliot's New Life.* New York: Farrar, Straus and Giroux, 1988.

Graver, David. *The Aesthetics of Disturbance.* Ann Arbor: University of Michigan Press, 1996.

Gray, Jeffrey. "Essence and the Mulatto Traveler: Europe as Embodiment in Nella Larsen's *Quicksand.*" *Novel: A Forum on Fiction* 27.3 (Spring 1994): 257–70.

Green, Christopher. "Expanding the Canon: Roger Fry's Evaluations of the 'Civilized' and the 'Savage.'" *Art Made Modern: Roger Fry's Vision of Art.* Ed. Christopher Green. London: Merrell Holberton, 1999.

Gregg, Veronica. *Jean Rhys's Historical Imagination.* Chapel Hill: University of North Carolina Press, 1995.

Griffith, D. W., dir. *The Birth of a Nation.* VHS. Republic Pictures Home Video, 1991 [1915].

Guinier, Lani. *The Tyranny of the Majority: Fundamental Fairness in Representative Democracy.* New York: The Free Press, 1994.

Gunning, Tom. *D. W. Griffith and the Origins of American Narrative Film: The Early Years at the Biograph.* Urbana: University of Illinois Press, 1991.

Habermas, Jürgen. "Modernity: An Incomplete Project." *New German Critique* 22 (Winter 1981): 37–44.

———. *The Philosophical Discourse of Modernity: Twelve Lectures.* Translated by Frederick G. Lawrence. Cambridge, Mass.: MIT Press, 1987.

Haller, William, ed. *Tracts on Liberty in the Puritan Revolution, 1683–1647.* Vols. 1–3. New York: Columbia University, 1933.

Halperín Donghi, Túlio. *The Contemporary History of Latin America.* Durham, N.C.: Duke University Press, 1993.

Hammond, John. "Between Ourselves." *New Masses* 8 November 1938, 2.

Hancock, Ian. *We Are the Romani People.* Hertfordshire: University of Hertfordshire Press, 2002.

Hannah, Matthew G. *Governmentality and the Mastery of Territory in Nineteenth-Century America.* Cambridge: Cambridge University Press, 2000.

Hansen, Miriam Bratu. "America, Paris, the Alps: Kracauer (and Benjamin) on Cinema and Modernity." *Cinema and the Invention of Modern Life.* Eds. Leo Charney and Vanessa R. Schwartz. Berkeley: University of California Press, 1995. 362–402.

Harlow, Barbara. *Resistance Literature.* New York: Methuen, 1987.

Harrison, Robert L. "The Manuscripts of *A Passage to India.*" Dissertation, University of Texas, Austin, 1964.

Hartman, Geoffrey H. *The Sympathy Paradox: Poetry, Feeling, and Modern Cultural Modernity.* Austin, Tex.: The Harry Ransom Humanities Center Research Center, 1996.

Harvey, David. *The Condition of Postmodernity.* Oxford: Blackwell, 1990.

———. "Cosmopolitanism and the Banality of Geographical Evils." *Public Culture* 12.2 (2000): 529–64.

Haviland, Beverly. "Passing from Paranoia to Plagiarism: The Abject Authorship of Nella Larsen." *Modern Fiction Studies* 43.2 (Summer 1997): 295–318.

Heater, Derek. *National Self-Determination: Woodrow Wilson and His Legacy.* New York: St. Martin's Press, 1994.

Hegel, G. W. F. *Lectures on the Philosophy of World History: Introduction—Reason in History*. Eds. Maurice Cowling, E. Kedourie, G. R. Elton, J. R. Pole, and Walter Ullmann. Trans. H. B. Nisbet. Cambridge: Cambridge University Press, 1998.

———. *The Philosophy of History* [1899]. Trans. John Sibree. New York: Dover, 1956.

Hegeman, Susan. *Patterns for America: Modernism and the Concept of Culture*. Princeton, N.J.: Princeton University Press, 1999.

Herrnstein Smith, Barbara. "Narrative Versions, Narrative Theories." *On Narrative*. Ed. W. J. T. Mitchell. Chicago: University of Chicago Press, 1980. 209–32.

Hill, Bridget, ed. *The First English Feminist: "Reflections upon Marriage" and Other Writings*. New York: St. Martins Press, 1986.

Hogan, Patrick Colm. *Colonialism and Cultural Identity: Crises of Tradition in the Anglophone Literatures of India, Africa, and the Caribbean*. Albany: SUNY Press, 2000.

Hokanson, Robert O'Brien. "Jazzing It Up: The Be-Bop Modernism of Langston." *Mosaic* 31.4 (December 1998): 61–82.

Horkheimer, Max, and Theodor W. Adorno. *Dialectic of Enlightenment: Philosophical Fragments*. Ed. Gunzelin Schmid Noerr. Trans. Edmund Jephcott. Stanford: Stanford University Press, 2002.

Hostetler, Ann E. "The Aesthetics of Race and Gender in Nella Larsen's *Quicksand*." *PMLA* 105.1 (January 1990): 35–46.

Hoxie, Frederick E. *A Final Promise: The Campaign to Assimilate the Indians, 1880–1920*. Lincoln: University of Nebraska Press, 1984.

Hughes, Langston. *The Big Sea: An Autobiography* [1940]. London: Pluto, 1986.

———. "Montage of a Dream Deferred" [1951]. *The Collected Poems of Langston Hughes*. Ed. Arnold Rampersad. New York: Random House, 1994. 387–429.

Hunter, Lynnette. "Blood and Marmalade: Negotiations between the State and the Domestic in George Orwell's Early Novels." *Rewriting the Thirties: Modernism and After*. Eds. Keith Williams and Steven Matthews. London: Longman, 1997.

Hurston, Zora Neale. *Tell My Horse: Voodoo and Life in Haiti and Jamaica*. [1938] New York: Harper & Row, 1990.

Hutcheon, Linda. "Circling the Downspout of Empire: Postcolonialism and Postmodernism." *Past the Last Post: Theorizing Post-Colonialism and Post-Modernism*. Eds. Ian Adam and Helen Tiffin. New York: Harvester Wheatsheaf, 1991. 167–89.

Hutchinson, George. "Subject to Disappearance: Interracial Identity in Nella Larsen's *Quicksand*." *Temples for Tomorrow: Looking Back at the Harlem Renaissance*. Eds. Geneviève Fabre and Michel Feith. Bloomington: Indiana University Press, 2001. 177–92.

Jabra, Jabra Ibrahim. "Modern Arabic Literature and the West." *Critical Perspectives on Modern Arabic Literature*. Ed. Issa J. Boullata. Boulder, Colo.: Three Continents Press, 1980. 7–22.

James, C. L. R. *The Black Jacobins: Toussaint L'Ouverture and the San Domingo Revolution* [1938]. New York: Random House, 1963.

———. "Existentialism and Marxism." Typescript of lecture presented in London. 8 October 1966.

Jameson, Fredric. "Cognitive Mapping." *Marxism and the Interpretation of Culture*. Eds. Cary Nelson and Lawrence Grossberg. Urbana: University of Illinois Press, 1988. 347–60.

———. *Fables of Aggression*. Berkeley: University of California Press, 1979.

———. "Literary Innovation and Modes of Production: A Commentary." *Modern Chinese Literature* 1 (1984): 67–77.

———. *The Political Unconscious: Narrative as a Socially Symbolic Act*. Ithaca, N.Y.: Cornell University Press, 1981.

———. *Postmodernism; or, The Cultural Logic of Late Capitalism*. Durham, N.C.: Duke University Press, 1991.

———. "Remapping Taipei." *New Chinese Cinemas: Forms, Identities, Politics.* Eds. Nick Brown, Paul G. Pickowicz, Vivian Sobchack, and Esther Yau. New York: Cambridge University Press, 1994. 117–50.

———. *A Singular Modernity: Essay on the Ontology of the Present.* New York: Verso, 2002.

Jarraway, David R. "Montage of an Otherness Deferred: Dreaming Subjectivity in Langston Hughes." *American Literature* 68.4 (December 1996): 819–47.

Jay, Gregory S. "Postmodernism in *The Waste Land:* Women, Mass Culture, and Others." *Rereading the New: A Backward Glance at Modernism.* Ed. Kevin J. H. Dettmar. Ann Arbor: University of Michigan Press, 1992. 221–46.

John, Augustus. *Chiaroscuro.* Oxford: Alden, 1952.

Johnson, Barbara. "The Quicksands of the Self: Nella Larsen and Heinz Kohut." *Female Subjects in Black and White: Race, Psychoanalysis, Feminism.* Eds. Elizabeth Abel, Barbara Christian, and Helen Moglen. Berkeley: University of California Press, 1997. 252–65.

Johnson, Michael. *All Honourable Men: The Social Origins of War in Lebanon.* London: Centre for Lebanese Studies and I. B. Tauris, 2001.

Joyce, James. *Dubliners.* New York: Modern Library, 1926.

———. "Ireland, Island of Saints and Sages." *The Critical Writings of James Joyce.* Eds. Mason Ellsworth and Guy Davenport. Ithaca, N.Y.: Cornell University Press, 1989. 153–74.

———. *A Portrait of the Artist as a Young Man.* Boston: St. Martin's, Bedford, 1993.

———. *Ulysses.* New York: Random House, 1986.

Kalaidjian, Walter. "The Edge of Modernism: Genocide and the Poetics of Traumatic Memory." *Modernism, Inc.: Body, Memory, Capital.* Eds. Jani Scandura and Michael Thurston. New York: New York University Press, 2001. 107–32.

Kant, Immanuel. "An Answer to the Question: 'What Is Enlightenment?'" *What Is Enlightenment?* Ed. James Schmidt. Berkeley: University of California Press, 1996. 58–64.

———. *The Critique of Judgment.* Trans. J. H. Bernard. Amherst, N.Y.: Prometheus Books, 2000.

———. *Kant: Political Writings.* Ed. Hans Reiss. Cambridge: Cambridge University Press, 1991.

Kaplan, Carla. "Undesirable Desire: Citizenship and Romance in Modern American Fiction." *Modern Fiction Studies* 43.1 (Spring 1997): 144–69.

Kern, Stephen. *The Culture of Time and Space, 1880–1918.* Cambridge, Mass.: Harvard University Press, 1983.

Kinney, Arthur F. *Humanist Poetics: Thought, Rhetoric, and Fiction in Sixteenth-Century England.* Amherst: University of Massachusetts Press, 1986.

Kliger, Samuel. *The Goths in England: A Study in Seventeenth and Eighteenth Century Thought.* Cambridge, Mass.: Harvard University Press, 1952.

Klug, Francesca. "'Oh to be in England': The British Case Study." *Women-Nation-State.* Eds. Nira Yuval-Davis and Floya Anthias. New York: St. Martin's Press, 1990. 16–35.

Koselleck, Reinhart. *Futures Past: On the Semantics of Historical Time.* Trans. Keith Tribe. Cambridge, Mass.: MIT Press, 1985.

Kozloff, Max. "Remembering Raghubir Singh." *Aperture* 156 (Summer 1999): 96.

Kraemer, Joel L. *Humanism in the Renaissance of Islam: The Cultural Revival during the Buyid Age.* Leiden: E. J. Brill, 1986.

Kupperman, Karen Ordahl. *Providence Island, 1630–1641: The Other Puritan Colony.* New York: Cambridge University Press, 1993.

Lang, Robert, ed. *The Birth of a Nation.* New Brunswick, N.J.: Rutgers University Press, 1997.

Larsen, Nella. *An Intimation of Things Distant: The Collected Fiction of Nella Larsen.* Ed. Charles Larson. New York: Anchor Books, 1992.

———. *Quicksand* and *Passing.* New Brunswick, N.J.: Rutgers, 1988.

Lawrence, D. H. *The Virgin and the Gipsy* [1925/30]. Baltimore: Penguin, 1967.

Laughlin, Charles A. "The Battlefield of Cultural Production: Chinese Literary Mobilization during the War Years." *Journal of Modern Literature in Chinese* 2.1 (July 1998): 83–103.

Lawal, Babatunde. *The Gelede Spectacle: Art, Gender, and Social Harmony in an African Culture.* Seattle: University of Washington Press, 1996.

Leavis, F. R. *The Living Principle: "English" as a Discipline of Thought.* London: Chatto and Windus, 1975.

Lee, Ken. "Orientalism and Gypsylorism." *Social Analysis* 44.2 (November 2000): 129–56.

Lee, Leo Ou-fan. *Shanghai Modern: The Flowering of a New Urban Culture in China, 1930–1945.* Cambridge, Mass.: Harvard University Press, 1999.

Lefebvre, Henri. *The Production of Space.* Trans. Donald Nicholson-Smith. Cambridge, Mass.: Blackwell, 1991.

Levine, June Perry. "An Analysis of the Manuscripts of *A Passage to India.*" *PMLA* 85 (March 1970): 284–94.

Lewis, Wyndham. *The Art of Being Ruled.* Santa Rosa: Black Sparrow, 1989.

———. "Physics of the Not-Self." *Wyndham Lewis: Collected Poems and Plays.* Ed. Alan Munton. Manchester: Carcanet, 1979. 193–204.

———. *Rude Assignment: An Intellectual Autobiography.* Santa Rosa: Black Sparrow, 1984.

———. *Time and Western Man.* Santa Rosa, Calif.: Black Sparrow, 1993.

Lewis, Wyndham, ed. *Blast.* No. 1 (June 1914). Santa Rosa, Calif.: Black Sparrow, 1981.

———. *Blast.* No. 2 (June 1915). Santa Rosa, Calif.: Black Sparrow, 1981.

Linebaugh, Peter, and Marcus Rediker. *The Many-Headed Hydra: Sailors, Slaves, Commoners, and the Hidden History of the Revolutionary Atlantic.* Boston: Beacon, 2000.

Lizst, Franz. *The Gipsy in Music* [1859]. Trans. Edwin Evans. London: New Temple Press, 1926.

Lloyd, David. "Race under Representation." *Culture/Contexture: Explorations in Anthropology and Literary Studies.* Eds. E. Valentine Daniel and Jeffrey M. Peck. Berkeley: University of California Press, 1996. 249–72.

Locke, Alain, ed. *The New Negro* [1925]. New York: Atheneum, 1992.

Lombroso, Cesare. *Criminal Man* [1876]. New York: Putnam, 1911.

Lyon, Janet. "Josephine Baker's Hothouse." *Modernism, Inc.: Body, Memory, Capital.* Eds. Jani Scandura and Michael Thurston. New York: New York University Press, 2001. 29–47.

———. "Sociability in the Metropole: Modernism's Bohemian Salons." *Changes of Address: Essays from the English Institute.* Ed. Barbara Johnson. New York: Routledge, forthcoming.

Lyotard, Jean-François. *Political Writings.* Trans. Bill Readings and Kevin Paul Geiman. Minneapolis: University of Minnesota Press, 1993.

Mack, Phyllis. *Visionary Women: Ecstatic Prophecy in Seventeenth-Century England.* Berkeley: University of California Press, 1992.

Mackinder, Halford J. "The Geographical Pivot of History." *Geographical Journal* 23 (1904). Reprinted in Halford J. Mackinder, *Democratic Ideals and Reality.* New York: Norton, 1962. 241–65.

———. "The Scope and Methods of Geography." *Proceedings of the Royal Geographical Society* (1887). Reprinted in Halford J. Mackinder, *Democratic Ideals and Reality.* New York: Norton, 1962. 211–41.

MacRitchie, David. "The Privileges of the Gypsies." *Journal of the Gypsy Lore Society*, New Series 1.4 (April 1908): 299–313.

Makdisi, George. "Inquiry into the Origins of Humanism." *Humanism, Culture, and Language in the Near East: Studies in Honor of Georg Krotkoff*. Eds. Asma Afsaruddin and A. H. Mathias Zahniser. Winona Lake, Ind.: Eisenbrauns, 1997. 15–26.

———. *The Rise of Humanism in Classical Islam and the Christian West with Special Reference to Scholasticism*. Edinburgh: Edinburgh University Press, 1990.

Malraux, André. *Picasso's Mask*. Trans. June Guicharnaud. New York: Holt, 1974.

Malti-Douglas, Fedwa. "Playing with the Sacred: Religious Intertext in *ʾAdab* Discourse." *Humanism, Culture, and Language in the Near East: Studies in Honor of Georg Krotkoff*. Eds. Asma Afsaruddin and A. H. Mathias Zahniser. Winona Lake, Ind.: Eisenbrauns, 1997. 51–52.

Manganaro, Marc. *Culture, 1922: The Emergence of a Concept*. Princeton, N.J.: Princeton University Press, 2002.

Martí, José. "The Abolition of Slavery in Puerto Rico." *José Martí: Selected Writings*. Ed. and trans. Esther Allen. New York: Penguin, 2002. 314–18.

———. "My Race." *José Martí: Selected Writings*. Ed. and trans. Esther Allen. New York: Penguin, 2002. 318–21.

———. "Oscar Wilde." *Prosas escogidas*. Ed. José Olivio Jiménez. Madrid: Editorial Magisterio Español, 1975. 59–70.

———. "Our America." *José Martí: Selected Writings*. Ed. and trans. Esther Allen. New York: Penguin, 2002. 288–96.

———. "The Truth about the United States." *José Martí: Selected Writings*. Ed. and trans. Esther Allen. New York: Penguin, 2002. 329–33.

———. "Versos sencillos." *José Martí: Selected Writings*. Ed. and trans. Esther Allen. New York: Penguin, 2002. 270–85.

Martin, Robert K., and George Piggford, eds. *Queer Forster*. Chicago: University of Chicago Press, 1997.

Marx, Karl. *Capital*. Vol. 1. Trans. Ben Fowkes. London: Penguin, 1976.

Mattera, Don. *Gone with the Twilight: A Story of Sophiatown*. London: Zed Books, 1987.

Mayall, David. *Gypsy-Travellers in Nineteenth-Century Society*. Cambridge: Cambridge University Press, 1988.

McClintock, Anne. "Angels of Progress: Pitfalls of the Term 'Post-Colonialism.'" *Social Text* 31/32 (1992): 84–98.

McClure, John. *Late Imperial Romance*. New York: Verso, 1994.

McDowell, Deborah E. "'That nameless . . . shameful impulse': Sexuality in Nella Larsen's *Quicksand* and *Passing*." *Black Feminist Criticism and Critical Theory*. Eds. Joe Weixlmann and Houston A. Baker, Jr. Greenwood, Florida: Penkevill, 1988. 139–67.

McElderry, Bruce. "Eliot's Shakespeherian Rag." *American Quarterly* 9 (Summer 1957): 185–86.

McEntee, Ann Marie. "The [Un]Civil Sisterhood of Oranges and Lemons: Female Petitioners and Demonstrators, 1642–53." *Pamphlet Wars: Prose in the English Revolution*. Ed. James Holstun. Portland, Ore.: F. Cass, 1992. 92–111.

McGee, Patrick. "The Politics of Modernist Form: Or, Who Rules *The Waves*?" *Modern Fiction Studies* 38.3 (Autumn 1992): 631–50.

McHale, Brian. *Postmodernist Fiction*. New York: Methuen, 1987.

McKay, Claude. "Home to Harlem." *Classic Fiction of the Harlem Renaissance*. Ed. William L. Andrews. New York: Oxford University Press, 1994. 105–237.

Melville, Herman. *Billy Budd, Sailor*. New York: Penguin, 1986.

Mendle, Michael, ed. *The Putney Debates of 1647: The Army, the Levellers, and the English State*. New York: Cambridge University Press, 2001.

Merleau-Ponty, Maurice. *The Visible and the Invisible.* Evanston, Ill.: Northwestern University Press, 1968.

Meyer, Stefan G. *The Experimental Arabic Novel: Postcolonial Literary Modernism in the Levant.* Albany: State University of New York Press, 2001.

Michaels, Walter Benn. "Anti-Imperial Americanism." *Cultures of United States Imperialism.* Eds. Amy Kaplan and Donald E. Pease. Durham, N.C.: Duke University Press, 1993. 365–91.

———. *Our America: Nativism, Modernism, and Pluralism.* Durham, N.C.: Duke University Press, 1995.

Middleton, Peter. "The Academic Development of *The Waste Land.*" *Demarcating the Disciplines: Philosophy, Literature, Art.* Ed. Samuel Weber. Minneapolis: University of Minnesota Press, 1986. 153–80.

Mignolo, Walter D. *Local History/Global Designs: Coloniality, Subaltern Knowledges and Border Thinking.* Princeton, N.J.: Princeton University Press, 2000.

Milton, John. *Paradise Lost.* Ed. Scott Eldridge. New York: Norton, 1975.

Monda, Kimberly. "Self-Delusion and Self-Sacrifice in Nella Larsen's *Quicksand.*" *African American Review* 31.1 (Spring 1997): 23–39.

Moore, David Chioni. "Is the Post- in Postcolonial the Post- in Post-Soviet? Toward a Global Postcolonial Critique." *PMLA* 116:1 (2001): 11–128.

Moore, Rachel O. *Savage Theory: Cinema as Modern Magic.* Durham, N.C.: Duke University Press, 2000.

Moran, Jo Ann Hoeppner. "E. M. Forster's *A Passage to India:* What Really Happened in the Caves." *Modern Fiction Studies* 34 (Winter 1988): 596–604.

Morrison, Toni. "Home." *The House That Race Built: Black Americans, U.S. Terrain.* Ed. Wahneema Lubiano. New York: Pantheon, 1997. 3–12.

———. "Unspeakable Things Unspoken: The Afro-American Presence in American Literature." *Within the Circle: An Anthology of African American Literary Criticism from the Harlem Renaissance to the Present.* Ed. Angelyn Mitchell. Durham, N.C.: Duke University Press, 1994. 368–98.

Mulvey, Christopher. 1990. "The Black Capital of the World." *New York: City as Text.* Eds. Christopher Mulvey and John Simons. London and Basingstoke: Macmillan. 147–65.

Naipaul, V. S. 1999. "Obituary" *L.A. Times* [online], April 24, 1999. DetNews, http://detnews.com/1999/obits/9904/27/04240049.htm [Accessed 08/05/01; the link has since been removed.]

Neal, Mark Anthony. *Soul Babies: Black Popular Culture and the Post-Soul Aesthetic.* New York: Routledge, 2002.

Newbigin, Marion I. *Modern Geography.* London: Williams and Norgate, 1911.

Ninkovich, Frank. *The Wilsonian Century: U.S. Foreign Policy since 1900.* Chicago: University of Chicago Press, 1999.

Nixon, Rob. *Homelands, Harlem, and Hollywood: South African Culture and the World Beyond.* New York: Routledge, 1994.

Nolan, Emer. *James Joyce and Nationalism.* London: Routledge, 1995.

Norbrook, David. *Writing the English Republic: Poetry, Rhetoric, and Politics, 1627–1660.* New York: Cambridge, 1999.

North, Michael. *The Dialect of Modernism: Race, Language, and Twentieth-Century Literature.* New York: Oxford University Press, 1994.

Al-Nowaihi, Magda M. "Committed Postmodernity: Muhammad Barrada's *The Game of Forgetting.*" *Tradition, Modernity, and Postmodernity in Arabic Literature: Essays in Honor of Professor Issa F. Boullata.* Eds. Kamal Abdel-Malek and Wael Hallaq. Leiden: E. J. Brill, 2000. 367–88.

Nunez, Zita C. "Phantasmatic Brazil: Nella Larsen's *Passing,* American Literary

Imagination, and Racial Utopianism." *Mixing Race, Mixing Culture: Inter-American Literary Dialogues.* Eds. Monika Kaup and Debra J. Rosenthal. Austin: University of Texas Press, 2002. 50–61.

Okely, Judith. "Constructing Difference: Gypsies as 'Other.'" *Anthropological Journal on European Cultures* 3.2 (1994): 55–73.

———. *The Traveller-Gypsies.* Cambridge: Cambridge University Press, 1983.

Okonkwo, Chidi. *Decolonization Agonistics in Postcolonial Fiction.* New York: St. Martin's Press, 1999.

Omi, Michael, and Howard Winant. "Racial Formation." *Race Critical Theories.* Eds. Philomena Essed and David T. Goldberg. Malden, Massachusetts: Blackwell, 2002. 123–45.

Ortega y Gasset, José. *The Dehumanization of Art and Other Writings on Art and Culture.* Garden City, N.Y.: Doubleday, 1956.

Owens, Louis. *Mixedblood Messages: Literature, Film, Family, Place.* Norman: University of Oklahoma Press, 1998.

Parry, Benita. *Delusions and Discoveries: Studies on India in the British Imagination, 1880–1930.* London: Penguin, 1972.

Patterson, Anita. "Jazz, Realism, and the Modernist Lyric: The Poetry of Langston Hughes." *Modern Language Quarterly* 61.4 (2000): 651–82.

Paul, Catherine. *Poetry in the Museums of Modernism: Yeats, Pound, Moore, Stein.* Ann Arbor: University of Michigan Press, 2002.

Pauly, Philip J. "'The world and all that is in it': The National Geographic Society, 1888–1918." *American Quarterly* 31 (1979): 517–532.

Peppis, Paul. *Literature, Politics and the English Avant-garde: Nation and Empire, 1901–1918.* New York: Cambridge University Press, 2000.

———. "Thinking Race in the *Avant Guerre:* Typological Negotiations in Ford and Stein." *Yale Journal of Criticism* 10.2 (1997): 371–95.

Petran, Tabitha. *The Struggle over Lebanon.* New York: Monthly Review Press, 1987.

Picard, Elizabeth. *Lebanon, A Shattered Country: Myths and Realities of the Wars in Lebanon.* Trans. Franklin Philip. New York: Holmes and Meier, 1996.

Pomerance, Michla. "The United States and Self-Determination: Perspectives on the Wilsonian Conception." *The American Journal of International Law* 70 (1976): 1–27.

The Post-Colonial Studies Reader. Eds. Bill Ashcroft, Gareth Griffiths, and Helen Tiffin. New York: Routledge, 1995.

Prakash, Gyan. "Postcolonial Criticism and Indian Historiography." *Social Text* 31/32 (1992): 8–19.

Prall, Stuart E., ed. *The Puritan Revolution: A Documentary History.* Gloucester, Mass.: Peter Smith, 1973.

Price, Sally. *Primitive Art in Civilized Places.* Chicago: University of Chicago Press, 1989.

Puchner, Martin. "Manifesto=Theater." *Theatre Journal* 54 (2002): 449–65.

———. "Screeching Voices: Avant-garde Manifestoes in the Cabaret." *European Avant-gardes: New Perspectives.* Ed. Dietrich Scheunemann. Atlanta: Rodolphi, 2000. 113–36.

———. *Stage Fright: Modernism, Anti-Theatricality and Drama.* Baltimore: Johns Hopkins University Press, 2002.

Rafael, Vincente. *White Love and Other Events in Filipino History.* Durham, N.C.: Duke University Press, 2000.

Rainey, Lawrence. *Institutions of Modernism: Literary Elites and Public Culture.* New Haven, Conn.: Yale University Press, 1998.

Rama, Ángel. *The Lettered City.* Durham, N.C.: Duke University Press, 1996.

———. *Transculturación narrativa en América Latina.* México, D.F.: Siglo Veintiuno, 1982.

Ramos, Julio. *Desencuentros de la modernidad en América Latina: Literatura y política en el siglo XIX*. México, D.F.: Fondo de Cultura Económica, 1989.

Rampersad, Arnold. *The Life of Langston Hughes*. Vol. 2: *1941–1967: I Dream a World*. New York: Oxford University Press, 1988.

Ransome, Arthur. *Bohemia in London* [1907]. Oxford: Oxford University Press, 1984.

Ray, Satyajit. "Foreword." *Henri Cartier-Bresson in India*. Foreword by Satyajit Ray. Introduction by Yves Vraequand. Trans. Paula Clifford. New York: Thames and Hudson, 1987.

Raymond, Joad. *Making the News: An Anthology of the Newsbooks of Revolutionary England, 1641–1660*. New York: St. Martins Press, 1993. Foreword by Christopher Hill.

Read, Herbert. "T. S. E.: A Memoir." *T. S. Eliot: The Man and His Work*. Ed. Allen Tate. New York: Delacorte, 1966.

Redfield, Marc. "Imagi-Nation: The Imagined Community and the Aesthetics of Mourning." *Diacritics* 29.4 (1999): 58–83.

Reed, Ishmael. *Mumbo Jumbo*. Garden City, N.Y.: Doubleday, 1972.

Renda, Mary. *Taking Haiti: Military Occupation and the Culture of U.S. Imperialism, 1915–1940*. Chapel Hill: University of North Carolina Press, 2001.

Restuccia, Frances. "'A Cave of My Own': The Sexual Politics of Indeterminancy." *Raritan* 2 (Fall 1989): 110–28.

Retamar, Roberto Fernández. *Calibán: Apuntes sobre la cultura en nuestra América*. México, D.F.: Diógenes, 1972.

Rhodes, Chip. *Structures of the Jazz Age: Mass Culture, Progressive Education, and Racial Discourse in American Modernism*. New York: Verso, 1998.

Rhys, Jean. *Letters 1931–66*. Eds. Francis Wyndham and Diana Melly. New York: Penguin, 1985.

———. *Voyage in the Dark*. New York: Norton, 1982.

Ricco, John Paul. *The Logic of the Lure*. Chicago: University of Chicago Press, 2002.

Richards, David. "Masks of Difference: Cultural Representations in Literature." *Anthropology and Art*. Cambridge: Cambridge University Press, 1994.

Richardson, Samuel. *Clarissa; or, The History of a Young Lady*. New York: Penguin Books, 1985.

Robbins, Bruce. *Feeling Global: Internationalism in Distress*. New York: New York University Press, 1999.

Rogers, J. A. "Jazz at Home." *The New Negro* [1925]. Ed. Alain Locke. New York: Atheneum, 1992. 216–24.

Rogin, Michael. "'The Sword Become a Flashing Vision': D. W. Griffith's *The Birth of a Nation*." Michael Paul Rogin, *Ronald Reagan, the Movie and Other Episodes in Political Demonology*. Berkeley: University of California Press, 1987.

Rojas, Rafael. *José Martí: La invención de Cuba*. Madrid: Editorial Colibrí, 2000.

Rousseau, G. S. "Nerves, Spirits, Fibres: Toward Defining the Origins of Sensibility." *Studies in the Eighteenth Century*. Vol. 3. Eds. R. F. Brissenden and J. C. Eade. Canberra: Australia National Press, 1976. 137–57.

Roy, Arundhati. *The God of Small Things*. New York: Random House, 1997.

Rushdie, Salman. *Mirrorwork: 50 Years of Indian Writing*. New York: Henry Holt, 1997.

Ryan, Katy. "Falling in Public: Larsen's *Passing*, McCarthy's *The Group*, and Baldwin's *Another Country*." *Studies in the Novel* 36.1 (Spring 2004): 95–119.

Ryan, Marie-Laure. "Cyberage Narratology: Computers, Metaphor, and Narrative." *Narratologies: New Perspectives on Narrative Analysis*. Ed. David Herman. Columbus: Ohio State University Press, 1999. 113–41.

Said, Edward. *Culture and Imperialism*. New York: Vintage, 1993.

Saliba, George. *A History of Arabic Astronomy: Planetary Theories during the Golden Age of Islam*. New York: New York University Press, 1994.

Sangari, Kumkum. "The Politics of the Possible." *Cultural Critique* 7 (1987): 157–86.

Sassen, Saskia. *The Global City: New York, London, Tokyo.* Princeton, N.J.: Princeton University Press, 1991.

Scandura, Jani, and Michael Thurston. "America and the Phantom Modern." *Modernism, Inc.: Body, Memory, Capital.* Eds. Jani Scandura and Michael Thurston. New York: New York University Press, 2001. 1–17.

Schumpeter, Joseph A. *Capitalism, Socialism, and Democracy.* 3rd ed. New York: Harper and Bros., 1950.

Schwarz, Roberto. *Misplaced Ideas: Essays on Brazilian Culture.* London: Verso, 1992.

Scott, Bonnie Kime, ed. *The Gender of Modernism.* Bloomington: Indiana University Press, 1990.

Segel, Harold B. *Turn-of-the-Century Cabaret.* New York: Columbia University Press, 1987.

Seidel, Michael. *Epic Geography: James Joyce's Ulysses.* Princeton, N.J.: Princeton University Press, 1976.

Seigneurie, Ken. "The Everyday World of War in Hassan Daoud's *House of Mathilde.*" *Crisis and Memory: The Representation of Space in Modern Levantine Narrative.* Ed. Ken Seigneurie. Wiesbaden: Reichert Verlag, 2003. 101–14.

———. "A Survival Aesthetic for Ongoing War." *Crisis and Memory: The Representation of Space in Modern Levantine Narrative.* Ed. Ken Seigneurie. Wiesbaden: Reichert Verlag, 2003. 11–32.

Seigneurie, Ken, ed. *Crisis and Memory: The Representation of Space in Modern Levantine Narrative.* Wiesbaden: Reichert Verlag, 2003.

Semple, Ellen Churchill. *American History and Its Geographic Conditions.* Rev. ed. New York: Russell and Russell, 1968.

———. *Influences of Geographic Environment.* New York: Henry Holt, 1911.

Seshagiri, Urmilla. "Orienting Virginia Woolf: Race, Aesthetics, and Politics in *To the Lighthouse.*" *Modern Fiction Studies* 50.1 (2004): 58–84.

Sharpe, Jenny. *Allegories of Empire: The Figure of Woman in the Colonial Text.* Minneapolis: University of Minneapolis Press, 1993.

Sheehan, Paul. *Modernism, Narrative and Humanism.* Cambridge: Cambridge University Press, 2002.

Sheppard, Richard. *Modernism—Dada—Postmodernism.* Evanston, Ill.: Northwestern University Press, 2000.

Shih, Shu-mei. *The Lure of the Modern: Writing Modernism in Semicolonial China, 1917–1937.* Berkeley: University of California Press, 2001.

Shohat, Ella. "Notes on the Post-Colonial." *Social Text* 31/32 (1992): 99–113.

Shoptaw, John. "Lyric Incorporated: The Serial Object of George Oppen and Langston Hughes." *Sagetrieb: A Journal Devoted to Poets in the Imagist/ Objectivist Tradition* 12.3 (Winter 1993): 105–24.

Silver, Brenda. "Periphrasis, Power and Rape in *A Passage to India.*" *Novel* 22 (Fall 1988): 86–105.

Silverman, Debra B. "Nella Larsen's *Quicksand:* Untangling the Webs of Exoticism." *African American Review* 27.4 (Winter 1993): 599–614.

Simmel, Georg. "The Sociology of Sociability" [1910]. *Simmel on Culture.* Eds. David Frisby and Mike Featherstone. London: Sage, 1997. 120–30.

———. "The Stranger." *The Sociology of Georg Simmel.* Trans., ed., and intro. Kurt H. Wolff. New York: The Free Press, 1950. 402–408.

Singh, Raghubir. *River of Colour: The India of Raghubir Singh.* London: Phaidon, 1998.

Sisney, Mary F. "The View from the Outside: Black Novels of Manners." *The Critical Response to Gloria Naylor.* Eds. Sharon Felton and Michelle C. Loris. Westport, Conn.: Greenwood, 1997. 63–75.

Sitwell, Osbert. *Great Morning!* Boston: Little, Brown, 1947.

Smith, George [of Coalville]. *Gipsy Life: Being an Account of Our Gipsies and Their Children.* London: Haughton, 1880.

Smith, P. C. "The Colours of India: Raghubir Singh." *Art in America* 88: 3 (2000): 98–103.

Soja, Edward. *Postmodern Geographies: The Reassertion of Space in Critical Social Theory.* New York: Verso, 1989.

Soper, Kate. *Humanism and Anti-Humanism.* London: Hutchinson, 1986.

Soyinka, Wole. *Death and the King's Horseman.* Ed. Simon Gikandi. New York: W. W. Norton, 2003.

———. *The Road: Collected Plays.* London: Oxford University Press [1965], 1973.

Spengemann, William C. *A New World of Words: Redefining Early American Literature.* New Haven, Conn.: Yale University Press, 1994.

Stearns, Marshall W. *The Story of Jazz* [1956]. New York: Oxford University Press, 1972.

Steele, James. *Rethinking Modernism for the Developing World: The Complete Work of Balkrishna Doshi.* New York: The Whitney Library of Design, 1998.

Stein, Gertrude. *The Geographical History of America; or, The Relation of Human Nature to the Human Mind.* Baltimore: Johns Hopkins University Press, 1995.

———. *Ida: A Novel.* New York: Vintage, 1941.

———. *Tender Buttons.* Los Angeles: Sun & Moon Press, 1991.

Stocking, George W., Jr. "The Ethnographic Sensibility of the 1920s and the Dualism of the Anthropological Tradition." *Romantic Motives: Essays on Anthropological Sensibility.* Ed. George W. Stocking, Jr. Madison: University of Wisconsin Press, 1989.

Stoker, Bram. *Dracula.* Eds. Nina Auerbach and David Skal. New York: Penguin, 1992.

Stoler, Ann. *Race and the Education of Desire.* Durham, N.C.: Duke University Press, 1995.

Strother, Z. S. *Inventing Masks: Agency and History in the Art of the Central Pende.* Chicago: University of Chicago Press, 1998.

Suleri, Sara. *The Rhetoric of English Empire.* Chicago: University of Chicago Press, 1992.

Symons, Arthur. "In Praise of Gypsies." *Journal of the Gypsy Lore Society,* New Series 1.4 (April 1908): 294–99.

———. "Sir Thomas Browne and the Gypsies." *Journal of the Gypsy Lore Society,* New Series 5.2 (Oct. 1911): 109–13.

Tagore, Rabindrath. *Angel of Surplus: Some Essays and Addresses in Aesthetics.* Ed. Sisirkuna Ghose. Calcutta: Visvia Bharati, 1978.

Taylor, Charles. *Sources of the Self: The Making of Modern Identity.* Cambridge, Mass.: Harvard University Press, 1989.

Themba, Can. *The World of Can Themba: Selected Writings of the Late Can Themba.* Ed. Essop Patel. Braamfontein, South Africa: Ravan Press, 1985.

Thomas, Nicholas. *Colonialism's Culture: Anthropology, Travel and Government.* Princeton, N.J.: Princeton University Press, 1994.

Thompson, John P. *The Media and Modernity: A Social Theory of the Media.* Stanford, Calif.: Stanford University Press, 1995.

Thompson, Robert Farris. "Fang Mask." *Perspectives: Angles on African Art—James Baldwin and Others.* New York: The Center for African Art, 1987.

Thompson, Thomas William. "Affairs of Egypt, 1909." *Journal of the Gypsy Lore Society,* New Series 5.2 (October 1911): 113–34.

Thurow, Lester. *The Future of Capitalism.* New York: William Morrow, 1996.

Tickner, Lisa. "The Popular Culture of *Kermesse:* Lewis, Painting, and Performance, 1912–1913." *Modernism/Modernity* 4.2 (April 1997): 67–120.

Tietjins, Eunice (E. T.). "Blast." *Little Review* 1 (September 1914): 33–34.

Todorov, Tzvetan. *Imperfect Garden: The Legacy of Humanism.* Trans. Carol Cosman. Princeton, N.J.: Princeton University Press, 2002.

Tolson, Melvin B. *Harlem Gallery.* New York: Twayne, 1965.

———. The Melvin B. Tolson Papers. Library of Congress. Washington, D.C. Container #8.

Tönnies, Ferdinand. *Community and Society (Gemeinschaft und Gesellschaft)* [1887]. Trans. Charles P. Loomis. New intro. John Samples. New Brunswick, N.J.: Transaction, 1988.

Torgovnick, Marianna. *Gone Primitive: Savage Intellects, Modern Lives.* Chicago: University of Chicago Press, 1990.

Trouillot, Michel-Rolph. "Anthropology and the Savage Slot." *Recapturing Anthropology: Working in the Present.* Ed. Richard G. Fox. Santa Fe: School of American Research Press, 1991. 17–44.

Trubowitz, Rachel. "Female Preachers and Male Wives: Gender and Authority in Civil-War England." *Pamphlet Wars: Prose in the English Revolution.* Ed. James Holstun. Portland, Ore.: F. Cass, 1992. 112–33.

Trumpener, Katie. "The Time of the Gypsies: A 'People without History' in the Narratives of the West." *Critical Inquiry* 18.4 (Summer 1992): 843–84.

Turner, John. "Purity and Danger in D. H. Lawrence's *The Virgin and the Gipsy.*" *D. H. Lawrence: Centenary Essays.* Ed. Mara Kalnins. Bristol: Bristol Classical Press, 1986. 139–71.

Unruh, Vicky. *Latin American Vanguards: The Art of Contentious Encounters.* Berkeley, Los Angeles and London: University of California Press, 1994.

Valente, Joseph. *Dracula's Crypt: Bram Stoker, Irishness, and the Question of Blood.* Urbana: University of Illinois Press, 2002.

Vidal de la Blache, Paul. *Principles of Human Geography.* Trans. Millicent Todd Bingham. New York: Henry Holt, 1926.

Wang, Jing. *High Culture Fever: Politics, Aesthetics, and Ideology in Deng's China.* Berkeley: University of California Press, 1996.

Wanklyn, Harriet. *Friedrich Ratzel: A Biographical Memoir.* Cambridge: Cambridge University Press, 1961.

Wees, William C. *Vorticism and the English Avant-garde.* Toronto: University of Toronto Press, 1972.

Weinstein, Barbara. *The Amazon Rubber Boom 1850–1920.* Stanford, Calif.: Stanford University Press, 1983.

West, Rebecca. "Indissoluble Matrimony." *Blast.* No. 1 (June 1914). Ed. Wyndham Lewis. Santa Rosa, Calif.: Black Sparrow, 1981. 98–117.

Wexler, Laura. "Tender Violence: Literary Eavesdropping, Domestic Fiction, and Educational Reform." *The Culture of Sentiment: Race, Gender, and Sentimentality in Nineteenth-Century America.* Ed. Shirley Samuels. New York: Oxford University Press, 1992.

Whitman, Walt. *Complete Poetry and Collected Prose.* New York: The Library of America, 1982.

Williams, Bettye J. "Nella Larsen: Early Twentieth-Century Novelist of Afrocentric Feminist Thought." *College Language Association Journal* 39.2 (Dec. 1995): 165–78.

Williams, Raymond. "The Metropolis and the Emergence of Modernism." *Modernism/Postmodernism.* Ed. Peter Brooker. New York: Longman, 1992. 82–94.

———. "What Was Modernism?" *The Politics of Modernism.* Ed. Tony Pinkey. New York: Verso, 1989.

———. *The Politics of Modernism: Against the New Conformists.* Ed. Tony Pinkey. New York: Verso, 1989.

Winslow, Barbara. *Sylvia Pankhurst: Sexual Politics and Political Activism.* New York: St. Martin's, 1996.

Wiseman, Susan. "'Adam the Father of All Flesh': Porno-Political Rhetoric and Political Theory in and after the English Civil War." *Pamphlet Wars: Prose in the English Revolution.* Ed. James Holstun. Portland, Ore.: F. Cass, 1992. 134–57.

Wood, Gordon S. *The Radicalism of the American Revolution.* New York: Knopf, 1992.

Woodhouse, A. S. P., ed. *Puritanism and Liberty: Being the Army Debates (1647–49) from the Clarke Manuscripts.* London: J. M. Dent & Sons, 1938.

Woolf, D. R. *The Idea of History in Early Stuart England: Erudition, Ideology, and 'The Light of Truth' from the Accession of James I to the Civil War.* Toronto: University of Toronto Press, 1990.

Woolf, Virginia. *The Diary of Virginia Woolf.* Vol. 3. Eds. Anne Olivier Bell and Andrew McNeillie. New York: Harcourt, 1980.

——. "The Narrow Bridge of Art." *Collected Essays of Virginia Woolf.* Vol. 2. New York: Harcourt, 1966. 218–29.

——. *Orlando.* New York: Harcourt, 1928.

——. *Roger Fry: A Biography.* New York: Harcourt, 1948.

——. *To the Lighthouse.* New York: Harcourt, 1981.

——. *The Voyage Out.* New York: Harcourt, 1948.

Wright, Richard. *12 Million Black Voices.* 1941. New York: Thunder's Mouth Press, 1988.

Young, Robert J. C. *Colonial Desire: Hybridity in Theory, Culture and Race.* New York: Routledge, 1995.

Yúdice, George. "Rethinking the Theory of the Avant-garde from the Periphery." *Modernism and Its Margins: Reinscribing Cultural Modernity from Spain and Latin America.* Eds. Anthony L. Geist and José B. Monleón. New York: Garland Publishing, 1999. 52–80.

Zaret, David. *The Heavenly Contract: Ideology and Organization in Pre-Revolutionary Puritanism.* Chicago: University of Chicago, 1984.

Zhang, Xudong. *Chinese Modernism in the Era of Reforms: Cultural Fever, Avant-garde Fiction, and the New Chinese Cinema.* Durham, N.C.: Duke University Press, 1997.

Zwerdling, Alex. *Improvised Europeans: American Literary Expatriates and the Siege of London.* New York: BasicBooks, 1998.

CONTRIBUTORS

GERARD ACHING is Associate Professor in the Department of Spanish and Portuguese at New York University. His most recent publications include *The Politics of Spanish American Modernismo* (1997) and *Masking and Power: Carnival and Popular Culture in the Caribbean* (2002). He is currently working on a book provisionally titled *Freedom from Liberation: Enslaved Subjectivities in 19th-Century Cuba.*

IAN BAUCOM is Associate Professor of English at Duke University. He is the author of *Out of Place: Englishness, Empire and the Locations of Identity* (1999) and of the forthcoming *Specters of the Atlantic: Finance Capital, Slavery, and the Philosophy of History.* He is editor of a special issue of *South Atlantic Quarterly* on "Atlantic Genealogies."

JESSICA BERMAN is Associate Professor of English and Women's Studies at the University of Maryland, Baltimore County. She is the author of *Modernist Fiction, Cosmopolitanism and the Politics of Community* (2001) and co-editor of *Virginia Woolf Out of Bounds: Selected Papers from the Tenth Annual Conference on Virginia Woolf* (2001).

SUNG-SHENG YVONNE CHANG is Full Professor of Asian Studies at the University of Texas, Austin. Her books include *Literary Culture in Taiwan: Martial Law to Market Law* (2004); *Modernism and the Nativist Resistance: Contemporary Chinese Fiction from Taiwan* (1993); and, as co-editor, *Bamboo Shoots after the Rain: Contemporary Stories by Women Writers of Taiwan* (1990).

PATRICIA E. CHU is completing a book titled *White Zombies: Literary Modernism and the State.* She has taught at The School of the Art Institute of Chicago, East-West University, and Brandeis University.

LAURA DOYLE is Associate Professor of English at the University of Massachusetts, Amherst. Her book *Bordering on the Body: The Racial Matrix of Modern Fiction and Culture* (1994) won the Barbara and George Perkins Award for the best book on narrative. She is editor of *Bodies of Resistance: New Phenomenologies of Politics, Agency, Culture* (2001) and a special issue of *Modern*

Fiction Studies on Virginia Woolf (2004). She is completing a book titled *Liberty's Empire: Race and the Force of Freedom in Atlantic Modernity.*

JUSTINE DYMOND holds a postdoctoral fellowship at the University of Massachusetts, Amherst, where she completed her doctoral work in transatlantic modernism and twentieth-century American literature. Her bibliography on Virginia Woolf scholarship appeared in the Spring 2004 issue of *Modern Fiction Studies.*

ARIELA FREEDMAN is Assistant Professor at the Liberal Arts College, Concordia University. She is the author of *Death, Men, and Modernism* (2003) and has published articles on Mary Borden, H.D., and the literature of World War I. She is currently at work on a book titled *Forbidden Zones: Modernism and the Home Front.*

SUSAN STANFORD FRIEDMAN is the Virginia Woolf Professor of English and Women's Studies at the University of Wisconsin–Madison. She is the author of *Psyche Reborn: The Emergence of H.D.* (1981); *Penelope's Web: Gender, Modernity, H.D.'s Fiction* (1990); *Mappings: Feminism and the Cultural Geographies of Encounter* (1998), winner of the Barbara and George Perkins Award for best book on narrative studies; and *Analyzing Freud: Letters of H.D., Bryher, and Their Circle* (2001). She is at work on a book on transnational modernism.

SIMON GIKANDI is Professor of English at Princeton University. He has written *Reading the African Novel* (1987); *Reading Chinua Achebe* (1991); *Writing in Limbo: Modernism and Caribbean Literature* (1992); *Maps of Englishness: Writing Identity in the Culture of Colonialism* (1996); and *Ngugi wa Thiong'o* (2000). He is editor of the Routledge *Encyclopedia of African Literature* (2003) and co-editor of *The Cambridge History of African and Caribbean Literature* (2004).

JANET LYON is Associate Professor of English and Women's Studies and co-director of the Disability Studies Program at The Pennsylvania State University. She is the author of *Manifestoes: Provocations of the Modern* (1999) and is at work on a book manuscript titled *The Perfect Hostess: Salons and Modernity.*

ALDON LYNN NIELSEN is the Kelly Professor of American Literature at The Pennsylvania State University. His books include *Reading Race: White American Poets and the Racial Discourse in the 20th Century* (1988); *Writing between the Lines: Race and Intertextuality* (1994); *Black Chant: Languages of African American Postmodernism* (1997); and *C. L. R. James: A Critical Introduction* (1997). Nielsen is also editor of *Reading Race in American Poetry* (2000) and author of four books of poetry.

FERNANDO J. ROSENBERG is Assistant Professor of Spanish at Yale University. He has written articles on modernism and avant-gardes in Latin America, poetry, and globalization, among other topics. He is the author of *Avant-Gardes and Geopolitics in Latin America* (forthcoming).

KEN SEIGNEURIE is Assistant Professor of English and Comparative Literature at Lebanese American University, Beirut. He is editor of *Crisis and Memory: The Representation of Space in Modern Levantine Narrative* (2003) and is currently working on a book titled *How British and American Literatures Remake the Human.*

ELUNED SUMMERS-BREMNER is Lecturer in English and Women's Studies at the University of Auckland, New Zealand. She has published numerous articles on literary and psychoanalytic topics. She is working on three book-length projects, including a cultural history of insomnia for *Reaktion.*

LAURA WINKIEL is Assistant Professor of English at Iowa State University. She has published articles on Djuna Barnes, Elizabeth Robins, and Valerie Solanas. She is completing a book project on manifestos, modernism, and race.

INDEX

"Humble Petition of Distressed Women," 58–59
Hungary, 196
Hunter, Lynnette, 178
Hurston, Zora Neale, 11, 175, 180–84; "Death of Leconte," 183–84; *Tell My Horse . . .*, 175, 181–84, 185n14
Hutcheon, Linda, 128n6
Hutchinson, George, 74n6, 76n20
Hybrid identities, 126–27
"Hypallage," 219
Hysteria, 258, 260

Identity: categories of, 220; collective, 180; education, 111; fragmented, 199; imperialism, 261; knowledge, 155–56; location, 282; mixed race, 302, 312n9; modernization, 224n12; nationalism, 170–84, 224n12; politics, 111n2; striations of, 190–91; topography, 290–91
Ideology: and culture, 143, 144; of Empire, 254; imported models, 148; racism, 18
Images, manipulation of, 207–208
Imagined community, 271
Imagism, 198
Imitation: and cultural formation, 152–60, 168n11, 238–39; excessive, 151–67
Immigrant Act (U.S.: 1924), 301
Immigration. *See* Migration/immigration
Imperial romance fiction, 224n11
Imperialism: chauvinism, 60; cultural parataxis, 246; democracy, 173; expansion, 211; identity, 261; mapping, 311; Metropole/metropolitanism, 6, 213–14, 219, 230, 246, 289; militarism, 215; modernism, 175, 212; (Neo)imperialism, 256; power disruption, 293; racial stratifications, 53, 74, 175, 214, 254, 257; sentimentalism, 299–301; and state power, 178
Imperialism, U.S., 52, 180; Haiti, 173, 181–84, 185n11, 186n15; and modernism, 175; Philippines, 171–74, 178
Impressionism, 49
Improvisation, 274
Incest, 252
Independence: and Christianity, 54; Cuban struggle for, 160–66
Indeterminacy, 98–99, 100, 107–108, 250
India, 114–27, 245–61; aesthetics, 116–18, 120–21; avant-garde, 126; Communist Party, 255, 256; Gypsies, 204n11; humanism, 120; Indian art and photography, 114–27, 128nn11,14,15; Indian cultural heritage, 47, 115, 117, 119–20, 204n10; nationalism/self-determination, 174, 178, 247, 250; use of color, 118–19, 121, 128n10
Indian policy (U.S.), 301–302, 305–306, 308, 312n9

Indifference, 85–87, 89–91
Indigenous traditionalism, 239, 244n16
Individualism, 91, 121, 185n6, 190, 209, 221, 222n3, 306
Industrial Revolution, 188, 213
Industrialism, 10, 41, 84, 137, 147, 194, 234, 312n6. *See also* Capitalism
Information technology, 147
"Inquiry, The," 174
Integration, 165, 302
Intellectuals: Brazilian, 77, 82, 85, 87, 90; Chinese, 136, 139, 143; migrant, 128n9; racialization/race thinking, 159
Intercaste eroticism, 256
Intercultural encounters, 106
Internal exile, 196–97
International film festivals, 142, 149
Internationalism, 87, 89, 125, 167n4
Intertextuality, 299
Iranian Revolution, 109
Iraq, 238
Ireland, 286–92; colonial status of, 61, 174, 185n11; Gaelic art and culture, 124, 287; Irish nationalism, 124, 286
Ireton, Henry, 60–62
Irigaray, Luce, 81
Isherwood, Christopher, 99
Islam/Islamic culture, 110, 129n20
Islam Renaissance, 112n12
Israeli social realism, 112n7
Iteration, 102–104, 107–108
Itinerancy, 193–94

James, C. L. R., 8, 17–21, 27–30; *The Black Jacobins*, 18, 172, 185n14; *Facing Reality*, 28; *Mariners, Renegades and Castaways*, 18, 23; *Notes on Dialectics*, 27
James I (King of England), 55
James, William, 296n2
Jameson, Fredric, 112n9, 126, 153, 203n7, 219, 228, 230
Jarr, Alfredo, 120
Jazz music/Jazz Age, 21, 23, 208–209, 238, 274–75, 278–79. *See also* Music
Jewish diaspora, 223n6
"Jewish race," 196–97
Jocelyn, John, 54
Johannesburg, 238
John, Augustus, 197, 199; *Chiaroscuro*, 199
Johnson, Barbara, 68, 75n15
Johnson, James Weldon, 25, 185n14, 190
Jones, LeRoi. *See* Baraka, Amiri
Joplin, Scott, 27
Journal of the Gypsy Lore Society, 187
Joyce, James, 1, 12, 32, 115, 124, 212, 251, 281, 290, 294, 296; "The Dead," 286–89; *Dubliners*, 285, 286; *Ulysses*, 126, 242, 286, 288–89
Judaism, 128n10

els, 136, 143, 148; depersonalizing forces, 191; English identity, 224n12; native cultures and, 170; racial distinctions, 212, 221; state-sponsored, 11; technological/administrative, 171
MOMA (Museum of Modern Art), 36
Mondrian, Piet, 45
Monleón, José, 3, 6
Monroe Doctrine, 172
Montage technique, 275, 277–80
Montana, 303
Moore, David Chioni, 128n11
Morality, 39, 42
Morrison, Toni, 29; "Home," 18
Moulin Rouge, 242
Mourning Dove. *See* Dove, Mourning
Moveable Dwellings Bill (England), 187, 193, 202n1
Mulatto, 164
Multiculturalism, 116, 120, 142
Multinational corporations, 256
Museums, 34–36
Music: Bebop, 274–75, 277, 279; black contributions to, 21; Jazz music/Jazz Age, 21, 23, 208–209, 238, 274–75, 278–79; popular music, 26–27; racial exchange in, 26–27; Ragtime, 27, 209
Musil, Robert, 32
Muslim fundamentalism, 125
Mya Than Tint, 125

Naipaul, V. S., 121, 125, 127
Napoleon, 109
Narayan, Uma, 246
Narrative models: absence of dialogue, 98, 100; anthropological, 302, 307; captivity narratives, 298, 301; English novel of manners, 247–48; fictive ethnicity, 10, 160, 167, 168n7; formula fiction, 298; freedom plots, 63–69, 72; indeterminant voice, 98–99; liberty plots, 8, 52–53, 63–69, 72; map-based, 286, 295–96; marriage plots, 298, 300, 307–308; national or government-based, 183–84; race-based, 53, 63, 67–68, 264; sea-crossing, 52–53, 65, 67, 212; seduction plots, 63, 66, 300; unemphatic tone, 100, 102, 107–108, 112n8
Nation-building: autochthony, 156; miscegenation, 159; modernism, 77, 80, 138; nonassimilation, 195–96; race, 154; representative democracy, 175–81, 209; self-determination, 172, 174–75, 180, 184
Nation-state: cynicism, 87, 108–109, 115–16; disintegration, 111n2; international legitimacy, 173
Nation, The, 173, 174
National Geographic, 171–72, 173, 178
Nationalism: anticolonialism in Haiti, 170–75, 181–84; anti-imperialism, 232; artistic

autonomy, 124; avant-garde, 224n10; categories of, 296; cultural formation, 175, 231–32, 243n9, 246, 294; geography, 284; identity, 224n12; landscape, 295; national elections, 171; national narrative, 183; nostalgia, 301; race, 5, 152, 166; sentimentalism, 203n9
Native Americans. *See* American Indians
Native/nativism/nativist: in British modernism, 198, 212–14; Hegel on, 60; liberty rhetoric, 58–59, 62; native culture and modernization, 170, 178, 312n6; native rights, 59, 61; native towns, 231–35; nativist artists, 213; property and power, 62; and race, 5, 11, 53, 60, 181, 222; in Taiwan, 5, 136–37, 141, 143, 145. *See also* Primitivism/primitive
Natural man, 159, 160, 163, 187
Naxos, 64–66, 74n6, 75n12
Nazism, 52, 284
Neal, Mark Anthony, 22, 25
(Neo)imperialism, 256. *See also* Imperialism
Neruda, Pablo, 95n24; *Canto general*, 93n11; "Heights of Macchu Picchu," 82–83
Networks, 57, 192–97
New Criticism/New Critics, 2, 135, 270
New Masses (journal), 22
New Negro, The (journal), 21–22
New Negroes, 24
New World: colonizing projects, 51, 57; discovery of, 54; New World Africans, 19, 22; social and economic organization in, 19
New York Times, 211
News, censorship of, 173–74
Nicolson, Harold, 294
Nielsen, Aldon, 8–10, 12, 17–30, 73, 266, 311
Nietzsche, Friedrich Wilhelm, 40, 44, 108, 209, 220
Nobel prize, 124
Nolan, Emer, 286, 288
Nomadology/nomadism, 194–95
Nord, Deborah, 189
Norman Conquest, 54
North Africa, 28
North, Michael, 25, 32–33, 265
Nostalgia, 263, 271–72, 276, 280, 301
Novel, as foreign modernity, 97–98
Al-Nowaihi, Magda, 107
Nunez, Zita C., 75n10

Obsessive-compulsive behavior, 105
Occidental modernity: African art forms, 21–26; paths of, 4, 9–10, 17–21, 29, 234–36; Western art museums, 34–36. *See also* Transatlantic/Atlantic modernism
Occidental rationalism, 17–18, 20–21
Occult, 189
Ogboni League, 43–44

Woolf, Virginia: Bloomsbury group, 50n11; and C. L. R. James, 29; concerns with geography, 281, 296; on end of Empire, 115; as high modernist writer, 251; on human character, 40; *longue durée*, 281; and modern subjectivity, 190, 222n1; *Mrs Dalloway*, 1–2; "The Narrow Bridge of Art," 2; *Orlando*, 292–94; possibilism, 12; and sentimental tradition, 299–300; *To the Lighthouse*, 300, 309–11, 312n10; *The Voyage Out*, 300; *The Waves*, 311
World Health Organization, 142
World island, 282, 284–92
World Trade Center, 256
Wright, Richard, 19

Xenophobia, 188

Yang, Edward (Yang Dechang), 141–42, 146–48; *The Terrorizer*, 147; *That Day, on the Beach*, 147; *Yi Yi (A One and a Two)*, 147
Yankeemania, 160–61, 169n16
Yeats, W. B., 190
Yoruba/Yoruban civilization, 43–44, 47–48
Young, Robert J. C., 224n12
Yúdice, George, 92n3
Yugoslavia, 109

Zambia, 234–37
Zaret, David, 62
Zhang, Xudong, 133
Zhang Yimou, 150n10
Zhu, Tianwen: *Notes of a Desolate Man*, 144
Zionism, 109, 112n7
Zwerdling, Alex, 270, 271